D1536682

Narrating Muḥammad's Night Journey

BP
166.57
C65
2008

NARRATING MUḤAMMAD'S NIGHT JOURNEY

Tracing the Development of the Ibn ᶜAbbās Ascension Discourse

FREDERICK S. COLBY

Withdrawn / Retiré

STATE UNIVERSITY OF NEW YORK PRESS

Published by State University of New York Press, Albany

© 2008 State University of New York

All rights reserved

Printed in the United States of America

No part of this book may be used or reproduced in any manner whatsoever without written permission. No part of this book may be stored in a retrieval system or transmitted in any form or by any means including electronic, electrostatic, magnetic tape, mechanical, photocopying, recording, or otherwise without the prior permission in writing of the publisher.

For information, contact State University of New York Press, Albany, NY
www.sunypress.edu

Production by Dana Foote
Marketing by Anne M. Valentine

Library of Congress Cataloging-in-Publication Data
Colby, Frederick Stephen, 1969–
Narrating Muhammad's night journey : tracing the development of the Ibn ᶜAbbas ascension discourse / Frederick S. Colby.
p. cm.
Includes bibliographical references and index.
ISBN 978-0-7914-7517-1 (hardcover : alk. paper)
ISBN 978-0-7914-7518-8 (pbk. : alk. paper)
1. Muhammad, Prophet, d. 632—Isra and Miᶜraj. 2. ᶜAbd Allah ibn al-ᶜAbbas, d. 688? Israᵓ wa-al-Miᶜraj. I. Title.
BP166.57.C65 2008
297.6'33—dc22 2007037534

10 9 8 7 6 5 4 3 2 1

Contents

Illustrations

Figures

Tables

Acknowledgments

This book presents the fruits of many years of labor, and it would never have been possible to harvest these fruits had it not been for the nurturing support of many individuals and institutions. First and foremost, I am grateful for the instruction I received from my teachers at Duke University and the University of North Carolina at Chapel Hill, especially Bruce Lawrence, Vincent Cornell, and Carl Ernst, who guided and mentored me and who offered invaluable suggestions as this project first took shape. I would like to thank Ebrahim Moosa, Lucas Van Rompay, Michael Sells, Marion Katz, and Christiane Gruber for reading and commenting on earlier versions of this work. I am also indebted to Wadad Kadi, Fred Donner, miriam cooke, Rkia Cornell, John Lamoreaux, Brannon Wheeler, and Th. Emil Homerin for their helpful advice during the research phase of this project. To my good friends, colleagues, and students from the University of Chicago, Duke University, and Miami University, and especially to Elizabeth Wilson, Allan Winkler, Matthew Gordon, Mary Denney, and Paula Ayad for their encouragement and assistance at Miami during the final months of writing, I offer my profound gratitude.

A number of institutions and individuals provided the resources that allowed me to carry out the research upon which this book is based. Part of the research for this study was supported by a Fulbright grant to Syria and by a Fulbright-Hays grant to countries on the historic "Silk Road." In addition, I received research fellowships from the American Research Institute in Turkey and the American Research Center in Egypt, as well as grants for international research from both Duke University and Miami University. Many libraries offered their generous cooperation in making manuscripts in their collections available for study, and I would like to thank in particular the directors and staff of Süleymaniye Kütüphanesi in Istanbul, Maktabat al-Asad al-Waṭaniyya in Damascus, Dār al-Kutub in Cairo, Bibliothèque Nationale in Paris, Staatsbibliothek in Berlin, and the British Library in London. A period of assigned research away from Miami University during the fall of 2006 greatly facilitated the completion of this work, and I am grateful to my good friends and colleagues at Indiana University, including David Brakke, Andrea Ciccarelli, Christiane Gruber, Carole Barnsley, and Liese van Zee for extending their valuable help and warm hospitality to me during my semester in Bloomington. I also owe a debt of gratitude to Nancy Ellegate, Dana Foote, and all the wonderful folks at State University of New York Press who shepherded this book through the stages of its production.

If all the earth's trees were pens and its seas were ink, they would still not be sufficient to express my appreciation to my family for their strong support of my work through the years. Special thanks go to my mother, Mary Colby, who carefully read through and edited an earlier draft of this book, and most of all to my wife and partner Jennifer Blue, who patiently kept the home fires burning and worked long hours to sustain us financially while I was away in pursuit of yet more *mi*^{c}*rāj* manuscripts. It is to Jennifer Blue that I dedicate this work, with much love.

Abbreviations

Amc.95/1	Istanbul Süleymaniye Kütüphanesi MS Amcazade Hüsayın Paša 95/1
Amc.95/2	Istanbul Süleymaniye Kütüphanesi MS Amcazade Hüsayın Paša 95/2
Ara.1931	Paris Bibliothèque Nationale MS Arabe 1931
Asad1426	Damascus Maktabat al-Asad al-Waṭaniyya MS 1426
Asad6093	Damascus Maktabat al-Asad al-Waṭaniyya MS 6093
Asad9608	Damascus Maktabat al-Asad al-Waṭaniyya MS 9608
Aya.867	Istanbul Süleymaniye Kütüphanesi MS Ayasofya 867
Aya.3441	Istanbul Süleymaniye Kütüphanesi MS Ayasofya 3441
b.	Ibn, "son of"
B.20919	Cairo Dār al-Kutub MS B 20919
EI^2	*Encyclopaedia of Islam, New Edition* (Leiden: E. J. Brill, 1960–)
Gaya.241	Madrid Real Academía MS Gayangos 241
IḤ	Ibn Ḥibbān's record of the Primitive Version of the Ibn ᶜAbbās ascension narrative, transmitted by Ṣuyūṭī in *al-Lālī al-maṣnūᶜa*
Ibr.852/3	Istanbul Süleymaniye Kütüphanesi MS Ibrahim Efendi 852/3
Ilah.1277	Istanbul Marmara Üniversitesı Ilahiyat Oğüt MS 1277
Maja.829	Cairo Dār al-Kutub MS Majāmīᶜ 829
Q	Qurᵓān, my own interpretive translation unless stated otherwise
QU	Qushayrī's record of the Primitive Version of the Ibn ᶜAbbās ascension narrative from "[*Kitāb al-miᶜrāj*]," Bankipore Kahuda Bakhsh Oriental Public Library MS 1891
T.T.738/8	Cairo Dār al-Kutub MS Tārīkh Taymūr 738/8
WA	Wāsiṭī's record of the Primitive Version of the Ibn ᶜAbbās ascension narrative from "*Sharḥ asmāᵓ Rasūl Allāh*," Damascus Maktabat al-Asad al-Waṭaniyya MS 6840

INTRODUCTION

Since the time that the Prophet Muḥammad lived, Muslim narrators have delighted in describing how angels took him on a fantastic journey by night from Mecca to Jerusalem, and from Jerusalem up through the heavens and back, a story that has captivated audiences with its fantastic descriptions of otherworldly wonders. The Qur˒ān contains only brief and cryptic allusions to such a journey, as exemplified first and foremost with the so-called night journey verse that opens the Qur˒ān's seventeenth *sūra* or chapter:

> *Glorified be the one who caused his servant to journey by night from the sacred place of prayer to the furthest place of prayer, whose precincts we have blessed, in order to show him some of our signs. Indeed [God] is the one who hears, the one who sees.* (Q 17:1).[1]

This famous qur˒ānic verse says little about the identity of the individuals taking part in the journey it describes and even less about the content of the "signs" revealed over its course. The brief mention in the night journey verse, as well as those in other qur˒ānic passages, required further explanation and elaboration before a coherent narrative of the event could emerge. Tracing the early history of these explanations and elaborations of the Prophet Muḥammad's night journey and ascension, especially those that continued to grow and expand over the centuries that followed Muḥammad's prophetic career, serves as the primary focus of this book.

Most versions of night journey and ascension narrative that Muslims subsequently narrate follow the same basic outline. They describe how Gabriel comes to Muḥammad one night in Mecca and takes him to Jerusalem on the back of the fantastic winged mount called Burāq. After riding Burāq to Jerusalem, Muḥammad meets figures whom the Islamic tradition considers to be prophets, including Abraham, Moses, and Jesus, and he leads these prophets in the Islamic ceremony of ritual prayer (*ṣalāt*). Then Gabriel takes Muḥammad ascending up through the seven levels of the heavens, where he meets a number of the prophets and angels in turn. Muḥammad eventually enjoys some type of audience with God at the climax of the ascent, during which he receives the duty for the Muslim community to pray such ritual prayers fifty times per day. On the advice of Moses, the Prophet bargains with God about the number of prayers required, and gets the requirement reduced from fifty to five. Muḥammad then returns to Mecca, and he tells his fellow Meccans of his experience the next morning. Although variations on this same story were told and retold countless times in the centuries that followed, Muslims came to consensus around this basic outline of the narrative within a couple of centuries after the lifetime of the Prophet.

One can learn a great deal about the interests and concerns of the Muslim community in the formative period of Islamic history (the first / seventh through the seventh / thirteenth centuries)[2] by studying the growth and diffusion of distinct versions of this key narrative. The night journey and ascension narrative became the subject of intellectual debate and struggle during the formative period of Islamic history because of the narrative's importance to Islamic thought. It remained a key focus for many Muslims because it describes the moment in which God made manifest his favor toward Muḥammad and revealed to him some of the secrets of the universe. Since the Qur᾿ān neither describes the journey in detail nor recounts the signs and secrets revealed that night, from the earliest period diverse Muslim traditionists, theologians, mystics, and storytellers took it upon themselves to fill in the gaps left by the Qur᾿ān. To interpret the narrative was to assume a position of power, because the content of this extra-qur᾿ānic revelatory experience could have an impact upon Islamic thought in general, and Islamic theology, philosophy, mysticism, and ritual practice in particular. The narrative could also be used as a powerful tool for Muslim propaganda and potential conversion among non-Muslims, providing a popular and accessible medium to highlight the special merits of Muḥammad over and against those of other religious figures. Precisely because of the narrative's importance, and its malleability, Muslim scholars of later centuries wrestled not only over the scope of the story but also over the particular details included therein.

This book delves into these debates over the night journey and ascension narrative, focusing particularly upon the construction of, and debates over, the influential version of the Islamic ascension narrative ascribed to Muḥammad's famous companion, the early scholar and exegete known as Ibn ᶜAbbās (d. ca. 68 AH / 687 CE). This particular version embellishes the story of the night journey and ascension with a series of new fantastic scenes and details, favoring rich and supple storytelling over dry scholarly conventions. For example, where most night journey and ascension narratives simply mention the idea that the otherworldly beast Burāq carried Muḥammad from Mecca to Jerusalem, frequently the Ibn ʿAbbās versions not only describe what Burāq looks like but they also recount the interaction and even conversation that took place between Muḥammad and Burāq. Where most narratives offer few details describing what Muḥammad experienced at the climax of his ascent other than the fact that he was given the duty of the daily ritual prayers, the Ibn ʿAbbās tales expand upon this encounter, often documenting the conversation between Muḥammad and God with specificity. These highly embellished accounts of Muḥammad's night journey and ascension, accounts that claim to be transmitting the story as Muḥammad conveyed it to Ibn ʿAbbās, and which I will collectively refer to as "the Ibn ʿAbbās ascension narratives," represent some of the most extensive and detailed of the Muslim ascension stories to have survived to the present. Despite the fact that a number of Muslim scholars throughout history have rejected these rich narratives as fabrications, seeing them as stories with no authentic chain of transmission linking them to the time of the Prophet, the Ibn ʿAbbās ascension narratives have been and remain tremendously influential, for they help to define the basic store of symbols that come to be used by the vast majority of subsequent Muslim accounts of the Prophet's otherworldly journey.

CONTESTING THE IBN ʿABBĀS NARRATIVES

Ascension narratives often form as discourses in the context of power struggles, struggles both between members of different religious groups and between competing members of a single religious group. Within a single group, one faction may appeal to the concept of orthodoxy and heresy as a way to promote its own doctrines and to attack those of its rivals. Pierre Bourdieu discusses how, when unspoken assumptions about the "way things are" are called into question, orthodoxy and heterodoxy emerge as competing possibilities, different ways of construing the truth of the matter relative to systems of power.[3] People who hold positions of power find their interests served by opinions that they define as orthodoxy, while conversely, people in subordinate positions sometimes promote heterodox or heretical positions (defined as such relative to a given articulation of orthodoxy) in order to challenge the power of those who dominate them. Bourdieu's model of the interplay between orthodoxy and heterodoxy is overly simplistic, of course, but it helps one to see how competing articulations of orthodoxy can each be interpreted as expressions of privilege that an individual or a group asserts in order to claim a position of power. This book will examine the development of the Ibn ʿAbbās ascension narrative in detail and over time during the formative period of Islamic history in order to illustrate how the struggle over the control of this ascension discourse originated in the very first centuries after the rise of Islam and how aspects of this struggle continue into the present.

Some Muslims who objected to the Ibn ʿAbbās ascension narratives in both the distant and recent past, for instance, claim for themselves the role of defender of Islamic orthodoxy, urging other Muslims to marginalize and reject this particular version of the tale. A contemporary example of such a critical discourse appears in the following attack by a Muslim scholar upon the Ibn ʿAbbās ascension "*ḥadīth* reports" (originally oral stories allegedly reporting something that Muḥammad said or did):

> While you are researching the story of the night journey and the ascension, beware of relying on what is called the *Miʿrāj* ("Ascension") by Ibn ʿAbbās. It is a book fabricated from a collection of false *ḥadīth* that have neither foundation nor chain of transmitters. Whoever forged it intended with his atrocious action to attach these lies to Ibn ʿAbbās. Yet every cultured person, indeed, every rational person already knows that Ibn ʿAbbās is innocent of [this forgery]. He never wrote any book on the *Miʿrāj* of the Prophet, and moreover the literary movement did not even begin until the final years of the Umayyad period [over half a century after Ibn ʿAbbās died]. Why would one stop cursing this book, when they find that it contains lies attributed to the Prophet that bring a shock to the faith of many people? They continue circulating it and urging [the reading of] it. . . . How quickly for them the lie turns into a sound truth when it contains things that muddle the thoughts of Muslims and deceive them about their religion.[4]

This condemnation of the account of the night journey and ascension narrative attributed to Ibn ʿAbbās makes clear that, according to this critic, the falsified narrative represents a threat to the orthodox belief of Muslims. The fantastic details the narrative conveys may indeed have caused concern among this and other Muslim scholars. Yet the outrage expressed in the quotation above probably largely stems from the narrative's depiction of the physical interactions between God and Muḥammad (e.g., God touching Muḥammad in an anthropomorphic manner) and the conversations that took place between them (e.g., God speaking intimately with Muḥammad on extra-qurʾānic topics, and promoting ideas that some Muslims do not accept, such as the ability of Muḥammad to intercede on behalf of wrongdoers). This scholar claims to be arguing in defense of sound orthodox Islamic belief by urging Muslims to reject all those accounts that purport to convey Ibn ʿAbbās' version of the events of Muḥammad's ascension.

This rejection of the Ibn ʿAbbās narrative contrasts sharply with the embrace of the narrative by another contemporary Muslim scholar:

> One should not be surprised that we have taken the Ibn ʿAbbās version as an Arabic base text. Its mythic quality gives it a highly significant status

> in the study of the marvelous. In any case, it is a text that has the consensus of the majority, allowing for both representations of the imaginary and respect for the fundamental provisions of the law.[5]

By "consensus of the majority," this scholar means that he considers the Ibn ᶜAbbās narrative to be one of the most widely circulated and recited of all Arabic ascension narratives. Acknowledging the narrative's "mythic quality," and hence its potentially dubious status as an authentic record of what Muḥammad actually narrated about his experience, the scholar nevertheless embraces it as a reflection of the collective Muslim construction of Muḥammad's journey and as a response to the needs and desires of the Muslim community over time. The diametrically opposite positions of these two Muslim scholars, then, illustrates how the struggle over whether or not to accept the Ibn ᶜAbbās ascension narratives revolves around the question over what constitutes legitimate Muslim narratives, and even what constitutes "orthodox" belief about Muḥammad and his legacy. Although ideologues today may pretend otherwise, one cannot deny that throughout Islamic history the question of what constituted legitimate Muslim stories about the Prophet Muḥammad and his experiences was very much open to debate.

According to both of these Muslim scholars, the history of the Ibn ᶜAbbās ascension narrative remains shrouded in obscurity. This obscurity leads the narrative's critic to reject the narrative outright as groundless and unworthy of consideration. In contrast, it leads the narrative's proponent to wish to know more about the narrative, for the sake of the history of Muslim ideas, and to therefore lament the state of our ignorance surrounding its origins and development: "It is impossible to specify when [the Ibn ᶜAbbās narrative] was composed, and whether it might have been taken as a model from which all the other [later ascension narratives] derive."[6] While the present study takes no position on the authenticity of this or any other ascension account, it seeks to solve key problems in the enigma of the narrative's early history, uncovering the development of the Ibn ᶜAbbās ascension narratives, and offering evidence to show that many later Islamic ascension narratives do indeed draw upon the Ibn ᶜAbbās versions. In addition, this study shows how the contemporary dispute between those who reject the Ibn ᶜAbbās narrative and those who embrace and/or develop the Ibn ᶜAbbās narrative can be heard echoing across numerous works on Muḥammad's night journey composed during the formative period of Islamic history.

While this book examines the early formation of the contentious discourse surrounding the Ibn ᶜAbbās narrative, it simultaneously traces over time how the discourse became part of a strategy for groups to oppose those ideas that they deemed objectionable in other accounts by appropriating and adapting—thereby rendering "harmless"—the stories of one's rivals. As Michael Sells points out, a group may not only critique a rival group or tradition, but also may appropriate the symbols or myths used by others "when it feels threatened by what another group is doing with that symbolic system."[7] In the particular case of the Ibn ᶜAbbās ascension narratives, for example, a strategy that some groups used to oppose how a rival group made use of these stories about the Prophet's night journey, aside from rejecting the rivals' stories as pure fabrications, was to appropriate them for their own purposes. For instance, we shall see that some early Shīᶜīs embraced the Ibn ᶜAbbās narrative, and some later Sunnīs appropriated and adapted portions of the narrative from these Shīᶜīs as a way to counter their rivals' use of the ascension story. Embracing a certain version of the ascension narrative thus implies an assertion of power and an implicit delineation of the boundaries of acceptable discourse as defined by a given religious position. The Ibn ᶜAbbās ascension narrative came to prominence in the formative period of Islamic history precisely because of its utility in helping groups of Muslims to define the status of Muḥammad and, by extension, to define their own status as faithful followers of Muḥammad.

By examining the development of the Ibn ᶜAbbās ascension narrative from its primitive version in the third/ninth century up through its complete expression in the seventh/thirteenth century, one becomes better able to understand the ways in which the early Muslims made use of the ascension narrative more generally. That is, this study of what may at first seem a tangential and obscure version of a pivotal Muslim story serves to illustrate the process by which Muslims developed ideas about what constitutes sound and authoritative oral narratives, a long and messy process that took place in the midst of a wide variety of competing accounts. Furthermore, it helps to explain why this particular account frequently came to displace other competing accounts at the end of the formative period of Islamic history, thus having a tangible impact upon the way that Muslims envisioned the structure of the universe and their particular place in it.

On the Scope of This Study

The choice to concentrate on the Ibn ᶜAbbās versions of the tale is prompted by the recognition of its influence upon the premodern development of Islamic ascension literature. Such an emphasis allows one to study the history of key narrative tropes as they become introduced into the discourse and to examine how certain passages become excised and others highlighted in subsequent versions of the story. Tracing the history of this particular genre requires that other types of ascension works, especially those of a primarily mystical (e.g., the ascent narratives ascribed to Abū Yazīd Bisṭāmī and Ibn ᶜArabī), literary (e.g., the work of Maᶜarrī and Niẓāmī), or scholastic nature (e.g., the studies by Qushayrī and Ibn Diḥya Kalbī) can only be discussed insofar as they serve to illuminate the history of the Ibn ᶜAbbās discourse. This study therefore makes no pretensions to offering a comprehensive survey of Islamic ascension literature in the formative period as a whole, but instead sheds light on the previously obscure history of this extremely influential genre of ascension texts circulated in the name of Ibn ᶜAbbās.

Whereas most previous studies of Islamic ascension narratives restrict themselves to a few texts or authors, this study examines the early development of a particular genre of texts, the Ibn ᶜAbbās ascension narratives, over a long stretch of time, from the first centuries of Islamic history through the end of the formative period in the seventh/thirteenth century. The large temporal and geographical territory covered in such a study necessitates that it minimize the attention paid to local histories and contexts, for such critical contextual work must be left to subsequent studies. What has been sacrificed in our ability to interpret specific texts through their local contexts is more than compensated by what has been gained in our knowledge of the overarching history of the development of this genre as a whole. The great advantage of a study of a particular phenomenon over several centuries, then, becomes apparent through the continuities and ruptures that such a study is able to uncover, noting and analyzing trends over the long term that more delimited studies would miss.

THE CONTRIBUTION THAT THIS STUDY MAKES

Until the beginning of the past century, many of those who found an interest in examining the otherworldly journeys of religious and heroic figures in other cultural spheres knew little of the story of Muḥammad's night journey and ascension. Due to the work of a few orientalist scholars in the past century, the most important of which will be discussed in the pages that follow, since then accounts of Muḥammad's journey have become more widely known, if not much better understood. Indeed, substantial studies dedicated to analyzing the narrative in the context of its formation and development have been quite rare, leading to a situation in which contemporary scholars of apocalyptic and ascension narratives in other religious traditions have largely ignored or dismissed the Islamic narratives.[8] The present work joins the work of other scholars at the dawn of the twenty-first century who have recognized the need for more studies dedicated to these Islamic narratives in their own right, especially more nuanced and detailed studies that acknowledge the vast number of texts that narrate discrete versions of Muḥammad's night journey.[9]

The examination of the Ibn ᶜAbbās ascension discourse offered in this study applies some of the insights of late twentieth-century critical theory as employed in literary and religious studies to the philological method of identifying, translating, and scrutinizing particular texts. Postmodernist thought has radically called into question any particular articulation of truth claims, yet a number of scholars of religion, particularly those in Islamic studies, have resisted exploring the implications of this postmodernist challenge with regard to expressions of orthodoxy. Herein I selectively employ elements of postmodernist theory in order to break away from the pattern of most previous studies on Muḥammad's night journey and ascension, which until recently have privileged those ascension narratives that appear primarily in the Sunnī collections of *ḥadīth* that a select group of scholars from the formative period deemed to be authentic and authoritative. In order to "de-center" such narratives and to suggest that they emerged both in opposition to and in dialogue with other competing narratives, I defer the discussion of these semicanonical reports until the second half of this book. Instead, I begin by focusing attention upon the roots of the Ibn ᶜAbbās narratives in ascension accounts that may not have enjoyed the same official status and yet may still have enjoyed the support of many Muslims, as suggested by their wide circulation. The following analysis of the Ibn ᶜAbbās discourse assembles narrative evidence from a large number of Arabic and a select number of Persian sources, compiled through the time-tested philological tools of the orientalist, while employing tools from critical theory in order to draw conclusions about the relationships between the texts and the broader significance of the data assembled.

Through such an approach, I demonstrate that the accounts told about Muḥammad's journey in the formative period of Islamic history were more varied and more intricate than have previously been recognized by historians of religion. I suggest that scholars need to look beyond the Sunnī sound *ḥadīth* collections to get a fuller sense of the way Muslims narrated this key story from Muḥammad's biography. This particular brand of revisionism does not go to the extreme of some contemporary revisionists who reject all Muslim accounts as inherently flawed. Rather, it follows the methodological lead of contemporary "reader response" approaches to the study of the Qurʾān, tracing the changing ways that Muslims over time have interpreted and adapted those narrative accounts that previous generations have passed on to them.[10]

This study thus takes a literary and an historical approach to the formative prose works on Muḥammad's night journey and ascension, those available in published works as well as those available only in unpublished manuscript collections throughout the world. Both the approach taken and the number and type of sources studied herein distinguish this work from the recent work of Brooke Vuckovic, whose useful thematic approach to Muḥammad's journey confines itself to those accounts recorded in published works.[11] I share Vuckovic's concern with focusing upon the legacy (i.e., reception and use) of the ascension discourse rather than attempting another positivistic search for its elusive historical truth. Yet unlike Vuckovic, I contend that to chart the development of the Islamic narrative, a diachronic rather than a synchronic approach is crucial. Moreover, many of the texts that preserve the legacy of Muslim ascension discourses have yet to be published or even properly identified. Since the history of the development of the Ibn ʿAbbās narrative hinges upon unpublished texts whose significance has been recognized only in the last decade, this study offers a model for future research, and it lays the groundwork for a series of new and more wide-ranging studies on Muḥammad's night journey and ascension that are already well underway.[12]

OVERVIEW OF THE CHAPTERS

The debate over the Ibn ʿAbbās ascension narratives takes place largely in the context of scholarly discussions of the Qurʾān and other oral narratives through the genres of Qurʾān commentary (*tafsīr*) and collections of prophetic sayings (*ḥadīth*). Before investigating the development and legacy of the Ibn ʿAbbās ascension narratives themselves, therefore, chapter 1 surveys those passages from the Qurʾān that Muslims most frequently associate with Muḥammad's night journey and ascension, namely the night journey verse (Q 17:1) and the opening verses of the Star chapter (Q 53:1–18). In addition, the chapter introduces other passages from the Qurʾān whose interpretation becomes especially significant in the development of the Ibn ʿAbbās ascension narrative.

Chapter 2 then introduces the earliest known version of this story, which I refer to as the "Primitive Version" of the Ibn ʿAbbās ascension narrative. The full text of this narrative appears for the first time in English in Appendix A. Chapter 2 analyzes this Primitive Version with an eye to highlighting its distinctive features and its elements that later texts further develop and appropriate. I have chosen to introduce this Ibn ʿAbbās narrative early in the book in order for the reader to become familiar with its basic framework and thematic tropes before examining other early narratives. I do not mean thereby to imply that the Ibn ʿAbbās ascension discourse necessarily represents the earliest Islamic ascension narrative outside the Qurʾān, despite the fact that some Muslim and non-Muslim scholars do date it to the first century of Islamic history. Rather, the decision is a strategic one, challenging typical approaches to the night journey and ascension that discuss the sound (*ṣaḥīḥ*) Sunnī *ḥadīth* reports (treated below, chapter 5) immediately after the qurʾānic passages. Such approaches tacitly accept the argument of those Sunnī scholars who hold that the latter reports reflect the earliest and most authentic oral traditions and therefore offer the best lens through which to view the Muslim responses to the qurʾānic allusions. Instead, by foregrounding the Ibn ʿAbbās version in chapter 2, I ask the reader to imagine how other early narratives, including the sound Sunnī reports, could be understood as contributing to and/or reacting against this remarkable account that highlights the "wonders of the ascension."

Chapter 3 turns to the earliest historical sources from the second/eighth and third/ninth centuries, composed prior to the compilation of the major *ḥadīth* collections, exploring how the evidence from Ibn Isḥāq and Ibn Saᶜd treat the events of the night journey and ascension in their biographical accounts of Muḥammad's life. These historical accounts of Muḥammad's experience demonstrate that the night journey and ascension reports were not always joined as a single event in the minds of Muslims. Rather, the early historical narratives suggest that the night journey to Jerusalem and ascension to the heavens were originally considered as the events of two separate occasions in the biography of the Prophet. These narratives furthermore illustrate that there were significant debates taking place among Muslims about Muḥammad's journey even in the earliest period, and at times these debates reflect political and theological disagreements among members of the Muslim community.

Select proto-Shīᶜī interpretations of the night journey and ascension discourse are examined in chapter 4. In many of the fragmentary ascension anecdotes by proto-Shīᶜī traditionists, Muḥammad's journey serves as a pretext for illustrating God's approval of the leadership of Muḥammad's young cousin and future son-in-law, ᶜAlī. The proto-Shīᶜī reports discuss not only Muḥammad's ascension but also those experienced by other individuals considered prominent among the partisans of ᶜAlī, especially those who come to be revered among Shīᶜīs as special leaders known as Imams (not to be confused with the more general title of "Imam" shared by those Muslims, Sunnī and Shīᶜī, who lead during Muslim ritual prayers). Although these proto-Shīᶜī reports about the ascension of the Prophet and the ascensions of the Imams may seem quite different from many Sunnī reports on Muḥammad's ascension, I endeavor to illustrate how subsequent Sunnī authors nevertheless appropriate a number of ideas from these narratives in their rival accounts of the story of Muḥammad's journey.

Despite the fact that some later Sunnī authors (including the transmitters of the later Ibn ᶜAbbās narratives) will be shown to embrace a number of esoteric and creative proto-Shīᶜī tropes, the Sunnī sound *ḥadīth* reports introduced in chapter 5 illustrate the manner in which many of these tropes are excluded from those *ḥadīth* collections that the majority of Muslims come to consider official or canonical. The chapter surveys the extended reports of Muḥammad's journey that are included in Bukhārī and Muslim's famous collections of sound *ḥadīth*. It goes on to investigate those more fragmentary anecdotes from the official Sunnī collections that later Muslim traditionists collate into their own ascension tales, especially those that build upon the framework of the Ibn ᶜAbbās ascension narrative.

Chapter 6 studies the ascension accounts presented in some of the pivotal Qurʾān commentaries from the formative period, demonstrating how Ṭabarī, ʿAlī Qummī, and Thaʿlabī all respond to the Ibn ʿAbbās ascension narrative in their *tafsīr* works. Ṭabarī refrains from recording the Primitive Version, although he alludes to it briefly in the context of his discussion of Muḥammad's vision, and he includes several other long ascension narratives not found in the official Sunnī collections, narratives that become influential in the development of later *miʿrāj* works. Ṭabarī's contemporary, the Imāmī Shīʿī exegete ʿAlī Qummī, includes an extensive account in his commentary on the night journey verse that combines the Primitive Version of the Ibn ʿAbbās ascension narrative with one of the longer narratives that Ṭabarī records. Likewise, the key Sunnī exegete from Nishapur, Thaʿlabī, combines the Primitive Version together with another one of these long accounts recorded by Ṭabarī in order to formulate a new composite full narrative. These exegetes demonstrate the movement in the third/ninth and subsequent centuries toward constructing increasingly detailed and extensive versions of the story of Muḥammad's journey that often substantially draw upon the Ibn ʿAbbās ascension narrative, combining it with other reports in order to create elaborate long and hybrid storylines.

One finds a surge in scholarly activity surrounding the story of Muḥammad's night journey and ascension in Thaʿlabī's home town of Nishapur beginning in the fourth/tenth century, and chapter 7 investigates those figures in and around this temporal and geographic context who wrote entire works dedicated to the subject of the Prophet's journey. These works, which treat the night journey and ascension as a subject worthy of consideration on its own, constitute some of the earliest known written works of their kind. The *Book of the Ascension* (*Kitāb al-miʿrāj*) of the Sufi traditionist Qushayrī represents a particular milestone in the development of written Islamic ascension texts. While its importance to early mystical interpretations of Muḥammad's ascension is undeniable, more critical here is the fact that Qushayrī's text brings together early versions of the story of Muḥammad's ascension, including the Primitive Version of the Ibn ʿAbbās narrative as well as what I identify as an Extended Cosmological narrative, that bear comparison with later Ibn ʿAbbās versions. In Qushayrī's work and those of some of his contemporaries, one finds all the required ingredients for the reformulating of the Primitive Version into a fuller and richer account, telling the tale of the Ibn ʿAbbās ascension narrative in what comes to be known as its "total and complete" version.

These "total and complete" reshaped versions of the Ibn ʿAbbās ascension narrative, recensions of which form the basis for the analysis in chapter 8, come to be associated with an elusive figure named Abū al-Ḥasan Bakrī. After briefly examining the evidence for the historicity of this figure, chapter 8 turns to the earliest extant text of Bakrī's ascension that was copied down at the end of the seventh/thirteenth century in or around Yemen (a substantial portion of which is translated in Appendix B), comparing it with other extant Bakrī recensions. This novelized version of Muḥammad's night journey and ascension offers one of the most elaborate prose accounts of the tale circulating at the time, one that pays a great deal of attention to formulaic expressions of praise for the divinity, offers an inordinate focus upon the manner in which God honors the Prophet above all others, and emphasizes eschatological images of final reward and punishment. This chapter argues that perhaps because of its accessibility as a teaching text and its literary appeal, this Bakrī reshaped version of the Ibn ᶜAbbās ascension narrative comes to dominate virtually all subsequent versions of this Ibn ᶜAbbās genre. Chapter 8 identifies the distinctive features of the Bakrī text in order to make a case for its influence upon a series of later ascension texts, some of which are analyzed in the final chapter.

Chapter 9 looks at a select number of these later texts individually, weighing them as evidence for the wide circulation of the reshaped version of the Ibn ᶜAbbās ascension narrative in both the eastern and western lands of Islamdom prior to and during the seventh/thirteenth century. From works both obscure and famous, this chapter builds a case that Bakrī's reshaped version of the Ibn ᶜAbbās ascension narrative played a critical role in presenting the story of Muḥammad's journey both to non-Muslim audiences in Spain and to recent Muslim converts in Persia and Central Asia. Two central arguments of this book, namely that the Ibn ᶜAbbās ascension texts play a pivotal role in the formation of the wider Islamic ascension discourse, and that these texts frequently reflect polemics between Sunnī and Shīᶜī Muslims, are borne out by the evidence that appears in these subsequent Bakrī texts.

Beginning with Bakrī's reshaped version in the seventh/thirteenth century, and for the following three centuries until the dawn of the early modern era, this new and expanded Ibn ᶜAbbās discourse served as the most influential narrative of its kind across a vast expanse of territory within Islamdom, despite the uneasiness that it may have caused to some Muslim traditionists. With the translation of the reshaped Ibn ᶜAbbās ascension narrative from Arabic into European and Persian languages in the seventh/thirteenth century, the history of the narrative enters a new phase: the spread of this ascension narrative into non-Arabic spheres, and the rise of the illustrated ascension manuals.[13] By this time the development of the premodern Arabic story of Muḥammad's night journey and ascension had already reached its climax with the Bakrī version of the Ibn ᶜAbbās tale, however, forming a highly detailed genre of narrative tradition out of scattered references in *ḥadīth* reports, reports which served to elaborate on largely cryptic references in the Qurʾān. The process of narrating the development of the Bakrī texts out of the earliest versions of the Ibn ᶜAbbās ascension discourse thus begins first with the Qurʾān, examining those passages that generations of Muslims came to interpret in light of the tale of Muḥammad's night journey as told in the name of the early authority known as Ibn ᶜAbbās.

1
MUḤAMMAD'S NIGHT JOURNEY IN THE QUR'ĀN

Those not familiar with the Qur'ān may find it difficult to locate the qur'ānic references to the night journey and ascension narratives, for the passages that Muslims have come to interpret as references to these narratives do not necessarily share common qualities or appear in close proximity in the text. There are two primary qur'ānic passages that serve as the major proof texts for the stories about Muḥammad's night journey and ascension: the first verse of the chapter called the "Night Journey" or "Children of Israel" (*al-isrā'* or *banī isrā'īl*, Q 17:1), and the opening verses of the chapter called "the Star" (*al-najm*, Q 53:1–18). In addition, there are a number of other words, phrases, and entire verses in the Qur'ān that some Muslims have collated into the night journey and ascension accounts. This chapter focuses on those verses that are foundational to an understanding of the development of the night journey and ascension narratives, especially the narratives that come to be associated with Ibn 'Abbās.

THE NIGHT JOURNEY VERSE

The opening verse of the Night Journey chapter of the Qur'ān (Q 17:1), which one may conveniently call the "night journey verse," presents something of an enigma, for it offers the most unambiguous reference to a journey by night while simultaneously maintaining a degree of ambiguity about exactly who journeyed and where. Let us examine the verse again:

> *Glorified be the one who caused his servant to journey by night from the sacred place of prayer to the furthest place of prayer, whose precincts we have blessed, in order to show him some of our signs. Indeed he is the one who hears, the one who sees.* (Q 17:1)

The nocturnal foray alluded to in the verse later comes to be known by the technical term "the night journey" (*isrāʾ*), a term that becomes synonymous with the idea of heavenly ascension as well. Most Muslim exegetes understand the verse as a proclamation of the divine voice as it describes the journey of one of God's servants. The voice shifts between describing the divinity in the third person ("the one" and "his") to the first person plural ("we" and "our") and back again, in a style relatively common in qurʾānic discourse.[1] It recounts how one of God's servants is sent out or taken by another (*asrā bi-ʿabdihi*) on a journey by night.

An important issue left open by the vague language of the night journey verse is the identity of the servant whom the verse describes as journeying by night. Muslim exegetes unanimously understand the reference to "his servant" as an allusion to the Prophet Muḥammad in his role as God's servant (*ʿabd*). Some non-Muslim scholars point out, however, that the term could also be understood as a reference to Moses.[2] They argue that the Qurʾān elsewhere connects the key verb in the night journey verse (*asrā*) to the journeying of Moses by night.[3] In addition, the verses following the night journey verse (Q 17:1) refer to Moses explicitly: "*And we gave Moses the book, and made it/him a guidance for the children of Israel*" (Q 17:2). Other scholars, such as Angelika Neuwirth, discount the identification of the servant in the night journey verse with Moses, seeing Muḥammad as the most likely referent.[4] While this debate about the original meaning of the night journey verse has its merits, the present study will not concern itself with the truth or original meaning of the night journey verse, but rather with how the verse came to be interpreted and understood by later Muslims.[5] Whether or not the first Muslims heard echoes or allusions to Moses in the night journey verse ultimately becomes of little consequence to the history of Islamic ascension literature, since no Muslim source that I have seen raises any doubt that the night journey verse refers to Muḥammad.

Unlike the question of the identity of the servant, one issue that Muslim sources do debate is the question of the origin and destination of Muḥammad's night journey. The verse states that he was taken from "*the sacred place of prayer*" (*al-masjid al-ḥaram*). This "place of prayer," which Muslims usually identify with the sacred enclosure in Mecca in general and the central shrine within it known as the Kaʿba in particular, serves as the basic beginning point for the journey in many Muslim narratives. Yet, Muslim narrators differ on the issue of where Muḥammad was when the angels (who are not mentioned in the night journey verse) first came to fetch him for the journey. For some he was sleeping inside the Kaᶜba itself, while for others he was sleeping elsewhere in the sacred enclosure, sometimes at the house of various friends or relatives. The versions of the night journey and ascension narratives that come to be associated with Ibn ᶜAbbās, the development of which will be the central focus of this study, tend to highlight the statement of Muḥammad's cousin, Umm Hāniʾ bint Abī Ṭālib (sister of ᶜAlī b. Abī Ṭālib, the latter of whom is the pivotal figure for most Shīᶜī Muslims), that Muḥammad had been sleeping in her house that night. While the significance of this detail remains open to debate, the important thing to recognize at this juncture is that even the fairly straightforward phrase "*sacred place of prayer*," which appears a dozen times in the Qurʾān in reference to Mecca,[6] still remains subject to a range of interpretations in the subsequent *ḥadīth* reports, Qurʾān commentaries, and night journey narratives told by storytellers.

If Muslims interpret the qurʾānic phrase "*the sacred place of prayer*" in diverse ways, one encounters even more debate over the destination of the night journey, the "*furthest place of prayer*."[7] From the earliest extant Muslim texts, it becomes clear that a group of Muslims from the beginning interpreted the "*furthest place of prayer*" (*al-masjid al-aqṣā*) with the city of Jerusalem in general and its Herodian/Solomonic Temple in particular.[8] It is equally clear that other early Muslims disputed this connection, identifying the "*furthest place of prayer*" instead as a reference to a site in the heavens.[9] Eventually a general consensus formed around the idea that Muḥammad's journey did indeed take him to Jerusalem. Even if the night journey verse were thought to refer first and foremost to the terrestrial portion of Muḥammad's journey, nevertheless for centuries scholars and storytellers also continued to connect this verse with the idea of an ascent through the levels of the heavens.

Indeed, how one interprets the location of the "*furthest place of prayer*" in the night journey verse hinges to some degree upon what one sees as the relationship between the terrestrial, horizontal journey to Jerusalem and the celestial, vertical journey to the heavens. The early sources differ on whether the terrestrial and celestial journey are in fact one and the same, or whether they refer to distinct events happening at different times.[10] When treated separately, the terrestrial journey to Jerusalem was frequently designated by the term "night journey" (*isrāʾ*), while the heavenly journey was frequently designated by the term "ascension" (*miᶜrāj*).[11] Numerous *ḥadīth* reports and early sources such as Ibn Hishām's recension of Ibn Isḥāq's prophetic biography prove, however, that Muslims connected the two journeys into one by the third/ninth century at the latest. After this time, Muslims come to use the terms "night journey" and "ascension" virtually interchangeably, often using either term to refer to a single composite journey over land (to Jerusalem) and through the heavens (to the seventh heaven and sometimes beyond) that Muḥammad experienced on a single night. In other words, the night journey verse, and the word "night journey" (*isrāʾ*) that derives from the key verb in that verse, both come to be employed by Muslims for the whole of Muḥammad's experiences on the night in question.

According to the night journey verse, the purpose of the journey was for God's servant (Muḥammad) to be shown some of God's signs (*āyāt*). The verse never provides any clues to the content of these signs. The term "sign" (*āya*) appears in the Qurʾān over three hundred times, often referring to something in creation that might remind one of the divine creator. Muslims also use the term "sign" as a technical term for a verse of the Qurʾān. One could imagine various reasons why the night journey verse does not explain the meaning of the signs that Muḥammad was shown. One might surmise that the early audience might have found the reference to signs self-explanatory, or that they would have turned to other verses or sayings to explain the meaning here. Alternatively, Muslims might interpret the lack of specificity in the verse as evidence that the content of the signs was meant to be a secret between Muḥammad and his lord, a position that some early Sufi mystics apparently took.[12] Even though the Qurʾān refrains from further elucidating the meaning of the "signs" mentioned in the night journey verse, later exegetes and storytellers will often supply the details that the qurʾānic account leaves out. The openness of the references in the night journey verse, references to a servant, places of prayer, and signs, allows later Muslims to interpret this key qurʾānic verse in a variety of ways.

VERSES FROM THE CHAPTER OF THE OVERTURNING

A passage from the chapter of the Qurʾān known as "the Overturning" (*al-takwīr*, Q 81), an apocalyptic chapter from the early period of Muḥammad's prophetic career, calls on celestial bodies to bear witness to the truth of Muḥammad's revelation in general and his visionary experience in particular. The portion of the chapter that most directly bears upon the narrative of Muḥammad's night journey and ascension is as follows:

15) *I swear by the stars that slide,*
16) *stars streaming, stars that sweep along the sky*
17) *By the night as it slips away*
18) *By the morning when the fragrant air breathes*
19) *This is the word of a messenger ennobled,*
20) *empowered, ordained before the lord of the throne,*
21) *holding sway there, keeping trust*
22) *Your friend has not gone mad*
23) *He saw him on the horizon clear*
24) *He does not hoard for himself the unseen.* (Q 81:15–24)[13]

This passage from "the Overturning" invokes the signs (*āyāt*) of the heavens and the earth in a manner characteristic of many Meccan revelations. The ostensible purpose behind the evocation of these signs rests upon their ability to testify to the veracity of the words brought by an "ennobled messenger" (*rasūl karīm*, Q 81:19), often understood as a reference to the angel Gabriel, who in Islamic belief represents the primary intermediary carrying the revelation from the divinity to Muḥammad. This reading of the passage suggests that the verse "He saw him on the horizon clear" (Q 81:23) alludes to Muḥammad's vision of the angel Gabriel, and one group of Muslim exegetes understand the verse in this way.

However, the title "messenger" (*rasūl*) applies to Muḥammad as well, so perhaps this passage from "the Overturning" has something other than Gabriel in mind. Perhaps Muḥammad himself, for instance, was "ordained before the lord of the throne" (Q 81:20). Indeed, some versions of the night journey and ascension narratives, especially those transmitted in the name of Ibn ᶜAbbās, depict Muḥammad as receiving verses of the Qur'ān and/or his prophetic commission at the foot of God's throne.[14] Moreover, as Josef van Ess proposes, the verse "He saw him on the horizon clear" (Q 81:23) may refer not to a vision of the angel Gabriel but rather to a vision of God.[15] These ideas do not represent the majority opinion about the meaning of these verses from the chapter of "the Overturning," but they do suggest exegetical trends that the Ibn ᶜAbbās ascension narratives will develop in detail.

One sees at the beginning of the above passage from "the Overturning" (Q 81:15–16) a predominance of celestial signs, particularly the stars or planets (*al-khunus*). This emphasis upon the celestial bodies and the skies causes one to wonder whether there may be some connection between celestial signs and prophetic or visionary revelations. Could such a connection explain why Muslim storytellers incorporated images from the above verses in their ascension narratives? This possibility becomes even more intriguing in light of the opening verses of chapter of the Star (*al-najm*, *sūra* 53) to which we now turn.

THE OPENING VERSES OF THE CHAPTER OF THE STAR

As in the night journey verse and the verses from the Overturning chapter cited above, the first eighteen verses of the chapter known as "the Star" (*al-najm*, Q 53) refer to a revelation of God's signs through a visionary experience. Some Muslims from the first centuries of Islamic history denied that the following verses had much of a connection to Muḥammad's night journey or ascension, as the compilation of early exegesis by the famous commentator Ibn Jarīr al-Ṭabarī (d. 310/923) proves.[16] Nevertheless other Muslims, especially those interested in fleshing out the bare-bones account of the heavenly ascension provided in other sources, found in the following passage a number of rich symbols and ideas.

1) *By the star when it sets*
2) *indeed your companion is not astray*
3) *nor does he speak vainly.*
4) *It is nothing less than a revelation revealed*
5) *taught to him by a being of intense power*
6) *possessing strength. He straightened up*
7) *while he was on the highest horizon,*
8) *then he drew close and descended*
9) *and he was a distance of two bows or closer.*
10) *He revealed to his servant what he revealed.*
11) *The heart did not lie in what it saw.*
12) *Will you then argue with him about what he saw?*
13) *He saw him another time*
14) *at the Lote Tree of the Boundary*
15) *next to the Garden of the Refuge*
16) *when the Lote Tree was covered by what covered.*
17) *His vision did not stray, nor was it excessive.*
18) *He saw some of the greatest signs of his Lord.*

As in the passage from the Overturning, these verses from the Star begin with an invocation of the authority of a celestial phenomenon as a sign. As in the night journey verse, here the divine voice speaks in the third person, appearing "to disclose a secret which, apart from [God] Himself, only the Prophet could have known."[17] In both the passage above from the Star chapter and in the night journey verse, the Qur᾿ān describes an experience granted to a "servant" (*ᶜabd*), understood by Muslims in both cases to be an allusion to Muḥammad. The above passage also shares with the night journey verse the idea that these experiences revealed to Muḥammad some of God's signs (*āyāt*). In the Star chapter, the signs are further described by the superlative adjective "greatest" (*kubrā*, feminine form of *akbar*). Just as in the previous two qur᾿ānic citations, the opening verses from the Star chapter contain a fair amount of ambiguous language.

The identity of the powerful being that the passage describes is especially cryptic, and the interpretation of these verses apparently shifted over time between viewing the being as God and viewing the being as Gabriel.[18] Much about how the verse is read hinges upon how one interprets the ambiguous pronoun "he" sprinkled throughout the following passage: "*He straightened up while he was on the highest horizon, then he drew close and descended and he was a distance of two bows or closer* [at which point] *he revealed to his servant what he revealed*" (Q 53:7–10). While some figure was on "*the highest horizon*" (Q 53:7), a phrase reminiscent of the "*clear horizon*" from the Overturning (Q 81:23), some being drew near and revealed something. Those Muslims intent on seeing in this passage a reference to Muḥammad's heavenly ascension could claim that the vision took place while Muḥammad had been raised to the "*highest horizon.*" Other Muslims, interpreting the ambiguous pronoun as referring to the angel Gabriel, often explained the verse as a description of Gabriel revealing himself to Muḥammad, perhaps for the very first time and/or perhaps in his immense true form.[19] The former exegetical trend holds particular interest in this study, for those early Muslims who interpreted the above verses from the Star as describing one or more visions of God frequently attributed their ideas to the famous companion of Muḥammad and exegete, Ibn ʿAbbās.[20] Nevertheless, the qur'ānic reference in this passage remains sufficiently vague to allow for a variety of interpretations of the content of the vision described.

The revelation or inspiration (*waḥy*) mentioned in the above passage from the Star chapter does not offer much more specificity to the account, although the passage does appear to suggest that the revelation consisted first and foremost of a vision, since it offers the assurance that Muḥammad's faculties correctly reported this vision: "*The heart did not lie in what it saw*" (Q 53:11). As with the night journey verse, the Qur'ān circumvents stating exactly what was revealed, here offering the even more elusive formulation, "*He revealed to his servant what he revealed*" (Q 53:10). The cautious explanations that Muslims give in many scholarly commentaries and sound (*ṣaḥīḥ*) *ḥadīth* reports about this elusive verse tend to understand it as saying either that Muḥammad was granted a vision of Gabriel in his true form or saying that during his journey he was told of the Muslim duty to perform the ritual prayer (*ṣalāt*) a set number of times per day. Muslim storytellers and more daring exegetes, on the other hand, explain that the vague language in this verse conceals the fact that Muḥammad had enjoyed a vision and conversation with God. The Ibn ʿAbbās ascension narratives wax especially poetic on this subject, reading the Star chapter's ambiguous statement "*He revealed to his servant what he revealed*" (Q 53:10) as an allusion to the climactic dialogue and vision at the highest point in Muḥammad's ascension.

Almost all accounts of Muḥammad's heavenly ascension make use of a less ambiguous yet no less mysterious reference from the opening verses of the Star chapter, the reference to a vision at the "*Lote Tree of the Boundary*" (*sidrat al-muntahā*, Q 53:14). Few details about this Lote Tree appear in the Star chapter, aside from the fact that it is located near the equally mysterious "*Garden of the Refuge*" (*jannat al-ma'wā*, Q 53:15), and that a vision took place at the tree when it was covered by something undefined (Q 53:16). Despite the paucity of specific referents in this passage, Muslims early on almost unanimously associated the tree with a heavenly location, and interpreted "*the boundary*" as a reference to some type of barrier or limit in one of the highest heavens. Most official Muslim accounts describe the boundary as an absolute limit, beyond which created beings cannot cross. In contrast, the more extensive Ibn ʿAbbās ascension narratives portray the Lote Tree as marking a limit that Muḥammad and a few select archangels are allowed to pass beyond, and they depict how Muḥammad leaves Gabriel behind at this point and travels on through yet higher realms to the divine throne itself. The Ibn ʿAbbās narratives exploit the vague language from the opening verses of the Star chapter, attempting to elucidate these otherwise obscure qurʾānic phrases.

Josef van Ess' discussion of the passage "*He saw him another time at the Lote Tree of the Boundary, next to the Garden of the Refuge*" (Q 53:13–15) raises key points about how both early and more recent scholars understood its meaning:

> This sounds like a code for paradise, the "*Garden of the Refuge*" being the abode where the blessed will find refuge during or after Judgment (cf. 32:19) and the "*Lote Tree*" marking the boundary of the *sanctissimum* where God Himself resides. But God could descend to it nevertheless, for in those early days paradise was frequently imagined to be on earth. We need therefore not follow the suggestion of early orientalists (starting with Grimme and Caetani up to Richard Bell and Régis Blachère), namely that the "*Garden of the Refuge*" was simply a plantation near Mecca and the "*Lote Tree*" some well-known tree marking the boundary of the Meccan Sanctuary. Muslim exegesis never saw any reason to deny that the encounter took place in paradise, even if it were somewhere on earth. The "*Lote Tree of the Boundary*" became something like the emblem of Muḥammad's ascension; even when reports of the *miʿrāj* make no other reference to *sūrat al-Najm* [the Star chapter], the *sidrat al-muntahā* [Lote Tree of the Boundary] remains as the threshold leading to God's own realm, the seventh Heaven; it is there that the four rivers of paradise originate.[21]

As van Ess states, some Islamicists have argued that the Lote Tree originally referred to a tree located somewhere in Arabia, perhaps marking the boundary of a sacred enclosure.[22] He dismisses this mundane identification in favor of a paradisiacal one, accepting the Muslim exegetical consensus that the Lote Tree should be seen first and foremost as a tree of paradise.[23] Van Ess is correct that the vision at the Lote Tree hints at the link between this site and God's abode or presence, and one strand of the Muslim exegetical tradition understands the cryptic qurʾānic reference to the tree being covered (Q 53:16) with the descent of God's presence to it.[24] In some ways, however, van Ess' treatment of the Lote Tree in the quotation above misses some subtleties that become especially important to more extensive Muslim ascension narratives. For instance, while many Muslim ascension accounts do treat the Lote Tree as a tree of paradise the way van Ess describes, those ascension narratives that include a more extensive and detailed tour of the various sections of paradise frequently distinguish between the Lote Tree at the boundary of this realm and a different tree[25] in the midst of the paradisiacal garden. Many Ibn ᶜAbbās narratives, as mentioned above, depict the Lote Tree less as an ultimate destination on the ascension and more as a boundary marker separating the preliminary stages of the journey in which Gabriel accompanies Muḥammad from its final and highest stages where Muḥammad must travel alone. Regardless of whether or not they accept these extra scenes and flourishes, however, as van Ess rightly asserts, for Muslim narrators, "The '*Lote Tree of the Boundary*' became something like the emblem of Muḥammad's ascension." Thus, despite the fact that the opening verses of the Star chapter never say anything explicit to connect them to a heavenly journey or ascension, in the minds of the vast majority of Muslims who comment or elaborate upon these verses, the verses' reference to what are assumed to be heavenly or paradisiacal locations imply such a connection.

THE APPROPRIATION OF TERMS AND PHRASES FROM THE QUR'ĀN

Just as with the "*Lote Tree of the Boundary*" and the "*Garden of the Refuge*," Muslims narrating the story of Muḥammad's ascension lift a series of other terms out of their qur'ānic context and collate them into their narratives. Neuwirth would call ascension narratives that draw upon qur'ānic terms and phrases in this fashion examples of "mythologizing exegesis," for this type of approach "dissolves the qur'ānic statements into its individual elements in order to construct out of these elements side-plots and background images."[26] I agree with Neuwirth that these terms have been lifted from their qur'ānic context and applied to a mythological extra-qur'ānic narrative. Such a collation process becomes more and more frequent in later stages of the ascension narratives, as in the portions of these narratives describing heavenly and paradisiacal locations. For instance, a vague qur'ānic oath invoking "*The Inhabited House*" (*al-bayt al-maᶜmūr*, Q 52:4) is understood in nearly every ascension narrative as standing for a type of celestial temple located in the seventh heaven,[27] often near the Lote Tree. A second tree located in the midst of paradise, mentioned above, sometimes bears the name "Goodness" (*ṭūbā*), drawn from a vague qur'ānic reference to "goodness" as being the reward for righteous behavior and belief (Q 13:29). Similarly a word is lifted from a qur'ānic passage proclaiming that Muḥammad (and by extension his community) has been given "abundance" (Q 108:1), applying this term to the name of one of the rivers of paradise, "Abundance" (*Kawthar*).[28] Even the widely accepted ascension narratives found in the major collections of Sunnī sound *ḥadīth* reports frequently contain interpolations of this kind.

Yet more examples of these types of appropriations of qur'ānic terms can be found in the detailed and extensive accounts of Muḥammad's heavenly journey ascribed to Ibn ʿAbbās. For instance, some of the stages of the journey beyond the Lote Tree in the Ibn ʿAbbās ascension narratives are given the name "Heights" (*ʿilliyūn*, Q 83:18–20), a term the Qur'ān somewhat puzzlingly links to the books containing the good deeds of righteous individuals. Muḥammad traverses these highest realms without Gabriel, usually carried aloft not by another angel but by a green "cushion" (*rafraf*, Q 55:76), a term appearing in the Qur'ān as one of the comforts of paradise, but here depicted as a type of flying carpet.[29] The three central and recurring themes that make up the bulk of Muḥammad's conversation with God in the Ibn ʿAbbās texts, the "Heavenly Host Debate," the "Final Verses of the Cow Chapter," and the "Favor of the Prophets" passages, all derive to varying degrees from explicit phrases in the Qur'ān. These appropriations of qur'ānic language and imagery may appear artificial or secondary to the narrative,[30] yet one should not be surprised that the highest stages of the journey would represent precisely those sections where Muslim narrators would seek to bolster their accounts with proof texts from the Qur'ān.

Whether to lend their stories greater legitimacy in the eyes of fellow Muslims, or to add a qur'ānic flavor to their mix, early Muslim narrators would often draw words and phrases from the Qur'ān to enrich their accounts of these otherworldly experiences through what Neuwirth calls "mythologizing exegesis." In the absence of passages in the Qur'ān presenting detailed descriptions of the places and beings Muḥammad encountered on his heavenly ascension, these narrators would imaginatively construct descriptions on their own, using references from the Qur'ān to a lesser or greater degree. The mythological use of the terms sometimes remains consistent with the meaning that the terms have in their qur'ānic contexts. At other times, however, it is difficult to see any direct connection between the mythological appropriation of qur'ānic references in the ascension narratives on the one hand and their original contexts in the Qur'ān on the other. Two of the three key tropes from the Ibn ʿAbbās narrative's dialogue between Muḥammad and God, the "Heavenly Host Debate" and the "Seals of the Cow Chapter," illustrate this point.

THE HEAVENLY HOST DEBATE

A passage from the Qur'ān that apparently has nothing to do with the night journey and ascension narratives but was subsumed into these narratives appears in an adaptation of a passage from the *Ṣad* chapter of the Qur'ān (Q 38:65–70) that I will be calling the "Heavenly Host Debate." In this passage the divine voice addresses Muḥammad, telling him to speak the following words:

65) *Say: I am a warner. There is no god except the one conquering God,*
66) *Lord of the heavens and the earth and whatever is between them, the one who is mighty and the one who forgives.*
67) *Say: It is a great prophecy,*
68) *one which you oppose.*
69) *I did not have knowledge of the heavenly host when they were debating.*
70) *It was only revealed to me that I am a clear warner.* (Q 38:65–70)[31]

Here the divine voice instructs Muḥammad to tell others that he is merely a warner,[32] not someone possessing knowledge of the secrets, such as the secret regarding the details of the debates between angels. From the verses immediately following the above passage (Q 38:71–85), one gets the sense that in the qur'ānic context the angels were "debating" (*yakhtaṣimūn*) about the creation of Adam and the command to bow down before him. Muḥammad is told to proclaim his ignorance of this event, and then the Qur'ān proceeds to instruct him and his audience about it. On the surface, these verses contradict the notion of there being any connection between this passage and Muḥammad's night journey and ascension, for the verses instruct Muḥammad to deny the claim that he possesses knowledge of hidden mysteries. Nevertheless, some Muslim exegetes will connect these verses with an extra-qur'ānic conversation between Muḥammad and his Lord, one in which Muḥammad learns from God the details about what the heavenly host debate. He learns in these imaginative passages, which circulate in *ḥadīth* reports and get later incorporated into ascension narratives, that the angels' debate has nothing to do with the creation of Adam, but rather it deals with the definition of pious behavior.[33] From a passing reference to a mysterious debate in the Qur'ān, therefore, an entire scene comes to develop in the oral reports, and this new scene is collated into the divine colloquy section of later ascension narratives.

THE FINAL VERSES (SEALS) OF THE CHAPTER OF THE COW

Another apparently unrelated passage from the Qur'ān that becomes appropriated into the divine colloquy section of a number of later ascension narratives appears in the final two verses that close the longest chapter of the Qur'ān, the so-called seals (*khawātim*) of the chapter of the Cow (Q 2:285–86). Muslims often portray the Cow chapter (*al-baqara*, Q 2) as the paradigmatic chapter revealed to the Muslim community at Medina. Since most Muslims date the night journey and ascension narratives to a time prior to the emigration of the Muslim community from Mecca to Medina in 622 CE, one wonders how the final verses of the Cow chapter could possibly relate to the events of that journey. Such a difficulty is not insurmountable, since the ascension narratives that collate this passage could claim that God gave Muḥammad these verses in the heavens even before they were revealed to him on earth.[34] This being as it may, these final two verses or "seals" of the Cow chapter outline the basic elements of Muslim beliefs, followed by a petitionery request for God's forgiveness and mercy.

> 285) *The Messenger believes what was sent down to him from his Lord. The believers all believe in God, his angels, his books, and his messengers. We do not differentiate between any of his messengers. They say, "We hear and obey." Forgive us, Lord. To you is the arrival.*
>
> 286) *God does not burden a soul beyond what it can bear. It has what it has earned, and upon it is what it earned. Lord, do not blame us when we forget or err. Lord, do not make us bear a heavy weight like the one you made those before us to bear. Lord, do not make us carry what we are not able. Forgive us and pardon us and have mercy on us. You are our master, so give us victory over the unbelievers.*

Authors of the ascension narratives modify this pair of statements and requests, turning them into the report of a dialogue between Muḥammad and God at the highest stage of the ascension. In this intimate and exalted station, Muḥammad's pleas on behalf of the Muslim community for God's forgiveness and mercy take on special significance, illustrating the degree to which some Muslims believe that Muḥammad will be able to intercede with God on their behalf. This particular dialogue is not easy to extrapolate from the way the verses appear in the Qur'ān. The petitionery dimension of the end of verse 285 and much of verse 286 possibly led some Muslims to consider these verses as part of the divine colloquy scene in ascension narratives. This "Seals of the Chapter of the Cow" trope becomes one of the most ubiquitous themes in the dialogue portion of the Ibn ʿAbbās ascension narratives, demonstrating how a certain theological issue, in this case belief in Muḥammad's intercessory power, may have caused some Muslim exegetes and storytellers to incorporate into their ascension tales certain qur'ānic verses that outwardly bear no relation to the story of the night journey and ascension.

Passing References to Ascension in the Qur'ān

The fact that so many disparate and diverse qur'ānic references become part of the night journey and ascension narratives in later centuries leads to the question of whether or not the Qur'ān contains even more explicit references to the idea of a night journey or heavenly ascension. Beyond the night journey verse (Q 17:1), the verses from the Overturning (Q 81:15–24), and the opening verses of the chapter of the Star (Q 53:1–18), all of which employ vague and ambiguous language to describe visionary experiences revealed to God's servant, the verses that mention the concept of ascension in passing seem either ambivalent to or even opposed to the idea of human beings ascending to the sky. The ambivalence or opposition of such verses lead Neuwirth to assert boldly that the Qur'ān offers an "explicit rejection of an ascension" insofar as it would be "inappropriate for a human messenger."[35] These verses do not rule out the idea that Muḥammad experienced a heavenly journey, however, but rather dwell on the idea that God refuses to provide explicit proofs to the unbelievers, for they would refuse to accept these proofs even were such proofs to be given to them.[36] The majority of these passages express the sentiment that unbelievers would not believe in God and the message of the Qur'ān, even were they themselves to be brought up into the heavens.

In addition to these qur'ānic passages that appear to reject the notion that it befits a human being to ascend to heaven, one finds allusions to the idea that God's enemies attempt to ascend to the heavens to overhear what those in the upper realms are saying. For instance, the following passage describes how certain satanic rebels attempt to spy on the upper realms, and how they are driven away to prevent them from doing so:

> 6) *We decorated the first heaven*[37] *with the decoration of heavenly spheres*
> 7) *protected from each rebel satan.*
> 8) *They do not hear the heavenly host and are pelted from each side,*
> 9) *driven off. They will [all] face continual torment*
> 10) *except for the one who steals a listen, for a piercing flame follows him.* (Q 37:6–10)

This passage presumes a certain knowledge of the mythological context that it does not give here. While intriguing parallels between the idea in the above passage of repelling an invasion of heaven and similar concepts in Jewish folklore and ascension narratives come to mind,[38] in the qur'ānic text the story of the rebellious angels—discussed above with regard to the Heavenly Host Debate—seems to provide the most fitting context. Note the parallel between the language in Q 37:8 above and the Heavenly Host Debate passage (Q 38:65–70): In the former, the rebel powers attempt to listen in on the discourse of the heavenly host; in the latter, Muḥammad is instructed to deny knowledge of the discourse of the heavenly host. Elsewhere in the Qur'ān, not only rebellious satans but also rebellious people attempt to hear the heavenly voices or at least claim to have done so. The Qur'ān instructs Muḥammad to ask his adversaries, "Do they have a ladder upon which they can hear? Let any who have heard bring clear authority (*ṣultān mubīn*)" (Q 52:38). Once again an allusion to heavenly ascension, here evoked through a reference to a ladder (*sullam*), contains a negative connotation, describing how impostors and enemies attempt to ascend through their own power in order to spy on the heavenly realm.

While the Qurʾān rejects any notion that the enemies of God can succeed in ascending to the heavens, just as it rejects the idea that an ascension would change the mind of unbelievers, nevertheless it does insist on God's supreme authority to allow beings to ascend from the earth up to the heavens and to descend from the heavens down to the earth. In these assertions, one finds some of the few instances in the Qurʾān in which the root of the Arabic word *miʿrāj*, namely *ʿ-r-j*, appears.[39] Two separate verses in the Qurʾān proclaim that God "*knows what goes into the earth and what exits from it, and what descends from the sky* [*heaven*] *and what ascends to it*" (Q 34:2, 57:4). The implication of this proclamation is not only that God has knowledge of all things, but also that God also allows for these movements to take place. The chapter of the Qurʾān known as "the Steps" (*al-maʿārij*, Q 70) is so called because it contains a description of God as "*Possessor of the steps*" (*dhū al-maʿārij*, Q 70:3), or translated differently, "*Lord of the ascensions*."[40] The same qurʾānic passage in which this epithet appears goes on to say, "*To him the angels and the spirit ascend, on a day whose span is fifty thousand years*" (Q 70:4). This verse from the chapter of the Steps bears comparison to the verses from the chapter of Destiny (Q 97), in which the angels and spirit (*rūḥ*) descend on a night "*better than a thousand months*" (Q 97:3–4).[41] In each case time collapses during the movement of the angels and spirit between heaven and earth, evoking a hyperbolic multiplication of the span of earthly time that expresses the magnitude of the event.[42] God commands his faithful heavenly servants to descend and ascend, just as he insures that his enemies will not succeed in doing so without his bidding.

Granted, these qurʾānic references detail the movements of angels and the spirit, and do not contradict Neuwirth's assertion that the Qurʾān offers an "explicit rejection of an ascension" insofar as it portrays such an ascension as "inappropriate for a human messenger."[43] In fact, depending on how one interprets the key passages that were introduced above, the night journey verse (Q 17:1), the verses from the Overturning (Q 81:15–24), and the opening verses of the chapter of the Star (Q 53:1–18), one may defensibly argue that not a single passage in the Qurʾān supports the idea that Muḥammad ascended up through the heavens and back, all within a single night. A reference to a terrestrial journey in the night, perhaps with a destination of Jerusalem, could certainly be seen in the night journey verse, but according to Neuwirth's study that uses the Qurʾān to explicate the Qurʾān, one finds little support for the concept of Muḥammad's heavenly journey in the text of the Qurʾān itself.

Even if one accepts that the Qur'ān offers little explicit support for the idea of Muḥammad's heavenly ascension, one cannot deny that, despite such lack of support, Muslims in the first three centuries of Islamic history not only accepted that Muḥammad experienced such a journey but also endeavored to tell the story of this experience and to explain its significance. Indeed, built into many Muslim extra-qur'ānic accounts of Muḥammad's journey, including those ascribed to Ibn ʿAbbās, is the idea that accepting the truth of Muḥammad's testimony about the journey serves as a test of faith for Muslims. From this point of view, the qur'ānic verse "*We only made the vision that we revealed to you as a strife* (fitna) *for people*" (Q 17:60), when understood as a reference to Muḥammad's journey, helps to explain why the Qur'ān does not recount the story in a more explicit fashion. Moreover, it can also be used to explain why Muslims argue over the meaning and significance of Muḥammad's journey.[44]

Unlike Neuwirth's attempt to examine "internal qur'ānic commentary,"[45] or any method claiming to uncover the original sense of the qur'ānic text, this study focuses on the historical development of the mythologizing trends within the vast storytelling genres of later centuries. That is, instead of endeavoring to explain the most correct interpretation of the qur'ānic verses, this book traces how Muslim interpretations of these verses, especially those associated with the Ibn ʿAbbās ascension narrative, take shape over time. Having examined some of the most important qur'ānic material on which these narratives will draw, the following chapters explore the extra-qur'ānic Muslim accounts of Muḥammad's journey, beginning with the earliest version of the ascension narrative ascribed to Muḥammad's cousin and companion, Ibn ʿAbbās.

2

ORALITY AND THE PRIMITIVE VERSION OF THE IBN ᶜABBĀS ASCENSION NARRATIVE

In the first two centuries of the Islamic era, the vast majority of the texts on Muḥammad's night journey and ascension were transmitted orally. Most Muslim accounts of the narrative place the event(s) in the early portion of Muḥammad's career; thus Muḥammad would have had years to tell his companions the story of what he experienced. These narratives represent what historian Jan Vansina would term "oral traditions," those accounts and tales that are passed on by later generations, beyond the lifetime of the transmitter.[1] Features of orality pervade these narratives; for instance, most ascension reports describe the same formulaic questions being asked at the gate of each of the heavens that Muḥammad and Gabriel approach, a type of repetition that one might expect to find in an oral tradition.[2] In oral traditions, as described by Vansina, even those narratives taken to be factual accounts nevertheless become subject to modification over time through the process of transmission: Disparate narratives or portions of narrative may fuse together, expand or contract, and/or have episodes rearranged, added, or subtracted.[3] Oral traditions tell the historian not only about the time that they claim to represent, but also about the period in which they were transmitted and the values of the transmitters. A transmitter preserves and passes on a narrative that she believes is relevant to her present age, simultaneously adapting and/or reinterpreting the narrative in accordance with her present perspectives and needs.[4] Vansina's insights into the fluid nature of oral tradition show how a study of changes in a particular pattern of Islamic ascension narratives over time also involves an exploration of the changing sensibilities, norms, and needs of different Muslim communities in different times and places. One way that oral traditions were transmitted by the early Muslims can be found in the form of what come to be known as *ḥadīth* reports.

Ḥadīth reports transmit what Muḥammad's followers passed on to later generations regarding what Muḥammad said or did on a certain occasion, and the best of these reports offer a source of Islamic teachings about the night journey and ascension that many Muslims place on par with the text of the Qurʾān. Since the Qurʾān does not offer a clear and full account of Muḥammad's night journey and ascension, Muslims needed to ask questions to gain a coherent understanding of what Muḥammad experienced, and while he was alive the most logical person to ask would have been Muḥammad himself. After Muḥammad's death, Muslims would naturally turn to other Muslims with their questions.[5] According to Muslim sacred history, Muḥammad's oral explanations of the details of the night journey and ascension were memorized by his companions and transmitted in the form of oral anecdotes that later scholars brought together and recorded to form written collections of *ḥadīth* reports.

As Muslim scholars in the early centuries following Muḥammad's death sought to understand the meaning and significance of both the verses of the Qurʾān and aspects of the life of Muḥammad such as the night journey and ascension, they turned to the *ḥadīth* reports and other oral accounts for interpretive guidance. The works by interpreters and historians composed in the second/eighth century and early third/ninth century, before the widespread acceptance of the newly developing science of *ḥadīth* criticism, frequently harmonized diverse accounts to form stories that flowed well, stories possessing a narrative coherence. One such early story recounting aspects of Muḥammad's journey appears in a report of the "wonders of the ascension" ascribed to a young scholar and companion of the Prophet Muḥammad named Ibn ʿAbbās.

APPROACHING IBN ʿABBĀS AND THE PRIMITIVE VERSION

Most historical studies of the night journey and ascension narrative begin with references to the Qurʾān, and then quickly move to recounting one of two genres of ascension report: either the versions of the narrative given in the early histories by Ibn Isḥāq and Ibn Saʿd (see chapter 3), or the oral narratives collected and deemed sound by the majority of later Sunnī scholars (see chapter 5). Other types of ascension reports were also in circulation in the early period, however, and instead of blazing the trails already well established by earlier studies, this study will take a new path by turning from the Qurʾān to the examination of one the earliest forms of the extended story of Muḥammad's journey, a version associated with the figure Ibn ʿAbbās.

Before examining that version of the ascension, however, let us briefly consider the life and legacy of Ibn ᶜAbbās. Abū ᶜAbd Allāh Ibn ᶜAbbās b. ᶜAbd al-Muṭṭalib was a cousin of the Prophet Muḥammad through his father, the Prophet's uncle ᶜAbbās.[6] He was said to have been born three years before the Muslim community's emigration from Mecca to Medina, and thus he would have only been a young child at the time when traditional sources say the night journey took place, and only thirteen years old when Muḥammad died. Ibn ᶜAbbās became one of the most important early Qur'ān scholars, and the early Muslims gave him honorific nicknames, including "Interpreter of the Qur'ān" (*tarjumān al-qur'ān*) and "The Sea [of Knowledge]" (*al-baḥr*). He was said to have died a hero's death while opposing a controversial claimant to the caliphate, Ibn Zubayr, in the year 68/687–68.[7]

The image and reputation that Ibn ᶜAbbās came to enjoy among both Sunnī and Shīᶜī Muslims represented a mythical projection of many of the ideals of the early Muslim community.[8] Later Muslim historians described the political role that he took in some of the early battles that divided the Muslim community, depicting him as fighting alongside ᶜAlī and his partisans.[9] Nevertheless, given Ibn ᶜAbbās' connection to the family of ᶜAbbās and the lineage claimed by the ᶜAbbāsid dynasty, he became embraced not only by later Shīᶜī scholars but also by later Sunnīs. Each of these groups was able to see in Ibn ᶜAbbās a model of proper Muslim behavior, and each attempted to claim Ibn ᶜAbbās as a forerunner to their interpretation of Islam.[10] Ibn ᶜAbbās' reputation as a paradigmatic figure and as the father of qur'ānic sciences help to explain why several works of Qur'ān commentary were ascribed to him, even though it remains doubtful that he himself authored any of these works.[11]

Ibn ᶜAbbās' name became associated early on with a type of Qur'ān commentary that drew on Jewish and Christian sources, later classified under the generic name "*Isrā'īliyāt*." He also became associated with those reports that claimed that Muḥammad actually saw God on the night of the ascension.[12] Such associations may have led to numerous otherwise unattributed reports becoming ascribed to him:

> Ibn ᶜAbbās was so important for the development of Qur'ān commentary, particularly the type called *Isrā'īliyāt*, that subsequent generations, confronted with the necessity of assigning attribution and authority to already accepted anonymously derived *Ḥadīth* reports, chose his name as the one figure who would not be controverted.[13]

The fame of Ibn ᶜAbbās as a scholar caused later unscrupulous transmitters of prophetic *ḥadīth* to circulate reports in his name, or to attach otherwise anonymous reports to his name in order to given them the air of legitimacy.

The present study foregrounds what I will be calling "the Ibn ᶜAbbās ascension narratives," oral reports that may not have been embraced by the scholarly establishment after the formative period of Islamic history, but detailed versions that arguably came to have a greater impact on the telling of the story of Muḥammad's ascension than any other versions. While no written sources prior to the fourth/tenth century preserve documented evidence for the earliest or "Primitive Version" of the Ibn ᶜAbbās ascension narrative, this and the chapters that follow offer evidence to suggest that this version was known early in the formative period.

Presently I am aware of three extant texts ascribed to Muḥammad's young companion Ibn ᶜAbbās that offer parallel accounts of the early Islamic ascension narrative I am calling the "Primitive Version."[14] The earliest explicit reference to this narrative was apparently recorded in a lost work by the Sunnī traditionist Ibn Ḥibbān Bustī (d. 354/965), a version he included in his collection of those oral reports that allegedly originated with the Prophet Muḥammad but that he considered inauthentic.[15] The fact that this first citation of the Primitive Version appears in a collection of *ḥadīth* reports whose authenticity was rejected demonstrates that this narrative was the subject of controversy: Some Muslims must have accepted the authenticity of this report for Ibn Ḥibbān to have considered it worthy of refutation. What specifically about this narrative was deemed so objectionable that it provoked the censorship of the Sunnī scholarly elite?

In order to approach this question, let us begin with an overview of the Primitive Version of the Ibn ᶜAbbās ascension narrative, the full text of which appears in Appendix A. The narrative commences not in Mecca but in the first stages of the heavenly journey, with no mention of a terrestrial journey to Jerusalem. It starts with a description of four major angels (figure 1), not necessarily the most elite of all the angels Muḥammad encounters, but those from the lower heavens who appear to have a particular lesson to teach the Prophet. The first of these four major angels is the Rooster angel, whose crowing resounds in praise of the divine, causing all the terrestrial roosters to echo its call.[16] The second is the angel formed half of fire and half of snow (which I will thus label the "Half-Fire-Half-Snow angel"), which not only serves as a proof of God's overwhelming power but also is said to offer an example of how believers should reconcile opposing elements in their own hearts.[17] The third major angel at the beginning of the Primitive Version is the Angel of Death, who explains to Muḥammad about the process of collecting the souls of the dead.[18] Finally, the fourth major angel with which the narrative commences is the Guardian of Hellfire, who upon Muḥammad's request uncovers the fiery pit of hell.[19] These four angels are certainly not unique to the Ibn ᶜAbbās ascension narrative, but their presence together in a single ascension narrative becomes one of the hallmarks of the Ibn ᶜAbbās ascension discourse in subsequent centuries. These angels set the tone of piety and repentance that one can trace throughout the Primitive Version, and their conjunction and juxtaposition at the head of the narrative underscore the importance of angelology in this text.

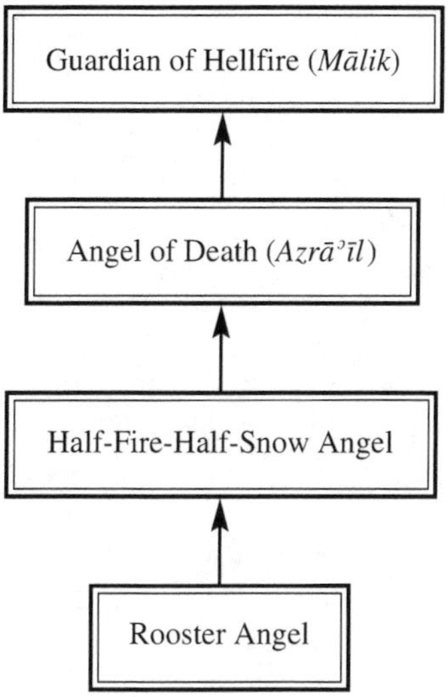

Figure 1 The Four Major Angels at the Beginning of the Primitive Version of Ibn ᶜAbbās and Near the Beginning of Muḥammad's Ascent in the Later Reshaped Version in Amc.95/2

In fact, the Primitive Version focuses almost exclusively on the angels whom Muḥammad meets and the environments in which he encounters them as he ascends to higher and higher spheres. The narrative glosses over the qur'ānic phrase "*No one knows the armies of your Lord except he himself*" (Q 74:31), as it quickly passes the angels of the first five heavens in order to describe in more detail the angels of the sixth heaven. These latter beings consist of a group of fearful angels that are focused intensely on their devotions to God, and Gabriel identifies them as the group called the *Karūbiyyūn* or "cherubim."[20] Muḥammad claims to have been forbidden to describe the angels of the seventh heaven, but he notes that he was granted great power in order to be able to look upon these angels despite the overwhelming intensity of their light. After the seventh heaven, Gabriel takes Muḥammad through ten stations of the High Realm (*ᶜiliyyūn*, a term drawn from Q 83:18), in each of which Muḥammad experiences new wonders greater than the last and repeatedly is overcome by terror so intense that only Gabriel's reassurances and God's blessings allow him to survive and continue to witness their splendor. These angels reside in and around oceans of darkness, fire, and light, bodies of water that symbolize both the grandeur and the terrible power of these upper realms that separate the heavenly spheres from God's throne. At the end of the tenth station of the High Realm, a green "vehicle" called the *rafraf* conveys Muḥammad out of Gabriel's

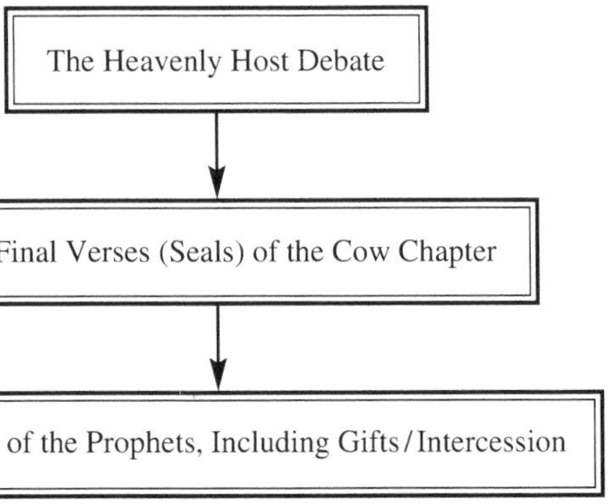

Figure 2 The Three Primary Topics of Conversation in the Intimate Colloquy Scenes of the Primitive Version and Reshaped Versions of the Ibn ʿAbbās Ascension Narratives

presence even higher into the presence of God, the highest station of all, at which no angel remains.

According to the Primitive Version of the Ibn ʿAbbās narrative, in this highest station Muḥammad sees God sitting on his throne, and God inclines toward Muḥammad and touches him between his shoulder blades with cool and comforting hands. Following that touch, all of Muḥammad's terror vanishes, and he begins to swoon as if in mystical ecstasy. God and Muḥammad converse together in an intimate dialogue, speaking on two main subjects: the subject I call the "Heavenly Host Debate" (springing from the commentary on Q 38:69), in which God teaches Muḥammad about the depths of pious behavior, and that which I call the "Favor of the Prophets," in which God informs Muḥammad of the manner in which his blessings exceed those of previous prophets. In the recension recorded by Qushayrī, the intimate dialogue also includes the passage that I have labeled the "Final Verses (Seals) of the Cow Chapter" (Q 2:285–86), yielding all three of the key topics of the intimate colloquy that become a conventional aspect of later Ibn ʿAbbās texts (see figure 2).[21] After these conversation topics run their course, God conveys some secret commission to Muḥammad, making no explicit mention of the daily prayers, and then God sits back down on his throne, concluding the scene.

The representation of God in such a human fashion is remarkable in this narrative. Although van Ess demonstrates that the situation was somewhat fluid in the earliest period of Islamic history,[22] the vast majority of Muslims disapprove of the idea of attempting to describe or represent God in a human form (anthropomorphism). The anthropomorphic aspect to the deity as depicted in the Primitive Version, therefore, offers one reason why many scholars would come to object to this *ḥadīth* report and come to reject its authenticity.

In the final sections of this Primitive Version of the Ibn ʿAbbās ascension narrative, Muḥammad receives a comprehensive tour of paradise, interrupted by Gabriel's explanations of the oceans, the classes of cherubim, and the veils that Muḥammad had passed while ascending into the divine presence. Gabriel shows Muḥammad the Lote Tree of the Boundary and the tree of *Ṭūbā*, the rivers of paradise and its residences and palaces. The only anthropomorphic beings Muḥammad sees in paradise are the heavenly "dark-eyed maidens" and the male attending youths, both of whom the Qurʾān describes.[23] This account of Muḥammad's journey ends with a brief description of Muḥammad's encounter with the previous prophets as he descends from heaven to heaven, with the prophets arranged in more of a chronological order than in other Islamic ascension narratives.[24] The fact that these prophets appear at the very end of the narrative, almost as an afterthought, raises the question of whether or not this final segment was appended to the narrative by a later transmitter who desired to reconcile it with other versions of Muḥammad's ascension that had subsequently gained currency.

As this brief summary of the Primitive Version has indicated, there are three central categories of fantastic wonders that this ascension narrative elucidates. First, the narrative describes in detail the personalities, ranks, and categories of angels that the Prophet encounters on his journey. Second, at the climax of the narrative the Primitive Version describes the nature of the meeting between Muḥammad and God and the content of their intimate conversation in that context. Third, the narrative depicts the bounties of paradise that await the believer in the afterlife, recounting the details of the residencies and delicacies that the inhabitants of paradise will enjoy. The ascension narratives accepted by those Sunnī scholars who focus their attention upon the "canonical" sound (*ṣaḥīḥ*) *ḥadīth* reports do not treat any of these three categories of wonders in detail.

COMPARATIVELY ANALYZING THE PRIMITIVE VERSION OF THE IBN ʿABBĀS ASCENSION NARRATIVE

One of the limitations of previous studies of the night journey and ascension is that they tend to emphasize the canonical Sunnī narratives, measuring all other narratives by that norm. Here the emphasis rests upon a different perspective, imaginatively taking the Ibn ʿAbbās ascension narrative to be the rule by which to measure other ascension narratives. In order to focus attention on the most significant features of the Primitive Version for the study of the development of early Islamic ascension narratives, we now turn to the consideration of eight key aspects of the Primitive Version of the Ibn ᶜAbbās ascension narrative. The eight points that follow raise a series of comparative issues with the goal of introducing and anticipating some of the arguments in this book.

The first significant point is that the scope and emphasis of the Primitive Version needs to be considered, for even though it presents the longest ascension narrative of the early period, the Primitive Version nevertheless concentrates upon select portions of the overall journey. As noted above, the Primitive Version presents a narrative that jumps immediately into a discussion of the wonders (*ᶜajāʾib*) that Muḥammad encounters in the heavens, with no attempt to set those experiences in any larger narrative framework. The Primitive Version does not provide answers to the issue of when the journey took place, where Muḥammad had been sleeping on the night he was taken on the journey, or how Muḥammad's contemporaries reacted to his news upon his return. Rather, one could imagine that such details were not especially important to the community that first circulated the Primitive Version, either because other narratives provided answers to these mundane questions or because this community was so focused on the otherworldly details that it did not take interest in such issues. From the perspective of subsequent and more full accounts of the Ibn ᶜAbbās ascension narrative, the Primitive Version appears fragmentary and incomplete, just as is the case with a number of other early reports.

The second significant point is that the Primitive Version focuses much more on angels than on prophets in the heavens, and several reasons could be offered to explain this emphasis. It could be traced to the fragmentary nature of the Primitive Version, based on the idea that this narrative was meant to supplement other ascension narratives, or on the speculative thesis that portions of the narrative that did include a mention of Muḥammad's encounter with other prophets were simply not preserved. Another possibility, however, is that the Primitive Version arises out of a community in whose "language world"[25] the angels were of paramount importance. One thinks, for instance, of the Jewish Merkabah and Hekhalot texts, in which learning the names and qualities of the angels in the heavens was of critical importance for a successful ascension journey.[26] The frequent use of the term *karūbiyyūn* (*cherubim*) in the text suggests that the connection between the Primitive Version and Jewish ascension narratives may be closer than previously thought. Along with this potential Jewish connection, a few select Islamic narratives in subsequent centuries also focused on angels in lieu of prophets, and the major examples were descriptions of the ascension ascribed to the mystic Abū Yazīd Bisṭāmī and the version of the Prophet's ascension discussed by the philosopher Ibn Sīnā (see chapter 9). The former of these two texts has been shown to bear comparison with Jewish texts, especially 3 Enoch, while the latter may well have drawn upon a version of the Ibn ᶜAbbās ascension narrative for the fundamental elements on which it based its allegory.[27] Be this as it may, the primary focus on angels in these Islamic ascension texts is certainly remarkable, and it sets them apart from the majority of other Islamic ascension narratives originating in the formative period. It suggests, in fact, that early on a certain group of Muslims used the ascension narrative as a context in which to explore the theme of angelology in greater detail.

As we have seen, while most other ascension texts describe the prophets in the heavens, the Primitive Version describes four main angels there: the Rooster angel, the Half-Fire-Half-Snow angel, the Angel of Death, and the Guardian of Hellfire. It locates these four major angels in the region simply called "*al-samāʾ*," a likely reference to the first of seven heavens. In almost all subsequent Ibn ʿAbbās ascension narratives, these four angels are likewise present, often appearing in close proximity to one another in the narrative. In contrast, most other ascension narratives rarely mention more than one or two of these four angels, and when they do mention them, they do not develop these angels as central characters in the story the way that the Primitive Version does.[28] Some early Shīʿī ascension narratives offer a partial exception to this rule, a fact that raises the question of whether or not the Primitive Version could have developed within or in response to a Shīʿī milieu (see chapter 4). Since the Primitive Version contains few overt Shīʿī characteristics or explicit Shīʿī sympathies, however, one might conjecture that the Primitive Version's preoccupation with angels has less to do with Shīʿī leanings and more to do with an emphasis on the extraordinary wonders of the ascension.

Besides its emphasis on the description of angels, a third important point is that the Primitive Version also concentrates on the upper regions of the creation and the highest stages of Muḥammad's journey. After describing the four wondrous angels at the beginning of its narrative, it goes on to recount Muḥammad's journey through the upperworldly heavens, beginning not with the first but with the sixth of these spheres. Proceeding beyond the seventh heaven, Muḥammad passes through ten separate stops within the uppermost High Realm (*ʿiliyyūn*), regions containing terrifying seas and mountains.[29] Some Shīʿī accounts take the journey higher than the seventh heaven, and some even up to the divine throne, just as in the Primitive Version. Most official Sunnī ascension narratives, in contrast, emphatically reject the idea that Muḥammad traveled higher than the seventh heaven and its famous sites, the celestial temple known as the Inhabited House *(al-bayt al-maʿmūr)*, and the immense tree known as the Lote Tree of the Boundary *(al-sidrat al-muntahā)*.[30] Outside the versions attributed to Ibn ʿAbbās, one looks in vain in both early Shīʿī and Sunnī ascension narratives for references to the numerous seas and mountains that Muḥammad passes on his journey in the Primitive Version. Although such seas and mountains most likely were known outside the Ibn ʿAbbās narratives, the Primitive Version goes the furthest among the ascension texts of the early period in interpolating these upperworldly heavenly locales into its storyline.

The fourth point is that the Primitive Version makes use of the concept of Muḥammad's fear much more than any other Islamic ascension narrative of its time, and his terrified reaction to each of the seas and mountains in the stations of the High Realm provides a good example of how the narrative portrays Muḥammad as being in the constant grip of this fear. In sharp contrast to the tone of joy and celebration that underlies the majority of other Islamic ascension narratives, aside from the brief tours of hell or trials that Muḥammad faces in the official narratives, in the Primitive Version the Prophet repeatedly finds himself on the verge of collapsing in terror. Only the intervention of Gabriel (or of God) sufficiently calms Muḥammad down, allowing him to steady himself and behold the otherworldly wonders.[31] In nearly every version of the Ibn ʿAbbās ascension story, Gabriel is forced at several stages of the journey to encourage Muḥammad to continue on despite the latter's fear. Unlike the other ascension narratives that report a conversation between Muḥammad and God, the Ibn ʿAbbās narratives invariably begin this colloquy scene with a reference to the manner in which God physically steadies Muḥammad (through touch, kind words, etc.), making him capable of looking at and speaking to God. In the Primitive Version, the touch of God's hand upon Muḥammad's back serves this function, allaying Muḥammad's fears and making him ready for the colloquy.

A fifth point also relates to this scene just prior to the colloquy, namely that it offers an example of possible mystical ideas informing the Ibn ʿAbbās ascension narrative, Muḥammad's swoon being reminiscent of the Sufi concept of "passing away" (*fanāʾ*). During the Primitive Version, Muḥammad states on several occasions that the intensity of what he experiences causes him to think that all created things outside his purview must have perished. When Muḥammad has such overwhelming experiences prior to his divine audience, Gabriel explains to him that other created things still exist, but that he has merely let himself become fixated on a certain created thing to the exclusion of all else. Gabriel gently eases Muḥammad out of these states of terrified fixation, settling him down and making him able to see created things for what they are.

In contrast, when Muḥammad enters the divine presence without Gabriel's companionship, Muḥammad receives the favor of witnessing the divinity and feeling the divine touch, experiences that once again cause him to think that everything else has died or vanished. This time, however, he sways back and forth in a swoon after experiencing God's touch, and he ultimately falls into an ecstatic and/or unconscious state that lasts until God revives him:

> [H]e placed one of his hands between my shoulder blades, and I felt the coldness of his fingers upon my heart for some time. With that I felt his sweetness, his beautiful fragrance, his cool pleasure and generous vision. All the terror that I had encountered vanished, and all my trembling was driven from me. My heart became calm, and it became filled with delight

> and consolation. Rejoicing and rapture came upon me, to the point that I began to incline and topple to the right and left, and something like slumber overtook me. I thought that all those who were in the heavens and earth had died, because I did not hear any of the angels' voices, nor did I see any of his creatures upon the vision of my Lord. My God left me this way as long as he willed, then he returned me to consciousness as if I had been dozing. I awoke and came to my senses, feeling calm in the knowledge of my location and my situation of awake nobility and evident affection.[32]

This passage compares Muḥammad's rapturous state to a state of sleep or dozing. Certainly this description could be interpreted in a variety of ways, but here it is presented as a type of mystical ecstasy or rapture in which Muḥammad loses his physical sense of self. Although the Primitive Version never uses the term that comes to be associated with the mystical state of "passing away," the Arabic term "*fanāʾ*," this particular scene offers what could be construed as an early description of this mystical idea.[33]

This situation brings to mind comparisons with other situations in which holy figures were said to collapse in the divine presence. For instance, one recalls the qurʾānic description of how Moses fell thunderstruck upon witnessing the divinity at Mount Sinai (Q 7:143), a passage that mystical exegetes sometimes associate with the state of passing away.[34] One might also compare this detail from the Primitive Version with the extended version of the Abū Yazīd ascension narrative, in which, upon reaching the divine presence and hearing of his favor, Abū Yazīd claims that "it was as if I were melting as melting lead."[35] Unlike in the Abū Yazīd narrative and some other sayings of the early Sufis, the passage from the Primitive Version contains no mystical play that derives from a breakdown of subject and object identities, and so one needs to exercise some caution before equating the above experience with the Sufi concept of *fanāʾ*.[36] Even so, this experience of beatific rapture or slumber presents a feature of the Primitive Version that one rarely finds in other ascension narratives, be they Sunnī or Shīʿī.

This idea introduces our sixth point, namely that other ascension narratives hardly ever offer any details about Muḥammad's encounter with the divinity beyond vague generalities. Often the official ascension narratives employ the passive voice, stating something to the effect of the idea that at the highest station "the duty of fifty ritual prayers day and night was revealed to Muḥammad." The narrators' use of the passive voice in those other narratives helps them to avoid the problem of how exactly to describe the highest station of the ascent, as well as the even more difficult question of how to portray God's appearance or to describe God's voice. In contrast to these passive constructions in other ascension narratives, the Primitive Version and subsequent Ibn ʿAbbās ascension narratives depict these episodes in a detailed and active voice. They also recount the dialogue between Muḥammad and God at length, often including all three central tropes: the Heavenly Host Debate, the Favor of the Prophets, and the Seals of the Cow Chapter. The Ibn ᶜAbbās narratives do not shy away from reporting exactly what Muḥammad experiences at this climax to his journey, and this aspect of the Ibn ᶜAbbās narrative becomes one of its most distinctive and intriguing dimensions.

Some early Shīᶜī narratives also recount the intimate colloquy between Muḥammad and God. For instance, a few Shīᶜī accounts draw upon the Final Verses of the Cow Chapter trope.[37] Furthermore, the intimate colloquy in ᶜAlī Qummī's Shīᶜī *Tafsīr* draws directly on the Ibn ᶜAbbās Primitive Version (see chapter 6). Aside from these few exceptions, however, the majority of early Shīᶜī ascension narratives that do describe a colloquy tend to focus on an entirely different sort of conversation, one revolving around specifically Shīᶜī themes such as the exalted status of ᶜAlī. The Primitive Version itself shows little trace of such partisan intra-Muslim debates, but such polemics surface in subtle ways in successive versions of the Ibn ᶜAbbās ascension narrative. In the latter, the Favor of the Prophets trope leads directly into a discussion of the gifts that God grants to the Muslim community, a scene that develops over time into an increasingly elaborate oral exchange in which Muḥammad intercedes to secure entrance to paradise for a specific proportion of his people. The identity of the people thus saved and thereby allowed to enter paradise remains open to debate and interpretation in the Ibn ᶜAbbās narratives, whereas similar passages in Shīᶜī accounts tend to reserve that privilege for the devoted followers of ᶜAlī and his descendents.

The seventh point to discuss with reference to the Primitive Version centers upon Muḥammad's extensive and colorful tour of paradise in that narrative, a chapter of the work that offers far more by way of description than any other similar passage in other early Arabic ascension narratives, Sunnī or Shīᶜī. A number of proto-Shīᶜī *ḥadīth* reports offer more brief anecdotes about Muḥammad's tour of paradise, many of which mention a specific Tree called *Ṭūbā* and its role in the birth of Muḥammad's daughter, Fāṭima. This same tree also appears in the Primitive Version of the Ibn ᶜAbbās narrative, and while it depicts no such role for *Ṭūbā*, it still offers a reference that may preserve a trace of Shīᶜī subtext: The Primitive Version states how the tree of *Ṭūbā* will provide shelter in the afterlife "for you and many of your people (*ahlaka*) and your community," the term "your people" perhaps separately designating the "People of Muḥammad's House," whom the Shīᶜīs particularly revere. Even if this phrase contains a hint of Shīᶜī partisanship, and the point is far from certain, still its additional reference to the broader community of Muslims suggests more of a Sunnī perspective. It may be that what we have here is an originally Shīᶜī symbol that the

Primitive Version appropriates and modifies in order to make it more suitable to a Sunnī worldview.

The detailed descriptions of paradise in the Primitive Version likewise reflect an early stage of what was to become an elaborately articulated tour of both paradise and hellfire in the reshaped versions of the Ibn ᶜAbbās ascension narrative. The Primitive Version's tour of paradise stands out, however, through its numerous allusions to qurᵓānic descriptions of the pleasures of paradise. These allusions in general and the second half of the narrative in particular (which contains the tour of paradise) demonstrate that the narrative's compiler must have been well versed in the sacred text.[38]

The eighth and final important point about the Primitive Version that I would like to make at this stage regards the way the narrative describes Muḥammad's encounter with the other prophets upon his descent. Having neglected to include the Jerusalem portion of the journey, which in other narratives includes Muḥammad's first meeting with the prophets, and having neglected to mention the prophets during the entire ascent portion of the journey, the narrative introduces a few of these prophets at its very end, upon Muḥammad's descent. In this way, it parallels the mystical ascension narrative ascribed to Abū Yazīd Bisṭāmī in which the Abu Yazīd similarly encounters the prophets at the very end of his vision, after the completion of his experience of union.[39] Aside from these two accounts, however, no other early Islamic ascension narrative represents Muḥammad's encounter with the prophets in such a fashion.[40]

The short passage describing Muḥammad's encounter with the prophets upon his descent at the end of the Primitive Version does not settle the question of which prophet resides in which heaven. However, it does present the prophets he meets in a roughly chronological order:

> I saw our father Adam, and I saw my brother Noah. Then I saw Abraham. Next I saw Moses. Then I saw his brother Aaron, as well as Enoch, in the fourth heaven, his back leaning against the archives of creatures in which are their affairs. Next I saw my brother Jesus in the [first] heaven.[41]

Adam and Noah appear in the highest sphere, and Muḥammad meets them first upon the start of his descent. They are then followed by four prophets in the reverse order in which they normally appear in the heavens in official Sunnī accounts: Abraham (normally in the seventh heaven), Moses (normally in the sixth heaven), Aaron (normally in the fifth heaven), and Idrīs / Enoch (normally in the fourth heaven). Finally, the Primitive Version places Jesus in the first heaven (normally with John the Baptist in the second heaven). Reconstructing an ascending sequence from the Primitive Version, Muḥammad would have encountered Jesus in the first heaven, Idrīs / Enoch in the fourth, Aaron in the fifth,

Moses in the sixth, and Abraham in the seventh along with Noah and Adam. The absence of prophets in heavens two and three defies explanation, but given the episodic nature of the narrative in the first place, and given its emphasis upon wonders, the inconsistency is not all that surprising. The presentation of Muḥammad's encounter with other prophets in the Primitive Version differs significantly from those of most other Islamic ascension texts, and the malleability of this type of sequence becomes yet another hallmark of the later Ibn ᶜAbbās ascension narratives.

AUTHENTICATING AND DATING THE CIRCULATION OF THE PRIMITIVE VERSION

Some Muslim scholars, like the Sunnī traditionist Ibn Ḥibbān mentioned above, transmitted the Primitive Version of the Ibn ᶜAbbās ascension narrative in their collections precisely in order to warn fellow Muslims about its inauthenticity. Rather than attacking the text of the narrative directly, the traditionists would often critically scrutinize the narrative's chain of transmitters (singular *isnād*, plural *asānīd*). For example, after quoting the Primitive Version at length, Ibn Ḥibbān negatively evaluates its authenticity with the remark, "It is forged, and its inventor was Maysara [Ibn ᶜAbd Rabbih, d. 170/786], a liar and fabricator [of *ḥadīth* reports]."[42] The Mamluk era compiler Jalāl al-Dīn Suyūṭī, who records Ibn Ḥibbān's report and his theory as to its origin, supplies a pair of additional chains of transmission from a different source in order to conclude that the narrative probably originates instead with an even earlier figure named ᶜUmar b. Sulaymān Dimashqī (d. 105/722), with whom the transmission of three reports at Suyūṭī's disposal converge.[43] One interesting feature of both of these Sunnī traditionists' approach to the Primitive Version of the Ibn ᶜAbbās ascension narrative is that, despite their assertion that it has no authentic basis as a saying of the Prophet, they each agree that the narrative circulated very early, certainly prior to the beginning of the third/ninth century.

In a famous early twentieth-century work comparing Islamic ascension narratives to the medieval Christian masterpiece by Dante, the first European scholar to comment on the Primitive Version of the Ibn ᶜAbbās ascension narrative, Miguel Asín Palacios, also attacks its authenticity. He builds his case for the forged nature of the narrative partially on its chain of transmission and partially on its content. Asín rejects the authenticity of the entire final portion of the narrative based on what he sees as its materialistic and Neoplatonic elements. Over and against Dante's work, Asín negatively compares the Primitive Version (which he refers to as "Redaction C of Cycle 2"), portraying the latter as overly repetitious and boring. Furthermore, he views its use of quotations from the Qurʾān as a transparent attempt to add Islamic legitimacy to essentially non-Islamic ideas and concepts:

> The monotonous style, overloaded with hyperbole and repetition, that characterizes this Redaction C of Cycle 2 of the *miʿrāj* [the Primitive Version] is of such a baroque taste, and the final episode that closes it, the visit to the mansions to the Qurʾānic paradise, contains such little spiritual character, that only with difficulty can one see in this legend some nexus with such a delicate and artistic poem as Dante's. . . . [T]he final episode of this Redaction C, which completely rips apart the entire body of the legend with its Qurʾānic materialism, ought to be considered as something artificial that the author cleverly introduces under the pretext of forced concession to the ideas current among [both] the populace and the orthodox clergy. . . . With this recourse, the author tries to guarantee before the public the authenticity and orthodoxy of his forged legend, which, far from revealing at its base and form the mentality of Muḥammad, a polygamist and warrior, clearly denounces its author as a Muslim contaminated with neoplatonism, that is, a mystic of the *Ishrāqī* and pseudo-Empedoclean school, so fond [is he] of luminous similes and circular geometric symbols in order to exemplify metaphysical ideas. One should not forget, as well, that the paternity of this legend was attributed, in the tenth century of our era, not to an ethnic Arab but to a Persian of the eighth century, Maysara b. ʿAbd Rabbih, that is to say, to a Muslim in whom the Qurʾānic faith had perhaps not blotted out some of the Zoroastrian beliefs of his country, recently converted to Islam by the force of arms.[44]

Clearly Asín has a certain preconceived idea about what a genuinely spiritual narrative should be like, as well as a preconceived idea about what kind of narrative the real "polygamist and warrior" Muḥammad would have transmitted. The Primitive Version meets neither of these criteria according to Asín's analysis of it. Without any more substantial evidence than the Persian origin of one suspect figure in the narrative's chain of transmission, drawn directly out of the polemical conclusion of Ibn Ḥibbān, Asín hypothesizes that the narrative either derives from or is strongly influenced by Zoroastrian sources. Although Asín's thesis remains plausible, proof of influence requires more than simply identifying the foreign origin of a figure in the chain of transmission.

Contemporary Islamicist Josef van Ess takes a similar approach to Asín but arrives at different conclusions, ascribing the composition of the narrative to an even earlier figure in the chain of transmission, Ḍaḥḥāk b. Muzāḥīm (d. ca. 105/723) based on a break in the chain between Ḍaḥḥāk and Ibn ʿAbbās.[45]

Van Ess furthermore suggests that Ḍaḥḥāk "may have discovered his inspiration in Iraq,"[46] and that he subsequently transmitted the report to Maysara who later "reimported the text to Basra."[47] While van Ess' reconstruction of the movement of the narrative is once again based solely on the names and biographies of the figures in its chains of transmission, his theory has the merit of proposing in detail how the early Primitive Version may have circulated. Although their conclusions differ, both Asín and van Ess draw their ideas about the origins of the Primitive Version from early lists of the narrative's transmitters, extrapolating from those sources to conjecture not only about who may have forged the Primitive Version but also about how widely it may have circulated during the second/eighth century.

Even though I am less inclined than Asín and van Ess to trust the chains of transmission recorded in later texts as a basis to reconstruct the origin and subsequent history of this early oral narrative, nevertheless the text of the Primitive Version does contain a number of features, such as its overwhelming emphasis on the heavenly portion of the journey, that do suggest an early provenance. The text offers an ascension report with no mention whatsoever of a night journey to Jerusalem. Certainly other early accounts completely separate the two portions of the journey, and even some extended narratives in the official Sunnī *ḥadīth* collections similarly omit the Jerusalem portion of the narrative. Still, beginning in the fourth/tenth century one finds a near unanimous consensus among scholars that the night journey to Jerusalem and the ascension to the heavens refer to connected events from the same night. One can tentatively conclude, therefore, that the Primitive Version was likely in circulation prior to the end of the third/ninth century.

One brief piece of written evidence from Ṭabarī's late third/ninth-century *Tafsīr* further supports this early dating of the circulation of the Primitive Version. Unlike Ibn Ḥibbān, Ṭabarī only mentions the Primitive Version in passing, citing it only to illustrate a position in the debate about whether Muḥammad was able to see the divinity during his ascension. He ascribes to Ibn ᶜAbbās the idea that Muḥammad did see God, and he cites the following anecdote as part of his supporting evidence:

> Aḥmad b. ᶜĪsā Tamīmī—Sulaymān b. ᶜUmar b. Sayyār—ᶜUmar b. Sayyār—Saᶜīd b. Zarbī—ᶜUmar b. Sulaymān—ᶜAṭāᵓ—Ibn ᶜAbbās—Messenger of God, who said, "I saw my Lord in the best form. He said to me, "Muḥammad, do you know what the heavenly host debate?" I said, "No Lord." So he placed his hand between my shoulder blades and I felt the coldness between my nipples. I knew what was in the heaven[s] and what was in the earth. I said, "Lord, [they discuss] the degrees (*al-darajāt*) and the penitential acts (*al-kaffarāt*), going on foot to the congregational prayers (*al-jumuᶜāt*) and waiting for prayer after prayer (*al-ṣalāt*)." I said,

> "Lord, you *took Abraham as an intimate friend* (Q 4:125) and you *spoke to Moses directly* (4:164), and you did this and that."[48] He said, "*Did I not open your breast? Did I not remove your burden from you?* (Q 94:1–2). Did I not do this and that with you?" [Muḥammad] said, "Then he informed me of things that he did not permit me to tell you about. He said: That is [God's] saying in his book that he does tell you: "*Then he drew closer and descended, and was a distance of two bows or closer. He revealed to his servant what he revealed. The heart did not lie in what it saw* (Q 53:8–11). He made the light of my vision in my heart, and I gazed upon him with my heart.[49]

The first thing to notice about this brief report is its chain of transmission, not only for the fact that it mentions Ibn ᶜAbbās as the companion reporting the narrative from Muḥammad, but also because the entire chain closely resembles a chain of transmission attached by another exegete a century later to what was likely the full text of the Primitive Version of the Ibn ᶜAbbās ascension narrative.[50] Therefore, it is possible that Ṭabarī had access to an early recension of the Primitive Version, even though he decided not to cite it at length.

Evidence from within the text of this short Ibn ᶜAbbās anecdote further supports the idea that Ṭabarī was aware of the Primitive Version. First and foremost, the scenes from the divine colloquy in this anecdote are identical to the parallel scenes in the Primitive Version. Ṭabarī also ends the colloquy with the phrase "he informed me of things that he did not permit me to tell you about," an expression nearly identical to a parallel phrase in the Primitive Version.[51] One could conjecture that Ṭabarī condenses this reference to an early recension of the Primitive Version both because he does not deem the latter narrative to be authentic and also because he was only interested in it in order to discuss the issue of the vision of God, as the context on the passage makes clear. Even though he refrains from transmitting the Primitive Version of the Ibn ᶜAbbās ascension narrative in full, however, Ṭabarī's reference to this colloquy scene from the narrative presents solid evidence to support the thesis that some manifestation of the Primitive Version (either oral or written) was in circulation by the end of the third/ninth century.

The text of the Primitive Version contains plenty of anomalous details that could indicate that this version circulated prior to the establishment of a mainstream consensus about the night journey and ascension. For instance, as discussed in the summary above, upon his ascent through the heavens, Muḥammad meets only angels, not encountering any of the human prophets until he descends back to earth.[52] The anthropomorphic detail in which God touches Muḥammad with his cold hand appears in a dream vision transmitted in Tirmidhī's collection of sound Sunnī *ḥadīth* reports, but with few exceptions, it only appears in ascension narratives that derive from the Ibn ᶜAbbās versions.[53]

Furthermore, while the vast majority of the Islamic ascension narratives relate how Muḥammad receives the duty to offer ritual prayers a set number of times per day on his heavenly ascension, the Primitive Version does not even mention the imposition of this duty. Examples of such anomalous details could certainly be multiplied. They each offer support to the idea that the Primitive Version may well have originated in the early centuries of Islamic history and / or may have circulated outside the control of mainstream Muslim scholars. If the chains of transmission can be taken as reliable accounts attesting to the general circulation of the narrative, one might then conjecture that the narrative was especially popular in the eastern lands of Islamdom.

Based upon Richard Bulliet's insight that "concocted" *ḥadīth* reports probably were formulated in answer to the questions that new Muslim converts were asking,[54] one might view the Primitive Version as an account that sought to answer the questions about Muḥammad's journey that other narratives left out, questions such as the following: Besides the prophets, what other remarkable beings did Muḥammad encounter on his journey? How did Muḥammad describe the topography of the heavens and the highest regions? Did Muḥammad see God, and if so, what did God look like? Did Muḥammad speak with God, and if so, what did the two talk about? Did Muḥammad visit paradise and hellfire, and if so, what did he witness in each? The answers to these questions and many more like them can be found in the Primitive Version of the Ibn ᶜAbbās narrative. Instead of necessarily serving first and foremost as an esoteric or elitist discourse, as Asín contends, therefore, the Primitive Version could be seen as satisfying the general curiosity of regular Muslims regarding the various wonders of the ascension. Such a perspective also suggests that Muslims considered the Ibn ᶜAbbās ascension narrative as a kind of supplement to other night journey and ascension accounts, one that responds to the questions of ordinary believers about the fantastic things that Muḥammad saw and experienced that night.[55]

ECHOES OF MUQĀTIL B. SULAYMĀN'S COMMENTARY IN THE PRIMITIVE VERSION

If Ṭabarī's *Tafsīr* suggests that the Primitive Version most likely was in circulation prior to the end of the third / ninth century, the *Tafsīr* of Muqātil b. Sulaymān (d. 150 / 767) suggests that it may not have been in wide circulation in the century prior. Muqātil's famous, albeit controversial, Qurᵓān commentary presents an intriguing articulation of how some of the earliest storytellers (*quṣṣāṣ*) may have narrated the tale of Muḥammad's night journey and ascension.[56] As with the early biographical works of Ibn Isḥāq and Ibn Saᶜd that are discussed in the next chapter, Muqātil's Qurʾān commentary focuses on the journey to Jerusalem much more than it does on the idea of a heavenly journey. It offers a full narrative exposition of the meaning of the night journey verse (Q 17:1), while merely glossing over select terms and concepts from the beginning of the Star chapter (Q 53:1–18) without offering any narrative exegesis of them. Muqātil's exegesis of the night journey verse stands out for its attention to fantastic details, dwelling at some length on those details at the expense of narrative flow. His commentary more generally comes to be associated with this embellished style of storytelling that disregards the conventional norms of Muslim scholarship.[57]

With regard to Muḥammad's journey to Jerusalem, Muqātil's commentary focuses on the theme of pious awe and wonder. For instance, Muqātil elaborates on the word beginning the night journey verse, "*subhāna*" (glorified be), with the concept of "wonder" (*ᶜajab*). He thus implies that the proper Muslim reaction to the verse consists of that sentiment.[58] His account of how Muḥammad tells Umm Hāniʾ of his experience the night before further reinforces this theme, for he tells her, "Indeed, I saw a wonder (*ᶜajab*) in the night."[59] Later, Muḥammad asks the skeptical leaders of the Quraysh, "Shall I not tell you of the wonder?" to which they reply, "Inform us, since everything to do with you is a wonder."[60] Even though the term "wonder" appears in only select portions of Muqātil's exegesis of the night journey verse, nevertheless both the tone and emphasis of his approach suggest that Muqātil is interested in exploring the wondrous aspects of the Prophet's journey.

The wonders that Muqātil recounts in his narrative exegesis only infrequently dovetail in an explicit fashion with the wonders presented in the Primitive Version. He identifies the meaning and content of the "*greatest signs*" (Q 17:1) that the Prophet witnessed on the journey with Muḥammad's description of the fantastic otherworldly mount Burāq,[61] with his seeing the Antichrist known as *al-Dajjāl*, with his encountering various angels, and with his leading the earlier Abrahamic prophets in prayer in Jerusalem.[62] Elsewhere, in Muqātil's gloss on verses from the Star chapter, he connects the "*greatest signs*" (Q 53:18) that Muḥammad sees to his vision of the green *rafraf*.[63] Muqātil also reports the idea that Muḥammad sees God on two different occasions over the course of the night journey, a position that comes to be associated with Ibn ᶜAbbās.[64] Moreover, Muqātil offers a rich description of the Lote Tree of the Boundary, which he equates with the heavenly tree of paradise *Ṭūbā*.[65] Though only a few of these aspects of Muqātil's commentary relate directly to the details of the Primitive Version, suggesting that the Primitive Version was probably not available to Muqātil when he composed his *Tafsīr*, the use of the term "wonder" connects the two accounts. Recalling that the Primitive Version later becomes transmitted under the general rubric "The Wonders of the Ascension" (*ajāʾib* *al-mi^crāj*), one might thus postulate that the storyteller who composed the Primitive Version could have had access to Muqātil's early work and not the other way around.

To offer one brief but telling example in support of such a hypothesis, Muqātil describes a wondrous angel outside the context of the night journey and ascension narratives, an angel whom he identifies with the qur'ānic concept of "the spirit" (*al-rūḥ*):

> [The Spirit] is the angel about whom God speaks [in the verse], "*They will ask you about the spirit . . .*" (Q 17:86). His face is the face of a human. Half of him is of fire, and half of snow. He glorifies and praises God, saying, "Lord, just as you join together this fire and snow, the fire [not] melting the snow and the snow not extinguishing the fire, so join together your believing servants." He is set apart from other creatures by his immensity.[66]

Besides this physical description, Muqātil tells the reader little about this "Half-Fire-Half-Snow" angel, presenting it as merely one of the incredible denizens of the angelic realm. Despite the fact that neither Muqātil nor the Sunnī compilers of the sound *ḥadīth* collections draw any sort of link between this angel and Muḥammad's otherworldly journey, the transmitters of the Ibn ʿAbbās ascension narratives, beginning with the Primitive Version, invariably do. Had Muqātil been aware of the Ibn ʿAbbās ascension discourse, I contend, he probably would have made this same connection. Instead, the Ibn ʿAbbās discourse appears to draw from Muqātil for its material, just as it borrows freely from other Islamic and extra-Islamic sources in the common ascension "language world." The Primitive Version arises out of the same type of exegetical storytelling milieu in which Muqātil composed his *Tafsīr*, but it probably was composed somewhat after the time of Muqātil and before that of Ṭabarī. This hypothesis points us in the direction of placing the formulation of the Primitive Version at between the second half of the second/eighth century and the second half of the third/ninth century. Comparisons with the early biographical and historical texts composed during this same period, some of which will be examined in the following chapter, can be likewise shown to support such a conjecture.

TRACING THE BEGINNINGS OF THE PRIMITIVE VERSION

In the early centuries of Islamic history, the stories about the lives of the prophets were often the domain not of scholars but of the popular storytellers known as the *quṣṣāṣ*.[67] Commenting on the general tenor of the Primitive Version, van

Ess states that the Primitive Version of the Ibn ᶜAbbās ascension narrative represents an account "worthy of the storytellers."[68] Likewise, in discussing the later versions of the Ibn ᶜAbbās ascension narrative, Nazeer El-ᶜAzmeh argues that the development of this discourse owes much to the storytelling movement.[69] Islamic sources tend to treat these storytellers as popular preachers who draw upon the Qur'ān, *ḥadīth*, and other oral sources both within and beyond the Islamic tradition, combining these accounts together in order to formulate tales for use in exhorting the masses. Scholars have proposed that the second/eighth century was a period in which the storytellers were particularly active, and clearly in the formative period the line between preacher and storyteller was often blurred.

I propose that the Primitive Version circulated as an independent narrative around the turn of the third/ninth century, perhaps in the form of a tale told by Muslim storytellers or *quṣṣāṣ*. Pellat contends that Muslim *ḥadīth* scholars came to treat the popular storytellers as a threat to the integrity of the Muslim oral reports:

> To enliven their narratives, the *ḳuṣṣāṣ* did not hesitate to quote from apocryphal traditions (and it is probable that they contributed to the propagation of the *ḥadīth*s put together from all sorts of different fragments), fabulous deeds and marvelous stories which the credulous masses took for gospel truth, thus placing the authentic Islamic tradition in real jeopardy.[70]

Mainstream *ḥadīth* scholars, both Sunnī and Shīᶜī, must have felt especially threatened by the Primitive Version. Aside from those who preserved such reports for posterity in their collections of weak and false *ḥadīth*, and the few who may have adapted short scenes from the Primitive Version for their own purposes, they generally excluded this Ibn ᶜAbbās narrative from their own discussions of Muḥammad's journey.

And yet, even as some scholars objected to the Ibn ᶜAbbās narrative and excluded the Primitive Version from their works, nevertheless there remained a group who chose instead to appropriate and transmit the Ibn ᶜAbbās ascension narrative, in whole or in part. This book endeavors to chart the course of that movement and to navigate the streams of Islamic ascension discourse as they intermingle in recognizable patterns. As one would expect, in the Primitive Version of the Ibn ᶜAbbās ascension narrative, as in the early narratives ascribed to Ibn Saᶜd and Ibn Isḥāq to which we turn in the next chapter, such patterns have yet to come to the surface. Only by examining this fluid discourse over an expanse of time is one able to recognize the ripples that flow and mingle between disparate versions of the story told on the authority of Ibn ᶜAbbās of the wonders that Muḥammad encountered while on his tour of the other world.

3
EARLY HISTORICAL DESCRIPTIONS OF MUḤAMMAD'S JOURNEY

Some of the earliest written narratives about Muḥammad's night journey and ascension appear in the two historical works on the life of the Prophet Muḥammad: first, the biography of the Prophet composed by Muḥammad Ibn Isḥāq (d. ca. 150/767) and preserved in the later versions by Ibn Bukayr (d. 199/814) and Ibn Hishām (d. 218/833); second, the biography of the Prophet in the larger collection of the biographies of his early followers in the work of Muḥammad Ibn Saᶜd (d. 230/845). As in the Primitive Version of the Ibn ᶜAbbās ascension narrative discussed in the previous chapter, the accounts of the night journey and ascension in these early historical sources combine to varying degrees the reports of different individuals to form what frequently becomes one single strand of narrative storyline. The following survey of the treatment of the night journey and ascension in the early works by Ibn Isḥāq and Ibn Saᶜd illustrates how historians made use of this storytelling technique, a technique also used by the storytellers (*quṣṣāṣ*) who similarly flourished in the formative period of Islamic history.

From Qur᾽ān and Oral Reports to Early Narrative History: Ibn Isḥāq

While Ibn Isḥāq may present one the earliest extant Muslim sources on the events of Muḥammad's life in his *Life of the Messenger of God* [*Sīrat Rasūl Al-lāh*], up until recently this work was known only through the recension by a scholar who lived a generation or two later, ᶜAbd al-Malik Ibn Hishām (d. 218/

833). However, fragments have surfaced from a second recension of Ibn Iṣḥāq's work by Yūnus Ibn Bukayr (d. 199/814) that now allow the historian to surmise what material from Ibn Hishām's account might have been original to Ibn Isḥāq's work, and to distinguish that material from the additions appearing in Ibn Hishām's recension.[1] A study of these two versions together thus provides valuable insight into the development of the story of Muḥammad's night journey and ascension between the second/eighth century and the third/ninth century.

Reading the two versions side by side, one notices immediately that Ibn Bukayr's version is shorter and more basic, while Ibn Hishām's version offers a wider variety of accounts and clearly devotes more attention to listing sources of transmission (see below). Both versions of Ibn Isḥāq's night journey section are preceded by a reference to Q 25:7, which asks why an angel had not been sent to accompany Muḥammad, suggesting that the night journey experience took place in response to the challenge of Muḥammad's opponents to prove the otherworldly source of his revelations.[2] Both Ibn Bukayr and Ibn Hishām's versions echo one another word for word in their opening discussion of the night journey, stating unambiguously that its destination was the site of the temple in Jerusalem. They mention the city of Jerusalem by its Latin name "Aelia," and report that the night journey took place "after Islam had already spread in Mecca and among all the tribes."[3] The recensions also coincide in their statement that the night journey serves as a test of faith for believers and that the journey offers an illustration of God's power.

Ibn Isḥāq's careful language in his account hints that by the second/eighth century the journey must had provoked a certain amount of debate and controversy: "*He caused [his servant] to journey by night* however he willed and just as he willed *in order to show him some of* his *signs* (Q 17:1) as he desired, until he saw what he saw."[4] That at least part of the debate hinged on the question of the nature of the journey becomes clear through the only other anecdote that the two recensions have in common, namely a report attributed to the Prophet's wife, ᶜĀʾisha, that Muḥammad's journey took place in spirit (*rūḥ*) only, his body never actually leaving Mecca.[5] This report clearly illustrates how in the first centuries after Muḥammad's death, different factions disagreed on whether the Prophet's journey had been a physical one, a visionary experience, or some type of dream. While Ibn Bukayr's recension suggests that the "journey in spirit" interpretation enjoyed significant support in these early centuries, the Sunnī consensus that emerges among later scholars was that Muḥammad's physical body was taken on the journey as a sign of the miraculous nature of the event.

The Ibn Bukayr and Ibn Hishām recensions of Ibn Isḥāq's account diverge at this point, for the former barely tells the story of the night journey to Jerusalem at all, while the latter tells several different versions of the story simultaneously. Aside from the report by ᶜĀᵓisha that Muḥammad's body stayed in Mecca, the main focus of Ibn Bukayr recension revolves around its description of the prophets whom Muḥammad encounters while in Jerusalem. Ibn Bukayr's version neglects to describe the rest of the night journey narrative, beyond the briefest of references to a scene in which Muḥammad is tested by being offered different cups of liquid, and the drink he chooses carries with it ultimate consequences for the fate of the Muslim community. This scene, which I will refer to as the "cup test," becomes a standard feature of most extended night journey and ascension narratives, even though its origin remains obscure. Ibn Bukayr's account summarizes the rest of the events of the journey with the following statement, attributed to the Prophet: "I was shown paradise and hell-fire, and I was shown in the heaven[s] this and that . . . and the ritual prayer was imposed upon me."[6] This reference makes it clear that a longer and fuller account was known to the transmitter, but he chooses to skim over its contents. Ibn Bukayr's gloss leaves open the question of whether or not this transmitter connects Muḥammad's journey to Jerusalem with his ascension through the heavens, a connection that was not always accepted in this early period, as other sources from the time demonstrate.

Some aspects of Ibn Bukayr's version give the impression that Ibn Isḥāq may not have originally connected the night journey to Jerusalem with the heavenly ascension as became common in later sources. Despite the gloss cited above in which Muḥammad reports having been shown "in the heaven[s] this and that," Ibn Bukayr's recension does not transmit a single account of the heavenly journey. The absence of ascension reports in Ibn Bukayr's version has led scholars such as Josef van Ess to postulate that the *miᶜrāj* section in Ibn Hishām's version, which will be discussed in what follows, likely reflects a later addition to Ibn Isḥāq's text.[7] The fact that Ibn Bukayr places Muḥammad's receiving the duty of the five daily prayers in Jerusalem rather than in the heavens[8] offers further evidence that for Ibn Bukayr and perhaps Ibn Isḥāq as well, the terrestrial journey was the major focus of the Prophet's experience described by Q 17:1, and while he may have been shown signs in the heavens, he never claims to have been taken on a heavenly journey.

Ibn Isḥāq's Account of the Prophet's Night Journey as Narrated by Ibn Hishām

Contrasting Ibn Bukayr's brief account of the night journey to Jerusalem and Ibn Hishām's full account of it, one is first struck by how much more Ibn Hishām's account concerns itself with sources of transmission. This focus in Ibn Hisham's work reflects the increased attention that scholars must have been paying to such issues in the third / ninth century, a time in which the science of *ḥadīth* criticism was beginning to make an impact. Ibn Hishām's version lists the various authorities from whom it draws, admitting that it intersperses their accounts in order to preserve the flow of the storyline:

> Ibn Isḥāq said, "From the account that reached me on [Muḥammad's] night journey from ᶜAbd Allāh Ibn Masᶜūd, Abū Saᶜīd Khudrī, ᶜĀᵓisha the wife of the Prophet, Muᶜāwiyya b. Abī Sufyān, al-Ḥasan b. Abūᵓl-Ḥasan Baṣrī, Ibn Shihāb Zuhrī, Qatāda and others among the traditionists (*ahl al-ᶜilm*), and Umm Hāniᵓ daughter of Abū Ṭālib, comes what is assembled in this account, each one reporting part of what was recollected about the matter of how he was caused to journey by night."[9]

Ibn Hishām's list mentions each of the parties who are quoted in the night journey discussion that follows, using these citations in an attempt to add greater legitimacy to its accounts. Unlike the storytellers who blend the various storylines into one without mentioning which detail comes from which source, however, a technique that becomes prominent in the Ibn ᶜAbbās ascension narratives, Ibn Hishām's recension of Isḥāq's account largely keeps the various transmitters and their positions separate.

From these separate sources, Ibn Hishām's recension at times presents multiple versions of a single scene or idea without attempting to harmonize the differences or taking a position on which version is most true. For instance, Ibn Hisham offers multiple versions of the cup test, the trial merely alluded to by Ibn Bukayr. In the first account, reported on the authority of Ibn Masᶜūd, Muḥammad is said to be tested with three cups: wine, water, and milk; in the following account, on the authority of al-Ḥasan, Muḥammad is only tested with two cups, wine and milk.[10] Ibn Isḥāq is portrayed as untroubled by such minor divergences, and indeed when faced with the surface disparity between ᶜĀᵓisha's assertion that the journey took place in spirit and Muᶜāwiyya's assertion that the journey took place in a dream vision, Ibn Isḥāq is reported to remark that neither one of these assertions contradicts the longer account of the journey that al-Ḥasan gives.[11] In contrast to Ibn Bukayr's recension, then, Ibn Hishām's recension of Ibn Isḥāq's discourse more closely resembles the *ḥadīth* collections and their separate accounts of the Prophet's journey. Ibn Hishām's version moves a step closer than the *ḥadīth* collections toward storytelling, however, in that it interweaves details from different accounts as it proceeds to recount the events of the narrative in sequence.

As mentioned above, both recensions of Ibn Isḥāq's discussion of the night journey treat the story as a test of faith, and Ibn Hishām's recension in particular stresses this concept. Not only does Ibn Hishām's version emphasize the concept of Muḥammad's trial through the cup test, but also it emphasizes Muḥammad's trial in the form of having to face doubting contemporaries upon his return to Mecca. For instance, Ibn Hishām recalls how Abū Ṭālib's daughter, Umm Hāniʾ, claimed that the Prophet spent the night in her house, and refused to listen when she begged him the next day to keep his experiences a secret.[12] In Ibn Hishām's version, when Muḥammad first tells the Meccans about what he experienced in the night, not only his opponents but even his loyal companion Abū Bakr initially questions the veracity of the account.[13] Abū Bakr and others challenge Muḥammad to describe Jerusalem to them, and the city is caused to rise into view in order for him to be able to remember it and provide more details.[14] As if such a miracle were not enough, the night journey section includes an account of how Muḥammad describes the physical attributes of the other prophets he met in Jerusalem, especially Abraham, Moses, and Jesus. This account of what each of the prophets looks like helps to explain the reason that such "description of the prophets" reports are often categorized together with night journey reports in the central Sunnī *ḥadīth* collections.[15] One can postulate that the connection between the night journey and the description of the prophets stems from the link between Muḥammad's encounter with the other prophets on his journey and the "*great signs*" mentioned in the night journey verse (Q 17:1), signs that attempt to prove to both friends and opponents alike that Muḥammad's account can be trusted.[16]

IBN ISḤĀQ'S ACCOUNT OF THE HEAVENLY JOURNEY AS NARRATED BY IBN HISHĀM

As mentioned above, Ibn Hishām's recension presents a whole series of narratives that do not appear in Ibn Bukayr's recension, and the entire account of the heavenly ascension represents one such additional narrative. One may surmise that Ibn Hishām's account of the heavenly ascension probably was added to the text some time between the completion of the work of Ibn Isḥāq (d. 150/767) and the time when Ibn Hishām (d. 218/833) transmitted his version. As with Ibn Saʿd's account of the ascension that will be described in what follows, Ibn Hishām's account of the ascension only appears after the night journey narrative has been told in its entirety from start to finish. This structure gives the impression that the ascension section was inserted into the narrative later, perhaps at the beginning of the third/ninth century, probably as a result of the way subsequent generations of Muslims connected the night journey to Jerusalem with the heavenly ascension.

Significantly, Ibn Hishām's new ascension section draws almost exclusively upon the report of a single transmitter, one Abū Saʿīd Khudrī. An ascension narrative ascribed to this same figure will later become developed and expanded by Qurʾān commentators in the generation following Ibn Hishām, including the ʿIbādī exegete Hūd b. Muḥakkam Hawārī and the famous Sunnī compiler Ibn Jarīr Ṭabarī.[17] Ibn Hishām uses the Abū Saʿīd Khudrī *ḥadīth* to fill in the details of the heavenly portion of the journey, inserting the account after the point where Muḥammad concluded the Jerusalem portion of his experience but before his return to Mecca.[18]

The Khudrī account may be summarized as follows. Muḥammad describes how a resplendent ladder is brought to him and he ascends upon it to the first heavenly gate, watched over by an angel named Ismāʿīl.[19] The narrative depicts Muḥammad meeting specific prophets in specific levels of the heavens, presenting the prophets in the order that becomes standard in the majority of later official accounts: Adam sits in the first heaven presiding over the judgment of souls, Jesus and John the Baptist appear in the second heaven, Joseph in the third, Enoch / Idrīs in the fourth, Aaron in the fifth, Moses in the sixth, and Abraham in the seventh heaven near the Inhabited House. The visit to the first heaven includes a brief tour of the tortures that various classes of evildoers have to suffer, scenes that could be classified as a tour of hellfire (although not explicitly labeled as such). Following his meeting with Abraham in the seventh heaven, Muḥammad is taken on a brief tour of paradise, where he meets a heavenly maiden destined for Zayd b. Ḥāritha.[20] These tours of paradise and hellfire in the Abū Saʿīd Khudrī narrative represent the earliest extant such tours in the Muslim sources, and they are particularly valuable for the study of the Ibn ʿAbbās ascension narratives, since many of the later versions greatly develop and expand upon these tours.

In addition to assimilating the Abū Saʿīd Khudrī *ḥadīth* into his version of Ibn Isḥāq's work, Ibn Hishām also includes an anonymous anecdote that bears close resemblance to a scene in the Primitive Version of the Ibn ʿAbbās narrative, namely Muḥammad's encounter with the Guardian of Hellfire. This encounter takes place shortly after Muḥammad arrives in the first heaven:

> Ibn Isḥāq said that a traditionist told [him] that the Messenger of God said, "The angels raised me up until I entered the lowest heaven. Every angel I met laughed in joyous welcome and greeted me with good wishes, until I met an angel who said similar sayings and wished me similar wishes but did not laugh. I did not see in him the same joy as I saw in the others. I said to Gabriel, 'O Gabriel, who is that angel who said what the other angels said, but did not laugh or show joy like the others?' He replied, 'Were he to laugh for anyone before or after you, he would have laughed for you, but he will not. This is Mālik, Guardian of the Hellfire.' I said to Gabriel, who was in a station with God described for you as '*holding sway there, keeping trust*' (Q 81:21) 'Command him to show me the hellfire.' He said, 'Of course. Mālik, show Muḥammad the hellfire.' He removed its cover, and [the fire] surged out and raised upward, to the point that I thought that what I saw would consume [me]. I said to Gabriel,

> 'Command him to return it to its place,' and he did so. [Mālik] said to it, 'Die down,' and it returned to the place from whence it had come. I can only liken its return to the falling of a shadow. When it entered from whence it had exited, he replaced its cover."[21]

This anecdote differs from the tour of hellfire passages described previously in that the experience here is a vision rather than an actual tour. In addition, the anecdote depicts Muḥammad as being frightened, conveying a sense of potential danger that one rarely finds elsewhere in official Islamic ascension narratives. Given that both the fear and the description of hellfire appearing in this account also appear in many of the ascension stories associated with Ibn ᶜAbbās, including the Primitive Version that was likely in circulation in the third/ninth century, one could conjecture that the anonymous transmitter of the above anecdote may be none other than Ibn ᶜAbbās. One could conjecture that his name was suppressed from Ibn Hishām's account at a time when many Sunnī scholars began to be suspicious of the Ibn ᶜAbbās ascension narratives, perhaps because they suspected them of being little more than Shīᶜī propaganda. While such a hypothesis must remain conjectural at this stage, there is no doubt that the Ibn ᶜAbbās narratives did circulate in Shīᶜī and other esoteric circles, as the following chapter will demonstrate.

THE EARLY ASCENSION NARRATIVE AS PRESENTED IN IBN SAᶜD'S HISTORY

Just as the night journey and ascension narratives appear to be distinct and separable units in Ibn Hishām's recension of Ibn Isḥāq's biography of Muḥammad, with the likelihood that the ascension portion of the text reflects a later interpolation, so too the two portions of the journey are distinct in the work of Ibn Hishām's contemporary, a man by the name of Ibn Saᶜd (d. 230/845).[22] The fact that Ibn Saᶜd discusses the two journeys one after the other in his biography of Muḥammad indicates that either he or a later editor considered the journeys connected enough to present them side by side, yet distinct enough to treat them separately. In fact, Ibn Saᶜd's text goes so far as to talk about the night journey to Jerusalem and the ascension to heaven as two completely different journeys, assigning them two different dates in the two years preceding the pivotal emigration of the Muslim community from Mecca to Medina (the *hijra*, the event thet establishes the year 1 AH on the Muslim calendar). According to Ibn Saᶜd, the ascension took place on the seventeenth day of the month of Ramadan approximately a year and a half before the *hijra*, while the night journey took place six months later on the seventeenth of the month of Rabīᶜ al-Awwal, one year before the *hijra*.[23] It is worth noting that Ibn Saᶜd understands the ascension (*mi*ᶜ*rāj*) as preceding the night journey to Jerusalem (*isrā*ʾ), for later Muslim scholars such as Ibn Kathīr attempt to explain details that might otherwise prove contradictory by similarly maintaining that the journey to heaven preceded the journey to Jerusalem.[24] In any case, Ibn Saᶜd's treatment of the two journeys proves that at the beginning of the third/ninth century Muslims had not yet come to the consensus position that the night journey and ascension took place on a single evening.

Ibn Saᶜd's extremely brief remarks on the heavenly ascension offer some intriguing details, some of which are unique to Ibn Saᶜd's account. Quoted here in full, the account presents what is essentially a summary of the events of that Ramadan night, sixth months before the night journey was to take place:

> Muḥammad b. ᶜUmar informed us that Abū Bakr b. ᶜAbd Allāh b. Abū Sabra and others said, "The Prophet used to ask his Lord to show him paradise and hellfire. On the night of the seventeenth of Ramadan, eighteen months before the *hijra*, while the Prophet was sleeping in his house at midday, Gabriel and Michael came to him. They said, 'Come away to what you asked of God!' So they brought him away with them to what is between the Station [of Abraham] and Zamzam.[25] He was brought the ladder, which was the most beautiful thing to behold. They ascended with him to the heavens, heaven by heaven. In them he met the prophets. He ended at the Lote Tree of the Boundary, and was shown paradise and hellfire."
>
> The Messenger of God said, "When I ended at the seventh heaven, I did not hear [anything] except the scratching of the pens (*ṣarīf al-aqlām*)."[26]
>
> The five prayers were imposed upon him. Then Gabriel descended and led the Messenger of God in the ritual prayers at their [appointed] times.[27]

In his section on Muḥammad's ascension quoted above, Ibn Saᶜd asserts that Muḥammad was taken on his journey to the heavens in response to his expressed desire to visit paradise and hellfire. As a completely separate experience from the night journey, Ibn Saᶜd depicts this heavenly journey as beginning and ending in the vicinity of Mecca, with no mention of Jerusalem. Despite the allusion to the well of Zamzam, the account contains no scene describing the opening of Muḥammad's breast and its subsequent purification with Zamzam water, a detail which becomes a standard element of many night journey versions beginning with the Sunnī *ḥadīth* accounts presented in the sound (*Ṣaḥīḥ*) collections by both Bukhārī and Muslim.[28] Interestingly, Ibn Saᶜd's summary account does not describe the heavens or indicate which prophet resides in which heaven. It does mention, however, that Muḥammad is shown paradise and hellfire (without giving any details) just as he requested, and this occurs prior to his divine audience and receiving the ritual prayers.

Ibn Saᶜd's account of Muḥammad's ascension mentions simply that "the five prayers were imposed upon him," with no mention of a dialogue with the divinity, and no concept that the five prayers might originally have been given as fifty. It is possible that despite Ibn Saᶜd's silence regarding the typical scene of God reducing the number of daily prayers for Muslims through Muḥammad's intercession, Ibn Saᶜd presumes a knowledge of this and other details which become familiar features of almost all the ascension narratives in the centuries that follow. It is just as likely, however, that Ibn Saᶜd was not aware of this idea, leaving open the possibility that it was developed only later. Even though Ibn Saᶜd claims that the purpose of the ascension was to satisfy Muḥammad's wish to tour paradise and hellfire, he refrains from recounting those tours, and instead ends the account with the imposition of the daily prayers and with Gabriel instructing Muḥammad on how to observe these prayers properly.

THE NIGHT JOURNEY AS NARRATED BY IBN SAᶜD

Prayer also forms a central thematic element of Ibn Saᶜd's account of Muḥammad's night journey, an event that Ibn Saᶜd describes as happening six months after the heavenly ascension. In contrast to the brevity with which Ibn Saᶜd summarizes the events of the heavenly ascension, Ibn Saᶜd paints a more elaborate picture of the night journey to Jerusalem. It begins with an anecdote ascribed to Muḥammad's cousin and Alī's sister, Umm Hāniᵓ, who recounts how the journey to Jerusalem both begins and ends with Muḥammad praying in Mecca. The narrative also comes to a climax in the middle with Muḥammad leading the other prophets in prayer in Jerusalem, and offers a second variant of this scene at the end of the account. Thus the performance of ritual prayer runs throughout Ibn Saᶜd's version of Muḥammad's night journey, and it serves as a major link between his previous discussion of the heavenly ascension and this discussion of his journey to Jerusalem.

Similar to Ibn Isḥāq's discourse on the night journey, and unlike the *ḥadīth* reports in the canonical collections, Ibn Saᶜd offers the names of those who transmit the anecdotes he uses, but does not shy away from combining these reports together. At the beginning, Ibn Saᶜd gives more elaborate chains of transmission than Ibn Isḥāq, and he goes further than Ibn Isḥāq in intertwining the disparate accounts to form what is largely one single unified storyline, uninterrupted by references to the different sources from which it springs. Out of the five chains of transmission that Ibn Saᶜd cites at the beginning of the account, intriguingly three of the five originate with female sources close to the Prophet: the aforementioned Umm Hāniᵓ, Muḥammad's young wife ᶜĀᵓisha, and Umm Salma. In addition, even more interesting for the purposes of this study is the fact that one of Ibn Saᶜd's five chains of transmission links his account of the night journey to Ibn ᶜAbbās.[29] Ibn Saᶜd states that he combines the different reports together, "one *ḥadīth* entering into the *ḥadīth* of another."[30] Ibn Saᶜd's night journey account, then, offers the earliest extant version of a composite night journey story like the ones we find in the Ibn ᶜAbbās accounts, a discursive story form in which scholarly conventions give way to the exigencies of a free-flowing narrative structure.

In Ibn Saᶜd's night journey story, three particular features command attention at this point: first, the references to the roles played by Muḥammad's household on the night in question; second, the depiction of Muḥammad's vision of Jerusalem after his return to Mecca; and third and finally, the portrayal of Muḥammad's encounter with Mālik, Guardian of Hellfire. Each of these features will be discussed in turn, with the particular goal of attempting to examine those themes and ideas that are especially important to later Ibn ᶜAbbās ascension narratives.

Regarding the roles played by Muḥammad's household in Ibn Saᶜd's narrative, the extra anecdotes that the narrative presents on this subject are remarkable for the way they highlight the special witness that Muḥammad's relatives provide for the bodily nature of Muḥammad's journey. In Ibn Saᶜd's story, Muḥammad's journey begins from the "Ravine of Abū Ṭālib,"[31] and it ends with the account of Umm Hāniᵓ (daughter of Abū Ṭālib, sister of ᶜAlī, cousin of the Prophet) who confirms that Muḥammad had slept with her household that night.[32] In an intervening anecdote in the narrative, Muḥammad's uncle ᶜAbbās (father of Ibn ᶜAbbās, after whom many ascension narratives are ascribed) joins others from the family of ᶜAbd al-Muṭṭalib in the search for Muḥammad through the night of his journey to Jerusalem, and ᶜAbbās finally discovers him at a place called "Dhū Ṭuwān." Brooke Vuckovic correctly asserts that these anecdotes may well have been added in order to support the idea that Muḥammad's journey involved him actually physically leaving, asserting this point against those who argued for a spiritual or dream journey.[33] Recalling that in both recensions of Ibn Isḥāq's narrative that very position was supported and defended on the authority of the Prophet's wife ᶜĀᵓisha (daughter of Abū Bakr), Vuckovic is right to see these two mutually exclusive positions "in dialogue."[34] Bearing in mind that ᶜĀᵓisha came into both political and military conflict with the partisans of ᶜAlī and his relatives after the death of Muḥammad, however, we might also expand Vuckovic's point to conjecture that the two positions may have been in "conflict-dialogue," and that there could have been a political dimension to this debate. At the very least, it is striking that Ibn Saᶜd does not ever mention the ᶜĀᵓisha anecdote that appears so central in Ibn Isḥāq's text, the idea that Muḥammad never physically left Mecca.

Such an omission is noteworthy especially given that Ibn Saᶜd claims to have used reports from ᶜĀʾisha among his major sources.

Ibn Saᶜd's narrative can be seen not only to support the idea of a physical bodily night journey, but also to support the idea that the "People of Muḥammad's House" were those most involved with Muḥammad on the night in question. We have seen above how Ibn Saᶜd claims that Muḥammad's uncle ᶜAbbās was the first to discover the Prophet the next morning; in the much later Sunnī exegetical work in a narrative transmitted by Ibn Kathīr, that same role gets assigned instead to Abū Bakr.[35] From this vantage point one begins to see that the question of where Muḥammad was sleeping on the night of the journey, as well as the question of who first talked to Muḥammad upon his return, could potentially be wrapped up in aspects of partisan debates.

The depiction of Muḥammad's conversation with his fellow Meccans upon his return from the night journey offers a second noteworthy aspect of Ibn Saᶜd's discourse, namely the way it portrays Muḥammad's miraculous vision of Jerusalem. Ibn Hishām's recension of Ibn Isḥāq recounts the basic idea that Jerusalem was raised up for Muḥammad to view while he described it, but a *ḥadīth* of Abu Hurayra given in Ibn Saᶜd's version depicts the Prophet's emotional trauma that preceded this miracle. In it Muḥammad recalls,

> I saw myself in the sacred enclosure while the Quraysh were asking me about my night journey, and they asked me about things in the House of the Sanctuary [Jerusalem] that I had not looked at in a concentrated fashion. I became deeply anguished in a way that I had not experienced before.[36]

This added emotional dimension offers a reason for why God chose such a dramatic manner in which to aid Muḥammad when he was plagued by the doubts of his contemporaries. Muḥammad had indeed been to Jerusalem, the anecdote contends, but he had not studied its details to the degree that would be convincing to his later critics. His concern over not being able to convince his critics registers in the anguish that he then feels.[37] In order to support the validity of his case, God reveals Jerusalem to the Prophet so that he could confidently assert, "Each thing they asked about, I informed them of it."[38] The presence of this anecdote in both Ibn Hishām and Ibn Saᶜd's accounts, along with its absence from the Ibn Bukayr recension, suggests that a new round of polemics and debate may have entered into the discussion of the night journey by the third/ninth century: the accuracy of Muḥammad's description of Jerusalem. Both the Sunnī and the Shīᶜī *ḥadīth* collections from this period contain reports to the effect that Muḥammad ascended directly to the heavens from Mecca, without first stopping in Jerusalem. One wonders if partisans of this alternate side of the

Muslim debate, or even Jewish or Christian skeptics, may have questioned the validity of Muḥammad's Jerusalem visit, giving rise to the defensive response that the above anecdote represents. Although the anecdote was never incorporated into the mainstream narratives told about Muḥammad's night journey as a way to verify Muḥammad's Jerusalem visit, it does get transmitted as an independent anecdote (separate from the extended night journey *ḥadīth* reports) in a canonical *ḥadīth* collection that is nearly identical to the *ḥadīth* on which Ibn Saᶜd draws.[39] In both cases, following the discussion of the confirmation of Muḥammad's visit to Jerusalem through this miraculous vision, there appears a description of the figures whom Muḥammad met in Jerusalem, presenting yet more evidence that Muslims could turn to in order to build a case for the truth of Muḥammad's Jerusalem account.

Muḥammad's encounter with the Guardian of Hellfire, Mālik, after meeting the prophets in Jerusalem forms part of the third theme from Ibn Saᶜd's work that merits attention here because of its prominence in the Ibn ᶜAbbās ascension narratives. Ibn Saᶜd's reports of Muḥammad's description of the prophets Abraham, Moses, and Jesus, which precede the encounter with Mālik, bear close resemblance to similar reports in both recensions of Ibn Isḥāq's work.[40] Ibn Bukayr's recension of Ibn Isḥāq, unlike Ibn Hishām's recension and unlike the Ibn Saᶜd text, contains a report stating that Muḥammad encountered the Antichrist *al-Dajjāl* shortly after meeting Jesus.[41] Of the three narratives, only Ibn Hishām's version mentions Muḥammad's meeting with Mālik in the first heaven, and this in the appended ascension narrative ascribed to Abū Saᶜīd Khudrī. In Ibn Saᶜd's version, by contrast, Muḥammad meets Mālik in Jerusalem as part of the night journey, which for Ibn Saᶜd is a completely separate event from the heavenly ascension. Ibn Saᶜd recounts that Muḥammad reported how he had led Abraham, Moses, and Jesus in ritual prayer, and then he stated, "When I finished the prayer, a voice spoke to me saying, 'Muḥammad, this is Mālik, Guardian of Hellfire, so greet him.' I thus turned to him, and he initiated the greetings."[42] Ibn Saᶜd's account of the night journey ends at this point, and the context for this final anecdote suggests that Ibn Saᶜd sees Muḥammad's encounter with Mālik and the prophets as testimonial evidence in support of the validity of the account. Unlike his description of the heavenly journey, an event he portrays as taking place six months prior to the night journey to Jerusalem, here Ibn Saᶜd says nothing about a vision or tour of hellfire. Instead, Mālik appears in this passage as merely one of a series of extraordinary individuals whom Muḥammad encounters during his trip to Jerusalem.

Ibn Saᶜd's two sections describing Muḥammad's ascension and night journey, respectively, thus appear to be remarkable not only for their treatment of the two journeys as separate, but also for the concise way in which they allude to the kernel of details that will grow into more fully developed tropes in later versions of the tale. Ibn Saᶜd's reference to Muḥammad's being shown paradise and hellfire, for instance, conveys the rough outlines of the idea that will expand into full-fledged tours of paradise and hellfire, a development that Ibn Hishām's narrative already begins to reflect.

Despite the similarities between Ibn Saᶜd's account and the two recensions of Ibn Isḥāq's account (that of Ibn Bukayr and that of Ibn Hishām), comparing these different versions of the story of Muḥammad's night journey and ascension helps to illuminate some of the political debates that appear to have been taking place in this early period. For instance, while both Ibn Saᶜd and Ibn Hishām's recensions transmit the *ḥadīth* from Umm Hāniᵓ to the effect that Muḥammad began the night of the journey by physically departing from her house, both recensions of Ibn Isḥāq's report privilege ᶜĀᵓisha's contention that Muḥammad never physically left Jerusalem. In contrast, anecdotes from Ibn Saᶜd's account suggest that Muḥammad's body was indeed absent from Mecca, and that circumstance explains the reason why the Prophet's immediate family members searched for him in the night.

Even though it would be premature to talk of a sharp and defined Sunnī/Shīᶜī split at the beginning of the third/ninth century, it seems clear that the Ibn Saᶜd and Ibn Isḥāq versions both represent the family of the Prophet as playing a role in Muḥammad's journey(s). They especially portray Muḥammad's family as active participants at the beginning and end of the drama. Because the group that becomes known as the partisans of ᶜAlī has a particular interest in foregrounding the Prophet's family in this manner, this common element merits further investigation. The next chapter explores proto-Shīᶜī accounts of the night journey and ascension in order to highlight the contrasts between these disparate versions and those versions that the majority of early Sunnī *ḥadīth* scholars in the middle of the third/ninth century deem authoritative (chapter 5).

4
PROTO-SHĪᶜĪ NARRATIVES OF HEAVENLY ASCENT

Many scholars who have studied Muslim ascension discourses have tended to downplay or ignore *ḥadīth* reports that are not recorded in official Sunnī collections. This chapter focuses primarily on the proto-Shīᶜī accounts of the night journey and ascension in order to highlight the contrasts between their disparate versions and those versions that many early Sunnī *ḥadīth* scholars in the middle of the third / ninth century deem most reliable, which are discussed in the following chapter. It makes logical sense to examine these proto-Shīᶜī narratives first, for the tropes that they introduce and the issues that they raise shed some light upon the context in which other ascension narratives emerge and circulate.

The Ascension Experiences of Proto-Shīᶜī "Extremists"

One problem with the sources that describe the beliefs and worldviews of the amorphous proto-Shīᶜī movement lies in the fact that these sources largely consist of polemical works opposed to the early Shīᶜīs, works that depict these early forerunners to the Shīᶜī movement as "extremists" (*ghulāt*) in order to discredit both them and their followers. Whether or not actual historical figures believed and acted the way these sources said they did, therefore, is an open question. What is clear, however, is that the polemical sources describe on the one hand what Muslims in the early period might conceivably have thought and done, and describe on the other hand what the authors of the works deemed to be extreme or objectionable beliefs and practices. With these comments about the nature of the sources in mind, we turn to two accounts of so-called extremists in order to illustrate how some Muslims may have claimed to have experienced journeys similar to those Muḥammad experienced, exploring these examples with the goal of charting the parallels between them and early versions of Muḥammad's journeys.

According to heresiographical sources, the proto-Shīʿī known as Abū Manṣūr ʿIjlī (d. ca. 120/738) claimed to have been taken up into the heavens, using the same general terminology used for Muḥammad's ascension: "He was caused to ascend to the sky" (*ʿurija bihi ilā ʾl-samāʾ*).[1] Reportedly Abū Manṣūr ʿIjlī claimed that during his ascension God told him to draw near, God addressed him in Syriac (or in another version, addressed him in Persian) as "my son," and God touched him (*masaḥahu*) on the head. After that, God commissioned him to tell his community about God, and about what he had experienced. From this journey, ʿIjlī was said to have become convinced that he was an equal of the prophets, for he had become an anointed individual (*masīḥ*) just like Jesus and an intimate friend of God (*khalīl*) just like Abraham.[2] Many of the details in this brief account of ʿIjlī's ascension can be compared to parallel details in the early version of the Ibn ʿAbbās ascension narrative: the command to draw near, the touch of God's hand, the commission to return and tell of the experience, and the sense of having achieved the status that other prophets had achieved. Such parallelism offers the first bit of evidence to suggest that the early Ibn ʿAbbās narratives were composed in an environment that was in dialogue with formative Shīʿī ideas.

One might explain the close connection between the ascension account ascribed to ʿIjlī and Muḥammad's ascension account ascribed to Ibn ʿAbbās in a variety of ways. Since ʿIjlī's account appears to borrow language directly from early accounts of Muḥammad's ascension, and in light of the fact that the entire story may have been manufactured by heresiographers in order to discredit ʿIjlī, it is thus intriguing to conjecture that the account ascribed to ʿIjlī may have drawn upon a very early version of the Ibn ʿAbbās ascension narrative. This hypothesis would suggest that the Ibn ʿAbbās ascension narrative was in circulation in the very first century following Muḥammad's death.[3] On the other hand, one might also argue that the Ibn ʿAbbās narrative adapts and modifies ideas from ʿIjlī's ascension account, or ideas from another source common to the two. The latter hypothesis would not necessarily tell the researcher anything about the date the Ibn ʿAbbās ascension narrative first circulated, but it would raise the possibility that it was composed either in Shīʿī circles or among those familiar with Shīʿī stories.

According to Sunnī polemical sources, the early Shīʿīs also circulated stories about the ascension experience of a mysterious figure known as Bazīgh. Like ʿIjlī, Bazīgh was accused of telling others that he was taken on a heavenly journey in a manner similar to Muḥammad's ascension. According to Muṭṭahir

b. Ṭāhir Maqdisī, Bazīgh "claimed that he had ascended to heaven, and that God had touched him and spat into his mouth, and that wisdom had grown in his breast like a truffle in the earth, and that he had seen ʿAlī sitting at the right hand of God."[4] Once again, this brief ascension anecdote refers to God physically touching the one who ascends into God's presence. This report contains the additional claim that God spit into Bazīgh's mouth, causing wisdom to spring forth in him. Both anecdotes could be compared to analogous passages in the Ibn ʿAbbās ascension narratives, especially the touch of God's hand. The idea that God spits in the aspirant's mouth resembles passages appearing in later versions of the Ibn ʿAbbās narrative that Muḥammad imbibes a "sweet drop" that falls into his mouth as he nears the divine throne (see chapters 8 and 9).[5] The claim that Bazīgh had looked next to God's throne and had seen Muḥammad's cousin and son-in-law, ʿAlī b. Abī Ṭālib, whom Shīʿīs consider the rightful leader and model for the Muslim people, anticipates the debate over the presence of revered Muslims in the heavens. It specifically echoes the claim that various Shīʿī leaders (Imams) reside near the divine throne. In the following century, proto-Shīʿī authors such as Ṣaffār Qummī and Furāt al-Kūfī transmit Shīʿī *ḥadīth* reports that elaborate on this very concept.

ASCENSION-RELATED SAYINGS IN ṢAFFĀR QUMMĪ'S COLLECTION

Muḥammad b. al-Ḥasan Ṣaffār Qummī (d. 290/902–3) compiled the first major Shīʿī collection of *ḥadīth* reports, a collection whose content has rendered it controversial to this day, despite the fact that its compiler had reportedly been a companion to the figure whom the Imāmī ("Twelver") Shīʿīs consider the eleventh Imam, al-Ḥasan b. ʿAlī ʿAskarī (d. 260/874).[6] The modern scholar of Shīʿī Islam Mohammad Ali Amir-Moezzi has described Ṣaffār Qummī's collection as a fine example of what he calls "the esoteric non-rational" trend in proto- or early Shīʿism. The collection contains a whole series of fragmentary and episodic reports describing not only Muḥammad's ascension but also the ascension experiences of some of the twelve Shīʿī Imams whom the Imāmī Shīʿīs admire. These short anecdotes often develop a single idea, such as the following report that draws a connection between Muḥammad's ascensions (in the plural) and his recognition of ʿAlī as his rightful successor:

> ʿAlī b. Muḥammad b. Saʿīd—Ḥamdān b. Sulaymān—ʿAbd Allāh b. Muḥammad Yamanī—Manbaʿ—Yūnis—Ṣabbāḥ Mizānī—Abū ʿAbd Allāh said, "The Prophet was caused to ascend to the heaven[s] one hundred and twenty times. Each time, God entrusted the Prophet with the authority (*walāya*) of ʿAlī and the Imams after him more than he entrusted duties (*farāʾid*) to him.[7]

This account offers a commentary on earlier ascension narratives through its insistence that the central point of Muḥammad's journeys was not the imposition of ritual duties upon Muḥammad but rather the revelation of the rightful status of ʿAlī and the other Imams in the eyes of God. It details how God repeatedly conveys this Shīʿī message to Muḥammad over the course of his 120 heavenly journeys, the number of which is, of course, a multiple of the number of Imams that the Imāmī Shīʿīs follow.[8] The contentious issue of the Imāma, namely who deserved to rule the Muslim community after Muḥammad and how that ruler was to be chosen,[9] became intertwined with the ascension discourse as a rejoinder to those Muslims who understood Muḥammad's ascension to be about the institution of duties such as the daily ritual prayers. In the above account, as with many similar accounts in Ṣaffār Qummī's work, the ascension discourse serves as a forum to illustrate the divine favor enjoyed by ʿAlī and his followers.

Another *ḥadīth* report preserved by Ṣaffār Qummī portrays God as not merely mentioning ʿAlī's name, but explicitly permitting Muḥammad to bring ʿAlī along on his ascension and to favor him with a share of the same revelation of signs:

> Muḥammad b. ʿĪsā—Abū ʿAbd Allāh al-Muʾmin—ʿAlī b. Ḥassān b. ʿAlī b. al-Jammāl—Abū Daʾūd al-Sabʿī—Burayda Aslamī—the Messenger of God, who said: "ʿAlī, God caused you to witness with me seven residences (*mawāṭin*)." He [then] mentioned the second residence: "Gabriel came to me and caused me to journey by night to the heaven[s]. He said, 'Where is your brother?' I said, 'I left him behind as my substitute (*khalafī*).' He said, 'Petition God to bring you [together] with him.' So I petitioned, and there you stood with me! He kept uncovering the seven heavens and the seven earths for me until I saw their residents and furnishings, and the location of every angel in them. Everything I saw he showed to both you and me."[10]

This *ḥadīth* report once again uses the ascension narrative as a foil to support ʿAlī's rightful status as Muḥammad's successor. During their shared heavenly ascension, which is portrayed as the second stage of a multipart journey,[11] ʿAlī receives the exact same knowledge that Muḥammad receives. Thus ʿAlī obtains information about the unseen from his own direct experience, and one might surmise that according to common Shīʿī belief, ʿAlī later passes these secrets on to his descendants, the Imams.

In another report, instead of Muḥammad's ascension, one finds Abraham's ascension serving as the paradigmatic example for ʿAlī to follow. The anecdote interprets the qurʾānic reference to Abraham's vision as an otherworldly journey experience revealed to Abraham:

> Muḥammad b. ᶜAbd Allāh—Muḥammad b. Hujjāl—Thaᶜlaba—ᶜAbd al-Raḥmān—Abū Jaᶜfar said about the verse, "*And thus we showed Abraham the angelic-realms* (malakūt) *of the heavens and the earth that he might be one of the devout*" (Q 6:75): "He uncovered the earth for him to the point that he saw it and those in it, and [uncovered] the heaven[s] to the point that he saw them and those in them, and the angel that carries them, and the throne and who is on it, and thus was your companion [ᶜAlī] shown."[12]

This report describes Abraham's ascension in a manner that resembles how the narratives ascribed to Ibn ᶜAbbās recount Muḥammad's ascension. In both accounts, the reports do not simply reveal the mysteries of the earth and the heavens, they also reveal the secrets of the divine throne and the divine presence. The final phrase claims that ᶜAlī was shown exactly what Abraham was shown, setting the two figures on par with one another. One could even read into the final phrase of the above quotation the idea that ᶜAlī might have been the figure who was allowed to sit on the throne. A second but clearly connected report expresses more explicitly the idea that ᶜAlī and the Imams ascended in a manner similar to the prophets before them:

> Aḥmad b. Muḥammad—his father—ᶜAbd Allāh b. al-Mughīra—ᶜAbd Allāh b. Miskan—Abū ᶜAbd Allāh said [regarding the verse] "*And thus we showed Abraham the angelic-realms of the heavens and the earth so that he might be one of the devout*" (Q 6:75): "He uncovered the seven heavens for Abraham, to the point that he looked upon what was above the throne, and he uncovered the earth to the point that he saw what was in the air. He did something similar with Muḥammad, and again something similar with your companion [ᶜAlī] and the Imams after him.[13]

This report that Ṣaffār Qummī transmits broadens the circle of otherworldly revelatory experience even further, for it includes the Shīᶜī Imams among those who ascend to the heavens to learn the mysteries of the unseen. In other words, it places the Imams on the same level as the prophets Abraham and Muḥammad in terms of knowledge of the other world.[14]

The aforementioned anecdotes from Ṣaffār Qummī's work all describe the visions and ascension experiences equally conveyed to the prophets and Imams, whereas other anecdotes portray ᶜAlī as enjoying an even higher status than the rest. One such *ḥadīth* report details how Muḥammad and ᶜAlī will ascend together on the last day, both receiving special praise, but ultimately ᶜAlī will be given the honor of deciding the fate of souls. In this report, the divine voice addresses the pair in the following fashion:

> [All] will say, "*Ṭūba is for* these two servants; how favored they are with God." A voice from God's presence that the prophets and creatures will hear [will say], "This is Muḥammad, my beloved, and ʿAlī, my friend. *Ṭūba is for* (Q 13:29) the one who loves him (i.e. ʿAlī), and woe to the one who hates him and spreads lies about him."[15]

After this experience, in which God reaffirms the importance of accepting ʿAlī's legitimacy and loving him, Muḥammad then encounters the angels Riḍwān (Guardian of Paradise) and Mālik (Guardian of Hellfire), who each give the keys of their respective kingdoms to Muḥammad for him to convey them to ʿAlī. The keys are meant for ʿAlī because ʿAlī retains the ultimate right to divide creatures between the two realms on judgment day.[16] This assignment may not seem like anything extraordinary, especially given the fact that in other more mainstream ascension narratives, the Prophet Adam appears in the first heaven carrying out the duty of distinguishing good souls from bad ones and sending them off to their respective destinations. The difference here, I would argue, is that ʿAlī carries out this role on the day of judgment, deciding upon the ultimate eschatological fate of creatures. ʿAlī thus wields a type of intercessory power, and even the ability to forgive and to admit to paradise those whom he wishes, powers sometimes also extended to the Shīʿī Imams. Later Ibn ʿAbbās ascension narratives will attribute some intercessory powers to Muḥammad, but they tend explicitly to deny him the power to decide the otherworldly fate of particular individuals. It is important to recognize that Muḥammad appears to ascend higher than ʿAlī in the above account, for he takes the keys that he is supposed to convey to ʿAlī from the angels Riḍwān and Mālik, suggesting that ʿAlī is no longer there to receive them himself. Nevertheless, anecdotes like the one above underscore ʿAlī's special status among creation, and they illustrate how this status was communicated to Muḥammad during his heavenly journey.

One final example of an ascension-related anecdote from Ṣaffār Qummī's work demonstrates how the ascension reports of proto-Imāmī Shīʿīs prior to the Buyid/Buwayhid period (334/945–447/1055) sometimes contain traces of the discourses of those "extremists" (*ghulāt*) who insisted that ʿAlī or one of his followers was virtually a manifestation of the deity. This particular version narrates how on the night of the ascension, God explains to Muḥammad during their intimate colloquy how ʿAlī appears to have taken on some of the divine qualities:

> Ibrāhīm b. Hāshim—Barqī—Ibn Sanān (and someone else on ʿAbd Allāh Ibn Sanān)—Abū ʿAbd Allāh [Jaʿfar al-Ṣādiq] said that the Messenger of God said, "My Lord caused me to travel by night. *He revealed* to me, *from behind a veil, what he revealed* (Q 53:10), *and he spoke* (Q 42:51) to me.[17] Among what he said to me was the following: 'Muḥammad, ʿAlī

> is *the first* and ᶜAlī is *the last*, [ᶜAlī is *the manifest* and ᶜAlī is *the hidden*,] and *he is of all things most knowing* (Q57:3).'[18] I said, 'My Lord, is that not you [described by that verse]? Is that not you?' He said, 'Muḥammad, *I am God, there is no god but me* (20:14): *the king, the holy, the peaceful, the faithful, the protector, the powerful, the omnipotent, the proud. Glorified be God above* [all] *that they associate* [with him] (Q 59:23). *I am God, there is no god but me*: *the creator, the fashioner, the shaper. To him are the most beautiful names with which those in the heavens and earths glorify him. He is the powerful, the wise* (Q 59:24; cf. 57:1). O Muḥammad, *I am God, there is no god but me*. I am *the first*, for there is nothing before me; I am *the last*, for there is nothing after me. I am *the outer*, for there is nothing above me, I am *the inner*, for there is nothing below me. *I am God, there is no god but me, of all things the most knowing*. O Muḥammad, ᶜAli is *the first*: the first of the Imams who accepted my covenant. O Muḥammad, ᶜAli is *the last*: the last of the Imams whose soul I will seize, which is a *mount that will speak with them* (Q 27:82). O Muḥammad, ᶜAli is *the manifest*: I will manifest to him all that I entrusted to you. You need not conceal anything from him. O Muḥammad, ᶜAli is *the hidden*: I will hide in him the secret that I kept with you. No secret between us will I conceal from ᶜAlī. About all things that I created, both permissible and forbidden, ᶜAlī is *the most knowing*.'"[19]

This remarkable account portrays a dialogue between Muḥammad and his Lord on the night of the ascension, a dialogue legitimized by combining a reference to a revelation from the Star chapter (Q 53:10) together with a reference to a verse that claims that God can speak to human beings directly through revelation (Q 42:51). In the exchange, Muḥammad expresses his confusion regarding ᶜAlī's status, for he hears God ascribing qualities to ᶜAlī that Muḥammad thought reserved for God alone.[20] God responds by assuring Muḥammad that while God remains unique in his transcendent status, nevertheless some divine qualities can be ascribed to ᶜAlī for different reasons. That is, God informs Muḥammad that the verses cited above can be correctly understood on both levels of meaning, the plain sense meaning and the symbolic esoteric level of meaning. The anecdote therefore offers an example of what Bar-Asher classifies as "allegory as supplementary interpretation of the qurʾānic text," for the plain level of meaning is not replaced but supplemented by the Shīᶜī allegorical level of meaning. Thus God and ᶜAlī do not become synonymous here, despite the fact that this "cosmic ᶜAlī" shares in certain aspects of the divine qualities. Similar ideas appear in the sayings ascribed to some of the earliest Sufis, as recorded by some of Ṣaffār Qummī's near contemporaries.[21] The above report promotes the concept of ᶜAlī as representing the highest being in God's creation. Ultimately, that is the message that Ṣaffār Qummī finds to be the most significant aspect of Muḥammad's night journey and ascension: not the number of daily prayers that Muḥammad receives, but the knowledge of ᶜAlī's exalted status that Muḥammad receives that night.

THE QUR'ĀN COMMENTARY OF FURĀT KŪFĪ

Somewhat less controversial than Ṣaffār Qummī's anecdotes described above, the early Imāmī Shīᶜī Qur'ān commentary by Furāt b. Furāt Kūfī (d. ca. 300/912) offers an additional early perspective on Shīᶜī versions of Muḥammad's night journey and ascension. According to a contemporary scholar, this Qur'ān commentary "has a unique Shīᶜī outlook, and [Furāt Kūfī] concentrates all his exegetical energy on verses that include Shīᶜī allusions, virtually ignoring other verses."[22] In other words, Furāt Kūfī selectively highlights those passages in the Qur'ān that Shīᶜī scholars have understood to have latent Shīᶜī content, verses that could be interpreted as presenting references to ᶜAlī, his family, his descendants, and/or his partisans.

As we have seen sporadically in Ṣaffār Qummī's work, Furāt Kūfī's text offers a whole series of anecdotes in which Muḥammad learns of ᶜAlī's exalted station while on his night journey and ascension. For example, it comments on the qur'ānic verse "*ask those who recite the book before you*" (Q 10:94) by explaining that Muḥammad led the angels, prophets, and true believers in ritual prayer in the fourth heaven, and afterward he asked them to what they bore witness, to which they replied, "We testify that there is no god but God, that you are the Messenger of God, and that ᶜAlī is the Commander of the Faithful."[23] Variations on such a testimony are relatively commonplace in Shīᶜī texts. Not only are these phrases inscribed on the walls of some Shīᶜī mosques,[24] but they also are described in night journey and ascension narratives as adorning otherworldly surfaces as well, such as the legs of the divine throne, the gates to paradise, and so on.[25] Thus the very heavens themselves are inscribed in such a way as to bear witness to ᶜAlī and his role as Muḥammad's rightful successor.

Furāt Kūfī's work contains a range of Shīᶜī ideas, some of which describe a quasi-divine "cosmic ᶜAlī" similar to the final anecdote of Ṣaffār Qummī reported above, while others depict ᶜAlī as merely an extraordinary human being, one often given a special role to play. The following anecdote, told by Muḥammad in the first person, illustrates this second idea:

> When I was made to journey by night to the heaven[s], there was neither near angel nor sent prophet between my Lord and me, and every need that I asked of my Lord was fulfilled even more generously than I had requested. Words fell upon my ears: "*Rather, you are a warner, and every people has its guide*" (Q 13:7). I said, "God of mine, I am a warner, but

> who is the guide?" God said, "That is ᶜAlī b. Abī Ṭālib, the best of guides, the Imam of the pious, leader of the select, the one who by my mercy will guide your community into paradise."[26]

In this scene, Muḥammad's successful intercession with God leads to a short exchange on the meaning of a qurᵓānic verse, with God explaining to Muḥammad how ᶜAlī's eschatological role will complement that of the Prophet. Muḥammad and ᶜAlī both successfully intercede on behalf of the righteous, and both are instrumental in securing paradise for the Muslim community. Although they clearly play an exalted role on behalf of humanity, the above anecdote does not imply that Muḥammad and ᶜAlī's ontological status is superior to that of other human beings.

In contrast, a series of anecdotes in Furāt Kūfī's *Tafsīr* describe the superhuman status of ᶜAlī and members of his household, a theme clearly illustrated in the accounts of the heavenly origin of Muḥammad's daughter and ᶜAlī's wife Fāṭima. Here the night journey and ascension narrative seems merely to serve as a backdrop for the action, explaining how Muḥammad came to be in possession of the heavenly seed from which Fāṭima was born. In one brief version of this Shīᶜī trope, Muḥammad justifies to his wives the reason why Fāṭima holds a special place in his heart:

> When I was caused to journey by night to the heaven[s], Gabriel took me to the limit at the tree of *Ṭūba*.[27] Gabriel was intent upon one of its fruits, which he rubbed between his fingers and then gave me to eat. Then he placed his hand between my shoulder blades.[28] He said, "Muḥammad, God brings you joyful tidings of Fāṭima from Khadīja bint Khuwaylid." When I descended to the earth, what happened happened, and Khadīja conceived Fāṭima. When I long for paradise, I draw close to her and smell the fragrance of paradise. She is a dark-eyed [maiden] among women.[29]

Even though the ascension context only serves as a legitimating device that is secondary to the main thrust of the anecdote, the above account links Muḥammad's journey to paradise with the birth of Fāṭima.[30] Indeed, the anecdote announces that Fāṭima continues to serve as a reminder of paradise for the Prophet, and suggests that Fāṭima retains characteristics that derive from her otherworldly origins. This report, and others like it, reinforces Fāṭima's status as an extraordinary woman, and by extension it raises up the status of her progeny, the line of Imams revered by both Imāmī and Ismāᶜīlī Shīᶜī groups.

Other anecdotes in Furāt Kūfī's commentary explore even further the issue of the ontological status of Muḥammad, ᶜAlī, Fāṭima, and the descendants of the latter couple, as illustrated in Furāt Kūfī's discussion of the final two verses of the Cow chapter (Q 2:285–86, the so-called seals). The account, attributed to the fifth Shīᶜī Imam, Muḥammad al-Bāqir, offers one of the earliest instances of these two qurʾānic verses being read as reporting a dialogue between God and Muḥammad:

> Muḥammad [Bāqir] reported that the Messenger of God said, "When I was caused to journey by night to the heaven[s], the Almighty said to me, 'Does *the Messenger believe what was sent down to him from his Lord?*' I replied, '*And the believers* [*all believe*]' (Q 2:285) He said, 'You speak the truth, Muḥammad, peace be upon you. Who have you left in your place for your community after you?' I said, 'The best of [the community] for its people.' He said, 'ᶜAlī b. Abī Ṭālib?' I said, 'Yes, Lord.'
>
> He replied, 'Muḥammad, I caused some to rise up upon the earth, and I chose you from among them. I split off for you a name from among my names. I am never mentioned anywhere without you being mentioned with me. I am "Maḥmūd" ("the praised one") and you are "Muḥammad" ("highly praised"). Then I caused a second one to rise, and I chose ᶜAlī. I split off for him a name from among my names. I am "al-Aᶜlā" ("the most high") and he is "ᶜAlī" ("high").
>
> 'Muḥammad, I created you, ᶜAlī, Fāṭima, Ḥasan and Ḥusayn as figures of light out of my light. I showed your authority to the heavens and their residents as well as to the earths and their residents. Those who accept your authority become close companions in my eyes, and those who struggle against it become unbelievers. Muḥammad, were a servant to serve me until he becomes cut apart or like a worn out waterskin, and then he struggles against your authority, I will not forgive him until he acknowledges your authority.'
>
> 'O Muḥammad, would you like to see them?' I said, 'Indeed, Lord!' He said, 'Turn to the right side of the throne.' I turned to the right side of the throne, and there I found myself with the reflections of ᶜAlī, Fāṭima, Ḥasan, Ḥusayn, and all of the imams until the Mahdi, in a pool of light. They began to pray, the Mahdi in their midst as if he were a shining star. He said to me, 'Muḥammad, these are the proofs, and this is the avenger of your stock. [I swear] by my power and grandeur, he is a necessary proof to my friends, one who takes vengeance upon my enemies.' "[31]

This remarkable passage, which appears to bring together several shorter Shīᶜī *ḥadīth* reports,[32] expresses a connection between the Imams and the divine light of God. In this respect it draws upon the idea of how God's primordial light gets passed on to Muḥammad, the so called light of Muḥammad (*nūr Muḥammad*).[33] The above report suggests that the exalted status that Muḥammad and the Imams enjoy derives from their sharing in the divine essence. It also shows how Muḥammad meets each of the Imams in their luminous forms during his ascension, and he prays with them next to the divine throne just as he prays with the other prophets in Jerusalem. Beyond merely hearing about the Imams, this report illustrates how Muḥammad joins together with them in this most sacred and exalted station. Furāt Kūfī's commentary on the final two verses of the Cow chapter thus interprets the intimate encounter between Muḥammad and God as a site for the communication of unmistakably Shīᶜī messages.

The above narrative demonstrates one way in which the proto-Shīᶜīs such as Furāt Kūfī made use of the ascension discourse in order to assert their partisan Imāmī position. It proclaims the God-given right for the Imams to lead the Muslim community based upon their primordiality and subsequent authority, hinting that those who refuse to accept the authority of the Imams are not true Muslims. This interpretation of the "seals" of the Cow chapter also introduces the figure of the Shīᶜī Mahdi, the final Imam who will return to restore God's justice on earth.[34] Perhaps most importantly, the anecdote takes the origin story of the Imams a step further by describing how the luminous essence of the members of the Prophet's household were created out of the preexisting light of the divine essence itself.

The same idea of the luminous forms of the Imams receives a slightly different treatment in one final passage from Furāt Kūfī's *Tafsīr* that I would like to examine at this point, his commentary on the verse "*Praise be to God, who spoke truly to us in his promise. . . . We may settle wherever we wish in paradise*" (Q 39:74). In each of the heavens, Muḥammad participates in a discourse with the angels, who share with the Prophet their intimate love of him and their deep longing for ᶜAli, to whom they invariably send their greetings. In fact, the *ḥadīth* report formulates an explanation of the qurᵓānic proof text by spinning an elaborate tale of how the angels have been in love with both Muḥammad and ᶜAlī since the beginning of time.

The *ḥadīth* report depicts the angels as sincere lovers, attracted to their beloveds through disinterested devotion. The passage illustrates this sincere devotion in a humorous scene in which Muḥammad expects the angels that he meets to ask him to intercede with God on their behalf, but instead they ask him only to convey a message to ᶜAlī on their behalf.[35] These angels care less about their own eschatological fate than about making sure that ᶜAlī is aware of their longing for him. Although the angels may now be cut off from access to the earthly ᶜAlī, they explain that they have intimate knowledge of all the Imams, since the latter were created from God's light even before the angels, and the angels learned the proper way to worship God from the Imams. As in the anecdote that Furāt Kūfī tells with reference to the final verses from the Cow chapter cited above, here too one finds a reference to the luminous reflected forms (*ashbāh*) of the Imams, who serve as guardians over the rest of the creation. The angels serve these Imams with sincere devotion, modeling for the emerging Shīʿī community the proper attitude of the community toward ʿAlī and his descendants.

Beyond this general station that all the Imams seem to enjoy, the passage implies that ʿAlī's station surpasses all the others in the eyes of the angels. In fact, in answer to the requests of the angels, God even creates an angel in the form of ʿAlī, as the angels themselves explain:

> We complained to God of [our love for] ʿAlī b. Abī Ṭālib, so he created for us an angel in his image (*fī ṣūratihi*). He caused it to sit on the right of his throne, on a high seat of gold adorned with pearls and jewels. . . . The owner of the throne said to [the angel in the form of ʿAlī], "Stand, by my power!" So it stood by God's command. Whenever we passionately yearned for a vision of ʿAlī on the earth, we gazed upon his likeness in the heaven[s].[36]

One might see in this "cosmic ʿAlī" the logical conclusion to the exaltation of ʿAlī, for he takes his seat (*sarīr*) as a type of "lesser divinity" at the right hand of God.[37] As if to combat the notion that ʿAlī could be mistaken for God, however, the luminous form of ʿAlī is commanded to stand instead of sit. While one could imagine other reasons why God might command this angelic figure to stand, comparison with similar passages in early Muslim and Jewish narratives[38] suggest that this interpretation is the correct one. In the above passage, the narrator describes the most noble and exalted of creatures with supreme hyperbole while seeking to avoid the danger of confusing this "cosmic ʿAlī" (here in angelic form) with the divinity.

Instead of all of the Imams appearing together next to God's throne, the above report places ʿAlī's form above the rest, and it assigns to him the messianic role that the previous report cited above ascribes to the Mahdī. In this *ḥadīth*, as described in other anecdotes, ʿAlī's high rank is inscribed onto the very surfaces of the otherworld. For instance, in it the angels of the sixth heaven describe a tree at the gate to the level of paradise known as *Firdaws* (Persian for garden or paradise), which has written upon each of its leaves, "There is no god but God, Muḥammad is the Messenger of God, ʿAlī b. Abī Ṭālib is God's solid grip, God's firm rope, whose eye is upon all creatures, the sword of his vengeance upon the idolaters."[39] Not only does such a description provide a sanction for ʿAlī's special status, attaching his name and titles after the first two portions of the Muslim testimony of belief (*shahāda*), but also it offers a militant image of ʿAlī as God's righteous avenger,[40] attributing to him a role often assigned to the messianic Mahdī.

This final anecdote from Furāt Kūfī's *Tafsīr* combines a number of proto-Shīʿī symbols, not only describing the primordial creation of Muḥammad and the Imams out of God's light and the special role that the angelic ʿAlī plays at the right hand of God's throne, but also detailing how the angels joyously greet Muḥammad, and ardently send their greetings to ᶜAlī through Muḥammad. The whole point of the narrative seems to be to demonstrate how the heavens resound with proclamations of love for ᶜAlī and his descendants, implying that righteous Muslims on earth should follow suit and join the partisans of ᶜAlī. The above ascension-related reports transmitted by Furāt Kūfī serve less as complete ascension narratives and more as a fragmentary anecdotes with specific partisan objectives. Undoubtedly, the same could be said of the vast majority of reports that we have surveyed from the early proto-Shīᶜī scholars discussed in this chapter.

This chapter draws upon material from a vast expanse of early Islamic history, and it is therefore useful to conclude it by discussing what connections can be made between the ideas of these disparate proto-Shīᶜī writers. On the one hand, we have examined ascension-related ideas ascribed to activist proto-Shīᶜīs from the second/eighth century; on the other hand, we have looked at the more developed ascension-related ideas of proto-Shīᶜī scholars from the end of the third/ninth century. In the intervening century, the first independent works dedicated to Muḥammad's night journey and ascension were compiled. The very first may well have been written by a proto-Shīᶜī, the companion of the sixth and seventh Shīᶜī Imams named Hishām b. Sālim Jawālīqī (d. after 148/765, the death date of the sixth Imam Jaᶜfar Ṣādiq).[41] Since Jawālīqī's *Kitāb al-miᶜrāj* is no longer extant, its contents remain a mystery. However, the mere fact of the work's composition demonstrates that proto-Shīᶜī authors took a distinct interest in the story at an early date. Perhaps the authors were attracted to the narrative of Muḥammad's ascension because of its potential as a legitimating device for Shīᶜī claims, as a convenient source for extraqurʾānic pronouncements from on high.

By placing these works together in the same chapter I am not asserting a direct dependency of the later scholars on the earlier material, nor am I claiming that these figures all shared a common theology or worldview. Instead, I wish to show that between the second/eighth and the third/ninth centuries, some esoteric reports on the night journey and ascension began to develop in a particularly partisan direction within Shīᶜī circles. They began to focus less on the journey to Jerusalem and more on the heavenly ascent, less on the meeting with prophets and more on the encounter with angels, less on the exaltation of Muḥammad's unique station and more on the exaltation of ᶜAlī with him or instead of him. That not all Shīᶜī ascension narratives developed in this same direction will become clear in the chapters that follow. Nevertheless, these partisan proto-Shīᶜī narratives must have been circulating in the third/ninth century, and one might hypothesize that other Muslim scholars writing about the night journey and ascension felt they had to respond to these narratives in some way: to adapt and appropriate them, to refute and reject them, or to ignore and marginalize them. The issue lies at the heart of the thesis of this book, for I contend that one of the ways the Ibn ʿAbbās ascension narratives developed was through Sunnī scholars and storytellers adapting, appropriating, and subverting these early esoteric themes for use in ascension narratives that were aimed at less esoteric and less Shīʿī-inclined audiences.

5

CANONICAL SUNNĪ *ḤADĪTH* REPORTS ON MUḤAMMAD'S JOURNEY

As we have seen, *ḥadīth* reports present accounts of what Muḥammad said or did on a certain occasion, and they offer a source of Islamic teachings about the night journey and ascension that many Muslims place on par with the text of the Qur'ān. Since the Qur'ān does not offer a clear and full account of Muḥammad's night journey and ascension, Muslims needed to ask questions to gain a coherent understanding of what Muḥammad experienced, and while he was alive the most logical person to ask would have been Muḥammad himself. According to Muslim sacred history, Muḥammad's oral explanations of the details of the night journey and ascension were memorized by his companions and transmitted to later generations of Muslims in the form of oral anecdotes that later were collected as *ḥadīth* reports.

Within decades of Muḥammad's death, however, the Muslim community was split by political and theological divisions, and it became clear that unscrupulous scholars could easily modify or fabricate wholesale those *ḥadīth* reports that supported their own particular agendas.[1] In light of the proliferation of distinctive and even mutually exclusive *ḥadīth* reports in the first two centuries after Muḥammad's death, Muslim scholars developed a science of *ḥadīth* transmission and criticism that attempted to distinguish authentic reports from spurious ones. To determine the relative validity of any given *ḥadīth* report, this science not only scrutinized the content of the report itself but also its chain of transmission (*isnād*), a list of figures who passed on the text (so-and-so heard from so-and-so, who heard from so-and-so, etc.), ideally stretching back to Muḥammad or one of his immediate companions. The science of *ḥadīth* criticism, while aiming to divine the objective truth of what Muḥammad "really said," ultimately relies upon a priori premises,[2] subjective judgments,[3] and the general consensus of later scholars.

Written collections preserve tens of thousands of *ḥadīth* reports, but only a small fraction of these were accepted as reliable by the majority of the "piety minded" of later generations of Muslims. Given the amount of subjectivity involved, in what follows I consider determinations of what might be called the "orthodoxy" or "heterodoxy" of given reports to be a particular discourse articulated within a specific political or theological context. It is useful for the historian of religion to bracket the issue of ultimate truth or accuracy, those issues that may be of the most concern to some Muslims, to examine instead the issue of the history and legacy of different mythologizing exegetical trends that the divergent reports illustrate.[4] Instead of asking "is this account the most true or most early version?" this approach seeks to ask "which accounts were transmitted by whom and to what purpose?" Taking this approach allows the historian to avoid the elusive search for origins, and to look at the construction of trends and orthodoxies in context over time, rather than having to treat as marginal those accounts that a certain group of Muslims might reject as spurious.

Interestingly, even within the smaller and more limited body of accounts that a certain community deems sound (*ṣaḥīḥ*), one still finds significant variations and even apparent contradictions among the narratives that recount the story of Muḥammad's night journey and ascension. This fact proves that even the early scholars, whose work played a major role in determining what later scholars would agree upon as authentic narratives, could not agree upon a single version of the night journey and ascension story as representing the most complete and unambiguously true account. In a study focusing on the development of one specific strand of Islamic ascension narrative, those accounts attributed to Ibn ᶜAbbās, it will not be possible to offer a comprehensive survey of the wide breadth of references to this narrative in the diverse Sunnī collections of *ḥadīth* reports. Instead of aiming at comprehensiveness, this chapter selects those reports that arguably played a major role in shaping the development of the Ibn ᶜAbbās ascension narratives.[5]

For the majority of those Muslims who came to call themselves Sunnīs, six collections of *ḥadīth* reports largely compiled around the third/ninth century came to be considered quasi canonical, containing those authentic reports upon which Sunnī scholars could rely. Of these, the two collections of Bukhārī (d. 256/870) and Muslim (d. 261/874) enjoyed the highest status for this Sunnī majority. By examining a selection of some of the ascension-related *ḥadīth* reports contained in the collections of Bukhārī and Muslim that many Sunnīs deem as most reliable, one gets a sense of some of the issues over which the early

Muslims wrestled, as well as some of the raw materials from which the early Muslim storytellers drew.

Night Journey and Ascension *Ḥadīth* Reports in Bukhārī and Muslim

The *ḥadīth* reports on the night journey and ascension contained in Bukhārī and Muslim's *Sound* (*Ṣaḥīḥ*) collections run the spectrum from brief and fragmentary anecdotes to extended and rhetorically seamless whole narratives,[6] the latter of which tell the tale of how Muḥammad received the duty of the daily ritual prayers directly from God. Even a cursory survey of the extended narratives from these collections demonstrates that they are largely limited to those reports transmitted by the companion of the Prophet by the name of Anas b. Mālik (d. ca. 91/709).[7] All the extended accounts in the *ḥadīth* collections of Bukhārī and Muslim focus on the heavenly ascension portion of the journey, refraining from narrating the specific details of the Mecca to Jerusalem portion of it, if mentioning that portion of the journey at all. The following summaries offer an overview of the features of the four most extended ascension narratives appearing in these two major Sunnī *ḥadīth* collections:

> [259] Anas b. Mālik from the Prophet.[8] A story told in the first person. It begins with the arrival of Burāq, without any mention of the opening of the chest or where the Prophet was sleeping. It contains a short account of the journey to Jerusalem, where Muḥammad meets the prophets and is told to select one of several beverages that symbolize the future fate of his community (the cup test). The heavenly ascent follows. The order of the prophets whom Muḥammad meets in the heavens is the order that comes to be standard in the majority of official accounts (Adam, John and Jesus, Joseph, Enoch, Aaron, Moses, Abraham). The narrative ends after Muḥammad receives the duty of the daily prayers as a revelation (drawing upon Q 53:10) and bargains the number of daily prayers from fifty down to five.
>
> [262] Anas b. Mālik, presumably from the Prophet.[9] A story told in the third person. Three angels come to Muḥammad before he has received revelation, while he is sleeping in the sacred place of prayer (*masjid al-ḥaram*; cf. Q 17:1). After opening his chest to purify his body and to fill him with faith, the angels take Muḥammad directly to the first heaven, with no mention of Burāq or the journey to Jerusalem. Aside from Adam appearing in the first heaven, the order of the prophets in the heavens

is uncertain. This *ḥadīth* contains the most descriptive account of the Prophet's encounter with the divinity found in either Bukhārī or Muslim's collections, drawing on the language in Q 53:8–10. After the fifty prayers are reduced to five, Moses tells Muḥammad to "descend in the name of God" and he wakes in the sacred place of prayer.

[263] Anas b. Mālik from Abū Dharr from the Prophet.[10] A story told in the first person. Gabriel opens the roof of the residence where Muḥammad is sleeping in Mecca, opens his chest to purify him, and then ascends with him to the heavens. After the fifty prayers are reduced to five, Muḥammad comes to the Lote Tree decked out in colors (Q 53:14, 16), and the account ends with a brief mention of the Prophet's entrance to paradise.

[264] Anas b. Mālik from Mālik b. Ṣaᶜṣaᶜa from the Prophet.[11] A story told in the first person. Muḥammad lies between wakefulness and sleep somewhere in Mecca when an unspecified number of angels arrive and opens his chest to purify him. Burāq arrives and carries Muḥammad on his back, after which he is brought to the heavens. The prophets appear there in the standard order. In the seventh heaven, Muḥammad arrives at the Inhabited House (*al-bayt al-maᶜmūr*, Q 52:4), and is given the cup test there. The narrative ends with the fifty prayers being reduced to five, and in the Bukhārī versions, the divine voice expresses satisfaction with the final resolution.

While these four extended narratives agree in the broad outlines of the story, they differ from one another in minor details. Beyond these differences, it is noteworthy that each of the extended narratives comes to a climax with the Prophet receiving the duty of the performance of the daily ritual prayers (fifty reduced to five) directly from God.[12] Only one of the extended accounts summarized above mentions Muḥammad's return to Mecca, and none of them describe the community's reaction to Muḥammad's story the following morning.[13] These facts lead one to conclude that according to Bukhārī and Muslim, the tale of Muḥammad's heavenly ascension primarily was important not as a legitimating device for Muḥammad and his role as prophet, but rather as a device to explain how the number of daily prayers was set at five, a number never specifically set in the Qur'ān itself.

Besides their focus on the revelation of the daily prayers, the different versions of Anas b. Mālik's night journey and ascension narratives reported by Bukhārī and Muslim also generally share in recounting the scene in which the angels open Muḥammad's chest.[14] The scene depicts how the angels extract Muḥammad's heart, cleansing it and replacing it in his chest prior to taking him on the journey. In connecting this trope to Muḥammad's ascension, these transmitters demonstrate their belief that Muḥammad must have experienced a type of physical purification before ascending to the heavens.[15]

The extended narratives in Bukhārī and Muslim also share the similar feature of describing the prophets and angels that Muḥammad encounters on his journey in only the briefest of fashions, a brevity that also appears in the independent and fragmentary anecdotes that Bukhārī and Muslim transmit.[16] One representative example of such a concise anecdote describing the prophets, quoted in full, appears in the following *ḥadīth*:

> Muḥammad b. al-Muthannā and Ibn Bashshār told us—Ibn al-Muthannā—Muḥammad b. Jaᶜfar—Shuᶜba—Qatāda—Abū al-ᶜĀliya—the paternal cousin of your prophet [Ibn ᶜAbbās?] said that the Messenger of God recounted when he was taken on a journey by night, saying: "Moses was a tall man, as if he were one of the men of the Shanūᵓa [tribe]. Jesus is curly-haired and medium in stature." Then he mentioned Mālik, guardian of [the hellfire,] Jahannam, as well as the Dajjāl [Antichrist].[17]

Bukhārī and Muslim's collections contain a whole series of these types of brief fragments of night journey narrative, whose main purpose seems to be Muḥammad's descriptions of these central prophetic predecessors (Abraham, Moses, and Jesus) and / or eschatological figures (Mālik, al-Dajjāl), perhaps as a device to verify his story that he saw them.[18] Some versions of these brief descriptive fragments imply that Muḥammad meets some of these figures on his path before arriving in Jerusalem, such as his vision of Moses in a "blue wadi"[19] or praying in his grave at a "red hill,"[20] details that make these fragments reminiscent of the "prayer stop" trope that one finds in Nasāᵓī's *ḥadīth* collection (see below), which depicts Muḥammad as descending and praying at holy places such as Medina, Sinai, and Bethlehem on his way to Jerusalem.[21] Unlike these types of fragments, however, the extended ascension *ḥadīth* reports ascribed to Anas by Bukhārī and Muslim rarely offer even this amount of description. They often tell us little about each prophet beyond the detail of which particular prophet appears in which heaven, and even that information is not always clear (e.g., nos. 262–63, above). In contrast to the Ibn Isḥāq versions, for instance, the sound *ḥadīth* reports appear to be interested less in telling a story and more in arriving at the ultimate moral of the story: Muḥammad meets his prophetic forebears and other noble figures on his fantastic journey, and at the climax of the journey he receives the ritual prayer duty directly from God.

One fragmentary *ḥadīth* report found in the collections of Muslim, Nasāᵓī, and Tirmidhī offers some significant additions to the idea that God revealed the prayers to Muḥammad on his ascension, a duty that this *ḥadīth* presents as but one of three "gifts" that God bestows upon his Prophet. It does not mention the journey to Jerusalem at all, rather it deals only with the Prophet's experiences at the highest stages of his ascension. This report's details strongly suggest that by the third/ninth century the notion that Muḥammad received specific gifts from God during the ascension had begun to have an impact upon reports in official Sunnī collections such as this one:

> Abū Bakr b. Abī Shayba—Abū Usāma—Mālik b. Mighwal—Ibn Numayr and Zubayr b. Ḥarb—ᶜAbd Allāh Ibn Numayr; Ibn Numayr—his father—Mālik b. Mighwal—Zubayr b. ᶜAdiyy—Ṭalḥa—Murra—ᶜAbd Allāh, who said: When the Messenger of God was taken on the night journey, he came to an end at the Lote Tree of the Boundary, which is in the sixth heaven. At it ends one who is caused to ascend from below it, and one who is caused to descend from above it, to the point that both become caught in it. [God] said, "*When the Lote Tree was covered with what covered*" (Q53:16), [a verse upon which Muḥammad] said, "Golden butterflies." He was given three [things]: the five ritual prayers, the seals of the Cow chapter, and the forgiveness of the errors of one who dies a member of his community [while] not ascribing partners to God at all.[22]

The first portion of this anecdote describes the Lote Tree, making use of conventions such as the "golden butterflies" (*farāsh min dhahab*) that become part of the standard exegetical lexicon surrounding this heavenly tree. More significant for our purposes here is the final sentence of this fragment, where it describes three gifts that God grants to Muḥammad at this exalted station. First among the three gifts are the five prayers, which are treated here as favors bestowed rather than duties imposed upon the Muslim community. Second are the two final verses or seals of the Cow chapter of the Qurᵓān (Q 2:285–86), verses whose content as petitionery prayers have given them a special place in Muslim piety, and verses that become treated as the report of a dialogue in the intimate colloquy scenes of accounts related to the Ibn ᶜAbbās ascension narrative. Third and finally, in this narrative fragment God promises to offer forgiveness to all who die as sincere Muslims. While this final gift does not explicitly mention the concept of Muḥammad's intercession, it does introduce the idea that at the culmination of Muḥammad's ascension, God makes pronouncements to Muḥammad dealing with the eschatological fate of the Muslim community. The special significance of this fragment from Muslim's *Ṣaḥīḥ*, which also appears in the *ḥadīth* collections ascribed to Nasāᵓī and Tirmidhī (more on these collections below), lies in its depiction of Muḥammad receiving multiple gifts from God at the highest point that he reaches in his journey. Such a depiction leaves room for those who go on to describe how God bestows such gifts upon Muḥammad in the context of a direct face-to-face encounter, the intimate colloquy.

The idea of Muḥammad's intercession with God is only ambiguously supported in the text of the Qur᾽ān, but the Sunnī *ḥadīth* collections such as that of Muslim offer a significant number of Muḥammad's sayings in support of the idea. Such accounts depict Muḥammad playing the role of intermediary between two parties, pleading with God on behalf of humanity in general and the Prophet's community in particular.[23] Interestingly, beyond the fragmentary "Three Gift" narrative cite above, Muslim does not make any connection in his collection of *ḥadīth* reports between the narrative of Muḥammad's heavenly journey and the concept of Muḥammad's intercession. He nevertheless records dozens of reports that demonstrate how Muḥammad will be given the power to intercede on behalf of Muslims on judgment day.[24] In one particularly widely attested account, the Prophet proclaims that seventy thousand Muslims will be allowed to enter paradise without having first to be judged or punished.[25] We shall see in what follows that this and other intercessory reports are collated into the night journey and ascension narratives recorded by other authoritative Sunnī traditionists.

ḤADĪTH REPORTS FROM THE COLLECTION OF NASĀ᾽Ī

Considered among most Sunnīs today to be of somewhat lesser status than Bukhārī and Muslim's collections yet nevertheless authoritative,[26] the work known as *Sunan* of Abū ᶜAbd al-Raḥmān Aḥmad b. Shuᶜayb Nasā᾽ī (d. 302/914) supplements a few of the same extended *ḥadīth* reports on Muḥammad's ascension familiar from Bukhārī and Muslim's works[27] with other reports not found in these collections. One such extended *ḥadīth* contains a trope of particular significance to this study due to its subsequent incorporation into many later ascension narratives, the account of the prayer stops that Muḥammad and Gabriel took on their way to Jerusalem:

> ᶜAmr b. Hishām—Makhlad—Saᶜīd b. ᶜAbd al-ᶜAzīz—Yazīd b. Abī Mālik—the Messenger of God, who said: I was brought a mount larger than a donkey and smaller than a mule, its step at the limit of its sight. I rode it, and Gabriel was with me. I went, and then [Gabriel] said, "Descend and pray." So I did. Then he asked, "Do you know where you prayed? You prayed at Tayba [Medina], the destination of the emigration." Then he said, "Descend and pray." So I prayed, and he said, "Do you know where you prayed? You prayed at Mount Sinai where Moses spoke with God." Then [later] he said, "Descend and pray," so I descended and prayed. He said, "Do you know where you prayed? You prayed in Bethlehem, where Jesus was born." Then I entered the house of sanctity [Jerusalem],

> where the prophets were assembled for me. Gabriel advanced me forward, so that I led them [in ritual prayers]. Then I was caused to ascend.[28]

The narrative goes on to list the different prophets whom Muḥammad meets in each of the heavens, his prostrating at the Lote Tree "above the seventh heaven," and his receiving the duty of the fifty prayers there. The most remarkable portion of this ascension narrative, however, is its account of Muḥammad's visiting Medina, Sinai, and Bethlehem on his way to Jerusalem. Gabriel also instructs Muḥammad to perform cycles of ritual prayer in each of these holy sites, seemly setting an example for sacred pilgrimage to these places.

When juxtaposing these prayer stops appearing in Nasāʾī's report with the idea of tempting voices from among the Jews and Christians that seek to lead Muḥammad from his path during the night journey that appear in other reports (such as those cited by Ibn Hishām and Ṭabarī), it becomes clear that the above account seeks to embrace the legacy of Moses and Jesus while distancing itself from what Muslims consider the "corrupted doctrines" that Judaism and Christianity form around these prophets. As such, this prayer stop *ḥadīth* offers a creative amplification on the account of the night journey to Jerusalem. It stresses that the journey to Jerusalem involved Muḥammad's being able to praise God at earlier holy sites, thereby endowing these holy sites with the blessing of Muḥammad's presence.[29] The account performatively suggests the incredible speed with which Burāq travels, and it argues that the stages of the terrestrial journey matter almost as much as the final earthly destination, Jerusalem.

In her discussion of Nasāʾī's report of the account above, Brooke Vuckovic calls this tour "through the geographic history of the sacred past" a type of lesson for the Prophet, one that emphasizes Gabriel's role "in training and initiating Muḥammad." She continues, "Perhaps more than any other narrative, this account highlights the apprenticeship relationship between Muḥammad and Gabriel."[30] While Muḥammad certainly plays the role of a novice being instructed by his teacher in these scenes, this same characterization fits many other scenes in the extended ascension narratives. Time and time again Gabriel instructs Muḥammad to go from this place to that, to greet various exalted individuals and creatures from the upperworlds, to take courage and forget his fear. From my point of view, then, this scene is not especially remarkable for its illustration of Muḥammad's apprenticeship, nor for its initiatic dimension. Instead, I would stress two elements: first, the tour aspect of the account, mentioned previously; and second, the prayer aspect of the account, in which Muḥammad is being called to perform cycles of ritual prayer at each of the sacred sites he visits.[31] In the later reshaped ascension narratives attributed to Ibn ʿAbbās, these ideas become incorporated into the account of Muḥammad's ascension to such a degree that one finds Gabriel instructing Muḥammad to pray two cycles of ritual prayer in each of the heavens that he visits during the ascension. Part of the "lesson" being taught in this *ḥadīth*, then, could be said to center around the instruction to Muḥammad in particular and to Muslims in general on the proper way to visit holy sites.

One should notice that in the portion of the *ḥadīth* cited by Nasāʾī and translated above, Muḥammad does not visit the abodes of every one of the previous prophets whom he was to meet in Jerusalem. Therefore, I disagree with the broad scope of Vuckovic's comment that the anecdote depicts Muḥammad as "traveling to the various holy spots of the previous religions . . . [thus preparing him] to meet the previous prophets."[32] Rather, the account emphasizes Muḥammad's direct connection with two other prophets in particular: Moses and Jesus. This fact may tell us something about the intended audience for this ascension account, namely Jews, Christians, and those Muslims who live among Jews and Christians. The significance of this idea will become more apparent in our examination of the Bakrī ascension narratives (chapters 8 and 9), where the number of holy sites Muḥammad visits prior to Jerusalem often shrinks from three down to one, leaving Mount Sinai as the only prayer stop on the Prophet's terrestrial night journey.[33] Here in the *ḥadīth* version, as well as in the subsequent ascension narratives reported in the Qurʾān commentaries of ʿAlī Qummī and Thaʿlabī (see chapter 6),[34] Muḥammad receives the instruction to stop a total of three times and offer ritual prayers in each of these three holy locations.

Ḥadīth Reports from the Collection of Tirmidhī

As with reports in Nasāʾī's collection, the *ḥadīth* reports in the *Ṣaḥīḥ* collection compiled by Abū ʿĪsā Tirmidhī (d. 279/892) offer important examples of how diverse ascension material, beyond those extended accounts transmitted by Bukhārī and Muslim, was both known to respectable Sunnī scholars and was transmitted by them in the formative period. For instance, we have seen how the extended reports in the *ḥadīth* collections of Bukhārī and Muslim describe the ascension to heaven in more detail than they do the night journey to Jerusalem, and some of these accounts even bypass the latter, depicting Muḥammad as ascending to heaven directly from Mecca. A *ḥadīth* report transmitted by Tirmidhī suggests that early Muslims debated the meaning of the night journey verse, and some may have even questioned whether or not the Prophet traveled to Jerusalem in the first place.[35] In this account, Zirr b. Ḥubaysh and Ḥudhayfa b. al-Yamān dispute whether or not Muḥammad prayed in Jerusalem during the night journey, and Ḥudhayfa convinces his interlocutor that were Muḥammad to have prayed there, the verse would have said something about the fact. Instead, Ḥudhayfa asserts, Muḥammad remained upon the back of his fantastic mount Burāq throughout his journey, taking him on a tour of paradise and hellfire, and returning him back home. This report, declared a sound *ḥadīth* by Tirmidhī, suggests that Muḥammad's tours of paradise and hellfire, along with his witnessing of the "threatening promise" (*al-wa*ᶜ*d*) of the afterworld, comprise some of the most notable aspects of the journey. Such a narrative could be seen as sharply contrasting with the "prayer stops" anecdote related in Nasāᵓī, for the former seeks to develop and expand the account of Muḥammad's terrestrial journey to Jerusalem, while the latter virtually denies the journey to Jerusalem and instead develops the eschatological dimensions of the heavenly ascent. Contrasting these two reports from the *ḥadīth* collections of Tirmidhī and Nasāᵓī, and noting that both of these collections came to be considered among the authoritative "six books" by most Sunnī scholars, one gets a sense of the divisions and debates that took place regarding the correct representation of Muḥammad's journey.

Despite the contrast between these two particular accounts from Tirmidhī and Nasāᵓī's collections, one finds shared details that one can trace through these and other Sunnī *ḥadīth* collections. Both Tirmidhī and Nasāᵓī transmit versions of the same *ḥadīth* about Muḥammad receiving three gifts that we discussed above in reference to Muslim's *ḥadīth* collection. Referring to Muḥammad's encounter at the Lote Tree, Tirmidhī's version states, "God gave him there three things that he had not given to a prophet before him: the five prayers were imposed upon him, he was given the final verses of the chapter of the Cow, and his community was forgiven [its] errors that did not involve associating anything with God."[36] Unlike the other recensions of the report, here the fragment introduces the idea that these three gifts were uniquely reserved for Muḥammad and his community. Despite this small detail, and minor variations in wording, the content of the report in the three collections is essentially the same. As mentioned above, in addition to the important allusion to the Seals of the Cow chapter, perhaps the most intriguing gift mentioned in this fragmentary *ḥadīth* is the idea that Muḥammad received the dispensation of forgiveness on behalf of his community. Other *ḥadīth* reports, including later versions of the Ibn ᶜAbbās ascension narratives, directly relate such a notion that God will forgive a portion of the Muslim community to Muḥammad's role as intercessor.

Tirmidhī seems particularly interested in this concept of intercession, and he transmits a number of *ḥadīth* reports on the subject that he connects to the narrative of Muḥammad's night journey, including the remarkable account in which God promises to let more than seventy thousand from Muḥammad's community enter paradise without having to pass through any reckoning.[37] This fragmentary anecdote, which also appears in the early *ḥadīth* collections of Muslim and Dārimī,[38] comes to have an impact upon several of the Bakrī versions of the Ibn ᶜAbbās ascension narrative, as well as later narratives that seem to draw upon Bakrī's work.[39] Above and beyond the rest of the "six books" that form the canon of sound Sunnī *ḥadīth* reports, Tirmidhī's collection contains a series of eschatological reports that describe paradise and hellfire, that detail what will happen on the day of judgment, and that depict Muḥammad's role as intercessor. Each of these themes represent prominent tropes that will be collated in the Ibn ᶜAbbās ascension narratives by in the seventh/thirteenth century at the latest.[40]

A *ḥadīth* from Tirmidhī's work attributed to Muḥammad's companion Abū Saᶜīd Khudrī, whom we first saw with reference to Ibn Hishām's recension of Ibn Isḥāq's work and about whom we will have more to say in chapter 6, takes up the theme of the events of the end of times, using it to illustrate Muḥammad's high station. The *ḥadīth* begins with Muḥammad proclaiming his superiority to other prophets, a claim he presents as a statement of fact and not an idle polemic: "I am the leader of the descendants of Adam on the day of judgment, and that is not a boast."[41] The report continues with a depiction of how desperate humans will travel from prophet to prophet on the last day, seeking their aid as an intercessor with God. Only Muḥammad's intercession will prove effective, however. After the people have consulted each of the other prophets, each of whom admits to some wrongdoing that prevents him to serve as an intercessor and thus passes the community on to another prophet, the group comes to Muḥammad, who is both able and willing to intercede on their behalf.[42] Major scenes in fully developed ascension narratives will adapt and develop the theme introduced here, one that provides a concrete illustration of Muḥammad's superiority to the rest of the prophets. Sometimes such scenes play out in Jerusalem, with each of the prophets stating how God has favored him and Muḥammad's claim being superior to the rest; other times, they form part of Muḥammad's conversation with God (in the trope I have been calling the "favor of the prophets"). The later and most highly developed Ibn ᶜAbbās ascension narratives include both, emphasizing the call for those hearing the story to ackowledge Muḥammad's superior status and thus to place their trust in Muḥammad and his message.

Tirmidhī's report of this eschatological scene continues with an additional anecdote attributed to Anas b. Mālik in which God explicitly invites Muḥammad to advance intercessory petitions.[43] Muḥammad states: "I fall to the ground in prostration, and God inspires me to eulogize and praise. I am told, 'Raise your head! Ask and be given! Intercede and receive intercession! Speak and have your speech heard!' "[44] After describing this scene, Tirmidhī's *ḥadīth* relates how Muḥammad tells his listeners that the qurʾānic verse "*Perhaps your Lord will send you to a praised station*" (Q 17:79) refers precisely to such an intercessory moment. In Ibn Māja's version of a closely related *ḥadīth*, Muḥammad prostrates multiple times, after each of which God mentions to Muḥammad some specific number of Muslims who will enter paradise, and Muḥammad continues the process to increase that number.[45] God's command for Muḥammad to "ask and be given" (*sal tuᶜṭa*) in order to receive intercessory dispensation becomes a common feature of the intercessory passages in the Ibn ᶜAbbās ascension narratives, usually appearing near the end of the divine colloquy scene and introducing an intercessory section. The above anecdotes prove that this concept of Muḥammad interceding with God to secure the eschatological reward of his followers circulated among Muslims as early as the third/ninth century.

One last detail to note about the Tirmidhī report quoted above is that the command for Muḥammad to "raise his head" will also appear as a recurring trope in the later versions of this Ibn ᶜAbbās narrative (see chapters 8 and 9). The sequence appears in these later narratives as Muḥammad first approaches God's throne (*ᶜarsh*). In these versions of the Ibn ᶜAbbās ascension narrative, Muḥammad follows the command, looks up, and beholds the divine throne for the first time. The compilers of the ascension narratives do not appropriate Tirmidhī's anecdote wholesale into their accounts; rather, this anecdote shares this and other select details with the Ibn ᶜAbbās ascension narratives, perhaps providing inspiration for them, drawing upon them, or drawing upon some source shared in common with them.

A final group of reports from Tirmidhī's collection that bears on our discussion similarly describes Muḥammad's audience with God. The context in Tirmidhī's reports differs from the one that becomes standard in the Ibn ᶜAbbās ascension narratives, but unlike the previous intercessory anecdote, the outlines of the heavenly host debate dialogue appearing in Tirmidhī's collection closely model the way this scene plays out in the descriptions of Muḥammad's divine audience at the climax of the Ibn ᶜAbbās accounts. Tirmidhī presents three separate versions of the *ḥadīth*, two of which are transmitted on the authority of none other than Ibn ᶜAbbās.[46] All three of Tirmidhī's versions of this story consist of Muḥammad recounting a nighttime visionary experience (perhaps a dream) in which God appears to him "in the most beautiful form" and questions him about the subject of the heavenly host debate.

As discussed in chapter 1, the qurᵓānic reference to the "*heavenly host debate*" (Q 38:69) instructs Muḥammad to say he has no knowledge of such a debate, and the scene in Tirmidhī's reports depict how Muḥammad learns about this and other secrets directly from the divinity. When Muḥammad expresses his inability to answer God's question, God instructs Muḥammad not only about the heavenly host debate but also about other secrets of heaven and earth. God conveys this instruction to Muḥammad by touching him with his cold hand, an anthropomorphic detail that seems shocking from the perspective of later mainstream Muslim theological sensibilities. After the divine touch, Muḥammad is able to describe how the heavenly host debate consists of a discussion of pious human devotion, here conveyed under the rubric of two rhyming catchwords: *al-kaffarāt* (the penances) and *al-darajāt* (the degrees).[47] After Muḥammad recites the meaning of these terms in rhymed prose, the *ḥadīth* report comes to a close, having provided an answer to the question raised by the Qurʾān's ambiguous "*heavenly host debate*" allusion.

This heavenly host debate *ḥadīth* raises some tantalizing issues for the scholar of comparative religion, such as the relationship between the scene it describes and similar "theophany" scenes in other religious traditions. For instance, the scene's depiction of the appearance of the deity to Muḥammad and his conveying to him secret knowledge is reminiscent of the key "*Sar Torah*" scenes in the Jewish Hekhalot texts where an angelic "prince" appears to the mystic and offers him otherworldly instruction. It remains beyond the scope of this study to explore the details of this possible example of interreligious influence or symbiosis. More significant for our purposes here is the issue of the way in which the *ḥadīth* depicts the interaction between Muḥammad and God during this intimate encounter, since one commonly finds similar details—and even wholesale importation of the heavenly host debate trope—in the disparate Ibn ᶜAbbās ascension narratives.

The *ḥadīth* accounts of the heavenly host debate in Tirmidhī, and some of the Ibn ᶜAbbās ascension narratives that incorporate them, seem to offer a blatantly anthropomorphic depiction of the deity. This fact supports van Ess' thesis that Muslims tolerated a certain amount of anthropomorphism in the early period of Islamic history.[48] The idea that God touches Muḥammad with his hand when the two meet appears in the brief discussion of the heavenly host debate passage (Q 38:67–70) transmitted in the Qurʾān commentary of the Shīᶜī exegete ᶜAlī b. Ibrāhīm Qummī (d. ca. 307/919).[49] Qummī explains away the anthropomorphic divine hand by interpreting it in a metaphorical fashion. In any case, Qummī's commentary presents the cold hand detail and accompanying heavenly host debate dialogue in relation to Muḥammad's ascension, just as many Ibn ᶜAbbās ascension narratives do. The anthropomorphic cold hand detail becomes expunged from some subsequent Sunnī ascension accounts of the Ibn ᶜAbbās ascension narrative, such as the one transmitted by the Sufi theologian ᶜAbd al-Karīm Qushayrī (d. 465/1072).[50] While a substantial number of later Ibn ᶜAbbās ascension narratives include the cold hand trope, interestingly enough it is largely absent from the Bakrī versions discussed in chapter 8. Clearly, then, a significant number of scholars from the fourth/tenth century onward, even those who transmit the Ibn ᶜAbbās ascension narrative, were strongly opposed to such anthropomorphic descriptions of the deity.

While there are a number of both intriguing and puzzling aspects to this heavenly host debate account cited in Tirmidhī's Sunnī *ḥadīth* collection, what is most crucial to recognize is that not only the cold hand detail but also many other details from the heavenly host debate dialogue become interpolated to form standard features of the Ibn ᶜAbbās ascension narratives. Qummī's early use of the heavenly host debate *ḥadīth* in connection with the ascension suggests that this process of interpolation likely took place prior to the beginning of the fourth/tenth century. Evidence from the Qurʾān commentary of Qummī and from that of his contemporary, the famous Sunnī exegete and compiler Ṭabarī, also supports this contention. The ascension narratives in these commentaries and others from this period that are pivotal to the development of the night journey and ascension narrative will be the subject of the following chapter.

6

THE USE AND APPROPRIATION OF THE IBN ᶜABBĀS DISCOURSE IN COMMENTARIES

Compared with the relatively fragmentary reports of Muḥammad's journey appearing in the majority of *ḥadīth* collections, starting near the beginning of the fourth/tenth century Qur'ān commentaries by both Sunnī and Shīᶜī exegetes collated much longer and more complete versions of the narrative into their exegesis of the key qur'ānic passages associated with it: the night journey verse (Q 17:1) and the beginning of the Star chapter (Q 53:1–18). The discussion that follows explores these extended narratives formulated around the fourth/tenth century, paying particular attention to their use of symbols and ideas from the Primitive Version of the Ibn ᶜAbbās ascension narrative. Examining the ascension reports in three formative Qur'ān commentaries, those of Ṭabarī, ᶜAlī Qummī, and Thaᶜlabī, one can discover how portions of the Ibn ᶜAbbās ascension discourse found their way into the ascension stories that they recorded, proving the growing influence of the discourse during this period.

Night Journey and Ascension Accounts in Ṭabarī's *Tafsīr*

Although his importance has perhaps been overstated by contemporary scholars who see Muḥammad b. Jarīr Ṭabarī (d. 310/923) as the pivotal exegete of the early period of Qur'ān commentary,[1] nevertheless Ṭabarī's encyclopedic *Jāmiᶜ al-bayān* remains indispensable for the study of early narratives, given the way that it compiles the opinions of the first generations of exegetes. A significant feature of Ṭabarī's work is the manner with which it consistently records his own opinions on the correct way to interpret a verse, while simultaneously recording diverse dissenting opinions as well. After citing one or more qur'ānic verses, Ṭabarī usually addresses whatever issues arise from the passage, selectively quoting from both those with whom he agrees and those with whom he disagrees. Investigating Ṭabarī's approach to the key verses understood to refer to Muḥammad's night journey and ascension (Q 17:1 and 53:1–18), therefore, tells us something about the range of interpretations known to Ṭabarī and the decisions he makes regarding this mass of material.

With regard to the issue of the heavenly host debate mentioned in the previous chapter with reference to Tirmidhī's *ḥadīth* reports, a brief reference in Ṭabarī's text proves that by the turn of the fourth/tenth century this anecdote was associated with an ascension narrative connected to Ibn ʿAbbās.[2] Ṭabarī only briefly mentions this report in the context of his discussion of the vision of God, and he does not argue in favor of its authenticity. Nevertheless, the passage draws on verses of the Star chapter of the Qur'ān and links them to two major themes of the divine colloquy from the Ibn ʿAbbās ascension narratives, the heavenly host debate and the favor of the prophets. Although Ṭabarī's citation begins in a manner that closely resembles Tirmidhī's dream vision *ḥadīth* cited above, it quickly turns to the colloquy scene, which closely resembles the Primitive Version as recorded by Ibn Ḥibbān. Parallels between the brief ascension anecdote Ṭabarī attributes to Ibn ʿAbbās and the Primitive Version of the Ibn ʿAbbās ascension narrative support the idea that Ṭabarī had access to the latter narrative.

Ṭabarī's discussion of the night journey verse shows that he is well aware of the extended *ḥadīth* reports favored by Bukhārī and Muslim, those ascribed to Anas b. Mālik mentioned in chapter 5, and yet his own interpretations venture beyond the limitations of the latter. For instance, when seeking to determine exactly what the qur'ānic phrase "the sacred place of prostration" (*al-masjid al-ḥaram*, Q 17:1) designates, the mosque of the Kaʿba specifically or its environs more generally, Ṭabarī supports the idea that Muḥammad was sleeping on the night in question in the house of Umm Hāni', citing her testimony to that effect:

> The Messenger of God only traveled by night when he was [staying] in my house, sleeping at my place that night. He prayed the final evening ritual prayers, then he slept, and we also slept. Just before daybreak, we woke the Messenger of God. When he prayed the dawn ritual prayers, and we prayed together with him, he said, "Umm Hāni', I prayed the evening ritual prayers with you in this valley, as you saw, then I came to Jerusalem and prayed in it, then I prayed the morning prayers with you as you now see."[3]

Recall that Ibn Saᶜd and Muqātil present similar ideas, but significantly here Ṭabarī explicitly prefers this reading over the narrative versions ascribed to Anas b. Mālik and Mālik b. Ṣaᶜṣaᶜa, those extended reports favored by Bukhārī and Muslim. Even though Ṭabarī does not limit himself to the latter reports, neither does he deny them recognition or legitimacy. In fact, after citing two variations on the beginning of the Mālik b. Ṣaᶜṣaᶜa narrative, and offering a fragment of the report attributed to al-Ḥasan b. Abī al-Ḥasan (cf. the Ibn Hishām recension of the Ibn Isḥāq text, discussed in chapter 3), he then cites at length a variant of the Anas b. Mālik report familiar from Bukhārī and Muslim's collections.[4] Despite the acknowledgment that Ṭabarī gives to the latter report, he still contends that the Umm Hāniʾ *ḥadīth* is the most sound of all the variants, proving that not all the early Muslims treated Bukhārī and Muslim's extended narratives as the best accounts of Muḥammad's journey.

Ṭabarī's report interprets the night journey verse in a broad fashion, which allows him to transmit extended narratives that range far beyond the reports recorded by Bukhārī and Muslim. He sets the stage for this approach to the narrative with the following summary:

> God caused [Muḥammad] to journey by night bodily. He caused him to travel at night upon Burāq, from his sacred house to his furthest house, until he brought him and showed him what he wished to show him of the wonders of his command, precepts, and rulership. Then he gathered him together with the prophets, and he prayed with them there. He caused him to ascend to the heaven[s] until he made him go up above the seven heavens, and there he revealed to him what he wished to reveal. Then he returned to the sacred place of prostration in that one night, and he prayed with him the morning prayer.[5]

Notice in this summary how Ṭabarī mentions that Muḥammad saw "wonders" (*ᶜajāʾib*) at or prior to his arrival to Jerusalem, scenes that Ṭabarī will detail in the extended anecdotes he reports in what follows. Furthermore, the summary asserts that Muḥammad goes on to ascend above (*fawqa*) the seven heavens, another idea that is foreign to the collections of Sunnī sound *ḥadīth*, which are nearly unanimous in their assertion that Muḥammad never journeyed beyond the Lote Tree in the seventh heaven. The above summary leaves room for the validity of stories that describe Muḥammad's experiences beyond this location, such as conveyed in the Ibn ᶜAbbās ascension narrative. Beyond his brief reference to the Primitive Version discussed in chapter 2, however, Ṭabarī remains enigmatically silent about the Ibn ᶜAbbās ascension narrative. He transmits instead two long reports that do not appear in any of the official Sunnī *ḥadīth* collections: one attributed to Muḥammad's companion Abū Hurayra and the other attributed to Muḥammad's companion Abū Saᶜīd Khudrī, each of which will be treated separately in what follows.

THE ABŪ HURAYRA ASCENSION NARRATIVE FROM ṬABARĪ'S *TAFSĪR*

Several contemporary Islamicists who translated early accounts of Muḥammad's night journey and ascension have focused on Abū Hurayra's version of the story as reported in Ṭabarī, for they claim that it presents a greater variety of discursive elements than other narratives of its time.[6] Neither the official Sunnī *ḥadīth* collections nor Ṭabarī's *Tafsīr* consider Abū Hurayra's narrative as an especially reliable account of Muḥammad's journey, however, and one reason given centers around the weakness of its chain of transmission. Even though Ṭabarī does accept Abū Hurayra as the narrative's transmitter, he also registers his own uncertainty on the attribution.[7] Despite his hesitancy about the chain of transmission, however, Ṭabarī proceeds to cite the entire Abū Hurayra narrative at length, thus making it the longest narrative on the night journey and ascension included in Ṭabarī's Qurʾān commentary.[8]

The Abū Hurayra narrative seems to treat the night journey and ascension as an experience from the very beginning of Muḥammad's prophetic career, rather than as an event that took place late in the Meccan period of prophecy.[9] Even though early sources such as Ibn Isḥāq and Ibn Saʿd advocated the latter position, dating the event(s) to the period just before the emigration to Medina as became the consensus of later Muslim scholars, select *ḥadīth* reports in the sound Sunnī collections also treat the journeys as taking place around the time of the first revelations. Clearly, then, the dating of the night journey and ascension still remained a subject of significant discussion and debate throughout the third/ninth century.

The Abū Hurayra ascension narrative contains anomalous details in its description of the night journey to Jerusalem, suggesting that it may have been compiled at a relatively early date. The narrative intriguingly refers to the Prophet's mount Burāq as a horse (*faras*), rather than the standard depiction of Burāq as "something between a mule and a donkey." The narrative introduces scenes of reward and punishment along the road to Jerusalem, and it also includes a dialogue between the divine voice and two personified voices attributed to paradise and hellfire.[10] Muḥammad meets and prays together with angels in Jerusalem, and rather than encountering the prophets in physical form in Jerusalem, he meets with some of their spirits there.[11] Finally, just prior to his ascent to the heavens when Gabriel offers Muḥammad the three cups to drink in the cup test scene, the Abū Hurayra *ḥadīth* offers a new twist on it: Muḥammad drinks both from the cup of water and from the cup of milk, and claims to refuse the cup of wine because he was already full, rather than out of inspiration or guidance to reject the drink that would later be made unlawful to Muslims. These types of details, along with others like them, illustrate how the night journey portion of the Abū Hurayra narrative contains fragments that differ from other versions of the narrative that Sunnī scholars came to vest with greater authority. It may be that these details preserve early versions of the story that later official accounts adapted or ignored. It also may be the case that the Abū Hurayra *ḥadīth* might not date earlier than other reports, but that it simply draws on a different set of sources than those employed in the other accounts. Its expansive and composite character, together with its uncertain origins—recalling Ṭabarī's doubt regarding the chain of transmission—suggest that this Abū Hurayra ascension narrative may well derive from the milieu of the early Muslim moralizing storytellers.

The reward and punishment scenes included on the road to Jerusalem would certainly fit well into this moralizing and storytelling milieu.[12] The single description of the merits reaped by those who piously struggle on behalf of God's religion (the *mujāhidūn*) is overshadowed by the seven scenes that follow, each of which illustrate a measure-for-measure punishments inflicted upon different classes of wrongdoers.[13] Some of these scenes appear in a number of divergent night journey and ascension narratives, such as the adulterous men who are depicted as refusing good cooked meat for raw spoiled meat, a scene that was part of the Abū Saᶜīd Khudrī narrative, and thus was incorporated into Ibn Hishām's recension of Ibn Isḥāq's biography of the Prophet.[14] Other such scenes are distinctive of the Abū Hurayra account, and their appearance in later narratives offers a clue that the compiler likely drew upon a version of Abū Hurayra's *ḥadīth*.[15] While the scenes could be said to express the morality of the educated elite, as Vuckovic argues, they might also be heard as speaking to the concerns of the wider Muslim society and its desire to have confirmation of the next-worldly system of justice.

Scenes from the Abū Hurayra narrative could also be interpreted as being composed in a missionary milieu, attempting to convince others of the superiority of the character and prophetic mission of Muḥammad to those of other religious figures, especially those revered by Jews and Christians. For instance, as Muḥammad ascends through the heavens, he sees in the fifth heaven a group from the children of Israel, gathered at Aaron's feet to hear him tell them stories.[16] These Israelites have reached a fairly high station in the heavens, and their major prophet Moses appears even higher, in the sixth heaven. When Moses sees that Muḥammad ascends even higher than he, the former begins to cry, and when asked to explain this behavior Moses responds,

> The children claimed that I was the most noble of the descendants of Adam in the eyes of God, but this descendant of Adam has succeeded me in the [lower] world while I remain here in the next world. Were it to be he alone I would not mind, but along with each prophet is his community.[17]

Moses' statement points to what the narrative depicts as a false claim among the Jews, namely that they enjoy a spiritual status superior to Muslims. This anecdote may well have been used as a device with which Muslims who were engaged in proselytizing among Jews could argue for the superiority of Muḥammad over Moses, and of the religion of Islam over the religion of Judaism.[18]

Viewing this ascension narrative through the lens of a missionary context helps to illuminate the purpose of a scene involving a comparison of prophetic merits that Abū Hurayra's narrative links to Muḥammad's encounter with the spirits of the prophets in Jerusalem. In this scene, Abraham, Moses, David, Solomon, and Jesus each offer a eulogy (*thanāʾ*) in praise of their own merits, after which Muḥammad proclaims his own merits at even greater length. Muḥammad thereby proves his superiority to the others, a station acknowledged explicitly by Abraham at the end of the scene. This "eulogy contest" scene offers a close parallel to the favor of the prophets trope from the divine colloquy scenes, discussed above. In the latter, Muḥammad lists how God has favored the other prophets and asks how God plans to favor him, whereas here in the eulogy contest Muḥammad himself recounts the ways he has received God's favor in direct comparison with the other prophets. Both tropes highlight Muḥammad's merits over and above those of the other Abrahamic prophets, and they point to the use of this narrative as a tool for interreligious disputation.[19] The fact that the Abū Hurayra narrative incorporates both the eulogy contest and the favor of the prophets scenes, despite the overlap between the two, suggests how important these ideas were to the narrative's transmitters and/or audience.

The favor of the prophets trope dominates the intimate dialogue section of the Abū Hurayra ascension narrative, which consequently neglects other tropes such as the heavenly host debate and the seals of the Cow dialogues. Since the favor of the prophets trope is a central feature of the Ibn ʿAbbās ascension narratives, this passage from Abū Hurayra's ascension narrative as given in Ṭabarī's commentary deserves quoting in detail:

> He came to the Lote Tree, of which it is said: "This is the tree to which will arrive those of your community who concentrate themselves upon your path (*sunna*). . . ." Angels covered it like birds when they land upon a tree. [God] spoke to him at that point saying, "Ask!" So he said, "You took *Abraham as an intimate friend* (Q 4:125) and you gave him a great kingdom. You *spoke to Moses directly* (Q 4:164). You gave David a great dominion, you softened iron for him, and gave him control over the mountains. You gave Solomon a great dominion, gave him control over the jinn and humans and satans, gave him control over the winds, and *gave him kingdom such as befits no one after him* (Q 38:35). You taught Jesus the Torah and the Gospel, and you made him cure the lame, blind, and raise the dead by your leave, and you protected him and his mother from the stoned Satan, who has no access to them."

> His Lord said to him: "I took you as both an intimate friend and beloved, as it is written in the Torah, 'Beloved of God.' I sent you to *all people as a herald and a warner* (Q 34:28). I *opened your breast for you, took your burden from you, and raised your mention* (Q 94:1–2, 4). I am never mentioned without you being mentioned with me. I made your community a middle community (Q 2:143), and made it both the first and the last. I made no sermon acceptable to your community unless they bear witness that you are my servant and my messenger. I made some among your community a people whose hearts are their gospels. I made you the first prophet to be created, the last to be sent, and the first to be judged. I gave you *seven of my rhymed verses* (*mathānī*, Q 15:87)[20] that I did not give to any before you. I gave you *abundance* (*kawthar*, Q 108:1).[21] I gave you the eight portions: Islam, *hijra*, *jihād*, almsgiving, ritual prayer, the fast of Ramaḍān, commanding the good, and forbidding the evil. I made you the opener and the sealer."
>
> The Prophet said: "My Lord favored me with six things: He gave me the openings of utterances and their seals. [He gave me] all the sayings. He sent me to all people as a messenger and warner. He cast terror into the hearts of my enemies, even at a distance of one month's journey. He made booty permissible to me, something he had permitted to none before me. The whole earth was made ritually pure and a place of prayer for me."
>
> He said: "Then he imposed upon me fifty prayers."[22]

This intimate colloquy begins with God commanding Muḥammad to "ask," that is, to request a favor of or to pose a question to the divinity. Not only is this formula familiar from the *ḥadīth* reports from Tirmidhī and elsewhere, but the expanded formula "ask and be given" (*sal tu*ᶜ*tā*) appears repeatedly in the colloquies from the Ibn ᶜAbbās ascension narratives. In the Ibn ᶜAbbās texts, the formula introduces the favor of the prophets trope just as seen above, and it also introduces intercessory passages where Muḥammad petitions God on behalf of his community. Such petitions almost always result in God bestowing gifts and dispensations upon the Muslim community, some of which appear in the narrative as allusions to or direct quotations from the Qurᵓān. In the above passage, many of the "gifts" that God grants to Muḥammad come in the form of specific portions of the revelation. God also gives Muḥammad and the Muslim community a series of duties and honors, listed in a series of eight and six items, each cited as evidence of God's favor. Some of the specific favors listed have direct parallels in the primitive version of the Ibn ᶜAbbās ascension narrative. What distinguishes both the Abū Hurayra colloquy scene and the colloquy scene from the primitive Ibn ᶜAbbās narrative from the later Ibn ᶜAbbās texts is the absence in the earlier texts of Muḥammad making a specific appeal for God to promise salvation to a certain proportion of the Muslim community. This direct intercessory appeal becomes an increasingly popular trope in the Ibn ᶜAbbās ascension narratives of later centuries. In the Abū Hurayra narrative, Muḥammad's response to God's command "ask" revolves less around other-worldly eschatological promises and more around this-worldly contemporary favors that God bestows upon the living Muslim community, favors that distinguish it from other human communities.

And yet, the Abū Hurayra ascension narrative recorded in Ṭabarī's *Tafsīr* does contain an earlier scene that directly bears upon the question of other-worldly forgiveness and salvation for the Muslim community: Muḥammad's encounter in the seventh heaven with two groups of believers, those with white faces and those with gray-tainted faces.[23] These two groups sit with Abraham, they apparently are members of his community of believers, whether narrowly or broadly defined it is difficult to say precisely from the text itself, although the reader gets the impression that these "folk" represent a group of Muslims. The inspiration for the scene likely springs from a passage in the Qurᵓān in which the wicked are described as black-faced and the righteous as white-faced, the latter of whom abide securely within the "*mercy of God*" (Q 3:106–7). The Abū Hurayra ascension narrative appropriates this imagery and adapts it to discuss the plight of those who fall in the middle of this absolute dichotomy, those whose faces remain colored or gray, a mixture of black and white. While some medieval Christian theologians addressed this problem of the tainted believer with the concept of purgatory, in this scene the problem of the tainted believer is solved in the Abū Hurayra ascension narrative with the concept of the purifying power of God's forgiveness, here symbolized by ritual bathing.

In Abū Hurayra's report, while those whose faces are as white as parchment remain seated with Abraham, those with some color on their faces enter three rivers, progressively washing themselves clean of the taint on their faces until they resemble their white-faced companions. Gabriel interprets the symbolism of the scene for Muḥammad by explaining that the taint comes by mixing pious actions with evil actions, something those whose faces are white never apparently did. Those who were guilty of this wrongdoing were said to have repented, and God thus forgives them and allows them to wash away their sins through his mercy, graphically illustrated by the names given to the two rivers: the first is called "the Mercy of God" (*raḥmat allāh*) and the second is called "the Blessing of God" (*niᶜmat allāh*). The narrative labels the third river, which enacts the final stage of cleansing, by a qurᵓānic passage that describes the bounties the righteous will enjoy in paradise, saying, "*Their Lord will give them a pure drink to imbibe*" (Q 76:21).[24] Although the narrative does not specify which types of deeds God forgives in this scene, clearly they are those that are not wholly evil, certainly not the major crimes (*kabīra*), but rather those that are somewhat evil, borderline cases that require an act of purgation. This remarkable scene depicts how those repentant believers who have a "tainted record" in life will receive God's forgiveness in the next world and will be made as pure as those who performed nothing but wholly righteous deeds, implying an eventual equality of the saved in the afterworld.

This scene of forgiveness in Abū Huraya's ascension narrative on the one hand represents a distinctive identifying characteristic of this particular ascension narrative, while on the other hand it bears comparison with related scenes in other ascension narratives. It serves as an identifying characteristic because it presents a detail rarely, if ever, included by other ascension narratives that do not draw from this *ḥadīth* directly. I would contend, therefore, that when this scene appears in a later ascension work, one can be fairly confident that the compiler or one of the compiler's sources collated the Abū Hurayra ascension narrative into their account.[25] Despite what one might expect given the maximalist approach to borrowing and inclusion taken by the compilers of the Ibn ᶜAbbās ascension narratives, the above scene does not become incorporated into the Ibn ᶜAbbās recensions. It was most likely ignored by the transmitters of the Ibn ᶜAbbās story because the scenes of Muḥammad's direct intercession with God served the same general function, solving the problem of the tainted believer by describing a mechanism whereby God promises to forgive a portion of the believers for their minor misdeeds.

The Abū Hurayra ascension narrative, like that attributed to Ibn ᶜAbbās, becomes one of the foundational narratives that a number of the later texts will transmit, analyze, and collate into even more detailed ascension accounts. For example, the extensive night journey and ascension tale recorded in Thaᶜlabī's *Tafsīr* (see below) clearly combines elements from the Abū Hurayra *ḥadīth* together with elements from the primitive Ibn ᶜAbbās narrative. Despite its importance to later ascension texts, numerous questions remain about the origins of this Abū Hurayra version, which Ṭabarī records despite his doubts about its authenticity. What individual or community circulated this *ḥadīth* in the early period of Islamic history? How did the narrative come to play such a major role in some scholarly Sunnī discussions of the ascension after Ṭabarī, while the Ibn ᶜAbbās narratives even in the later period refrained from incorporating many of its features? While I suggest tentative answers to a few of the latter questions in the chapters that follow, solid conclusions about the origins and early circulation of this *ḥadīth* will have to await future research into the complexities of this key narrative.

THE ABŪ SAᶜĪD KHUDRĪ ASCENSION NARRATIVE FROM ṬABARĪ'S *TAFSĪR*

As we have seen in chapter 3, Ibn Hishām's version of Ibn Isḥāq's ascension account combines a number of different *ḥadīth* reports together to form a single narrative, and one of the authorities whom Ibn Hishām cites more than any other is a figure by the name of Abū Saᶜīd Khudrī. Khudrī's *ḥadīth* in Ibn Hishām's version contains a minimum of detail, and Ibn Hishām enriches it with supplemental details from al-Ḥasan's *ḥadīth* and from another anonymous source. Ibn Hishām draws upon Khudrī's *ḥadīth* in order to establish the standard sequence of the prophets in the seven heavens that was to gain widespread approval in official circles: Adam in the first, Jesus and John in the second, Joseph in the third, Idrīs (Enoch) in the fourth, Aaron in the fifth, Moses in the sixth, and Abraham in the seventh heaven. Given the presence of the Khudrī *ḥadīth* in Ibn Hishām's narrative, there remains little doubt that at least an early version of this *ḥadīth* had been in circulation by the beginning of the third/ninth century. The Ibn Hishām version of the Abū Saᶜīd Khudrī *ḥadīth* omits a number of key scenes that come to be widely associated with it in later versions. Three of these scenes in particular deserve particular attention: Muḥammad's encounters on the road to Jerusalem, his experience with the gray-cloaked people near the Lote Tree, and his brief tour of paradise.

If scenes from the Abū Hurayra *ḥadīth*, such as the eulogy contest and the favor of the prophets scenes, could be said to demonstrate the utility of the ascension discourse to Muslim missionaries, the scenes along the road to Jerusalem in Khudrī's *ḥadīth* bear even more obvious signs of originating in such a missionary environment. On his way to Jerusalem on the back of Burāq, with Gabriel strangely absent from the narrative at this point, Muḥammad encounters missionaries from the other two religions of the book.[26] A Jewish missionary (*dāᶜī al-yahūd*) calls Muḥammad from the right of the path, requesting him to slow down for a question. A Christian missionary (*dāᶜī al-naṣārā*) similarly calls Muḥammad from the left of the path. Muḥammad ignores both, and Gabriel later informs him that he made the correct choice. Had he inclined toward either of these voices, Gabriel tells him, he and his community would have inclined toward Judaism or Christianity instead of Islam. While this passage from the Khudrī report serves to portray Islam as the middle and straight path, it also suggests that the narrative circulated in an environment in which Jewish, Christian, and Muslim voices vied for converts among each other's religious communities.

At first glance, Muḥammad's third encounter on the road to Jerusalem that immediately follows the missionary voices seems to undercut this interpretation of this scene. Muhammad's path is blocked by a beautifully adorned woman who calls him to slow down and pay attention to her.[27] Gabriel later explains that this woman symbolizes the world here below (*al-dunyā*), and had Muḥammad inclined to her, his community would have inclined to this world rather than the hereafter. This third encounter could be seen to serve a different function than the other two, even though the consequences for Muḥammad's community may have been equally as dire. Muḥammad's avoidance of becoming ensnared by "the world" not only proves Muḥammad's devotion to an ascetic path of devotion, but it also must be interpreted in light of the fact that it appears in the midst of a narrative in which Muḥammad actually leaves behind this lower world to journey to otherworldly realms. In other words, this final encounter foreshadows Muḥammad's successful ascension to the heavens that follows soon after it.[28]

After Muḥammad passes the guardian angel Ismaᶜīl in the gate to the first heaven and exchanges greetings with Adam, Jesus and John, Joseph, Idrīs (Enoch), Aaron, and Moses in their respective heavens, Muḥammad meets Abraham in the seventh heaven near the celestial temple known as the Inhabited House (*al-bayt al-maᶜmūr*). Muḥammad enters this House, and performs the ritual prayer inside it. The narrative cites Q 3:68 at this point to justify the idea that Muḥammad's community will find its ultimate place there with Abraham. The Khudrī ascension narrative thus presents the celestial journey through the seven heavens as somewhat analogous to his terrestrial journey to Jerusalem, with Muḥammad leaving behind other religious communities to find his way to what the narrative depicts as the hierarchically superior prophetic stage, that represented by Abraham. The scene depicts the Muslim community as the true inheritors of Abraham's original monotheism, with ritual prayer as one of its central components.

Ibn Hishām and Ṭabarī's versions of the Khudrī *ḥadīth* are silent about one detail regarding this heavenly worship that becomes prominently associated with this *ḥadīth* in later years, namely Muḥammad's encounter with two different groups of Muslims present with Abraham, those wearing white robes and those wearing gray robes.[29] The people wearing white robes, the purely righteous, enter the celestial temple, while those in gray robes, those who mix good and evil deeds, refrain from entering. In Abū Hurayra's *ḥadīth* we have seen a variation of this same color-coded symbolism, the separation of the pure from the tainted believers. Without a doubt these parallel scenes from the Abū Hurayra and Khudrī reports are related to one another,[30] but it is important to notice that the two serve different purposes and draw different conclusions: Abū Hurayra's *ḥadīth* illustrates how the tainted Muslims progressively purify themselves in order to join their companions; in contrast, Khudrī's *ḥadīth* describes how only the purely righteous can pray in the heavenly temple, while the tainted Muslims are excluded. In the former, the distinction gradually washes away in the purifying water, while in the latter, the distinction between the two groups of Muslims appears fixed. The washing in the river of God's mercy performed by the tainted group in Abū Hurayra's *ḥadīth* appears in a transformed fashion in Khudrī's *ḥadīth*, portraying instead Muḥammad washing himself, thereby washing away all his misdeeds, past and future.[31] Since the two variants seem to have been in circulation at approximately the same time, one could conjecture that the scenes reflect different interpretations placed upon the ascension narrative by different groups of storytellers with different sets of theological assumptions about the possibility of the believer being able to redeem himself or herself through acts of ritual purification, through God's mercy.

The final scene of Abū Saᶜīd Khudrī's narrative in Ṭabarī's account begins with a brief tour of paradise, introduced from the previous river scene by Muḥammad being given the river named "Abundance" (*kawthar*, from Q 108:1), which Muḥammad follows into a garden paradise that contains an abundance of large edible fruit and fowl.[32] Here Muḥammad meets a servant girl (*jāriya*) who claims to be reserved for Muḥammad's adopted son Zayd b. Ḥāritha.[33] In the traditional biography of the Prophet, Muḥammad takes a fancy to and later marries Zayd's former wife; this scene, as if a commentary on the latter anecdote, illustrates how Zayd is promised a more beautiful partner in paradise, perhaps as partial recompense for losing his earthly partner.[34] Ṭabarī's narrative cuts directly from this paradisiacal scene to the bestowal of the fifty prayers, and at this point the key distinctive aspects of Abū Saᶜīd Khudrī's narrative draw to a close.

Despite all their extra detail, both Khudrī's narrative and the Abū Hurayra narrative in Ṭabarī's *Tafsīr* ultimately end just as the extended *ḥadīth* in the official Sunnī collections typically end, with the reduction of the duty of the daily prayers from fifty to five while Muḥammad remains in the upper heavens. The actual return to Mecca and aftermath of the night journey and ascension, therefore, does not seem to have been of great interest to these early Sunnī traditionists. One might conclude that the revelation of the daily prayers serves as a kind of climax to these versions of the ascension narrative, versions partially designed to explain the origin of this Muslim ritual. On the other hand, the extra details added to the official accounts seem to have been designed both to entertain and to argue in a polemical fashion for the superiority of the Prophet Muḥammad over the rest of God's creatures. The earliest extended Primitive Version of the Ibn ᶜAbbās narrative develops a similar polemic, but through a very different set of narrative tropes. Furthermore, storytellers and commentators beginning at the end of the third/ninth century combine various scenes from either the Abū Hurayra or the Abū Saᶜīd Khudrī *ḥadīth* reports together with scenes from the Ibn ᶜAbbās ascension narrative in order to begin to create more complex and rich ascension tales (chapter 7). This synthesizing process reaches something of a climax with the versions ascribed to a figure named Abu al-Ḥasan Bakrī (chapter 8), a stage that reflects the full elaboration of the Ibn ᶜAbbās ascension discourse.

The Appropriation of the Primitive Version in Other Early Commentaries

We have seen that in the first three centuries of the Islamic era, between the collation of the Qurʾān and the compilation of Ṭabarī's famous Qurʾān commentary, the story of Muḥammad's night journey and ascension gradually expanded, and later versions of the tale bring together elements from disparate accounts to form composite narratives of greater richness and complexity. Chapter 2 demonstrated that the Primitive Version of the Ibn ᶜAbbās ascension narrative had been in circulation prior to the time of Ṭabarī. It is likely that this Ibn ᶜAbbās narrative influenced other ascension narratives in the early period, an influence apparent through its appropriation as part of a specific type of composite ascension account, one in which the Ibn ᶜAbbās ascension narrative is combined together with one of the two reports discussed above, that ascribed to Abū Hurayra or that ascribed to Abū Saᶜīd Khudrī. Multiple examples of such composite narratives appear in works of Qurᵓān commentary by ᶜAlī b. Ibrāhīm Qummī (d. ca. 307/919), Aḥmad b. Muḥammad Thaᶜlabī (d. 427/1035), and Abū al-Futūḥ Rāzī (d. ca. 525/1116). The earliest of these appropriations of the Primitive Version appears in the ascension narrative of the foundational Imāmī Shīᶜī exegete named ᶜAlī b. Ibrāhīm Qummī, who is one of Ṭabarī's contemporaries.

THE USE OF THE PRIMITIVE VERSION IN ᶜALĪ QUMMĪ'S *TAFSĪR*

Abū al-Ḥasan ᶜAlī b. Ibrāhīm Qummī (d. ca. 307/919) devotes nearly his entire commentary on the Night Journey verse to a single *ḥadīth* report ascribed to a famous scholar and Shīᶜī Imam by the name of Abū ᶜAbd Allāh Jaᶜfar Ṣādiq (d. 148/765).[35] Even though this Jaᶜfar Ṣādiq report never mentions Ibn ᶜAbbās, a close examination of the text makes it clear that the *ḥadīth* largely consists of a combination of two main sources: the Primitive Version of the Ibn ᶜAbbās ascension narrative (see chapter 2) and the Abū Saᶜīd Khudrī narrative (see earlier in this chapter).[36] The close connection between Qummī's Jaᶜfar Ṣādiq ascension narrative and that ascribed to Abū Saᶜīd Khudrī has already been noted by Mohammad Ali Amir-Moezzi,[37] and the parallels include many of the distinctive characteristics of the Khudrī narrative, such as the meeting at the heavenly Inhabited House with people wearing differently tinted cloaks. Because of the fairly strong connection between the two narratives, I will limit my discussion here to those portions of Qummī's Jaᶜfar Ṣādiq narrative that diverge from the Abū Saᶜīd Khudrī account.

Some of the extra details in Qummī's Jaᶜfar Ṣādiq narrative represent those portions that undoubtedly were drawn from the Primitive Version of the Ibn ᶜAbbās ascension narrative, and the synthesis between the Abū Saᶜīd Khudrī narrative and the Primitive Version becomes especially clear in its elaboration of the individuals whom Muḥammad encounters in the first heaven. The discussion of the first heaven in Qummī's version of the Jaᶜfar Ṣādiq *ḥadīth* follows the general pattern of the Abū Saᶜīd Khudrī narrative closely, describing the angel Ismaᶜīl and his host, the encounter with Mālik, the Guardian of Hellfire (*khāzin al-nār*), meeting the prophet Adam, and witnessing some of the tortures of different classes of evildoers.[38] To that general account, Qummī's Jaᶜfar *ḥadīth* contains a description of several of the "wonders" reminiscent of the opening passages of the Primitive Version of the Ibn ᶜAbbās ascension narrative. For instance, in addition to the Guardian of Hellfire, the Jaᶜfar narrative places in the first heaven two of the other major angels that are introduced at the beginning of the Primitive Version: the Angel of Death (*malik al-mawt*) and the angel composed half of fire and half of snow.[39] As in the Primitive Version, the Jaᶜfar *ḥadīth* recounts how Muḥammad interrogates the Angel of Death regarding how the latter goes about harvesting the souls of people on earth. Furthermore, the Jaᶜfar *ḥadīth* from Qummī's *Tafsīr* concludes its account of the first heaven with a description of the Cherubim whose manner of worship is so concentrated and intense that they never interrupted their devotions since the day they were created, angels who similarly appear in the Primitive Version.[40] The account of the first heaven, therefore, shows unmistakably how details from both the Abū Saᶜīd Khudrī narrative and from the Primitive Version combine to form the resulting ascension narrative, an account which Qummī ascribes here to the pivotal Imāmī figure, Jaᶜfar Ṣādiq.

After recounting the Prophet's encounter with the various other prophets in a manner closely resembling the Khudrī *ḥadīth*,[41] this Jaᶜfar Ṣādiq narrative draws once again from the Primitive Version to add supplementary details to its account of the seventh heaven and beyond. This new section of interpolation begins with a concise summary of the highest oceans that are made out of light, darkness, snow, and so forth, which instill a terror in Muḥammad just as described in the Primitive Version.[42] Thereafter, an explicit reference to God's "wonders" (*ᶜajāʾib*) in the Jaᶜfar narrative, a key term given at the opening of the Primitive Version, precedes the discussion of the only other major angel from the beginning of the latter narrative not included in the description of the first heaven in the Jaᶜfar narrative, the angel in the form of a rooster.[43] The narrative next turns back to the Khudrī account in its description of the Prophet's encounters at the Lote Tree, the rivers of Mercy and Abundance, and his brief tour of paradise (in which he meets the servant girl belonging to Zayd), interspersing these scenes with details about the tree called Goodness (*Ṭūbā*) and about the intimate colloquy that derive from the Primitive Version. This climactic conversation with God includes the two topics familiar from the Primitive Version, an extended dialogue arising out of the final verses of the Cow chapter, and a more abbreviated reference to the favor of the prophets trope.[44] After his dialogue with God, Muḥammad leads the angels of the heavens in prayer, just as he had led the prophets in prayer in Jerusalem. These details, along with other interpolations such as the descriptions of the wondrous angels, together offer convincing evidence of the textual connection between the Primitive Version of the Ibn ᶜAbbās ascension narrative and the Jaᶜfar Ṣādiq *ḥadīth* as it is given in ᶜAlī Qummī's *Tafsīr*.

Despite the fact that many of the additions to the Ja^cfar Ṣādiq narrative can be traced to the Ibn ʿAbbās ascension narrative, it nevertheless contains some unique details, such as in the opening segment of the *ḥadīth*:

> My father—Muḥammad b. Abī ʿUmayr—Hishām b. Sālim—Abū ʿAbd Allāh [Jaʿfar Ṣādiq] said that Gabriel, Mikāʾīl, and Isrāfīl brought Burāq to the Prophet. One of them took the reins, another the stirrup, and the third adorned him with his garment (*thiyāb*). Burāq was skittish, and Gabriel slapped it, saying, "Settle down, Burāq. No prophet who rode you before him nor any who rides you after him will be like him." So it relented to him. It raised him up a little way, and Gabriel was with him, showing him the signs (*āyāt*) in the heaven[s] and the earth.[45]

In this opening of the Jaʿfar Ṣādiq *ḥadīth* from Qummī's *Tafsīr*, as with the Abū Saʿīd Khudrī ascension narrative and official Sunnī reports like it, one finds nothing specific about where Muḥammad was when the angels came to him, what precise day it was, nor what he was doing at the time. The opening of the breast scene is missing here, just as it is missing from the Abū Saʿīd Khudrī version as transmitted by Ṭabarī. The account quoted above depicts each of the three angels as having a role when they come to him, one of them helping him to put on a garment or cloak, a detail that takes on greater significance among those who claim that the special cloak Muḥammad wore during the journey was passed on in specific circles, such as among the descendants of the Prophet.[46]

The depiction of Gabriel striking Burāq in the above opening remains largely anomalous, although the trope of Gabriel having to convince Burāq more gently of Muḥammad's worthiness to ride it will become more developed in later versions, some of which record a whole dialogue between Gabriel and Burāq. In any case, the language used here for how Muḥammad was shown the "signs" after mounting Burāq not only alludes to the key qurʾānic prooftext which this report seeks to elucidate,[47] but also foreshadows all the mysteries and secrets that the journey will reveal to Muḥammad and that Gabriel will interpret for him. Similar language appears in the Ibn Isḥāq ascension narrative,[48] and both distantly reflect the statement from the Primitive Version of the Ibn ʿAbbās ascension discourse that Muḥammad was shown some of the wonders (*ʿajāʾib*) of the heavens and the earth.[49]

Qummī's report of the night journey goes beyond the details from the Primitive Version, however. Among the wonders of his journey mentioned in this Jaʿfar account are the prayer stops that Gabriel commands Muḥammad to make in Medina, Sinai, and Bethlehem, collating the Nasāʾī *ḥadīth* into the narrative at this point just as one finds in the Abū Hurayra account.[50] By the end of the third/ninth century, therefore, there appears to be a broad consensus that this anecdote belongs in the full account of the night journey. The trope becomes collated into Bakrī's "total and complete" version of the Ibn ᶜAbbās narrative, analyzed in chapter 8. There are other interesting features of Qummī's discussions of the night journey and ascension beyond what is contained in the Jaᶜfar Ṣādiq *ḥadīth* analyzed here,[51] yet for our purposes, the latter narrative has sufficiently illustrated the point that a proto-Imāmī scholar at the turn of the fourth/tenth century transmitted reports assembled from several extended sources, including the Primitive Version of the Ibn ᶜAbbās ascension narrative.

The Use of the Primitive Version in Thaᶜlabī's *Tafsīr*

It was not only Imāmī Shīᶜī scholars such as Qummī who interpolated large excerpts from the Ibn ᶜAbbās ascension narrative into their own versions of the ascension story, for without a doubt the Sunnī storyteller and traditionist by the name of Abū Isḥāq Aḥmad b. Muḥammad Thaᶜlabī (d. 427/1035) similarly drew upon the Primitive Version in his exegesis of the Night Journey verse (Q 17:1).[52] Just as the Jaᶜfar Ṣādiq *ḥadīth* from Qummī's *Tafsīr* constructs its narrative largely by adding scenes from the Primitive Version to the Abū Saᶜīd Khudrī version of the ascension, likewise the composite *ḥadīth* from Thaᶜlabī's *Tafsīr* constructs its narrative largely by adding scenes from the Primitive Version to the Abū Hurayra version of the ascension. This process demonstrates that the Jaᶜfar *ḥadīth* was not anomalous in its use of the Primitive Version of the Ibn ᶜAbbās ascension narrative, rather the latter narrative enjoyed a wide circulation and was understood to offer supplementary details that could be used to enrich the telling of the story of the Prophet's journey.

Thaᶜlabī prefaces his account of the night journey with some introductory remarks that proclaim his rationale for combining the Primitive Version with the Abū Hurayra *ḥadīth* in this fashion:

> As for the *ḥadīth* of the journey, I have abridged it along with the famous transmitted reports, aside from those objectionable *ḥadīth* that have weak chains of transmission. I collected them together as a summary into a single sequence in order that it may be more sweet to listen to and more beneficial.[53]

With this introduction, Thaᶜlabī clearly articulates both his method of combining disparate reports together into a "single sequence" and the purpose behind his method, namely the attempt to make the narrative flow more easily, and the attempt to render it more useful for those who read or hear it. While such a process might horrify a careful *ḥadīth* specialist, such an approach is not without precedent, for one may recall that the early traditionists Ibn Isḥāq and Ibn Saᶜd (see above, chapter 3) claim to have used a similar type of procedure in constructing their narratives. Unlike these two early authorities, here Thaᶜlabī anticipates criticism and attempts to mollify his critics by assuring them that he refrains from including into his mix any reports that were not authenticated by a strong chain of transmission.

To substantiate his claim that he only makes use of authentic reports, Thaᶜlabī begins his account by listing no less than seventeen different chains of transmission (*asānīd*, singular: *isnād*) that allegedly derive from the individual reports that Thaᶜlabī combined and summarized in the process of constructing his own narrative.[54] Many of the chains do represent *isnād*s that link to the famous ascension reports from the sound collections of Sunnī *ḥadīth*. For instance, Thaᶜlabī leads off with a number of chains of transmission that originate with the companion of the Prophet named Anas b. Mālik, whom nearly all the full ascension reports in the official Sunnī collections cite as the one who transmitted the story from Muḥammad. Anas' name appears in six of the chains of transmission that Thaᶜlabī gives, over a third of the total list. Other chains of transmission appearing in the list, however, might cause later traditionists to question Thaᶜlabī's claim to having omitted reports connected to weaker chains of transmission. Over a third of the list, for instance, originate with the figures Abū Hurayra (two *isnād*s) and Ibn ᶜAbbās (four *isnād*s).[55] This fact suggests that reports from these latter two traditionists were indeed central to Thaᶜlabī's construction of his narrative, and a close study of Thaᶜlabī's composite ascension account clearly demonstrates his heavy reliance on both the Primitive Version and the Abū Hurayra ascension *ḥadīth*.

The section of the narrative describing the night journey to Jerusalem in Thaᶜlabī's version bears a close resemblance to many of the details found in the Abū Hurayra ascension *ḥadīth*. For instance, those who struggle in God's path (*mujāhidūn fī sabīl Allāh*) appear to Muḥammad in both narratives as farmers who reap the good works that they sow.[56] In both, Muḥammad hears the personified voice of both paradise and hellfire carry on a dialogue with God about how many souls they contain.[57] In Jerusalem, Muḥammad is said to have met the prophets not in their physical bodies but as spirits, and he engages with them in what I have termed the eulogy contest.[58] A comparison between the Abū Hurayra ascension *ḥadīth* and the ascension *ḥadīth* in Thaᶜlabī's *Tafsīr* demonstrates without a doubt that Thaᶜlabī primarily relies on the former *ḥadīth* in the first portion of his own narrative.

As in the Jaᶜfar Ṣādiq *ḥadīth* from Qummī's *Tafsīr*, Thaᶜlabī collates scenes from the Ibn ᶜAbbās ascension narrative into his narrative beginning with the description of the denizens of the first heaven. In fact, Thaᶜlabī's version even more than Qummī's version reflects the Primitive Version in these scenes. Thaᶜlabī's account of the first heaven is composed of a sequence of encounters and descriptive language almost exactly parallel to the Primitive Version: the Prophet meets the Rooster angel, the Half-Fire-Half-Snow angel (here given the name "*Ḥabīb*"),[59] the Angel of Death, the Guardian of Hellfire, and finally some other angels with many faces that are sometimes described as Cherubim. The remarkable parallelism between Thaᶜlabī's *Tafsīr* and the Primitive Version in this section suggests that Thaᶜlabī extracted this passage virtually wholesale from the Primitive Version of the Ibn ᶜAbbās ascension narrative, collating it into his composite work at this point.[60]

The thesis that this angelic section was imported virtually wholesale from the Primitive Version and inserted into the Abū Hurayra *ḥadīth* is given further support by the fact that immediately after this section the two texts sharply diverge once again. Thaᶜlabī's report shifts to a discussion of the prophets in the various heavens drawn largely from Abū Hurayra's *ḥadīth*. As in the latter, Thaᶜlabī includes in his description of the heavenly temple in the seventh heaven the "gray face" folk, some of whom are forced to cleanse themselves in the heavenly rivers to wash away the taint on their faces before they are allowed to enter the temple.[61] We can see, therefore, that Thaᶜlabī relies upon the Abū Hurayra *ḥadīth* as his "base text," supplementing it at key points with further details provided by the Ibn ᶜAbbās narrative.

At the Lote Tree of the Boundary, where the Abū Hurayra *ḥadīth* turns to an abbreviated intimate colloquy scene, Thaᶜlabī again draws upon different ascension narratives, including that of the Ibn ᶜAbbās ascension discourse, to describe the realms Muḥammad was able to traverse beyond the Lote Tree, leaving Gabriel behind him. For an example of the supplementary experiences in these higher realms, Muḥammad passes beyond the Lote Tree through a series of veils, and at each an angel reaches underneath the veil and pulls Muḥammad to the other side.[62] When he first looks up and sees the divine throne, a drop of sweet liquid falls from the throne and lands upon Muḥammad's tongue, calming him of his fear and bestowing upon him the knowledge of all things that have happened and all things that will happen.[63] These two motifs, passing beneath the veils and tasting the sweet drop, both become relatively standard features in later versions of the Ibn ᶜAbbās ascension narrative. The portion of Thaᶜlabī's narrative that most clearly derives from the Primitive Version of the Ibn ᶜAbbās ascension narrative is the intimate colloquy scene that follows shortly after the aforementioned motifs.

Thaᶜlabī's version of the intimate colloquy scene follows the Primitive Version closely, containing all three of the major thematic sections present in the Primitive Version and in later Ibn ᶜAbbās narratives, following them with an elaboration of the gifts that God bestows upon Muḥammad and the Muslim community. Thaᶜlabī's account of this section mirrors nearly to the letter the account of the intimate colloquy scene in the Primitive Version as recorded by a scholar of Nishapur from the generation after Thaᶜlabī, namely ᶜAbd al-Karīm Qushayrī (d. 465/1072).[64] These Ibn ᶜAbbās ascension narratives transmitted by Thaᶜlabī and Qushayrī draw upon a common source, the Primitive Version as recorded by Ibn Ḥibbān Bustī (d. 354/965).[65] By collating multiple strands of narrative, both ᶜAlī Qummī and Thaᶜlabī enrich and expand their telling of the story of Muḥammad's fantastic journey beyond the detailed accounts in the Abū Saᶜīd Khudrī and Abū Hurayra reports, respectively.

Although Thaᶜlabī's own composite version did not come to be as widely circulated as the later versions of the Ibn ᶜAbbās narrative reshaped by Bakrī (chapter 8), nevertheless it was translated into Persian a century later and included with only minor variations in the Shīᶜī commentary on the night journey appearing in the Persian *Tafsīr* of Abū al-Futūḥ Rāzī (d. ca. 525/1131).[66] While it is beyond the scope of this work to analyze Abū al-Futūḥ Rāzī's translation of Thaᶜlabī's ascension *ḥadīth* in detail,[67] it is difficult to overstate the significance of the fact that this Imāmī Shīᶜī work, one of the earliest Shīᶜī Qurʾān commentaries in Persian, imports a narrative that is largely constructed out of a synthesis of the Abū Hurayra *ḥadīth* and the Primitive Version of the Ibn ᶜAbbās *ḥadīth*. Rāzī replaces Thaᶜlabī's extensive list of chains of transmission at the head of his narrative with two fragmentary chains of transmission,[68] one of which traces the account to the "Commander of the Faithful" ᶜAlī, thereby claiming a legitimate Shīᶜī provenance for the narrative. It appears, then, that both Sunnī and Shīᶜī scholars incorporated the Ibn ᶜAbbās ascension discourse into their accounts of Muḥammad's journey, and they each traced the origin of their accounts through chains of transmission that their constituent communities would consider authentic and authoritative.

As we have seen with this brief look at the extended ascension narratives in the Qurʾān commentaries of Ṭabarī, ᶜAlī Qummī, and Abū Isḥāq Thaᶜlabī, both Shīᶜī and Sunnī scholars in the eastern lands of Islamdom transmitted accounts of Muḥammad's otherworldly journey that were formed by combining the Primitive Version of the Ibn ᶜAbbās ascension narrative together with one of two other extended narratives in circulation in the third/ninth century and recorded in *Ṭabarī*'s commentary. While such narratives were embraced by some Shīᶜī and Sunnī scholars, they were also disputed by other Shīᶜī and Sunnī scholars in the very same milieu. The fact that these Ibn ᶜAbbās narratives provoked such controversy suggests that this ascension discourse represented a locus of struggle and contestation between competing groups of Muslims in the middle periods, a competition that the following chapter explores in more detail by focusing upon scholars who, like Thaᶜlabī, hail from the eastern city of Nishapur.

7

CONTESTING THE PRIMITIVE VERSION IN NISHAPUR

There is much that one can learn about the development of the Primitive Version of the Ibn ᶜAbbās ascension narrative by studying the disparate writings on the narrative by the scholarly elite of Nishapur.[1] Before its destruction during the Mongol invasions of the seventh/thirteenth century, the city of Nishapur represented a major intellectual center in the eastern Iranian region known as Khurasan. The concentration of important early treatises and books on Muḥammad's ascension composed in and around Nishapur during its florescence suggests that the topic of the Prophet's journey had become the focus of scholarly debate there.

The early middle period was one of major transition in the city of Nishapur as it was for much of Islamdom, with various groups of Sunnīs and Shīᶜīs vying for power and influence. According to Richard Bulliet, there is evidence that Shīᶜī sentiments grew among the patrician class in Nishapur during this period.[2] This rise in Shīᶜī influence in Nishapur corresponds with the more general flourishing of Shīᶜī intellectual thought during the so-called Shīᶜī century (mid-fourth/tenth until mid-fifth/eleventh centuries).[3] The central caliphal authority, already in a weakened state by the fourth/tenth century, was forced in the middle of that century to cede the control of the capital Baghdad and major western Iranian territories to the Shīᶜī Buyid (Buwayhid) dynasty. The ruler of Nishapur at the end of that century, Maḥmūd of Ghazna, like the rulers of the Seljuq dynasty that followed, promoted a staunch Sunnī partisanship in opposition to the partisanship of the Shīᶜīs. Debates and rivalries between various Sunnī and Shīᶜī factions may explain to some degree why the Prophet's night journey and ascension became a particular focus of attention in medieval Nishapur, especially given the fact that some Shīʿīs used the ascension discourse as a device to argue for the legitimacy of ʿAlī and his descendants as Muḥammad's rightful successors.

Beyond sectarian debates between Sunnīs and Shīʿīs, however, during this period Nishapur witnessed a rise in tension between competing groups of Sunnīs. For example, there is evidence of conflict in Nishapur between rival Sunnī legal schools, most markedly between Hanafīs and Shāfiʿīs. Strife and actual clashes between the partisans of these legal methodologies intensified largely as a result of the political struggle underlying this intellectual struggle.[4] Other intra-Sunnī strife revolved around rival theological positions, with the opposition between the Karrāmīs and the Ashʿarīs coming to the fore.[5] Nishapur was the center of an active Karrāmī group during the Ghaznavid period, and this group largely had the support of the Ghaznavid leaders, as well as the first of their Seljuq successors. The Karrāmīs were accused by their opponents of being anthropomorphists, claiming that God had a physical anthropoid body that was limited to a particular location in space. Clearly battles over competing conceptions over how to depict the deity might well have been waged using the ascension discourse as a battlefield. This intellectual and political history, therefore, is important to take into account as we examine the works of pivotal authors who wrote about Muḥammad's night journey and ascension in middle periods Nishapur.

IBN ḤIBBĀN'S REJECTION OF THE PRIMITIVE VERSION

Muḥammad b. Aḥmad Ibn Ḥibbān Bustī (d. 354/965), the Shāfiʿī traditionist of Nishapur who was introduced in chapter 2 as the earliest scholar to have recorded the Primitive Version of the Ibn ʿAbbās ascension narrative at length and in writing, transmits the Primitive Version in his work on weak *ḥadīth* reports in order to expose the narrative as a forgery. Ibn Ḥibbān was said to have traveled far and wide in the eastern lands of Islamdom, collecting sayings attributed to the Prophet. Even with all these travels, historians record that he lived for many years in and around the city of Nishapur.[6] Ibn Ḥibbān composed a series of scholarly works,[7] including a collection of Sunnī sound *ḥadīth* reports known as *al-Musnad al-ṣaḥīḥ ʿalā al-taqāsīm wa'l-anwāʿ* that attempts to organize those reports deemed authentic in a systematic way.[8] In addition to this collection, Ibn Ḥibbān is credited with at least two works that discuss unreliable transmitters and weak *ḥadīth* reports: *Kitāb al-majrūḥīn*, and *Gharāʾib al-akhbār*.[9] The first of these two works includes a reference to the Primitive Version of the Ibn ʿAbbās ascension narrative in its entry under the figure by the name of Maysara b. ʿAbd Rabbih "the Persian," the individual from the chain of transmission of the narrative whom Ibn Ḥibbān accuses of fabricating it.[10]

The very fact that Ibn Ḥibbān records the Primitive Version in order to argue for its baselessness proves that the Primitive Version must have achieved a wide enough circulation and/or gained a significant enough following to merit Ibn Ḥibbān's attention and disapproval of it. When we recall that Ibn Ḥibbān lived only a generation after the Shīᶜī exegete ᶜAlī Qummī, the Imāmī Shīᶜī whose major ascension *ḥadīth* (ascribed to Jaᶜfar Ṣādiq) draws substantially upon the Primitive Version, and only a generation after the Sunnī exegete Muḥammad b. Jarīr Ṭabarī, who clearly is familiar with the Primitive Version (even though he does not transmit more than a summary of it), then the hypothesis that the Primitive Version may have enjoyed a wide circulation by the middle of the fourth/tenth century is not difficult to support.

Ibn Ḥibbān seems to be mainly concerned with proving that the *ḥadīth* is a fabrication rather than a genuine saying from the Prophet. Were he to have considered the *ḥadīth* to be truly dangerous or subversive, he might not have quoted the report at such length. In any case, his text offers few clues to indicate whether a specific group of Muslims was championing the Primitive Version in the middle of the fourth/tenth century in the vicinity of Nishapur, leading Ibn Ḥibbān to oppose the narrative in an active fashion. It is possible that the Primitive Version had become popular among both a certain segment of Shīᶜīs and a certain segment of Sunnīs by the time that Ibn Ḥibbān composed his work, and writers from the generations immediately after that of Ibn Ḥibbān offer evidence to support this hypothesis.

SULAMĪ AND HIS COMPILATION OF SUFI SAYINGS ON MUḤAMMAD'S ASCENSION

A Sufi scholar from Nishapur of the generation after Ibn Ḥibbān, the famous biographer Abū ᶜAbd al-Raḥmān Muḥammad b. Ḥusayn Sulamī (d. 412/1021), compiled a collection of early Sufi sayings on the Prophet's ascension that offers a valuable window through which to examine how Sulamī and his early contemporaries viewed Muḥammad's ascension.[11] The collection proves that the early Sufis did not restrict themselves to commenting on *ḥadīth* reports from the sound Sunnī collections, and in fact the base narratives that some of the Sufis must have been commenting upon contain singular details, such as the idea that lights came down from above and enveloped the Prophet on the night of the ascension.[12] One saying describing the latter event makes it clear that at least a few of the early Sufis, such as the pivotal Baghdādī scholar Junayd (d. 297/910), connected the heavenly host debate with the night of Muḥammad's ascension, just as the Shīᶜī exegete ᶜAlī Qummī does: "Do you not see how when Muḥammad was asked about what the heavenly host debate, when the lights of his descriptions alighted upon him and he stripped him of his description, he spoke about all places and reported about them?"[13] This saying, ascribed to Junayd, suggests that both Sunnī and Shīʿī scholars of the third/ninth century had collated the heavenly host debate trope together with the narrative of Muḥammad's ascension, and the circulation of the Primitive Version of the Ibn ʿAbbās narrative might have facilitated this process.[14]

Even though the early Sufis likely had access to the Primitive Version, that does not mean that they accepted every aspect of it uncritically. In fact, some of Sulamī's sayings demonstrate that a few Sufis chose to rework aspects of this version to suit their own purposes. For example, a saying that Sulamī attributes to the famous early mystic Ḥallāj offers a new spin on the familiar "Ask and be given" trope that the Ibn ʿAbbās ascension discourse commonly places in the intercession segment of the intimate dialogue. According to Sulamī, Ḥallāj alleges that Muḥammad responded to God's command "Ask and be given" with a refusal to ask for anything: "He said, 'What shall I ask for, since I have been given? What should I request, since I have been satisfied?' "[15] Ḥallāj suggests that Muḥammad would not stoop to petition God to grant him any boons, nor would he stoop to complain to God for the injustices his community may face. The force of this mystical interpretation largely derives from the typical accounts of this intercessory scene, such as the one circulated in the Primitive Version, which generate the expectation that Muḥammad will respond with pleas on behalf of his community. Regardless of whether or not the Sufis were in sympathy with the Primitive Version and its perspective, nevertheless Sulamī's collection of Sufi sayings offers further proof that interest in Muḥammad's night journey and ascension appear to have reached a new peak in Nishapur near the beginning of the fifth/eleventh century.

QUSHAYRĪ AND HIS *KITĀB AL-MIʿRĀJ*

A generation after Sulamī and his contemporary from Nishapur, the exegete Thaʿlabī (chapter 6), Sulamī's student and fellow Shāfiʿī Sunnī by the name of Abū al-Qāsim ʿAbd al-Karīm Qushayrī (d. 465/1072) composed one of the most significant Arabic works of the formative period dealing extensively and almost exclusively with the subject of Muḥammad's ascension.[16] This *Kitāb al-miʿrāj* covers a broader range of genres and topics than Sulamī's short collection of mystical sayings, the latter of which Qushayrī largely incorporates into his own work.[17] Unlike the manner in which Sulamī limits his collection to mystical interpretations of the ascension, Qushayrī's work offers a more general scholarly and theological approach to the study of the theme of ascension in the Islamic tradition. An interesting feature of Qushayrī's work is that it does not restrict itself to discussions of Muḥammad's ascension, but it also briefly considers the question of the ascension visions ascribed to Sufi saints (*awliyāʾ*),[18]

and the ascensions experienced by prophets other than Muḥammad.[19] The majority of the work, however, focuses on the interpretation of qur᾿ānic verses and *ḥadīth* reports dealing with matters related to Muḥammad's ascension, and these sections are most relevant to this study.

Near the beginning of his *Kitāb al-miᶜrāj*, Qushayrī quotes a number of Sunnī *ḥadīth* reports in a chapter entitled "The Received Reports on the Ascension," and he opens this chapter by supporting the claim that the most sound reports are those transmitted by the early traditionist Anas b. Mālik.[20] Instead of recording entire extended narratives, Qushayrī constructs a composite and ideal Sunnī narrative that draws its anecdotes from a series of reports, strung together in a chronological sequence, together recounting the events of the night of the ascension. Qushayrī does not limit himself to the official extended reports in the Sunnī sound collections, but rather he supplements these extended reports with details from other collections.[21] Since Qushayrī quotes the entire Primitive Version of the Ibn ᶜAbbās ascension narrative in his book, clearly he has no problem with citing ascension narratives that other scholars reject.

The inclusion of unconventional and potentially suspect ascension reports in Qushayrī's work raises the issue of Qushayrī's reporting apparently Shīᶜī ascension anecdotes, especially given his strong commitment to Shāfiᶜī Sunnism. Although the Nishapur in which Qushayrī lived much of his life was dominated by staunchly Sunnī dynasties,[22] there remained a sizeable Shīᶜī population in the city. Portions of the Iranian plateau had been dominated by the Shīᶜī Buyid dynasty until the end of the fourth / tenth century, when Qushayrī was being raised and educated. As it stands in its unique manuscript form, Qushayrī's *Kitāb al-miᶜrāj* transmits several sayings that may be seen as in sympathy with, or at least creative dialogue with, ostensibly Shīᶜī ascension narratives.

The *Kitāb al-miᶜrāj* contains references to suggest that its author opposes the Shīᶜī use of Muḥammad's ascension, yet that evidence is somewhat ambiguous. From the outset, Qushayrī argues against those who hold that the ascension took place only in a dream vision, a group who thus disputes the notion that the ascension took place bodily. Qushayrī connects this position that he finds objectionable as reflecting the teachings of the Shīᶜīs (*al-Rawāfiḍ*) and the Muᶜtazilīs.[23] Despite his clear opposition to those who completely deny the bodily ascension, Qushayrī nevertheless recognizes that some trustworthy ascension reports describe Muḥammad's journey as a dream, and he thus concedes that the latter may describe other ascensions that Muḥammad may have experienced on different nights, in addition to the bodily ascension.[24] This compromise position denies the centrality of the nonbodily visionary ascent, yet it does leave room for recognizing the legitimacy of those *ḥadīth* reports, Shīᶜī or otherwise, that describe such a visionary ascent. Similar types of ambiguity appear later in Qushayrī's work as well. For instance, Qushayrī transmits several passages praising Abū Bakr, sometimes in a way that almost certainly was designed to respond to the Shīʿī use of ascension narratives to extol ʿAlī and his blessed station.[25] Nevertheless, the work also contains passages that call into question setting apart Abū Bakr in this fashion, thus appearing also to take issue with partisan Sunnī use of the discourse.[26] The position of Qushayrī's *Kitāb al-miʿrāj* in the struggle between Sunnīs and Shīʿīs over the control of the ascension discourse in medieval Nishapur, therefore, remains less straightforward that it first might appear.

Even more evidence for the ambiguous position of Qushayrī's work comes with its inclusion of ascension reports that seem to have originated in Shīʿī circles. For instance, the *Kitāb al-miʿrāj* contains two ascension anecdotes that trace their chain of transmission to a central figure among the Zaydī Shīʿīs, the descendant of the Prophet named Zayd b. ʿAlī [Zayn al-ʿAbdidīn] b. al-Ḥusayn, from reports originating with his great grandfather, ʿAlī b. Abī Ṭālib.[27] Qushayrī significantly records these two bits of narrative after he completes his section on the ascension reports from the sound Sunnī collections, perhaps implying that these Shīʿī reports potentially supplement the Sunnī narratives.[28] The first of these two "Zaydī" anecdotes describes how God responds to each of the phrases in the call to prayer when an angel proclaims the *adhān* in the heavens.[29] The second report that Qushayrī's work connects to this Zaydī Shīʿī Imam tells the story of how Muḥammad travels on a visionary tour of hellfire and paradise in which Gabriel postpones his explanations of the wonders that Muḥammad encounters en route.[30] After receiving the explanations for what he had seen, a voice at the Lote Tree calls upon Muḥammad to "Ask and be given!" He is only able to petition God on behalf of himself and the "People of the House" (*ahl al-bayt*) after angels comfort him by placing their hands upon his chest and between his shoulder blades.[31] Since Qushayrī would most likely have looked upon the Zaydī Shīʿīs as his intellectual adversaries in Nishapur, especially during the Ghaznavid and Seljuq periods, the appearance in Qushayrī's work of these "Zaydī" ascension anecdotes remains something of a mystery.[32] It unlikely that Qushayrī records these anecdotes to promote a Zaydī interpretation of the ascension; rather, he may have recorded these accounts in order to co-opt them, and to cause those in Nishapur who accepted them to understand them in a different (Ashʿarī Sunnī) light.

THE EXTENDED COSMOLOGICAL ASCENSION *ḤADĪTH*

If the two *ḥadīth* reports ascribed to Zayd seem anomalous among the Sunnī narratives in Qushayrī's work, the same could be said for the longest ascension narrative in his entire collection, a report that will be called hereafter the "Extended Cosmological *ḥadīth*."[33] Qushayrī connects this lengthy narrative to two figures named Sulaymān Aʿmash and ʿAṭā b. Sāʾib, claiming that the report originally derives from the sayings of ᶜAlī b. Abī Ṭālib, Muḥammad Ibn Isḥāq, and Ibn ᶜAbbās.[34] Given the importance of this narrative to the study of the later reshaped versions of the Ibn ᶜAbbās ascension narrative to be analyzed in chapters 8 and 9, a brief summary of its highlights is in order.

The narrative begins in the house of Umm Hāniᵓ, ᶜAlī's sister and Muḥammad's cousin, where Gabriel appears to Muḥammad near his bed after the evening prayers. Muḥammad does not recognize Gabriel, a detail which suggests that this encounter takes place at the beginning of his period of prophecy. He nevertheless obeys him unhesitatingly, tightening his girdle and donning his cloak, allowing himself to be led outside where Burāq waits. The description of Burāq here is particularly detailed, and she is said to have a human face and a human spirit inside her, despite her composite quadrupedal body. When Burāq carries Muḥammad through the lands of Palestine, Muḥammad is beckoned by a woman and a man from either side, the tempting figures who first appeared in Ibn Hishām's recension of Ibn Isḥāq's narrative. Unlike in most other versions of this scene, however, Muḥammad turns toward each of these figures until Gabriel explains who each of them represents and the dangers they pose to him. Upon arrival in Jerusalem (here given its Roman name, "*Aelia*," as in Ibn Isḥāq's narrative), Gabriel ties Burāq to the rock, and then calls up to heaven requesting the angels to lower the *miᶜrāj*-ladder. Not only does the ladder itself receive a detailed description in the Extended Cosmological version, but also its individual steps and the angels that reside upon each are mentioned: The ladder consists of some fifty-five steps, each positioned a four-hundred-year[35] journey away from the next. The narrative's editor interjects at this point that he omits many of the other fantastic details of the wonders (*ᶜajāᵓib*) that this narrative otherwise includes, fearing its excessive length.[36]

Despite this caveat, numerous new details beyond what one finds in the earliest ascension narratives appear in this Extended Cosmological *ḥadīth*. Before arriving at the gates of the first heaven and meeting its gatekeeper, Ismāᶜīl,[37] Muḥammad encounters a group of angels praising God unceasingly, hiding their faces and crying due to their fear of God. Here as in each successive heaven, the narrative gives not only the name of the angelic gatekeeper but also the name and material composition of the heaven itself.[38] In the first heaven the angel Mālik, Guardian of Hellfire, appears before Muḥammad, uncovering the fires of hell for Muḥammad in a fashion parallel to the Abū Saᶜīd Khudrī narrative. Shortly after that encounter, Muḥammad meets the prophet Adam, and surveys the tortures of various classes of evildoers.[39] He meets other prophets in their typical locations in the heavens: Jesus and John in the second heaven, Joseph in the third, Enoch in the fourth, Aaron in the fifth, Moses in the sixth, and Abraham in the seventh. In addition to this official hierarchy, also found in the Abū Saᶜīd Khudrī version, the Extended Cosmological *ḥadīth* inserts some less common scenes. For instance, in the fourth heaven Muḥammad spies a series of palaces, each one designated for one of the women considered religious heroines by Muslim traditionists: Mary mother of Jesus, the unnamed mother of Moses, Āsiya wife of Pharoah, Khadīja wife of Muḥammad, and Fāṭima daughter of Muḥammad.[40] Such scenes may appear incidental to the narrative as a whole, but such details reflect a process whereby longer and more complex accounts were becoming fabricated.

Even more important are the insertions into the Extended Cosmological report regarding the seventh heaven, insertions that include a description of the divine throne and footstool, the towering angelic scribe of the all-merciful divinity who goes by the name Spirit (*Rūḥ*),[41] the different layers of paradise, and the locations in the vicinity of the Lote Tree. Regarding the last of these, the narrative reports that there are five curtains or pavilions (*sarādiqāt*)—of light, fire, snow, darkness, and cold—separating the Lote Tree from the carriers of the throne, protecting the denizens of the Lote Tree from the light of the throne bearers.[42] Presumably somewhere near the Inhabited House, Gabriel descends into a river called Eastern (*al-Sharqī*) to wash himself, and when he emerges and shakes his wings, a new angel is created from each of the seventy-thousand drops that fall from his feathers.[43] Also at the Inhabited House, Muḥammad leads the rest of the prophets in ritual prayer, an event that many other ascension narratives place instead in Jerusalem.[44] The Extended Cosmological *ḥadīth* ends much as the narrative in Ibn Hishām's recension of Ibn Isḥāq's narrative ends, with a certain number of Muslims leaving the fold of the faithful because of their incredulity at Muḥammad's story, and with Muḥammad proving the truth of his journey to Jerusalem by accurately describing it, facilitated by Gabriel raising it up for Muḥammad to see as the Prophet enumerated its features for the Quraysh.[45]

Like the extended and composite ascension narratives from ʿAlī Qummī and Thaʿlabī's Qurʾān commentaries discussed in the previous chapter, the Extended Cosmological *ḥadīth* could be considered an intermediate step in the development of the reshaped versions of the Ibn ʿAbbās ascension narrative. As with ʿAlī Qummī and Thaʿlabī's accounts, this report supplements the early extended narratives (in this case, the Abū Saʿīd Khudrī narrative drawn from Ibn Hishām's recension of Ibn Isḥāq) with additional fantastic details from the Primitive Version and elsewhere. Although this *ḥadīth* does not incorporate some of the key elements of the Ibn ʿAbbās ascension narratives, such as the detailed encounters with the Angel of Death and other heavenly luminaries (Rooster angel, Half-Fire-Half-Snow angel, etc.), the descriptions of the realms beyond the Lote Tree, or the elaboration upon the specifics of Muḥammad's intimate conversation with God, nevertheless its inclusion of supplementary cosmological details offers the general type of framework on which later Ibn ʿAbbās narratives build. The Extended Cosmological *ḥadīth* provides yet another example of how traditionists in the early middle period continue to draw on the earlier ascension accounts to form increasingly intricate and rich versions of the tale.

Qushayrī transmits the Extended Cosmological *ḥadīth* at great length, just as he transmits the Primitive Version at substantial length, and he indicates to his reader that he is aware just how long these reports are. Speaking about the Extended Cosmological *ḥadīth*, which spans over 10 percent of the text of his *Kitāb al-miᶜrāj*, Qushayrī claims to have "left out details," ostensibly out of the fear of allowing the narrative to take up even more of the text.[46] At the conclusion of the narrative, Qushayrī reports that his teacher Abū Daqqāq shared his opinion about it with the following statement: "These are the sayings of the exegetes (*ahl al-tafsīr*), and we left off the chains of transmission for fear of making [the narrative too] long."[47] The Extended Cosmological *ḥadīth* was clearly being circulated in and around Nishapur during this period, and despite its great length, Qushayrī deemed it worthy of quotation in his work.

Another piece of evidence to prove that the Extended Cosmological *ḥadīth* was circulating in Nishapur in the fifth / eleventh century appears in the work of the Qushayrī's contemporary and fellow Shāfiᶜī from Nishapur, Aḥmad b. Ḥusayn Bayhaqī (d. 458 / 1066).[48] Bayhaqī does not include a citation of the Extended Cosmological *ḥadīth* in his collection, but he does record how an earlier traditionist by the name of Abū ᶜAbd Allāh Muḥammad b. ᶜAbd Allāh Ḍābī Naysabūrī (d. 405 / 1014) first learned of the report:

> We were informed from Abū ᶜAbd Allāh [Muḥammad b. ᶜAbd Allāh Ḍābī] Ḥāfiẓ—ᶜAbdān b. Yazīd b. Yaᶜqūb Daqqāq in [the city of] Hamadān—Ibrāhīm b. Ḥusayn Hamadānī—Abū Muḥammad Ismaᶜīl b. Mūsā Fazārī—ᶜUmar b. Saᶜīd Baṣrī, of the people of Naṣr b. Quᶜayn—ᶜAbd al-ᶜAzīz and Layth b. Abī Sulaym—Sulaymān Aᶜmash—ᶜAṭā b. Sāʾib . . . —ᶜAlī b. Abī Ṭālib and ᶜAbd Allāh Ibn ᶜAbbās; also, Muḥammad b. Isḥāq b. Yasār [author of the *Sīra*]—Ibn ᶜAbbās; and also Sulaymān or Salma ᶜUqaylī—ᶜĀmir Shaᶜbī—ᶜAbd Allāh Ibn Masᶜūd—Juwaybir—Ḍaḥḥāk b. Muzāḥim [— Ibn ᶜAbbās], who said, "The Messenger of God was lying down to sleep in the house of Umm Hāniʾ, having completed the evening ritual prayer. . . ."
>
> Abū ᶜAbd Allāh [Muḥammad b. ᶜAbd Allāh Ḍābī] said, "The Shaykh [ᶜAbdān b. Yazīd b. Yaᶜqūb Daqqāq] told this [*ḥadīth*] to us. He recounted the *ḥadīth*, and I wrote down its text from the copy from which he had heard it. He recounted a long *ḥadīth* in which was mentioned a number of spirits, angels, and other things. It is among those [reports] that would not be objectionable at all, were its [chain of] transmission to be sound."[49]

In the anecdote above, Muḥammad Ḍābī describes having received and later transmitted the Extended Cosmological *ḥadīth*. The chains of transmission given in the above anecdote include the mention of ᶜAlī b. Abī Ṭālib, Ibn Masᶜūd, and Ibn ᶜAbbās among those who form the earliest transmitters of the report. The presence of ᶜAlī seems particularly significant, suggesting that not only Sunnīs but also some Shīᶜīs circulated this report. Muḥammad Ḍābī became suspicious of it, not because of its contents but because of the problems he sees in its chains of transmission. Such problems might well have also led Bayhaqī to refuse to cite the narrative, unlike Qushayrī's decision to include a lengthy citation of it in his text.

Not only did these Shāfiᶜī scholars of Nishapur call the authenticity of the Extended Cosmological *ḥadīth* into question, but also a contemporary Muslim scholar who studied Qushayrī's ascension work took the same critical approach. Qassim Samarrai, in his brief survey of Qushayrī's *Kitāb al-miᶜrāj* in his work *The Theme of Ascension in Mystical Writings*, regards this Extended Cosmological *ḥadīth* as a clear forgery, a malicious interpolation into the body of Qushayrī's text. Samarrai evaluates the origins of the report in the following fashion:

> This tradition, incorporated with part of the Tradition found in [Ibn Isḥāq's] *Sīra*, covers more than eighteen folios. We have enough evidence to state safely that this tradition, marked by extreme exaggeration and incredible descriptions of the Heavens and Hell, reveals how fanciful and imaginative the writer was. . . . The forger appears to be a very learned Persian story-teller, [who is able] to incorporate the *ḥadīth* mentioned in the *Sīrā* with his [own] and make them appear as an integral part of the whole story-like tradition.[50]

Samarrai offers little evidence for his assertion that the author of the *ḥadīth* may be of Persian origin, aside from a Persian figure appearing in the chain of transmission (blamed by Ibn Ḥibbān and others for the forgery), and minor grammatical mistakes appearing in the Arabic text.[51] In any case, he ultimately postulates that either members of a rival theological faction inserted the text into Qushayrī's work, or that Qushayrī deliberately employed the weapons of his rivals to wage an intellectual battle with them.[52]

We have seen how a number of scholars, including ᶜAlī Qummī and Thaᶜlabī, transmit narratives like this Extended Cosmological *ḥadīth* that derive from the combination of earlier ascension reports. Such a process of story development appears to have been a creative technique utilized through much of the history of Muslim ascension narratives, and not just by scholars outside the Sunnī mainstream. Popular storytellers may indeed have led the way in weaving disparate fragments of narrative together into a single account, giving the resulting weave the appearance of an integral whole. Nevertheless, the storytellers did not have a monopoly on this process, and even more rigorous scholars made use of this storytelling process when they related the account of Muḥammad's night journey and ascension.

In examining the Extended Cosmological ascension *ḥadīth* in Qushayrī's *Kitāb al-miᶜrāj*, more important than the issue of the *ḥadīth*'s fabrication and/or possible interpolation is the question of what purpose the narrative serves in the work. In other words, supposing the narrative to be an authentic part of Qushayrī's original work, why might Qushayrī have included it? Samarrai postulates that Qushayrī may have turned to this and other "popular" ascension reports in order to fight against a competing group, namely the Karrāmīs, over the support of the common people in Nishapur:

> It is true that he wrote this book as a counterblast to and in refutation of the argument of the Muᶜtazilites and the Karrāmites of Khurāsān who denied the corporeal ascension and claim[ed] that, "If it was so, then God must be 'up there' and confined to a particular spot in heaven. . . ."
>
> It is a fact that the ordinary ignorant Muslim was incredibly credulous, and the instances quoted above illustrate how easy it was for a rascally Karrāmite to turn the laity of Nishapur against Qushayrī. This might have been the reason behind his compilation of *Kitāb al-miᶜrāj*, in which he, if we accept that he incorporated some rejected or weak traditions, used the same weapon that was turned against him of appealing to the laity through their ignorance.[53]

We have seen how narratives on Muḥammad's night journey serve as contested spaces within the ascension "language world" in the formative period of Islamic history, and given the many-layered and complex theological and political divisions in fifth/eleventh-century Nishapur, Samarrai may be correct that Qushayrī included narratives in his work that recommended themselves by their being widespread more than their being officially certified as authentic, with the goal of convincing a more general public of the superiority of the Shāfiᶜī Sunnī interpretation of these narratives. Whatever Qushayrī's purpose may have been, by including several *ḥadīth* of apparently Shīᶜī origin in his work, Qushayrī indicates that these narratives were no longer seen as exclusively "Shīᶜī *ḥadīth*," but rather clearly were appropriated and accepted by some of the scholars within the Sunnī circles of Nishapur of which Qushayrī was a part.

BAYHAQĪ'S REJECTION OF THE EXTENDED ASCENSION NARRATIVES

Just as Qushayrī's work includes the text of the Extended Cosmological *ḥadīth* while the text of his colleague Bayhaqī chooses not to, so also Qushayrī includes the citation of the Primitive Version of the Ibn ᶜAbbās ascension narrative in his work, which Bayhaqī declines to include beyond the listing some of its chains of transmission.[54] Along with this difference in strategy, which may point to a disagreement among the Shāfiᶜīs of Nishapur about the best way to deal with these controversial ascension narratives, these contemporaries treat the contents of the Primitive Version with different levels of caution. Prior to his citation of the Primitive Version, Qushayrī states:

> A *ḥadīth* of the ascension has been transmitted via Abū Ḥudhayfa Isḥāq b. Bishr Qurashī Bukhārī through chains of transmission that they discussed and with additions that the people of this craft, the leaders of the traditionists, did not accept. Abū Ḥudhayfa did not [actually] advance this *ḥadīth*. We mention [in what follows] some of the additions that it transmits which do not reach the point of being objectionable.[55]

Qushayrī's recension of the Primitive Version condenses some of the passages in the narrative, and it omits those details, such as the anthropomorphic touch of God's hand, that he considers too objectionable to include.[56] Qushayrī acknowledges that the experts in *ḥadīth* reports, probably a reference to the Shāfiᶜī traditionists over and against their opponents, do not accept certain aspects of this narrative.

Bayhaqī breaks from Qushayrī on the issue of the advisability of quoting from ascension reports whose authenticity remains open to question. While he does quote the Abū Huyayra and Abū Saᶜīd Khudrī ascension reports (see chapter 6) at length at the beginning of his section of ascension narratives with weak chains of transmission,[57] he registers his disapproval of even these versions. He expresses this disapproval not only by attacking their chains of transmission, but also by relating the following report of a dream vision of the Prophet:

> Imam Abū ᶜUthmān ᶜIsmāᶜīl b. ᶜAbd al-Raḥmān—Abū Nuᶜaym [Isfarāʾinī]—Aḥmad b. Muḥammad b. Ibrāhīm Bazzāz—Abū Ḥāmid b. Bilāl—Abū al-Azhar—Jābir b. Abī Ḥakīm said, "I saw the Messenger of God in a dream. I said, "O Messenger of God, regarding a man from your community named Sufyān Thawrī, is he not bad [as an authority]?" The Prophet answered, "No, he is not bad." [I said,] "Abū Hārūn told us from Abū Saᶜīd Khudrī that regarding the eve you were taken on a night journey, you said, 'I saw in the heaven[s] . . .' and he related the *ḥadīth*." [The Prophet] replied, "Yes." I said, "O Messenger of God, the people of your community are talking about your journey with wonders (*ᶜajāʾib*)." He replied to me, "That is the report of the storytellers (*dhāka ḥadīth al-quṣṣāṣ*)."[58]

This vision of the Prophet serves two functions, only the second of which relates to Bayhaqī's present discussion of Muḥammad's ascension. First, the dream vision establishes the legist and mystic Sufyān Thawrī as a reliable authority. Second, it calls into doubt the reliability of the ascension narrative attributed to Abū Saᶜīd Khudrī, the very same Khudrī *ḥadīth* discussed in chapter 6. Bayhaqī's critique of the Khudrī *ḥadīth* is apparent in the anecdote's reference to the storytellers, for the term "storyteller" by this period was synonymous with someone who fabricated *ḥadīth* reports. Moreover, in light of the fact that the Primitive Version of the Ibn ᶜAbbās ascension narrative often became connected to the title "The Wonders (*ᶜajāʾib*) of the Ascension," one might conjecture that the critique leveled against "storyteller" versions of the ascension in the above report might also be aimed at the Ibn ᶜAbbās ascension narratives. By ending his discussion of the night journey and ascension with the account of this dream vision, Bayhaqī advances what he registers as the Prophet's direct condemnation of weak ascension narratives, a category in which Bayhaqī undoubtedly includes the Primitive Version.

Bayhaqī's critical evaluation of these types of extended ascension narratives recalls Ibn Ḥibbān's critique of the Primitive Version of the Ibn ᶜAbbās ascension narrative a century earlier.[59] The insistent condemnation of these ascension narratives by the majority of Sunnī Shāfiᶜī scholars from Nishapur leads one to suspect that these narratives had taken hold of the imagination of a segment of the population of this city (or region?) between the fourth/tenth and fifth/eleventh centuries. While it is possible that other opponents of the Shāfiᶜīs of Nishapur, such as the Hanafīs, the Muᶜtazilīs, or the Karrāmīs, could have been circulating these rival traditions, it is likely that the narratives also appealed to the Shīᶜīs of the region. Thaᶜlabī's formulation of his composite version and Qushayrī's inclusion of both the Extended Cosmological *ḥadīth* and the Primitive Version of the Ibn ᶜAbbās *ḥadīth* together confirm the degree to which Shāfiᶜī scholars of Nishapur were forced to take these fantastic stories into account. They adapted details from these narratives to suit their own interpretations and sensibilities, perhaps as a way to subvert these narratives, or as a way to win converts to Shāfiᶜī Sunnī Islam. The process of adaptation and appropriation was to continue a step further with the formulation of the "Total and Complete" ascension narratives, composed by reshaping the more developed Ibn ᶜAbbās narratives together with other wondrous details. Controversy continued to surround these reshaped Ibn ᶜAbbās narratives, and yet the narratives continued to find an audience, for they spread far beyond Nishapur and the eastern lands of Islamdom in the years that followed.

8
BAKRĪ'S TOTAL AND COMPLETE IBN ᶜABBĀS DISCOURSE

The Primitive Version of the Ibn ᶜAbbās ascension narrative, with its focus on the fantastic angels and wondrous upper regions that Muḥammad encountered on his heavenly ascent, sparked the imagination of both the common folk and the learned official scholars in fifth / eleventh-century Nishapur in the eastern lands of Islamdom, and in the following two centuries in the lands of Islamdom further west this same spark kindled a blaze of creativity in an anonymous writer who assumed the persona of an early traditionist by the name of Abū al-Ḥasan Bakrī.[1] Until further evidence comes to light, it will not be easy to identify this mysterious source with any precision. Nevertheless, this chapter examines the traces of the narrative ground once traversed by this elusive author (or group of authors). The investigation will necessarily be speculative, for the remains have scattered and diminished over the centuries. Yet I would maintain that this speculative work remains critical for our understanding of the climax reached between the fifth / eleventh and seventh / thirteenth centuries by the prose Arabic ascension literature. In what follows, I will suggest that much of the credit for reaching this high point in the development of the Ibn ᶜAbbās ascension discourse should go to a series of texts, oral and written, transmitted in the name of Abū al-Ḥasan Bakrī.

As previous chapters have discussed, narrative versions of Muḥammad's night journey and ascension that ignore the conventions of scholarly discourse, resulting in historical short stories or novellas on the subject, probably were in circulation by the third / ninth century, and likely even earlier. The stories tended to elaborate on the celestial and wondrous aspects of the story more than its mundane features. So although some of the scenes in the night journey did expand, these ascension stories focused to a greater degree on the fantastic details about the compositions of the heavens, the names of the angels, the descriptions of upperworldly spheres beyond the seventh heaven, the tours of paradise and hellfire, and Muḥammad's encounters in the court of the divinity. Based on the later texts ascribed to Abū al-Ḥasan Bakrī, and speculatively imagining Bakrī as an early historical figure who drew upon the work of the early Muslim historians such as Ibn Isḥāq,[2] it appears that such fantastic and wondrous details, some drawn from the apocalyptic language worlds of related traditions and neighboring cultures,[3] was this storyteller's specialty. In order to make the case for this hypothesis, the best approach will be to begin from the later series of texts unambiguously attributed to Abū al-Ḥasan Bakrī that began to circulate in the seventh/thirteenth century, working backward from there toward earlier fragments of evidence that might suggest an earlier date for the beginnings of this type of ascension narrative.

Despite the vagueness that Bakrī's biography presents, thankfully the textual evidence for the existence of an ascension narrative attributed to Bakrī is amply provided in at least five extant manuscripts that preserve four separate recensions of the story.[4] Three of the four recensions bear the title *Ḥadīth al-mi*ᶜ*rāj* ᶜ*alā 'l-tamām wa 'l-kamāl* (*The Report of the Ascension, Total and Complete*),[5] which nicely describes the extensive scope of the work compared to other ascension works of the early and middle periods of Islamic history. A comparison of the chains of transmission included in these four recensions demonstrates that the "Bakrī" to whom these works are ascribed appears to represent a figure of the early period, only a few generations removed from the alleged source of the report, Ibn ᶜAbbās. Two of the four mention Bakrī in the same breath as the famous early author of the biography of Muḥammad, namely Muḥammad Ibn Isḥāq (d. ca. 150/767), and one even suggests that Bakrī transmits the narrative directly from this historian.[6] Whether an historical figure or a literary invention, then, these texts present an image of Abū al-Ḥasan Bakrī as a figure who flourished in the second/eighth or third/ninth century. A brief overview of the distinguishing characteristics of these Bakrī recensions will help to define the parameters of this genre of ascension narrative, only after which will it be possible to theorize about the geographical and historical growth and spread of this narrative.

A distinguishing feature of Bakrī's ascension narrative portrayed in the four recensions at our disposal lies in its attention to dramatic elements, including descriptive detail, emplotment and suspense. These characteristics apply to Bakrī's work (or the works associated with him) more generally, as Boaz Shoshan's study of the biography of the Prophet ascribed to Bakrī demonstrates.[7] A review of the scenes from Bakrī's night journey narrative, from the appearance of the angel Gabriel to the events of their journey together from Mecca to Jerusalem, illustrates the dramatic features that set Bakrī's version apart from other ascension narratives.

THE EVENTS PRIOR TO THE NIGHT JOURNEY IN TEXTS THAT INVOKE BAKRĪ

In its most complete recension, which may be among the earliest recensions of the text,[8] the Bakrī narrative recounts how Muḥammad describes in vivid detail the night in which he experienced his fantastic journey to Jerusalem and beyond:

> I had entered the house of my cousin Umm Hāniᵓ, daughter of Abū Ṭālib, after the last evening prayers. I found her already in her sleeping quarters asleep, so I performed the ritual prayers and then I wanted to seek shelter in [the comfort of] my bed. Suddenly I was in the presence of my beloved, Gabriel. It was a night of intense darkness, the moon having been hidden behind clouds and gloom. Indeed it was a gloomy night, one of thunder and lightning, one in which not a rooster crowed nor donkey brayed nor dog barked.[9]

Bakrī's description of this pitch black night in which thunder pealed and lightning flashed lucidly evokes the symbolism of mysterious and powerful forces at work, a night on which major and significant events take place. This particular night, according to Bakrī's description, is charged with both danger and expectation. The silence of all the animals heightens the anticipation of the audience, communicating to them the fact that the normal worldly order of things will presently be disrupted by an otherworldly visitation.

This visitation proceeds immediately after the above scene is set, supplementing the usual reference to the Angel Gabriel with an exhaustive inventory of his features:

> The roof of my house was split, and there descended Gabriel in his form. [He wore] the brightest of gowns, lightning of pleat, white of body. His hair was [in braids] like ropes, white like snow. His feet were immersed in yellow. Upon him was a cloak decorated with pearls and native gold. Upon his forehead two lines were written, gleaming and shining in light: "There is no god but God" [and] "Muḥammad is the Messenger of God." He had seventy whiskers of musk. His form filled everything between the east and the west. He has five hundred wings. I woke warily, trembling, afraid. He said, "Do not be anxious, Muḥammad, for I am the faithful spirit, the messenger of the Lord of the worlds." Then he embraced me and kissed me between my eyes.[10]

This description of Gabriel paints a vivid picture of the messenger archangel in the minds of those hearing the story of Muḥammad's journey. Gabriel physically embodies the truth of Muḥammad's message, having the testimony of Muslim faith emblazoned in light upon his forehead in a manner similar to the one we have seen the proto-Shīʿī authors use to sectarian effect (appending a line about ʿAlī's station to the end of the testimony).

The idea that Gabriel appeared to Muḥammad in this "true form" springs from a debate in the early Muslim community over the question of whether Muḥammad saw God during his heavenly ascent, or whether the pair of verses from the chapter of the Star that reports that "*he saw him another time at the Lote Tree of the boundary*" (Q 53:13–14) in fact describes Muḥammad's vision of Gabriel in the latter's true form. In this case Bakrī's narrative attempts to have it both ways, for it here describes Muḥammad's vision of Gabriel in his true form, while later in the narrative it reports that Muḥammad did in fact see God, even if only with the "eye of the heart."[11] With regard to his vision of Gabriel's form, the narrative implies that Muḥammad has never seen Gabriel this way before, for the initial shock of this vision terrifies him to the core.

The scene of Gabriel's appearance captures the sense of a recurring trope in Bakrī's narrative that was already introduced in the Primitive Version of the Ibn ʿAbbās ascension narrative, namely that Muḥammad receives the rare privilege of witnessing some of the splendors and wonders of the universe, and generally these otherworldly experiences scare him out of his wits. In response Gabriel, or some other being that takes his place as guide, interpreter, and comforter, reaches out to Muḥammad, touching or embracing him, telling him not to be afraid. The fear that grips Muḥammad here and in later scenes heightens the dramatic effect that the narrative produces. Unlike the celebratory tone set by the majority of official ascension narratives, with Muḥammad's journey being a pleasurable discovery of hidden realms, in the Primitive Version and Bakrī's reworking of the Ibn ʿAbbās ascension narrative, Muḥammad's journey on the night of the ascension resembles something closer to an amusement park ride in which the audience knows that all will turn out fine in the end, and yet they are thrilled by disturbing sights and life-threatening danger along the way. Gabriel does not threaten or menace Muḥammad directly in this scene, but the shock of having an enormous and unfamiliar being rip through his roof at night was enough to make him cower in fear, and the narrative's audience both sympathizes with the Prophet's plight and comforts him right along with Gabriel. The scene leaves Muḥammad and the Muslim audience with the message that things may appear terrifying upon first glance, but God remains in complete control of the situation, and God would not allow for harm to befall his beloved Prophet (and by extension, the Muslim community as a whole). Given the trial by fire that Muḥammad passes through in overcoming his fears, the night journey and ascension could be said to serve the function of a rite of passage, and with Gabriel's appearance its liminal phase has begun.

After clarifying that he did not come to Muḥammad to reveal a passage from the Qurʾān but rather to bring him into the presence of his Lord, Gabriel instructs Muḥammad to get up, prepare himself, and wrap himself well in his belt and cloak.[12] With regard to Muḥammad's clothing, we have seen how the proto-Shīᶜī reports tended to emphasize the importance of Muḥammad's cloak more than those of the Sunnīs, perhaps because according to Shīᶜī tradition the Prophet blessed the family of ᶜAlī with the very cloak that he wore (or received) during the heavenly journey. The recensions of the Bakrī narrative make reference to the Prophet's clothing far more frequently than do other early ascension narratives, and the majority of the Bakrī versions even go so far as to specify that he donned his Yemenī garments (*burda*s) to wear during the journey.[13] Reference to Muḥammad's clothing may have been inserted for verisimilitude, but given the later veneration of Muḥammad's effects, it becomes more likely that Bakrī inserted this detail into his narrative in response to the popular cult of the Prophet.

Except for the most extensive and developed of the Bakrī recensions given in Amcazade 95/2, surprisingly none of the other Bakrī versions makes any reference to the famous trope of the opening of Muḥammad's chest. Even the former recension gives only the briefest of references to the scene.[14] Given its absence from the majority of the Bakrī recensions, it is safe to postulate that the scene was not included in the simplest versions of Bakrī's narrative, and this omission requires explanation. One first should keep in mind that this opening of the chest scene, despite its importance to later scholars, does not appear in all of the early versions of the night journey recorded in the official collections of sound *ḥadīth* reports. In the early period, therefore, there was not yet consensus that the trope belonged as part of the story of Muḥammad's journey. And yet, the trope does form a part of the composite and extended versions of the story, at least those recorded by Sunnī exegetes such as Ṭabarī and Thaᶜlabī since the late third/ninth century. Since this ritual cleansing of the Prophet plays a role in the later theological debates over the Prophet's inerrancy (*ᶜiṣma*), one could suppose that the absence of the scene from the majority of Bakrī's ascension narratives suggests either that its original version was composed in the early centuries of the Islamic era, or else it draws upon a position like that of the Imāmī Shīᶜī exegete Faḍl b. Ḥasan Tabarsī (d. 548/1153) that because Muḥammad was born inherently pure and clean, the opening of the heart scene is rendered not only superfluous but even objectionable.[15]

In great contrast to the Bakrī narrative's relative neglect of the opening of the chest scene, the same narrative's scene introducing and describing the Prophet's fantastic mount Burāq takes a prominence rarely found in other narratives, prior or since. One could conjecture that Bakrī treats the description of Burāq as one of the "wonders (*ᶜajāʾib*) of the ascension," and as such it ranks up with the descriptions of the archangels in narrative importance. Since the earliest reports, Muslim traditionists agree on the fact that Burāq is "larger than a donkey and smaller than a mule," but does that mean that Burāq looks like a miniature horse? Furthermore, in many accounts Burāq is depicted as initially refusing to let Muḥammad ride upon it, relenting only after Gabriel upbraids Burāq. Can one assume that Burāq is a relatively dumb beast of burden, or does it show signs of higher intelligence? In response to these questions, Bakrī's narrative satisfies the audience's desire for a minute appraisal of Burāq's ornate bejeweled appearance.[16] Further, Burāq's full-fledged conversation with Gabriel about the reason why Burāq flinched from Muḥammad's touch makes clear the case that Burāq must be a creature endowed with rational intelligence. In some Bakrī versions, Burāq's scruple has to do with Burāq's pride in having served as the mount to previous prophets, and the idea that Burāq is not aware of Muḥammad's high station that earns him the merit to ride.[17] In others Burāq claims that Muḥammad might be ritually impure, for Burāq can sense that Muḥammad has touched an idol.[18] Despite these variations, two common elements unite these disparate recensions of Bakrī's description of Burāq: First, in nearly every case, Bakrī describes Burāq as having both a human face and a human soul (*nafs*);[19] Second, in absolutely every case, Burāq pleads with Muḥammad to include it in Muḥammad's intercession with God on the day of judgment, and Muḥammad's acceding to this request leads directly to Burāq's allowing Muḥammad to mount Burāq and to proceed on the journey.[20] Bakrī's depiction of Burāq thus humanizes the mount, separating it from all other worldly riding beasts, and underscoring the need for even such a heavenly creature to secure the blessing of Muḥammad's intercession.[21]

While the exchange between Gabriel and Burāq clearly foregrounds intercession as one of the primary ways in which God has favored Muḥammad, a theme that gains increased prominence in subsequent versions of Bakrī's narrative, it also makes clear that creatures must correctly follow Muḥammad's teachings in order to receive the benefits of his intercessory entreaties. The narrative portrays Burāq as plainly stating that Muḥammad's supporters will be saved and his detractors will be damned: "Whoever believes him enters paradise, and whoever calls him a liar enters hellfire."[22] Gabriel agrees with the correctness of this simple equation, essentially supporting the idea that one must be a Muslim to merit salvation in the next world. The narrative goes even further, however, suggesting that a central aspect of "believing in him" and his message consists of following Muḥammad in a certain way, the way favored by the Sunnī majority: "To [Muḥammad] is the *qibla* of Islam, the favor of [all] beings (*al-anᶜām*); the way and the consensus (*al-sunna wa 'l-jamāᶜa*), and the response during the intercession (*al-shafāᶜa*)."[23] Granted, these phrases appear in only one recension of the extant manuscripts that are explicitly attributed to Bakrī, and they therefore may not represent the earliest stratum of the Bakrī narrative. Nevertheless, they demonstrate that Sunnī Muslims since the seventh/thirteenth century at the latest made use of Bakrī's ascension narrative to support their own particular position over and against that of their non-Sunnī rivals, and we will find further evidence for this particular Sunnī use of the ascension narrative elsewhere in this and other texts, especially those connected with Bakrī's version.[24] The wider message presented in every recension of Bakrī's text remains the idea that one must reject other religions and accept Islam in order to avoid the punishments of hellfire, and this message illustrates the narrative's utility as an instrument for proselytization by presenting the story in the form of a moralizing conversion narrative.[25]

MUḤAMMAD'S NIGHT JOURNEY TO JERUSALEM IN TEXTS THAT INVOKE BAKRĪ

This moralizing and proselytizing theme is developed further in Bakrī's narrative through its depiction of Muḥammad's journey from Mecca to Jerusalem on the back of Burāq, which expands on the trope of Muḥammad's facing and overcoming a series of three temptations along the path, a trope familiar from the Abū Saᶜīd Khudrī *ḥadīth*.[26] Foreshadowing the drama of the scene and the danger facing the Prophet on the road ahead, in Bakrī's version Gabriel warns Muḥammad to stick close to Burāq and not to respond to any who address him on the way to Jerusalem. Subsequently voices symbolically representing the tempting call of the Jews and Christians cry out to Muḥammad, attempting to entice him from his path by claiming to offer him good advice, and following Gabriel's instructions Muḥammad refuses to heed their call. Gabriel later praises Muḥammad, explaining that had he responded to the first or second voices, Muḥammad's community would have been led to become Jews or Christians respectively. The third temptation comes in the form of an alluring woman in the road, symbolically representing the attractions of the world, who attempts to block Burāq's path no matter how it tries to avoid her. Unlike in Khudrī's version, in more than half of the recensions of Bakrī's account, Muḥammad shows some sign of weakness or fallibility in this last encounter, for he indicates that he momentarily wished to respond to this woman, succumbing to her worldly attractions.[27] Gabriel informs Muḥammad that as a consequence of his temptation, his community will likewise be tried by the temptations of the love of the world, which may draw believers away from devotion to the next world and may thus lead them into hellfire. While Bakrī's version of this trope builds on the ascetic message of the Khudrī version, its depiction of Muḥammad's temptation helps to acknowledge the difficulties of the ascetic path, and it portrays Muḥammad as a mere mortal who is not infallible but rather capable of slight error and lapse in judgment, a theme that Bakrī introduces here in the night journey account and reiterates in more subtle ways throughout the rest of the narrative.[28]

In addition to this depiction of Muḥammad's temptation on the road to Jerusalem, Bakrī's account of Muḥammad's journey to Jerusalem is distinctive from other accounts in three major ways, the first of which has to do with Muḥammad's "prayer stop" along the path. Not only does Muḥammad face the three tempters on the way to Jerusalem, but he also is instructed to descend from the back of Burāq and perform two cycles of ritual prayer at Mount Sinai. This trope was apparently first circulated as an independent anecdote in the official Sunnī *ḥadīth* collection of Nasāʾī,[29] and was later collated into the extended ascension narratives in the Qurʾān commentaries of Ṭabarī, Qummī, and Thaʿlabī.[30] In these contexts, Muḥammad is called to descend and pray in three separate sacred locations, namely Medina, Mount Sinai, and Bethlehem. In several Bakrī recensions Gabriel instructs Muḥammad to descend and pray in only one of these sacred sites, Mount Sinai.[31] This fact may be significant in deciphering Bakrī's emphasis in the narrative, for he appears to be favoring particular details of relevance to a Jewish audience, as will be discussed further below. Whether or not one accepts such a reading of Bakrī's use of the trope, this abbreviated prayer stop scene serves as a marker to identify other texts that later draw upon Bakrī's version of the story of Muḥammad's journey.

The second distinctive detail about versions of Bakrī's night journey narrative is that they nearly always include an account of how Muḥammad hears the sound of a rock falling into the pit of hellfire as he approaches Jerusalem, a trope indebted to the idea that the Valley of Jahannam (Gehennom in Hebrew) lies in the near vicinity of that city. One finds variations in the minor details presented in this trope in the different Bakrī recensions, such as variations in the exact number of years that the rock has been falling in this deep pit.[32] Nevertheless, the significant point for our purposes here is that the trope apparently does not appear in night journey narratives, as far as I am aware, prior to the account by Bakrī. Along with Muḥammad's temptation by the woman and the single prayer stop, this feature could be used to help identify other narratives related to Bakrī's reshaped version of the Ibn ʿAbbās ascension narrative.

The third and perhaps most significant distinctive detail from the night journey found in the majority of Bakrī recensions is the appearance of a handsome youth (*shāb*) who embodies "belief," embracing Muḥammad near the outskirts of Jerusalem.[33] This trope represents an analog to the three tempting figures on the path to Jerusalem, each of whom offer an allegorical representation of a belief system (Jewish, Christian, worldly) embodied in the form of a figure whom Muḥammad is called to embrace or rebuff, with significant consequences not only for Muḥammad but also for his community as a whole. Given Gabriel's command to avoid those who address him on the road, the appearance of the youth could be seen to represent a final test, determining whether or not Muḥammad will be able to distinguish truth from falsehood, whether he will know when not only to avoid an evil influence but also when to embrace a positive influence. This scene completes the logic of what Asín Palacios sees as the "allegorical aspect" of the earlier encounters on the road to

Jerusalem, since just as Muḥammad allegorically rejects the allure of Judaism, Christianity, and the world, so here he allegorically embraces the young and handsome allure of Islam. The attractive youth, who is belief personified, approaches Muḥammad after the Prophet's successful completion of the terrestrial portion of his journey, signifying that he has completed this phase of his "rite of passage" and has sufficiently overcome its trials to merit the rewards of true belief. At the moment that Muḥammad hugs the youth the figure vanishes, perhaps thereby revealing its miraculous nature (for Muḥammad thought it was a real person, not just another form of test), or perhaps thereby spiritually merging with Muḥammad. I see this final distinctive detail as especially significant, for it not only offers a new and creative anecdote into the narrative of Muḥammad's night journey, but it also reflects the eschatological language world common to some of the eastern Islamic lands, especially the Iranian regions.[34] Bakrī's version of Muḥammad's journey to Jerusalem, as summarized and analyzed above, contains some creative interpretations on familiar tropes, as well as the inclusion of some new tropes that do not seem to have earlier precedents among the extant Islamic ascension narratives. The peculiar combination of these new and old tropes gives the Bakrī recensions their distinctive character, and they help to illustrate how Bakrī has shaped select elements from other narratives to turn his version of the night journey into something of a fantastical historico-mythological novel.

In order to maintain audience interest and suspense, the hero must continue to face and overcome challenges and/or dangers, and Bakrī's novelized version of Muḥammad's experiences in Jerusalem offers no exception, for even though he has successfully arrived in the city, he still has further difficulties to overcome there. Similar to most ascension narratives that depict Muḥammad's experiences in Jerusalem, the majority of Bakrī's recensions describe how Muḥammad encounters and leads the earlier prophets in prayer, something that Bakrī depicts Muḥammad as somewhat reluctant to do, and something he has Muḥammad assure his listeners represents "no boast" on his part.[35] At the famous rock (*sakhra*) in Jerusalem, Muḥammad faces another trial in the form of the cup test. In Bakrī's version of the latter scene, unlike in previous versions, the amount of fluid that Muḥammad drinks from the cup that he correctly selects has eschatological consequences:

> There I found myself among three cups, the first of wine, the second of milk, and the third of water. Suddenly a voice called out from above my head, "If Muḥammad drinks the water, his community after him will drown. If he drinks the wine, his community after him will go astray." So I reached out my hand for the milk, and I drank all except a little of it. Then another voice said, "Had Muḥammad drunk all the milk, none of his community would have entered hellfire." I said, "Gabriel, return the

> milk to me." He replied, "Impossible, Muḥammad, the matter has been set, and the pen has written what will be." I asked Gabriel if that were set down in the Book, and he replied that it was.[36]

As in the version of the cup test in Ibn Isḥāq's biography of the Prophet,[37] a mysterious voice from above informs Muḥammad the results of the choices before Muḥammad is forced to choose. According to Shoshan, this "invisible speaker" also appears in Bakrī's biography of Muḥammad and other works, in each instance "directing the heroes to the right decision or action."[38] Although the voice here does lead Muḥammad to make the correct choice, it does not inform him of the result of his correct choice, nor how to proceed with it (i.e., how much milk to drink). Since it is only after the fact that Muḥammad learns he could have secured the assurance of paradise for his entire community had he finished the whole cup of milk, he remains powerless to change the fated result. The inclusion of this detail reflects Bakrī's larger preoccupation with the question of salvation and damnation, which relates to his emphasis upon Muḥammad's role as intercessor on behalf of his followers. Gabriel's introduction of Muḥammad to Burāq with the title "intercessor," and Burāq's subsequent request for Muḥammad's intercession introduces this idea, as was discussed above, and the idea of Muḥammad's intercession will culminate with Muḥammad's direct intercession with God during the intimate colloquy scene at the climax of the heavenly ascent. Bakrī depicts Muḥammad as savior and hero, therefore, but he also illustrates once again in the scene at the rock in Jerusalem that Muḥammad's actions fall short of perfection, for he remains merely human and cannot foresee all ends.

Bakrī Versions of Muḥammad's Journey through the Heavens

The preceding summary of Bakrī's narrative of Muḥammad's night journey from Mecca to Jerusalem has illustrated some of the distinctive features of Bakrī's elaborate storytelling, and while it is not possible here to offer such a detailed summary of Bakrī's subsequent treatment of Muḥammad's ascension, it is important to discuss some of those features of Bakrī's ascension narrative that set it apart from other earlier accounts. The elaboration of these features in the discussion that follows does not presume that the features always appear the same way in each recension of Bakrī's narrative. Indeed, the degree of variation found in the separate recensions of the Bakrī narrative is remarkable, perhaps suggesting its being transmitted orally more than in a written form, a theory that will be examined near the end of this chapter. Despite the variations, clearly many of the features that we will now examine, including the descriptions of the *miʿrāj* ladder and the four wondrous angels, the narration of Muḥammad's journey past seas and veils beyond the seventh heaven without the guidance of Gabriel, and the account of Muḥammad's colloquy with God and tours of paradise and hellfire, serve as critical blocks of narrative out of which every Bakrī ascension narrative is built.

The first distinctive feature one notices in Bakrī's *miᶜrāj* account appears at its outset with Bakrī's description of the ladder itself and his narration of the various wonders that Muḥammad sees while ascending to the gates of the first heaven via this ladder. Bakrī describes the *miᶜrāj* as a physical ladder that connects the heavens to the earth at the rock in Jerusalem, and he provides more details about this ladder (and the incredible visions Muḥammad witnesses while ascending it to the first heaven) than found in any of the previous ascension narratives that we have discussed. He depicts the ladder as being composed of precious gems and metals, and offers comments on its individual steps or rungs (*mirqāt*).[39]

In most recensions of Bakrī's account, Muḥammad encounters wondrous angels "in the air" before his arrival in the first heaven. At times the descriptions of these angels are generic, but at other times they are quite specific, and occasionally they are recognizable personalities that we have seen in earlier ascension narratives. For instance, in one important recension of Bakrī's narrative, that recorded in Amcazade 95/2 that currently represents the earliest dateable complete Bakrī recension, the wondrous angels appearing between earth and the heavens are none other than the four major angels introduced at the opening of the Primitive Version of the Ibn ᶜAbbās ascension narrative: the angelic Rooster, the Half-Fire-Half-Snow angel, the Angel of Death known as ᶜAzrāʾīl, and the Guardian of Hellfire known as Mālik.[40] In other Bakrī recensions, these same angels almost invariably appear at some point in Muḥammad's ascent through the seven heavens, sometimes together in a small cluster. For instance, Asad 6093 depicts the Angel of Death, the angelic Rooster, and the Half-Fire-Half-Snow angel as appearing together in the second heaven.[41] Moreover, a fair number of Bakrī recensions depict the Angel of Death in the fourth heaven, and the Guardian of Hellfire in the fifth.[42] Even in those narratives in which these four angels appear in different locations in the heavens, their descriptions are similar enough to those of the other Bakrī recensions to show that all four of these angels formed an indispensable component of Bakrī's ascension narrative. A connection between the Bakrī account of Muḥammad's ascension and the Primitive Ibn ᶜAbbās ascension narrative (or to a later text, such as the ascension narrative in Thaᶜlabī's *Tafsīr*, that itself draws upon the latter) can thus be established.

Bakrī's version goes far beyond the Primitive Version, however, in its depiction of the specific makeup of the seven realms of the heavens, and its descriptions of the specific prophets residing in each (see table 1). For instance, just as the Thaᶜlabī and Extended Cosmological ascension *ḥadīth* reports provide

Table 1 The Seven Heavens in Texts Related to the Ibn ᶜAbbās Ascension Narrative

MANUSCRIPT (DATE)	AUTHOR/RAWI	FIRST HEAVEN	SECOND HEAVEN
Primitive Version of the Ibn ᶜAbbās Ascension Narrative (pre 354/965) [Appendix A]	Muḥammad b. Sudūs on Ḥamīd on Muḥammad on ᶜAlī on Maysara on ᶜUmar on Ḍaḥḥāk on Ibn ᶜAbbās	m: none n: none p: Rooster angel, Half-Half angel, Angel of Death, Guard. of Hellfire; [Jesus, on descent]	(missing)
Qushayrī Ext. Cosmological *Ḥadīth* (pre 465/1072)	Sulaymān Aᶜmash and ᶜAṭā b. Sā᾿ib on ᶜAlī, Ibn ᶜAbbās and Ibn Isḥāq	m: obstruct. waves n: al-Rafīᶜ p: Ismāᶜīl, Adam, Guard. of Hellfire	m: copper n: Batītā (or Tītā?) p: Rafā᾿īl, Jesus and John
Istanbul Suleymaniye Ayasofya 3441 (685/1286)	[Ibn ᶜAbbās, among others cited in midst of the text]	m: emerald n: Barqīᶜa p: Ismāᶜīl; Rooster, Adam	m: white silver n: Aflūn p: Qiyayīl, Half-Fire-Half-Snow angel; Joseph
Istanbul Suleymaniye Amcazade 95/2 (ca. 679/1280) [Appendix B]	Abū Ḥasan **Bakri** (Ibn Isḥāq, Muqātil & Ibn ᶜAbbās, etc.)	m: smoke n: al-Rafīᶜa p: Angel of Death, Rooster, Half-Half, Guard. of Hellfire; Ismā᾿īl; Noah	m: iron n: Qaydūm p: ᶜIliyyūn, Jesus and John
Damascus Asad 6093 (ca. 1156/1743–44)	Aḥmad b. ᶜAbd Allāh **Bakri** (Ibn Isḥāq)	m: none n: none p: Ismā᾿īl, Jesus and John, Adam	m: none n: none p: Angel of Death, Rooster, Half-Half
Istanbul Suleymaniye Ayasofya 867 (886/1481)	Abū Ḥasan [**Bakrī]** (Ibn ᶜAbbās)	m: smoke n: al-Rafīᶜa p: Ismāᶜīl	m: iron n: al-Māᶜūn p: Jesus and John
Cairo Dar al-Kutub Tarikh Taymur 738/8 (n.d.)	Abū Ḥasan **Bakri** (IbnᶜAbbās)	m: smoke n: none p: Ismāᶜīl	m: iron n: al-Māᶜūn p: Jesus and John

Key: m = material composition of the heaven, n = name of the heaven, p = prophet and/or prominent angel(s) in the heaven

THIRD HEAVEN	FOURTH HEAVEN	FIFTH HEAVEN	SIXTH HEAVEN	SEVENTH HEAVEN
(missing)	(missing) [p: Idrīs/Enoch, on descent]	(missing) [p: Aaron, on descent]	m: none n: none p: Karūbiyyūn; [Moses, on descent]	m: none n: none p: creatures unable to discuss [Adam, Noah, Abraham, on descent]
m: silver n: Zaylūn p: Kawkabyalīl, Joseph	m: yellow gold n: al-Maᶜūn p: Muᵓminyālīl, Idrīs/Enoch	m: red ruby n: Shuqḥīn p: Shaṭghatyālīl, Aaron	m: green emerald n: Ghazaryūn p: Rawᶜanyālīl, Moses	m: light n: Marshamaᶜū p: Nūryālīl, Rūḥ, Abraham
m: red gold n: Qaydūn p: Kukiyaᵓīl, Jesus and John	m: ruby n: Maᶜūm p: Mumyaᵓīl, Solomon, Angel of Death	m: emerald n: ᶜAydūn p: Saqtiyayīl, Guardian of Hellfire, Aaron	m: white pearl n: ᶜAzriyūn p: Ruᵓyaᵓīl, Rūḥ, Moses	m: light n: ᶜArniyya p: Nuryaᵓīl, Abraham
m: copper n: Mākūn p: David and Solomon	m: white silver n: al-Zāhira p: Raḥmānaᵓīl, Moses	m: red gold n: al-Muzayyana p: Shahrabaᵓīl, Mikāᵓīl, Idris/Enoch, Abraham	m: gems n: al-Khālisa p: Yaᵓīl, Shajaᵓīl, Prophet Hūd	m: white pearl n: al-Dami'a p: Rūḥaᵓīl, Adam, Rūḥāniyūn
m: none n: none p: Marjayaᵓīl, David and Solomon	m: none n: none p: Abraham, Joseph	m: none n: none p: Aaron	m: none n: none p: Moses	m: none n: none p: Ruḥyaᵓīl
m: copper n: al-Muzayyana p: David and Solomon	m: white silver n: al-Zāhira p: Angel of Death, Abraham	m: red gold n: al-Munira p: Idris/Enoch, Guard. of Hellfire	m: gems n: al-Khāliṣa p: Half-Fire-Half-Snow angel, Moses	m: ruby n: al-Lāmiᶜa p: Adam
m: copper n: al-Muzayyana p: David and Solomon	m: white silver n: al-Khāliṣa p: Angel of Death, Adam	m: gold n: al-Zāhira p: Half-Half angel, Guard. of Hellfire	m: none n: none p: Moses	m: ruby n: al-Lāmi'a p: Abraham, Mikāᵓīl, Rooster

(*continued*)

Table 1 *Continued*

MANUSCRIPT (DATE)	AUTHOR/RAWI	FIRST HEAVEN	SECOND HEAVEN
Paris Biblitheque Nationale, Arabe 1931 (n.d.)	Abū Ḥasan **Bakri** (Ibn ᶜAbbās)	m: smoke n: none p: Ismāᶜīl	m: iron n: al-Māᶜūn p: Jesus and John
Liber Scale Machometi (663/1264)	(Abū Bakr and Ibn ᶜAbbās)	m: iron n: none p: Angel of Death, Rooster, Half-Half, Guard. of Hellfire; Jesus and John	m: copper n: none p: Joseph

Key: m = material composition of the heaven, n = name of the heaven, p = prophet and/or prominent angel(s) in the heaven

the names of each heaven, their material composition, and/or the names of their angelic guardians, so the majority of the Bakrī ascension narratives also provide such information at the beginning of their descriptions of each of the seven heavens. Furthermore, the Bakrī narratives depict prophets residing in the heavenly spheres, similar to the manner that they appear in both official narratives and popular narratives. In this respect Bakrī's narrative appears to draw inspiration from earlier narratives that combine the Primitive Version with other ascension reports that describe the prophets in the heavens. Recall, for instance, how the narrative from Qummī's *Tafsīr* combined the Primitive Version with the Abū Saᶜīd Khudrī *ḥadīth*, and how Thaᶜlabī's *Tafsīr* combined the Primitive Version with the Abū Hurayra *ḥadīth*, as analyzed in chapter 6. The ascension narratives associated with Bakrī follow a similar pattern of incorporating the prophets into the heavens, but unlike the Qummī and Thaᶜlabī narratives, they resist incorporating the relatively fixed "official order" of the prophets in the heavens established by Khudrī and other early traditionists. Instead, Bakrī's ascension narrative largely leaves the prophetic heavenly hierarchy much more fluid and subject to variation, with one exception. The exception appears in the depiction of two prophets in the heavens that normally do not appear there, namely, David and Solomon, prophets whom the Bakrī narrative almost invariably places in the third heaven.[43] The significance of David and Solomon's relatively fixed position in the heavens in the Bakrī recensions, despite the fluidity in which these texts place other prophets elsewhere in the heavens, will be

THIRD HEAVEN	FOURTH HEAVEN	FIFTH HEAVEN	SIXTH HEAVEN	SEVENTH HEAVEN
m: copper n: al-Muzayyana p: David and Solomon	m: white silver n: al-Khāliṣa p: Angel of Death, Adam	m: gold n: al-Zāhira p: Half-Half angel, Guard. of Hellfire	m: none n: none p: Moses, Jesus	m: ruby n: al-Jama'a p: Abraham, Mikāʾīl, Rooster
m: silver n: none p: Enoch and Elijah	m: pure gold n: none p: Aaron	m: pearl n: none p: Moses	m: emerald n: none p: Abraham	m: ruby n: none p: Adam

discussed below. Suffice it to say here that the Bakrī recensions further develop scenes and symbols drawn from the Primitive Version, as well as from later composite narratives, such as those transmitted by Qummī and Thaᶜlabī, that clearly build upon the Primitive Version.

MUḤAMMAD'S JOURNEY BEYOND THE SEVEN HEAVENS IN BAKRĪ TEXTS

The manner in which the Bakrī ascension narrative expands upon the Primitive Version of the Ibn ᶜAbbās ascension narrative becomes even more clear when we examine the way each describes Muḥammad's journey through the highest realms prior to his arrival at God's throne. Recall how in the Primitive Version, in the highest spheres beyond the seventh heaven Muḥammad leaves Gabriel and climbs on a green vehicle called the *rafraf* just prior to the Prophet's audience with God. Bakrī's version of the ascension takes the basic format of the Primitive Version and expands on the scenes that Muḥammad describes between the time he leaves Gabriel and the point at which he enters into the divine presence. Bakrī modifies the Primitive Version's depiction of the upperworldly seas, focusing less on their material composition (Light, Darkness, Fire, Water, etc.) and more on their color (White, Green, Yellow, Black). Just as Muḥammad becomes afraid upon his vision of the Sea of Darkness in the Primitive Version, he is wracked with terror upon his vision of the Black Sea in the Bakrī recensions. In the former version, Gabriel still accompanies Muḥammad and is thus able to comfort him and decrease his terror, but in the latter Muḥammad has left Gabriel far behind at the Lote Tree, and thus Bakrī relies upon a "voice from above" or an intervention by archangels Mikāʾīl (Michael) or Isrāfīl to serve in the role of Muḥammad's comforter. The scenes describing these archangels and Muḥammad's interactions with them become typical features of the majority of Bakrī-inspired ascension narratives. Mikāʾīl usually appears in or near one of the terrifying seas,[44] comforting Muḥammad and explaining to him the names of the greatest angels; Isrāfīl usually appears subsequently near the realms of the multiple veils, pointing Muḥammad to glance upward for his first view of God's throne, explaining to him the mysteries of God's speech, and sometimes leading him past a number of the veils between Isrāfīl's regular station and the throne.[45] Muḥammad's leaving not only Gabriel but also Michael and Isrāfīl behind thus proves his ability to proceed even further than these highest of archangels. In the Bakrī recensions, after leaving the archangels behind Muḥammad finally arrives at a veil named the Veil of Oneness (*waḥdāniyya*), a stage immediately preceding his audience with God. In the majority of Bakrī recensions, a sweet drop lands in Muḥammad's mouth as he approaches the throne, and this liquid conveys to him some type of knowledge and strengthens him for his encounter with the divinity.[46] Many of these details do not appear in extant ascension narratives that can be definitively dated prior to the seventh / thirteenth century, and thus it is possible to conjecture that Bakrī's ascension narrative was among the first, if not the first, to collate these details into the story of Muḥammad's ascension.

As in the approach to the throne, Bakrī's depiction of the intimate colloquy between Muḥammad and God at the divine throne expands on the Primitive Version and all other early ascension narratives, developing and modifying some of the previous tropes and including several new tropes not seen in previous narratives. It covers the principle conversation topics familiar from the Primitive Version, namely the final verses of the Cow chapter, the heavenly host debate, and the favor of the prophets dialogue themes. However, it briefly precedes these major colloquy tropes with the inclusion of other details, such as the formulaic phrases that Muḥammad and God use to greet one another.[47] In the earliest dated recension, we find a trope that was to gain prominence in later Ibn ʿAbbās ascension narratives, the idea that God instructs Muḥammad to keep wearing his sandals instead of taking them off the way Moses had done in God's presence.[48] In a few more recensions of Bakrī's narrative, God asks Muḥammad about how the latter recognized that he was in the presence of the divinity, and / or to explain the latter's vision of God, remarkable queries in that they satisfy the curiosity of the theologically inclined members of the audience but do so by making God appear less than all-knowing and forced to ask Muḥammad questions.[49]

These additions to the intimate colloquy scene serve several purposes at once. First, they instruct the Muslim audience on the proper way to greet one another.[50] Second, they reemphasize the supreme favor that God granted to Muḥammad on the night of the ascension. Third, they answer the objections of some scholars about the nature of Muḥammad's vision of God, an issue debated since the earliest period of written ascension narratives. The fact that only the first of these tropes appears in all the extant Bakrī recensions (that of the greetings exchanged at the beginning of the colloquy) suggests that the majority of those who circulated the Bakrī ascension narrative were more interested in the requirements of good storytelling than in the subtleties of scholarly debate.

With regard to storytelling, all the recensions of the colloquy scene directly ascribed to Bakrī contain a short anecdote that uses allegorical symbolism to express the idea that God sanctions and in fact requires the violence that besets the Muslim community. Chapter 4 discussed a Shīᶜī ascension narrative in which Muḥammad sees a representation of the messianic Mahdi and/or Imam ᶜAlī in the heavens wielding a sword, and one version specifically calls the sword that ᶜAlī wields a "Sword of Vengeance." Here the same anecdote has been appropriated and transformed, for in this instance no figure wields the sword that Muḥammad sees, rather it merely appears on its own, suddenly hanging on the side of God's throne. Muḥammad asks for this bloody sword, often also named in the Bakrī recensions the "Sword of Vengeance" (*sayf al-naqma*), to be lifted from his community, a request that God refuses to grant on the pretext that the sword serves a specific function in God's plan (especially in expanding the Muslim community through military victory).[51] This hanging sword anecdote graphically makes use of the storyteller's art to convey a message about the necessity, if not the desirability, of sacred warfare. It differs significantly from other portions of the intimate colloquy scene in that it depicts God as denying Muḥammad's wishes, in direct tension with God's promise to "give [Muḥammad] contentment and beyond contentment."[52] By God refusing this request but wishing to bring the Prophet satisfaction nonetheless, this sword anecdote prepares the reader for Muḥammad's success in interceding with God for the ultimate salvation of a portion (but not the whole) of his community.

The Bakrī colloquy scene develops the intercession scene, as well as its related favor of the prophets and bestowal of gifts dialogues, in innovative ways not seen before this version of the ascension narrative. Just as the Bakrī narratives almost invariably include David and Solomon in Muḥammad's description of the third heaven, so too they nearly always mention these figures as prophets with whom Muḥammad compares himself in the favor of the prophets conversation, with Muḥammad being granted dominions that surpass even those of these great kings of Israel. God gives David a portion of God's revelation, so God gives Muḥammad superior revelations in the form of the Opening *sūra* of the Qurᵓān (*al-Fātiḥa*, Q 1), as well as the entire Qurᵓān itself.[53] Furthermore, a couple of the Bakrī recensions mention how God responds to Muḥammad's complaint that Adam and/or Jesus was created directly through God's agency by recounting how Muḥammad was originally created out of God's light.[54] Among the gifts that God grants to Muḥammad, beyond the heavenly rivers of *Kawthar* and *Salsabīl*, is the power to intercede on behalf of his community. Although the power will only be fully exercised on judgment day, the Bakrī recensions illustrate examples of Muḥammad requesting God's assurances of the salvation of his community. In the earliest recension, Muḥammad asks God to forgive his community, and God promises paradise to seventy Muslims who otherwise deserve to go to hellfire.[55] In another Bakrī recension copied approximately two centuries later, God grants paradise to seventy million, and Muḥammad follows this boon with the request to God, "Increase it for me (*zidnī*)."[56] While in the latter recension God refuses to specify the exact number that he will forgive, two undated recensions describe how God responds to Muḥammad's request for increase by granting Muḥammad salvation for seventy thousand times seventy thousand (4,900,000,000).[57] A comparison between the early Bakrī recensions and the later versions of the Ibn ᶜAbbās ascension narrative demonstrates that over time the numbers become more and more hyperbolic, depicting Muḥammad as petitioning God for the salvation for an increasingly larger proportion of his community. He returns again and again with the request "Increase it for me," to the point that in later versions Muḥammad requests, unsuccessfully, to be granted the ability of being able to decide who among his community will go to paradise and who among them will go to hellfire.[58] Despite God's withholding this final boon, maintaining his own prerogative over judgment, God nevertheless promises Muḥammad to be beneficent toward the Muslim community. Such intercession passages illustrate the zeal with which later copyists and transmitters of the Bakrī version of the Ibn ᶜAbbās ascension narrative expanded the intercession scenes and their increasingly exaggerated depictions of God's promise for the eschatological welfare of the Muslim community.

Along with the generous gifts with which God showers the Muslim community in the ascension narratives attributed to Bakrī, these narratives also depict God as imposing duties on the Muslim community that go beyond the fifty daily ritual prayers (which are eventually reduced to five through Muḥammad's pleas) familiar from other ascension narratives. Most interestingly, Bakrī claims that God originally imposes six months of fasting upon the Muslim community, only decreasing it to one month (the month of Ramaḍān) following Muḥammad's pleas for a reduction of the duty.[59] One might conjecture that this trope was added to Bakrī's recension in order to portray the Muslim duty to fast for a month as a merciful reduction from the much heavier duty that God originally intended to impose. In later recensions of the Ibn ᶜAbbās ascension narrative, other central Muslim devotional duties will be added to the list that God reveals to Muḥammad at the conclusion of their intimate colloquy scene, including the pilgrimage to Mecca (*ḥajj*) and the struggling in the way of God (*jihād fī sabīl Allāh*).[60] These citations could be explained by a desire to portray God as imposing many of Islam's central "pillars" all at once, in a clear and unambiguous fashion, and perhaps to elevate the call to struggle on the par with other central Muslim devotional duties. No matter how one interprets these extra duties that God imposes upon Muḥammad on the night of the ascension, one must recognize that they are rarely found outside the group of texts associated with the Ibn ᶜAbbās ascension genre, and the imposition of extra fasting months may reflect a particular innovation conceived by the compiler of the Bakrī ascension narrative.

Before examining the early development of the Bakrī narrative, let us conclude this exploration of the narrative's distinctive features by simply noting that the texts attributed to Bakrī contain some of the most developed and extended tours of paradise and tours of hellfire of all the premodern Islamic ascension narratives. In the earliest Bakrī recension, these tours appear sequentially immediately after the intimate colloquy, at the very end of the heavenly ascension account.[61] In this recension, Muḥammad describes his tours in some detail, listing such features as the names of the eight gardens, the phrases written over each gate to paradise, the way the birds of paradise reappear after being eaten, and so on, as well as the names of each level of hellfire and its respective type of punishment. In the majority of other Bakrī recensions the tour of hellfire is launched from the fifth heaven, occasioned by Muḥammad's encounter with Mālik, the Guardian of Hellfire, or with his finding of a door that leads from the fifth heaven to the lowest depths of Jahannam. In any case, the tour of both paradise and hellfire from the earliest recension becomes supplemented,[62] substituted,[63] and greatly expanded,[64] by other Bakrī recensions. While it is beyond the scope of this work to explore these tour scenes in detail,[65] the extant evidence shows that these scenes gained greater and greater prominence in the ascension narrative beginning around the seventh / thirteenth century. Although one should also not underestimate the importance of the rise of illustrated *Miᶜrājnāma* collections at about the same time, and their influence on these scenes of eschatological reward and punishment, nevertheless one might conjecture that the Bakrī ascension narratives served as another impetus contributing to this new eschatological turn.[66]

DATING THE ASCENSION NARRATIVES ASCRIBED TO ABŪ AL-ḤASAN BAKRĪ

So far this chapter has proceeded under the assumption that the five extant manuscripts attributed to a figure named Abū al-Ḥasan Bakrī can be studied as a collectivity, and that they offer a window onto a new narrative approach to Muḥammad's night journey and ascension that can be associated with Bakrī's name. The remainder of this chapter will explore the available evidence justifying such an assumption, beginning with the evidence from the Istanbul manuscript which suggests that this Bakrī ascension genre was in circulation by the end of the seventh / thirteenth century at the latest. Although other versions of the ascension narrative explicitly attributed to Bakrī date from later centuries, the next chapter will argue that versions of this Bakrī narrative were known in western Islamic lands by the sixth / twelfth century.

The long and detailed Bakrī text that serves as the basis for the overview of the Bakrī ascension narrative above, *Ḥadīth al-mi*ᶜ*rāj* ᶜ*alā al-tamām wa'l-kamāl* found in Istanbul Süleymaniye Kütüphanesi MS Amcazade Hüsayın Paşa 95 / 2, appears to have been copied in the last quarter of the seventh / thirteenth century in the Rasūlid court of what is now Yemen. Even though this ascension text does not itself have a colophon giving information about when and where it was copied, comparisons between it and the text that precedes it in the same manuscript, *Kitāb* ᶜ*arba*ᶜ*īn ḥadīth al-muẓaffariyya* (Istanbul Süleymaniye Kütüphanesi MS Amcazade Hüsayın Paşa 95 / 1, fols. 1r–26r), offer some proof for such a provenance.[67] The work *Kitāb* ᶜ*arba*ᶜ*īn ḥadīth* with which the manuscript opens is a collection of forty *ḥadīth* reports collated by the Rasūlid Sultan Abū Manṣūr Yūsuf (al-Muẓaffar) b. ᶜUmar b. ᶜAlī b. Rasūl (d. 694 / 1295).[68] This Rasūlid Sultan's name appears in the text on the frontispiece to the first work,[69] and it also appears in an *ijāza* statement appended to the end of the same and dated 679 / 1280.[70] The Arabic handwriting throughout the entire manuscript can be said to be from a single hand, written in a *naskh* style typical of the seventh / thirteenth-century Mamluk era.[71] Moreover, the frontispieces decorating both texts have the exact same dimensions and a nearly identical layout, and they resemble other Mamluk-style frontispieces from the same century.[72] Given these correspondences, one can fairly safely conclude that the Bakrī ascension work copied immediately after the Muẓaffar collection of forty *ḥadīth*, and in the same hand, was most likely also copied in or around the Rasūlid court in the last quarter of the seventh / thirteenth century. If this dating can be sustained, it offers for the very first time proof that a figure named Abū al-Ḥasan Bakrī, or someone transmitting *ḥadīth* in his name, composed this ascension text prior to the end of the seventh / thirteenth century. When one recalls that the Vatican copy of Bakrī's biography of Muḥammad, Vatican MS Borg 125, dates from 694 / 1295, and that polemics against Bakrī and his work first appear at the beginning of the eighth / fourteenth century,[73] one gets the impression that these Bakrī texts achieved a certain degree of circulation in the seventh / thirteenth century.

One needs to be clear that the other extant copies of the Bakrī ascension narrative either are dated to after the seventh / thirteenth century or remain completely undated, and they preserve variant recensions that diverge from Amcazade 95/2 to greater or lesser degrees. The next recension whose date can be established definitively, based upon the evidence from its colophon, was copied two centuries after Amcazade 95/2.[74] Nevertheless, I have treated the "Bakrī ascension narratives" together for the simple reason that their shared features, detailed throughout this chapter, outweigh their divergences. These similar features show how the Bakrī narratives take the basic framework of the Primitive Version of the Ibn ᶜAbbās ascension narrative, adding to it the account of Muḥammad's night journey to Jerusalem, and expanding the whole into what its compiler terms a more "total and complete" narrative, as illustrated in the following chart (table 2).

We have seen that other ascension narratives, such as those provided by Qummī and Thaᶜlabī in their Qurᵓān commentaries, similarly supplement the Primitive Version with other reports in order to form a more complete narrative. What is distinctive about the Bakrī versions of the narrative centers less around this method and more around the details added to the story. The Bakrī narrative almost invariably contains certain stock narrative elements. It contains a rich description of the otherworldly beings that Muḥammad encounters (e.g., the extensive description of Burāq, or his long conversations with angels such as the polycephalous angel, Mikāᵓīl, Isrāfīl, and the Angel of Death). It provides illustrations of the fallibility and/or humanity of the Prophet (e.g., his initially being tempted by the beautiful woman on the path to Jerusalem, or his failure to drink all the milk in the cup test, or his fearing for his life during the ascension). If offers details about the highest heavens (e.g., leaving Gabriel at the Lote Tree before preceding to the highest stages of the journey, the specifics about the veils and seas that Muḥammad crosses on his way to the throne). It supplements the core narrative elements of the intimate colloquy scene, supplementing them with other details (e.g., the sweet drop, the sword, and the highly developed intercession scenes). The Bakrī versions differ from one another, but they contain enough common elements to justify classifying them as a distinctive category of Islamic ascension narrative.

Dating the earliest Bakrī ascension report to the last quarter of the seventh/thirteenth century has provided further evidence in support of the argument of Rosenthal and others that Abū Ḥasan Bakrī must have lived prior to 694/1295, and perhaps even earlier.[75] Since the basic contours of the Bakrī narratives were established prior to the end of that century, and since one of the longest and most detailed versions of these narratives was in circulation by then, the fact that the majority of the extant manuscripts that mention Bakrī by name either have no date or were copied later does not invalidate the thesis that this distinctive "Bakrī genre" of ascension narratives can be treated as examples of the types of reports about the Prophet's journey that circulated in Bakrī's name near the end of the formative period of Islamic history.

Table 2 Comparison and Contrast between the Primitive and the Bakrī Versions

P.V. OF IBN ʿABBĀS ASCENSION NARRATIVE	FEATURES OF THE BAKRĪ ASCENSION NARRATIVES
• No night journey to Jerusalem present in the Primitive Version	• Dark night, house of Umm Hāniʾ, Gabriel in True Form wakes Prophet • Opening of Chest largely absent • Burāq described in detail, has human face, and has conversation with Gabriel • On road to Jerusalem, Muḥammad addressed by Jews and Christians • Muḥammad attracted by woman • Descends and prays at Sinai (only) • Encounter with youth near Jerusalem • Meets all prophets in Jerusalem • Refrains from drinking all the milk
• *Miʿrāj*-ladder not described	• *Miʿrāj*-ladder and steps described
• No material or names of heavens given	• Material and/or names of heavens often given
• Meets Rooster and wondrous angels	• Meets Rooster and wondrous angels
• Encounter Mālik, has vision of hellfire	• Encounters Mālik and tours hellfire
• Meets ʿAzrāʾīl, asks about methods	• Meets ʿAzrāʾīl, asks about methods
• Meets no prophets during the ascent; some upon descent	• Meets prophets during ascent, David and Solomon in the 3rd heaven
• Meets immense angels, e.g., Cherubim	• Meets immense angels, e.g., Cherubim, sometimes given specific names (e.g., guardians) and often meets in the seventh heaven 70,000-headed angel with as many mouths, tongues, etc.
• Muḥammad does not pray with angels	• Muḥammad leads the angels, and sometimes the prophets of each heaven, in two cycles of prayer
• Seas of light, fire, darkness, water	• Seas of different colors, and/or seas of light, fire, darkness, water
• Gabriel stops after the seas, before the throne	• Gabriel stops before the seas, often at the Lote Tree of the Boundary
• No encounter with Mikāʾīl or Isrāfīl	• Detailed encounters with both Mikāʾīl and Isrāfīl in the highest realms
• Vision of God in heart, God touches Muḥammad with his cold hand	• Vision of God in heart, rarely cold hand, sometimes adds sweet drop
• Colloquy: Heavenly Host Debate, Seals of Cow Chapter, Favor of the Prophets, Gifts	• Colloquy: Greetings, Heavenly Host Debate, Seals of Cow, Favor of the Prophets, Sword, Gifts, Intercession
• No mention of duties (no fifty prayers)	• Receives fifty prayers, six months fasting
• Detailed tour of paradise	• Detailed tour of paradise
• Abrupt conclusion	• Return to Mecca described
• No mention of debates in Mecca	• Debates in Mecca, Vision of Jerusalem

9

THE CIRCULATION AND DIFFUSION OF BAKRĪ'S VERSIONS

Without entering into the debate over the historicity of Bakrī himself, let us turn to evidence for the wide circulation of Bakrī versions of Muḥammad's ascension prior to the end of the seventh/thirteenth century, as well as evidence for the broad circulation of similar narratives up through the end of this formative period. The creative spark for this new discourse can be credited to Bakrī even though only a handful of texts mention Bakrī by name, for each of the texts in this group bears a family resemblance to the others. Assembling and examining this disparate evidence sheds new light on the historical development and spread of this influential genre. Together, the texts offer evidence for what essentially constitutes a watershed moment in the development of the Islamic ascension discourse, the formation of a reshaped and widely dispersed version of the Ibn ʿAbbās ascension narrative. This reshaped version, while put to distinct uses in different contexts, appears to have appealed especially to Sunnī scholars beginning in the seventh/thirteenth century, who championed it as a means to propagate a particular Sunnī approach to the interpretation of Muḥammad's night journey and ascension.

The extant evidence suggests that the first strands of this ascension discourse were woven in the eastern lands of Islamdom, beginning with the narrative threads spun in accounts like the Primitive Version that focused on angelology and the wonders of Muḥammad's heavenly journey. An examination of the *isnād* chains appended to the extant copies of the Primitive Version point to its eastern circulation, as does the fact that this particular narrative was first recorded by Ibn Ḥibbān and Qushayrī in and around Nishapur (chapters 2 and 7). The Primitive Version may have emerged out of the eastern lands, but the discourse gradually spread to the other end of Islamdom as well.

Two early narratives from the opposite geographical extremes of Islamdom help to demonstrate the existence of a more developed "Bakrī" narrative prior to the seventh/thirteenth century, one that collated the "wonders of the ascension" together with a fuller account of Muḥammad's journey. One appears in an early narrative used by the famous Muslim philosopher of the eastern lands, Ibn Sīnā, as the base text for his discussion of the night journey and ascension as a Neoplatonic allegory. The second appears a century or so after Ibn Sīnā's work, represented by Madrid MS. Gayangos 241, which was copied in the western Islamic lands and appears to possess many of the features of the Bakrī versions. Other *ḥadīth* reports had previously told full and rich accounts of Muḥammad's journey (especially those discussed in chapters 6 and 7), yet Ibn Sīnā's text and Gayangos 241 point to the early development of an independent narrative strand that fills out the broad pattern set by the Primitive Version in order to tell an angelically focused yet complete night journey and ascension story that relates closely to the Bakrī versions described in chapter 8. It is to the examination of these two early and widely dispersed "Bakrī" narratives that we now turn.

THE BASE NARRATIVE BEHIND IBN SĪNĀ'S ALLEGORICAL TREATISE

As mentioned above, the pivotal Muslim philosopher Abū ᶜAlī Ḥusayn Ibn Sīnā (known in Europe as Avicenna, d. 428/1037) composed a treatise drawing upon Muḥammad's night journey and ascension as a philosophical allegory illustrating his Neoplatonic thought.[1] Ibn Sīnā served under Būyid (Buwayhid) prince Shams al-Dawla (d. 412/1021) of Hamadhan, and he then served at the court of ᶜĀlāᵓ al-Dawla Kākūyī (d. 433/1041–42) in Isfahan. According to Peter Heath, Ibn Sīnā probably composed his Persian-language *Miᶜrājnāma* soon after arriving at the latter Kākūyid court in the last fifteen years of his life (ca. 413/1022).[2] Learned discussions of the Prophet's journey and its interpretation were circulating in the region during this period,[3] which likely served as an impetus for Ibn Sīnā to explore the underlying spiritual truths behind the narrative.[4] Apart from the allegorical meanings Ibn Sīnā finds in the narrative, more relevant to this study is the "base narrative" on which he constructs his philosophical edifice.[5] Key elements of this narrative extracted from the midst of Ibn Sīnā's commentary, forming a story of the Prophet's ascent that must have been in circulation by the beginning of the fifth/eleventh century, bear a striking resemblance to the Bakrī version of the Ibn ᶜAbbās ascension narrative.

The precursor to and description of Muḥammad's night journey from Mecca to Jerusalem, absent in the Primitive Version, appears in Ibn Sīnā's narrative with details quite similar to the Bakrī versions described in chapter 8. As in the Bakrī versions, Ibn Sīnā's base text describes the initial setting of the tale as a dark, stormy, yet mysteriously silent night, in which Gabriel descends to Muḥammad in his true created form (with the testimony of Muslim witness known as the *shahāda* emblazoned on his forehead).[6] As in the Bakrī versions, in Ibn Sīnā's base text Gabriel shows affection to the Prophet upon his arrival: "He embraced me and kissed me between my two eyes and said, 'O Sleeper, arise!"[7] As in almost every Bakrī version extant, Ibn Sīnā's base text offers no reference to the idea that the angels opened Muḥammad's heart prior to his journey. Instead, Gabriel brings Muḥammad directly to Burāq, who as in the Bakrī versions is described as having a human face.[8] These parallel details from the opening of the story in both Ibn Sīnā's base text and in the Bakrī versions make probable some sort of connection between the two accounts.

Both the Ibn Sīnā base narrative and the Bakrī versions demonstrate the limits of Muḥammad's guidance and insight during the cup test in Jerusalem, for as in the Ibn Hishām recension of Ibn Isḥāq's night journey account, they depict the angels as leading Muḥammad to the correct choice of the cup full of milk. Recall that in the Bakrī versions, Muḥammad selects the milk on the advice and guidance of the angels, but he misses an opportunity to secure paradise for all his followers, for he fails to drink all the milk. While not mentioning such eschatological consequences, Ibn Sīnā's base narrative depicts Muḥammad's own personal temptation as being more serious, for it records the Prophet as saying, "I wanted to take the wine [but] Gabriel did not allow [this]. He pointed to the milk, so I took [it] and drank."[9] Given that Ibn Sīnā interprets this detail in his commentary as an allegory for the human tendency to obey the natural and animal souls rather than the rational soul,[10] it is certainly possible that Ibn Sīnā modified the base narrative slightly in order for it better to fit his philosophical system. The Prophet's temptation to fall prey to his desire for wine here resembles his temptation depicted in most recensions of the Bakrī version to respond to the calls of the beautiful woman on the road to Jerusalem.[11] Despite the different context for Muḥammad's temptation, the Ibn Sīnā narrative shares with the Bakrī versions the idea of Muḥammad as fallible, as subject to temptation. Such a position contrasts sharply with the vast majority of other early ascension narratives, which depict Muḥammad's unfailing correct selections and choices as evidence of his perfect natural disposition (*fiṭra*). The parallel once again offers support for the idea that the Bakrī versions and the Ibn Sīnā base narrative come from a similar intellectual milieu.

The parallels between the Ibn Sīnā base text and the Bakrī versions become even more evident in their accounts of the Prophet's journey through the levels of the heavens. Some of these parallels may be explained by the fact that both texts draw upon the Primitive Version of the Ibn ʿAbbās ascension narrative, for figures such as the Half-Fire-Half-Snow angel, the Guardian of Hellfire named Mālik, the devotedly worshipping angels known as the Rūḥāniyyūn, and so on, all find their place in the heavens in Ibn Sīnā's base text.[12] Yet Ibn Sīnā's base text goes beyond the Primitive Version by placing many of these angels in distinct levels of the seven heavens (in lieu of placing a single prophet in the heavens, as done by other narratives that incorporate the Primitive Version), and their order resembles one familiar from a number of Bakrī narratives. For example, the angel Isma^cīl appears in the first heaven, sitting on a throne.[13] In the fifth heaven, Muḥammad meets the Guardian of Hellfire, and learns about that realm by witnessing Mālik tormenting its inhabitants.[14] After passing four seas of different colors (again, familiar from the Bakrī recensions), Muḥammad comes to a boundless sea in which he meets the archangel Mikā'īl, who answers Muḥammad's questions.[15] The way that Ibn Sīnā's base narrative supplements the Primitive Version with these angelic tropes found in the Bakrī version, while nevertheless dwelling exclusively on the angels and not collating the descriptions of any human prophets into its text, gives the impression that Ibn Sīnā's angelically focused base narrative reflects an early stage in the development of the Ibn ᶜAbbās ascension narratives.

The place of Ibn Sīnā's base narrative as a stage in the development of the Ibn ᶜAbbās ascension, related to both the Primitive Version and the Bakrī Versions but identical with neither, can be illustrated through an examination of its concise intimate colloquy scene.

> When he brought me to the Presence of Glory, the command came to me: "Draw nearer!" I did not see sensation or movement in that Presence. I only saw tranquility, stillness, and sufficiency. From being in awe of God, I forgot everything that I had seen and known. Such unveiling, grandeur, and pleasure from proximity was produced that you would say that I was intoxicated. So affected was I by proximity that I began to tremble. The command was coming, "Draw nearer!" When I drew nearer, He said, "Fear not, be calm!" When I drew nearer, God's greeting came to me through a voice the like of which I had never heard. The command came, "Praise!" I said, "'I do not enumerate your praises, for you have praised yourself.' I am unable [to say] the like of what you yourself have said." The command came, "Desire something!" I said, "Give permission that whatever [problem] I encounter, I [can] ask until its difficulties are solved."[16]

The first half of this passage closely resembles the corresponding passage in the Bakrī versions, especially in its depiction of the disembodied divine voice calling from above, commanding Muḥammad to advance, and instructing him not to fear.[17] The second half of it, however, which briefly describes two topics of conversation in the intimate colloquy, diverges from the Bakrī versions. The initial divine command "Praise!" invokes in Muḥammad the *ḥadīth*, "I do not enumerate your praises, for you have praised yourself," a trope appearing in other ascension anecdotes and treatises ascribed to Sufi masters, but otherwise not frequently attested in ascension literature.[18] Presumably some of the Sufis had collated that *ḥadīth* into their accounts of the ascension, and Ibn Sīnā's base narrative follows suit. The other command that God gives in the intimate colloquy of Ibn Sīnā's Persian base narrative, "Desire something!" (*chīzī bikhwāh*)[19] here takes the place of the phrase familiar from the Arabic Ibn ᶜAbbās ascension narratives, "Ask and be given!" (*sal tuᶜṭā*). Nevertheless, Muḥammad's response in the Ibn Sīnā passage, his request for the ability to solve difficulties, appears unique to this text within the Islamic ascension tradition.[20] It nicely fits with the worldview of the *falāsifa*, lovers of wisdom who continually pose and seek answers to philosophical questions. Given this close fit with Ibn Sīnā's own positionality, it is again possible that Ibn Sīnā inserted this detail into the base ascension narrative in order to serve his allegorical interpretation and philosophical agenda, which could help to explain the degree to which it differs from the Bakrī versions of the Ibn ᶜAbbās ascension narrative.

These minor differences aside, the base narrative of Muḥammad's ascension that Ibn Sīnā uses in the composition of his allegorical *Miᶜrājnāma* demonstrates some intriguing correspondences with both the Primitive Version and the Bakrī versions of the Ibn ᶜAbbās ascension discourse. Perhaps its most intriguing feature is its lack of human prophets, similar to their virtual absence from the Primitive Version.[21] Also noteworthy is its description of Mālik, the Guardian of Hellfire, in the fifth heaven, and of the archangel Mikāʾīl in the upper ocean close to the divine throne, both of which correspond closely with the description of these figures in the majority of the Bakrī texts. The base narrative that Ibn Sīnā uses for his allegory (but not his allegorical ideas themselves) therefore appear to represent something of an intermediate position between the Primitive Version and the Bakrī versions of the Ibn ᶜAbbās discourse.

Let us conclude our discussion of Ibn Sīnā's philosophical treatise by noting that such an allegorical approach to the Prophet's ascension is by no means unique, as illustrated by the similar approach recorded in a number of treatises and chapters of famous works attributed to the celebrated western Sufi, the "Grand Shaykh" Ibn ᶜArabī (d. 638/1240). Scholars interpret a short treatise known as *al-Isrāʾ ilā al-maqām al-asrāʾ* as describing Ibn ᶜArabī's own visionary ascension at the end of the sixth/twelfth century, its symbolic stages clearly drawing their inspiration from Muḥammad's journey.[22] In his celebrated work *Futuḥāt al-makkiyya*, several chapters also explore Ibn ᶜArabī's allegorical approach to Muḥammad's journey, basing their commentary largely upon those versions of the narrative reported in the canonical Sunnī *ḥadīth* collections.[23] A short treatise attributed to Ibn ᶜArabī that is of particular interest to our discussion of Ibn Sīnā's allegorical work is one entitled "*Shajarat al-Kawn*," for while the entire treatise is not dedicated to Muḥammad's ascension, its final section offers a philosophical and mystical commentary on an account of the night journey and ascension that bears significant resemblances to the "base narrative" of Bakrī's versions. It depicts Gabriel as coming to Muḥammad on the night of the ascension and commanding him to arise (and as later asking for the Prophet's intercession), depicts Muḥammad interacting with Mikāʾīl, Isrāfīl, and the Throne, and depicts the intimate colloquy scene as beginning with the sweet drop episode and the standard exchange of greetings.[24] As one finds in Ibn Sīnā's colloquy scene, "*Shajarat al-Kawn*" quotes Muḥammad as expressing his inability to praise as God has praised God's self.[25] Although "*Shajarat al-Kawn*" is an obscure treatise that may or may not represent an authentic work of Ibn ᶜArabī, it nevertheless attests to the spread and influence of the reworked Ibn ᶜAbbās narrative in western circles of Islamdom.

EVIDENCE FROM SIXTH/TWELFTH-CENTURY NORTH AFRICA

By drawing on the distinctive "Bakrī" features outlined in chapter 8, one can compare these features to those from a fragmentary early text in order to support the conjecture that the basic framework of the Bakrī narrative must predate the seventh/thirteenth century. The text in question appears in a manuscript fragment summarized a century ago by Miguel Asín Palacios, Madrid MS Gayangos 241.[26] The style of its Arabic calligraphy and the vertical chain watermarking on its paper support Asín Palacios' proposed dating of the manuscript to the sixth/twelfth century. Its calligraphic peculiarities, however, may well point to a North African provenance, rather than the Andalusian provenance that Asín Palacios proposed.[27] Whether copied in North Africa or al-Andalus, the important fact for our purposes remains that Gayangos 241 predates our earliest dated recension of Bakrī's ascension narrative, Amcazade 95/2, by a century or more.

Unfortunately both the beginning and ending of Gayangos 241 are no longer extant, and what is left of the text describes Muḥammad's journey from his encounter with ᶜAzrāʾīl, the Angel of Death, in the fourth heaven[28] up through a portion of the favor of the prophets trope in the midst of the intimate colloquy scene. Even with such fragmentary remains, and even without an introduction or colophon that could help to situate this particular ascension fragment in a specific milieu, the text contains enough details in common with the Bakrī ascension narrative to merit the exploration of the meaning of this commonality. A likely explanation is that the original full narrative of this text, of which a portion survives in Gayangos 241, has at its base either an early recension of the Bakrī version or else another highly developed Ibn ᶜAbbās ascension narrative.

To test out this hypothesis, one merely needs to examine Gayangos 241 with reference to the features of the Bakrī versions described above in chapter 8. For example, in the former's account of the fourth heaven at the start of its fragmentary text, Gayangos 241 contains the trope familiar since the Primitive Version of the Ibn ᶜAbbās ascension narrative in which Muḥammad meets ᶜAzrāᵓīl, the Angel of Death, and he questions this angel briefly about his methods in harvesting the souls of the dead.[29] Just as in Gayangos 241, this scene takes place in the fourth heaven in the majority of the Bakrī recensions.[30] Muḥammad meets the prophet Idrīs (Enoch) in the fourth heaven and is commanded to lead him and the angels of the fourth heaven in two cycles of ritual prayer. With its account of the fifth heaven missing,[31] Gayangos 241 goes on to describe how in the sixth heaven Muḥammad sees a polycephalous angel on a throne made of light, here given the name Dardayaᵓīl.[32] This Dardayaᵓīl has seventy thousand faces, each with seventy thousand mouths, each with seventy thousand tongues, each praising God with seventy thousand different languages, a repetitive and hyperbolic image well established by the identically featured polycephalous angel who often appears in the seventh heaven in the Bakrī narratives.[33] Gabriel commands Muḥammad to advance and lead this angel, together with the other angels of the sixth heaven and the prophet Aaron (Hārūn), in two cycles of ritual prayer.[34] With Muḥammad leading these two cycles of prayer in each of the heavens, it becomes clear that the account of these heavens in Gayangos 241 follows the exact pattern that one finds over and over again at the end of the account of each heaven in the majority of the Bakrī texts. Such examples of parallels between the Bakrī versions of Muḥammad's ascension and Gayangos 241 could easily be multiplied.

Throughout the fragmentary narrative in Gayangos 241 one continues to find such parallels as the narrative progresses to the highest levels of Muḥammad's journey. The parallels range from the colorful seas that Muḥammad crosses after passing the Lote Tree, to his paradigmatic encounters with Mikāᵓīl and Isrāfīl, from the veils that he traverses on his way to the divine throne, to the specifics of his intimate colloquy with God (which includes the greetings, the discussion of the vision of God, and the sword anecdote, among others). As the fragmentary text of Gayangos 241 comes to an abrupt and premature end, God is in the midst of describing the favors that he has bestowed upon Muḥammad. In this version of the favor of the prophets passage, God informs Muḥammad that he will receive favors that are just as desirable and even better than those that he has bestowed upon David and Solomon.[35] Gayangos 241 even contains some less common details found in only select Bakrī versions, such as its extensive description of the enormous snake that God created around the divine throne as a way to humble it.[36] The accumulated depth and breadth of the correspondences between Gayangos 241 and the ascension narratives attributed to

Bakrī offer sufficient evidence that an early version of the reshaped Ibn ʿAbbās narrative circulated in the western lands of Islamdom even prior to the beginning of the seventh/thirteenth century.

Although it is impossible definitely to link Gayangos 241 with Abū al-Ḥasan Bakrī, especially given its fragmentary condition, without a doubt this sixth/twelfth-century text shares many features not only with the Primitive Version of the Ibn ʿAbbās ascension narrative but also, and more importantly, with Bakrī ascension narratives such as the one found in Amcazade 95/2. Amcazade 95/2, which was discussed in some detail above in chapter 8, was likely copied in the last quarter of the seventh/thirteenth century in Yemen, Egypt, or one of the other central Arab lands dominated by the Mamluks. There is reason to believe that a version of the same narrative was used in the western lands as the central basis for the complex composite text that comes to be known as the *Liber Scale Machometi* [*Book of Muḥammad's Ladder*].[37]

LIBER SCALE AND THE DIFFUSION OF THE BAKRĪ VERSIONS IN THE SEVENTH/THIRTEENTH CENTURY

The now relatively well-known *Liber Scale* was translated into Castilian at the Spanish court of Alfonso X the Wise (r. 1252–1284), translated into Old French in 1264 CE, and translated into Latin probably around the same time.[38] Since the original Arabic and Castilian versions of the famous *Liber Scale* are no longer extant, and the Latin versions appear to have been made somewhat later, one must turn to the surviving French version for the earliest extant recension of the text.[39] Even a cursory reading of the *Liber Scale* shows that Bakrī's version of the ascension narrative must have been one of its original Arabic sources. Some of the major commonalities appear when one compares central details from these narratives side by side (see table 3).

The *Liber Scale* reports the story of Muḥammad's ascension in the first person, as do all the Bakrī versions.[40] As in almost all the recensions of the Bakrī ascension narrative, the *Liber Scale* insists that Muḥammad was sleeping in the house of Umm Hāniʾ on the night of his journey.[41] Gabriel descends in his true form and tells Muḥammad to arise and put on his belt and shawl, but makes no move to perform the ritual opening of the heart.[42] The *Liber Scale* describes Burāq as having a human face, a detail only rarely seen in the formative period outside the Bakrī texts.[43] While riding Burāq on the way to Jerusalem, Muḥammad encounters the beautiful woman in the road and is tempted to stop for her, but when she approaches he changes his mind and refuses to speak to her: "I waited for her, and when she was near me and wished to speak to me further, with great disdain I left her behind and resumed my course."[44] Upon arriving in Jerusalem, Muḥammad leads the prophets in prayer, and after-

Table 3 Comparison and Contrast between the Bakrī Versions and *Liber Scale*

FEATURES OF THE BAKRĪ ASCENSION NARRATIVES	**FEATURES OF THE FRENCH ED. OF *LIBER SCALE***
• Dark night, house of Umm Hāniʾ, Gabriel in true form wakes Prophet	• Begins in house of Umm Hāniʾ, here: his wife; Gabriel reveals true form
• Opening of Chest largely absent	• No opening of chest
• Burāq described in detail, has human face, and has conversation with Gabriel	• Burāq described in detail, has human face, conversation with Gabriel
• On road to Jerusalem, Muḥammad addressed by Jews and Christians	• On road to Jerusalem, Muḥammad addressed by Jews and Christians
• Muḥammad attracted by woman	• Muḥammad attracted by the woman
• Descends and prays at Sinai (only)	• No command to descend and pray
• Encounter with youth near Jerusalem	• No encounter with youth
• Meets all prophets in Jerusalem	• Meets all the prophets in Jerusalem
• Refrains from drinking all the milk	• Cup Test after divine colloquy, drinks all of each of the four cups except the wine
• *Miʿrāj*-ladder and steps described	• *Miʿrāj*-ladder and steps described
• Material and/or names of heavens often given	• Material of the heavens given, but not names
• Meets Rooster and wondrous angels	• Meets Rooster and wondrous angels
• Encounters Mālik and tours hellfire	• Encounters Mālik; later tour of hell
• Meets ʿAzrāʾīl, asks about methods	• Meets ʿAzrāʾīl, asks about methods
• Meets prophets during ascent, David and Solomon in the third heaven	• Meets prophets during ascent, David and Solomon not there, but Adam in seventh heaven
• Meets immense angels, e.g., Cherubim, sometimes given specific names (e.g., guardians) and often meets in the seventh heaven 70,000-headed angel with as many mouths, tongues, etc.	• Meets immense angels, e.g., Cherubim, and meets in the first heaven 70,000-headed angel with as many mouths, tongues, etc.; one in eighth heaven with as many eyes, pupils, etc.
• Muḥammad leads the angels, and sometimes the prophets of each heaven, in two cycles of prayer	• No mention of leading others in prayer until reaching seventh heaven, leads angels
• Gabriel stops before the seas, often at the Lote Tree of the Boundary	• Gabriel stops at Lote Tree, tells Muḥammad he cannot advance further
• Seas of different colors, and/or seas of light, fire, darkness, water	• Passes seas of light, rivers of light, water, snow, delicious water, in second visit to seventh heaven
• Detailed encounters with both Mikāʾīl and Isrāfīl in the highest realms	• Encounters Raphael and Auquotrofins
• Vision of God in heart, rarely cold hand, sometimes adds sweet drop	• Vision of God revealed to the blessed; no sweet drop, but cold hand
• Colloquy: Greetings, Heavenly Host Debate, Seals of Cow, Favor of the Prophets, Sword, Gifts, Intercession	• Multiple colloquies: Greetings, Duties; then Seals of Cow chap., Heavenly Host Debate, Gifts (entire Qurʾān), Duties
• Receives fifty prayers, six months fasting	• Receives fifty prayers, two months fasting
• Detailed tour of paradise	• Detailed tour of paradise; tour of hell
• Return to Mecca described	• Return to Mecca described
• Debates in Mecca, Vision of Jerusalem	• Debates in Mecca detailed, Gabriel revealing the entire world

ward each of the prophets greets Muḥammad individually, and "and every one of them showed me openly that he desired very much for our Lord God to do me great good and honor."[45] Upon ascending the *mi^crāj* ladder but prior to entering the first heaven, Muḥammad meets the wondrous angels from the beginning of the Primitive Version: the Angel of Death, the Rooster angel, the Half-Fire-Half-Snow angel, and the Guardian of Hellfire. These angels appear in *Liber Scale* in a manner very similar to the way they appear in Amcazade 95/2, and Muḥammad interacts with these angels in a similar fashion in both texts.[46] The parallels run the gamut between rare details found in only select Bakrī texts (e.g., the angels in the form of cows, present only in *Liber Scale* and Amcazade 95/2)[47] to those largely limited to explicitly Bakrī texts and the *Liber Scale* (such as the need to reduce the number of fast days from the initial duty to fast multiple numbers of months down to the final duty simply to fast the month of Ramaḍān).[48] Many more elements could be cited as commonalities between the *Liber Scale,* on the one hand, and the Bakrī texts (and especially the near contemporary of *Liber Scale*, Amcazade 95/2), on the other. These examples should be sufficient, however, to illustrate the depths of the correspondences.

Of course, the *Liber Scale* also presents details not found in any extant Bakrī texts, especially in its lengthy descriptions of eschatological secrets near the end of the narrative's long tour of hellfire. Clearly the *Liber Scale* is a composite text, bringing together narrative elements from multiple sources, to such a degree that some scenes appear multiple times in variant forms throughout the narrative.[49] The point in drawing the above comparisons is not to suggest that the Bakrī ascension narratives represent the missing Arabic source that was translated and thus transformed into the *Liber Scale*. Rather, the quantity and quality of the parallels between the *Liber Scale* and the Bakrī versions prove beyond a reasonable doubt that extensive passages in these texts overlap. Taken together with the evidence from Gayangos 241, these sites of overlap suggest the likelihood that the Bakrī version served as one of the major Arabic sources at the base of the magnificent and complex *Liber Scale* that was translated into European languages in the second half of the seventh/thirteenth century.[50]

AN ANONYMOUS EASTERN PERSIAN *MI^cRĀJNĀMA*

About the same time that *Liber Scale* made its way around the western lands, another version of the Bakrī narrative was translated into Persian in the eastern lands, forming the basis for a recently discovered anonymous prayer manual that was copied circa 685/1286.[51] If the connections between these three key texts can be proven, with the Bakrī versions serving as their common link, the implications would be profound. It would establish that variations of the Bakrī ascension narrative gained such currency that they were being discussed and translated in various elite circles during the second half of the seventh/thirteenth century in disparate regions of Islamdom: the far west, the central lands, and the east. Recently, Christiane Gruber has highlighted the significance of the remarkable Persian text, Istanbul MS. Ayasofya 3441, that she argues represents an Ilkhanid prayer manual copied in the year 685/1286.[52] Gruber makes a convincing case that the narrative differs from other ascension accounts in its attention to the ritual and devotional aspects of the story, emphasizing throughout its narrative the importance of repentance, prayer, and the invocation of pious formulae. She summarizes what she sees as the four basic functions of the text as follows:

> First and foremost, it is a prayer manual used to teach non-native Arabic speakers parts of the Qur'ān and a variety of oral prayers (*duʿā's*). Secondly, it appears as an elaborate forewarning of what lies ahead for those who stray from the right path. Thirdly, it promotes the acceptance of Muḥammad's prophetic miracles and conversion to the Islamic faith through the lessons learned upon the Quraysh's doubting. Lastly, it advances traditional, Sunnī Islam over all other forms of religion and Islamic "heterodox" movements.[53]

While I would not dispute the importance of the first two dimensions that Gruber explores in the narrative, and especially their utility in helping to make sense of Ilkhanid-era ascension paintings, here I would like to examine in more detail the last two dimensions that Gruber identifies, both of which revolve around the use of the ascension narrative as a polemical tool in this anonymous Sunnī author's disputations with members of different religious factions, be they Muslim or non-Muslim.

The ascension text in Ayasofya 3441 offers a complex amalgamation of scenes drawn from earlier narratives, not unlike the approach in the *Liber Scale*, but here the author has supplemented his collation of disparate reports with detailed scholarly excurses. Even before it begins with the telling of the tale, for example, Ayasofya 3441 offers a long philosophical discourse on the ascension of pure bodies and the journeys of the souls of people in sleep, prayer, and mystical ecstasy, insisting that Muḥammad's journey on the night of the ascension was of a different character than that of other human beings.[54] This philosophical preface establishes a pattern that the author returns to throughout the text, privileging his elaborate commentary on the meaning and moral of the story of Muḥammad's ascension over and above preserving the "readability" and narrative coherence of the basic storyline.

The text hardly mentions the idea that the angels open Muḥammad's chest and clean his heart of various desires, for example, when the author launches into what appears to be a curious digression, namely an inquiry into the "two aspects to the *mi*ʿ*rāj*": demonstrating God's power, and demonstrating Muḥammad's exalted station.[55] Denying either aspect of the *mi*ʿ*rāj*, the text asserts, is tantamount to infidelity. It would entail nothing less than supporting the denier's position as represented by Abū Jahl, rather than supporting the believer's position as represented by Abū Bakr.[56] Using rhetorical techniques that suggest the context of religious debate, the anonymous author seeks to establish himself as the defender of the true (and only) faithful Muslim point of view. Just at the point that the reader begins to wonder why Ayasofya 3441 digresses into dichotomous polemics in this way, the text provides an answer: Some critics of the story of Muḥammad's ascension apparently object to the idea of the splitting of Muḥammad's breast, charging that according to the rules of logic, the splitting of Muḥammad's chest should have left the Prophet seriously wounded. Although it remains difficult to determine the religious or philosophical perspective of this unidentified interlocutor, he or she apparently represents the position of one who rejects the idea of prophetic miracles, or one who wishes each element of the tale to conform to the rules of human logic.[57] The anonymous author replies to this objection by highlighting one of the aspects of the *mi*ʿ*rāj* that he had just introduced in his digression, the idea that with the events of the *mi*ʿ*rāj*, God demonstrates God's supreme power over all things. The anonymous author here and elsewhere in the text takes pains to demonstrate how details from the story of Muḥammad's ascension confirm what human reason and experience dictate. The opening of the heart example thus illustrates how Ayasofya 3441 abandons the pattern established in the Bakrī recensions of telling the narrative of Muḥammad's ascension first and foremost as an entertaining and unified story. Its author instead uses the story as the basis for seeking to establish the truth of Muḥammad's ascension (as presented and interpreted by the author) and by extension the truth of Muḥammad's prophecy more broadly.

The author makes it clear that almost every aspect of the ascension narrative contains some kind of moral lesson that could be explored, and it is not uncommon to find him interject "digressions" into the text after recounting only a line or two of the basic storyline. He states plainly, "The story of the ascension contains a more subtle knowledge/science (ʿ*ilm*) than in every other story. Every step that the Prophet took on that night contains a valuable lesson (*ḥikma*)."[58] While other scholarly works on the Prophet's ascension of the middle periods, by the likes of Qushayrī, Ibn Diḥya Kalbī (d. 633/1236), and others, almost invariably separate the telling of the tale from their discussions of its moral lessons, the author of Ayasofya 3441 combines these sections. The best way to compare the "base text" of this narrative with its parallel Bakrī sources would be to follow the same method as used in looking at the Ibn Sīnā *Mi*ʿ*rājnāma*, namely, examining its narrative elements as distinct from the author's philosophical commentary. In this way, the similarities and differences between the two works become clearer, as illustrated in table 4.

Table 4 Comparison and Contrast between the Bakrī Versions and Ayasofya 3441

FEATURES OF THE BAKRĪ ASCENSION NARRATIVES	FEATURES OF AYASOFYA 3441'S "BASE NARRATIVE"
• Dark night setting, house of Umm Hāniʾ	• Begins in house of Umm Hāniʾ, here: his aunt
• Muḥammad told to arise, put on his robe, and/or tighten his belt	• Muḥammad told to arise; he puts on his robe
• Gabriel reveals his True Form to Muḥummad	• Gabriel reveals his True Form to Muḥummad
• Opening of Chest trope largely absent	• Contains Opening of Chest trope
• Burāq described in detail, has human face, and has an entire conversation with Gabriel (asks for Muḥammad's intercession)	• Burāq described in detail, has human face, and has short conversation with Gabriel (asks for Muḥammad's intercession)
• On road to Jerusalem, Muḥammad addressed by voices from the Jews and Christians	• On road to Jerusalem, addressed by the Jews, Christians, Zoroastrians, and Polytheists
• Muḥammad initially attracted by the woman	• Muḥammad initially attracted by the woman
• Descends and prays at Sinai (only)	• Descends and prays at Sinai (only)
• Encounter with youth near Jerusalem	• No encounter with youth
• Generally meets all the prophets in Jerusalem	• Meets the *souls* of all the prophets in Jerusalem
• Refrains from drinking all milk in Cup Test	• Refrains from drinking all milk in Cup Test
• *Miʿrāj*-ladder and steps described in detail	• Ladder not described
• Material and/or names of heavens often given	• Material and names of the heavens given
• Meets Rooster and other wondrous angels	• Meets Rooster and other wondrous angels
• Encounters Mālik and has long tour of hell	• Encounters Mālik and has long tour of hell
• Encounters ʿAzrāʾīl, asks about methods	• Encounters ʿAzrāʾīl, asks about methods
• Meets prophets during ascent in most or all heavens, David and Solomon in the third heaven	• Meets prophets during ascent in most or all heavens, Solomon in the fourth heaven
• Meets immense angels, e.g., Cherubim, sometimes given specific names (e.g., guardians) and often meets in the seventh heaven 70,000-headed angel with as many mouths, tongues, etc.	• Meets immense angels, e.g., Cherubim, given specific names (e.g., guardians) and meets in the sixth heaven 70,000-headed angel with as many mouths, tongues, etc.
• Muḥammad leads the angels, and sometimes the prophets of each heaven, in two cycles of prayer	• Generally prays two cycles of prayer at the end of the account of each heaven; no mention of leading others until reaching House of Life
• Gabriel stops before the seas, often at Lote Tree, tells Muḥammad it is Gabriel's "Known Station"	• Gabriel stops at Lote Tree, before the seas, tells Muḥammad it is Gabriel's "Known Station"
• Passes seas of different colors, and/or seas of light, fire, darkness, water	• Passes seas of light, fire, darkness, water, many analogous to the Primitive Version
• Detailed encounters with both Mikāʾīl and Isrāfīl in the highest realms	• Detailed encounters with both Mikāʾīl and Isrāfīl in the highest realms
• Vision of God in heart, cold hand trope less common, sometimes adds sweet drop	• Vision of God in heart, no cold hand trope but adds sweet drop

(*continued*)

Table 4 *Continued*

FEATURES OF THE BAKRĪ ASCENSION NARRATIVES	FEATURES OF AYASOFYA 3441'S "BASE NARRATIVE"
• Intimate colloquy: Greetings, Heavenly Host Debate, Seals of Cow chapter, Favor of the Prophets, Sword, Gifts, Intercession	• Intimate colloquy: Greetings, Seals of Cow, Favor of the Prophets, Gifts
• Receives fifty prayers and six months of fasting	• Receives only fifty prayers
• Detailed tour of paradise	• Detailed tour of paradise
• Return to Mecca described	• Return to Mecca described, supplemented by a visit to communities of the Righteous Jews
• Debates in Mecca detailed, with Gabriel revealing Jerusalem to Muḥammad	• Debates in Mecca detailed, with Gabriel revealing Jerusalem to Muḥammad

As with Ibn Sīnā's *Mi*ᶜ*rājnāma*, a large number of the features of the "base narrative" that undergird the philosophical and theological discussions in Ayasofya 3441 show a remarkable resemblance to parallel features from the Arabic Bakrī texts. Some of these details may originate in the Primitive Version of the Ibn ᶜAbbās ascension narrative, and as such were incorporated into a number of subsequent ascension texts (e.g., the accounts in the commentaries of Qummī, Thaᶜlabī, etc.). Some of the details, however, are so distinctive to the Bakrī versions such as Muḥammad's temptations by the woman on the road to Jerusalem, his failure to drink all the milk in the cup test, his leading the angels in prayer, his paradigmatic encounters with Mikāʾīl (who explains to Muḥammad the names of angels) and Isrāfīl (who shows Muḥammad how near the latter has reached to the throne) that one is forced to conclude that Ayasofya 3441, as with the *Liber Scale*, either draws directly on one or more Bakrī versions for its source of inspiration, or else it shares with the Bakrī versions some other hitherto unknown common link.

From the basic comparisons given in table 4 and discussed above, a number of correspondences between Ayasofya 3441 and the Bakrī texts appear, yet it is important not to overstate these similarities. Some of the details, such as the introduction of the specific eastern references (e.g., Muḥammad being called by a Zoroastrian tempter on the night journey), the more abbreviated colloquy scene, and his visits to the lands of the righteous Jews near the end of his journey, represent obvious surface differences. Other differences, however, are not as immediately apparent through the simplified comparison inherent in the chart's tabular format. Just as with the *Liber Scale*, the eschatological sections near the end of Ayasofya 3441 tend to be more detailed and expansive than any single version of the Bakrī narratives,[59] although substantial correspondences can be traced between elements from these sections and the Bakrī narratives. The Bakrī versions and Ayasofya 3441 share the same basic narrative movements, and they share enough specific details to suggest that the author of Ayasofya 3441 either had access to one of these versions, or else drew on another source (in Arabic or Persian) that adapted substantial passages related to Bakrī's ascension narrative.

As with the western Spanish "language worlds" in the seventh/thirteenth century, then, the Bakrī narrative had also penetrated into Persian and Turko-Mongolian circles by the end of that same century. A series of Ilkhanid *miᶜrāj* paintings analyzed by Gruber may have accompanied a text similar to Ayasofya 3441, as Gruber argues.[60] However, many of the images in these paintings derive more broadly from descriptions shared by many texts recording the reshaped version of the Ibn ᶜAbbās ascension discourse, which enjoyed a wide circulation by the end of the seventh/thirteenth century.

The novel approach to telling the story of Muḥammad's night journey and ascension that in the Arabic sources comes to be associated with Ibn ᶜAbbās, and that appears to be connected to versions circulated by the elusive Abū al-Ḥasan Bakrī, clearly made a significant impact on Islamic ascension narratives both within and outside the Arab world, in the east as well as the west. From its modest beginnings in the east around the third/ninth century to its rise to prominence around the seventh/thirteenth century, the development of this distinctive movement within Islamic ascension literature tells us a great deal about the growth of Muslim storytelling in the formative period. It reveals something not only about the process whereby oral narratives were formulated and reformulated, but it also reveals something about the way that disparate groups sought to control the articulation of such narratives in order to control their limits and to channel their expression in order to serve particular, especially partisan, ends.

CONCLUSION

A long process of development connects the earliest anecdotes and stories springing from the brief references in the Qur'ān with the much more detailed and intricate narratives of the reshaped version of Muḥammad's ascension ascribed to Ibn ʿAbbās in the final centuries of the formative period. This type of process certainly has parallels in other religious traditions, for example in the diverse and lengthly accounts of Enoch's heavenly journey that grew out of the biblical reference that mentions that Enoch "walked with God" (Gen. 5:22, 24), or the tales of Paul's ascension that derive from a mention in his letter of a "man of Christ who . . . was caught up to the third heaven" (2 Cor. 12:2). The fact that a single and vague reference in a sacred text could engender such a wealth of exegetical narrative material should not strike those who read such texts today as all that remarkable. What is more remarkable is that outside of a handful of short studies and translations, the variety and richness of Islamic ascension narratives has passed largely unnoticed by scholars, despite the pivotal importance of these narratives to the history of Muslim thought and practice.

Even scholars of early Islamic history and literature have essentially ignored the ascension narratives described in this book, perhaps because they have internalized the bias that an account that does not appear in one of the sound Sunnī collections of *ḥadīth* must be marginal and/or unworthy of serious consideration. I would contend that the development and diffusion of the Ibn ʿAbbās ascension narrative, especially as it later circulated in its reshaped form by storytellers and traditionists such as Abū al-Ḥasan Bakrī, has not received the attention it deserves. This study proves that the Ibn ʿAbbās ascension discourse was far from being a marginal phenomenon among the Muslims of the formative period of Islamic history. Even though it frequently has been rejected as a weak narrative by many traditionists, Sunnī and non-Sunnī alike, a substantial number of Muslim scholars from both the mainstream and the margins clearly embraced and expanded upon this particular account of Muḥammad's night journey.

The evidence suggests that the narrative's early versions first caught hold of the imaginations of Shīᶜīs, Sufis, and disparate Qurᵓān exegetes from diverse backgrounds in the eastern lands of Islamdom (see table 5). We have seen how select early scholars from the Iranian plateau, especially ᶜAlī Qummī, Qushayrī, and Thaᶜlabī, drew upon the Primitive Version of the Ibn ᶜAbbās ascension narrative in the reports that they circulated. Not long after these versions flourished, a fuller and more detailed version of the tale had made its way westward, presumably via the central lands of Islamdom, where the Christian European Crusades had recently captured Jerusalem and its surrounding territories.[1] The first textual evidence for the spread of the Ibn ᶜAbbās discourse to the far west appears in the sixth/twelfth century. Three different works from the following century, originating in and around al-Andalus (now the country of Spain) in the west of Islamdom, the Mamluk lands in the center (Egypt, greater Syria, and much of the Arabian peninsula), and the region recently come under Turco-Mongol control in the east (Iraq, Iran, and further east), together demonstrate that what comes to be called Bakrī's "total and complete" narrative became so well known as to gain the attention of rulers across the breadth of Islamdom. Despite scholarly censure, then, the Bakrī approach to telling the story of Muḥammad's night journey and ascension had managed to gain a wide and influential audience. Due to the narrative's appeal and broad applicability, that audience was only to grow in the centuries that followed.

The night journey and ascension discourse became widely circulated and discussed partially because it was an entertaining tale, but also partially because of what was at stake, namely the empowerment that one gains by controlling the content of otherworldly secrets. Nearly every act of telling of the story of Muḥammad's night journey involves the implicit claims to reveal the truth about what the Prophet experienced on that special night. Beyond that, however, each telling implicitly reflects the position of its author, editor, or transmitter regarding the narrative's limits: its scope, its form, its style, and its content. The Ibn ᶜAbbās ascension discourse is characterized by its expansive scope, its prose form, its hyperbolic descriptive style, and its maximalist approach to content. It took the isolated, fragmentary, and rudimentary story elements present in the earliest *ḥadīth* reports and other oral narratives, combined many of them, and supplemented them with other details from the ascension language world. It supplied gems of anecdote that would have been of great interest to a Muslim audience, for instance the names and descriptions of the beings and realms that Muḥammad encountered, the trials that Muḥammad faced after passing the seventh heaven, and especially the conversations that took place between Muḥammad and God at the climax of the journey. The Ibn ᶜAbbās discourse reveled in revealing these details, and other details as well, placing special emphasis on the intimate colloquy scene because of that scene's potential for determining the central meaning of the story as a whole. The role of narrating Muḥammad's night journey was a position of power and authority, for the narrator arrogated to him or herself the right to determine exactly what message God communicated to Muḥammad that night, and its ultimate significance.

The official Sunnī *ḥadīth* reports shied away from describing anything specific about this encounter, partially out of concerns over the anthropomorphic representation of God, but also out of an insistence that the only exchange taking place between Muḥammad and God that night was the imposition of the five daily ritual prayers. In these official accounts, while the night journey and ascension serve as a miracle tale that underscores the status of the Prophet, their main function seems to be to explain how the number of daily ritual prayers came to be set at five. The narrative thus functions to regulate communal orthopraxy, the norms of correct behavior. While the Ibn ᶜAbbās discourse preserved this regulative function, it largely overshadowed it with its concern to depict Muḥammad as God's most favored creature, and the only being allowed to intercede with God on behalf of the salvation of others. Sound Sunnī reports did not accept the legitimacy of these intercession scenes as part of the ascension narrative, and such scenes consequently did not appear anywhere in their accounts of Muḥammad's journey.

During its long period of development, the Ibn ᶜAbbās ascension discourse repeatedly came under attack by Muslim scholars for being a fabrication, a compilation of lies told about the Prophet and his journey. The scholarly attacks often took the form of criticisms of the discourse's chains of transmission, or its lack thereof. In addition, the discourse's supplementary content, with its discussion of the secrets of the divine colloquy and other features not reported in other ascension narratives, also must have played a factor in the repeated scholarly rejection of the Ibn ᶜAbbās ascension discourse.

Despite its rejection and censure by a series of Muslim official scholars, one of the reasons for the ubiquity and popularity of the Ibn ᶜAbbās ascension discourse was its very claim to reveal heavenly secrets, to fill in the gaps of the official *ḥadīth* reports in order to construct a more complete account. Stories in which a hero is taken on a tour of the otherworld in order for an angelic guide to reveal to him or her the mysteries of the universe form a subdivision of an established genre of works classified under the rubric of apocalyptic narratives. Muslim ascension narratives certainly fit the description of the apocalyptic genre, and they continue to be described by contemporary scholars as largely deriving from Jewish apocalyptic works, despite the obvious differences, as well as the similarities, between the Jewish and Muslim narratives.[2] Muslim and Jewish apocalyptic texts certainly do share some similar features; for

Table 5 Temporal and Geographical Chart of Authors, Transmitters, Historical Events

	WESTERN ISLAMDOM AND EUROPE	CENTRAL ISLAMDOM	EASTERN ISLAMDOM AND ASIA
	Night Journey and Ascension supposed date (ca. months before AH/621 CE)		
		Muḥammad (d. 10/632), Prophet of Islam, dies	
		Ibn ʿAbbās (d. ca. 68/687), companion of Prophet	
100 AH/719 CE			
		[ʿAbbasids take power in Baghdad, 132/750]	
	Muqātil b. Sulaymān (d. 150/767), Qurʾān commentator (*mufassir*) and Ibn Isḥāq (d. 150/767), biographer		
200 AH/816 CE		Yūnus Ibn Bukayr (d. 199/814), transmitter from Ibn Isḥāq	
		Ibn Hishām (d. 218/833), other transmitter from Ibn Isḥāq	
		Ibn Saʿd (d. 230/845), historian and biographer	
		Bukhārī (d. 256/870) & Muslim (d. 261/874), compilers of Sound Sunnī *ḥadīth*	
		Tirmidhī (d. 279/892), compiler of Sound Sunnī *ḥadīth*	
			Ṣaffār Qummī (d. ca. 290/902), Shīʿī *mufassir*
300 AH/912 CE			Furāt Kūfī (d. ca. 300/912), Shīʿī *mufassir*
			ʿAlī Qummī (d. ca. 307/919), Shīʿī *mufassir*
			Ṭabarī (d. 310/923), Sunnī *mufassir* and historian

[Shīᶜī Buyid dynasty begins in Baghdad, 334/945]

Ibn Ḥibbān (d. 354/965), compiler of Sunnī *ḥadīth*

400 AH/1010 CE

Sulamī (d. 412/1021), Sufi mystic, Sunnī *mufassir*

Thaᶜlabī (d. 427/1035), Sunnī *mufassir*

Ibn Sīnā (d. 428/1037), philosopher

[Sunnī Seljuq Turks move from eastern lands westward, take Baghdad in 447/1055]

Qushayrī (d. 465/1072), Sufi mystic, Sunnī *mufassir*

[First Christian Crusades from Europe to Central Islamdom, capture Jerusalem, 492/1099]

500 AH/1107 CE

Abū al-Futūḥ Rāzī (d. 525/1131), Persian Shīᶜī *mufassir*

Approximate period MS. Gayangos 241 was copied

[Salāḥ al-Dīn takes Jerusalem from the Christian Crusaders, 583/1187]

600 AH/1204 CE

[Mongols devastate eastern Islamdom, ca. 624/1227]

[Mongols sack Baghdad, 656/1258]

Liber Scale translated and copied

Bakrī Reshaped Version (MS. Amc.95/2)

Anon. Eastern Persian *Miᶜrājnāma* (MS. Aya.3441) copied

700 AH/1301 CE

instance, they both claim to reveal heavenly secrets via the ascension of a hero, who braves terrifying otherworldly realms in order to reach the vicinity of the divine throne.

This is not the place to analyze the merits of the comparison between Jewish and Muslim ascension texts, and yet examining the manner in which contemporary scholars of Jewish and Muslim apocalyptic works have wrestled with the question of how to determine the authorship of such works can provide suggestions for how to formulate educated conjectures about the authors of the Ibn ᶜAbbās ascension texts, the majority of whom remain anonymous. For instance, David Halperin identifies the Hekhalot authors with the general masses, the common folk of the earth, who sought to use the knowledge gained from their rituals to secure their own power and religious authority over and above those of the elite official scholars.[3] From this point of view, the apocalyptic text is a type of revolutionary document for the magical empowerment of the disenfranchised. Taking a slightly different tack in his comparative study of Muslim and Jewish apocalyptic works, Steven Wasserstrom characterizes Muslim apocalypticists as consisting of "semi-erudite intellectuals operating as marginal elites."[4] In other words, according to Wasserstrom, the apocalyptic authors are not the common folk, but rather those scholars who find themselves on the margins of official power. He theorizes that these marginal elites, by resorting to apocalyptic literature, seek to empower themselves vis-à-vis more powerful scholars. Although Halperin and Wasserstrom reach different conclusions about the authorship of Jewish and Muslim apocalyptic texts, both agree that the purpose of this genre of writing has something to do with the empowerment of those originally disempowered.

Building upon the reasoning of Halperin and Wasserstrom, one might theorize that Bakrī and the others responsible for the development of the Ibn ᶜAbbās ascension narratives might be sought among Muslims from the common folk or marginal elites of Islamdom. Such a conjecture appears especially appealing given the degree of opposition that these figures faced and the little that was recorded in official sources about them. Such a theory necessarily remains a mere hypothesis, open to dispute and contingent on the discovery of further evidence. What cannot be disputed is that the ascension discourse was and remains a discourse of power, and those who controlled the discourse were able to use it to obtain and maintain a position of power.

Unfortunately, it is difficult to connect the development and early circulation of the Ibn ᶜAbbās ascension discourse to a particular region, legal school, or sect of Muslims. Perhaps as a consequence of the official censure, some of the individuals who transmitted the Ibn ᶜAbbās ascension narrative refrained from attaching their names to the work, making the process of identification more difficult. Furthermore, to illustrate the difficulties in identifying the parties involved, one merely needs to recall that several Nishapuri Shāfiᶜī scholars in the fourth/tenth to fifth/eleventh centuries seem to have played pivotal roles in transmitting the text, but the Primitive Version preceded them, and the reshaped version likely postdated them. The role that these transmitters played in developing the text, if any, is far from clear. Moreover, the Bakrī narrative was copied and circulated in multiple royal courts in the seventh/thirteenth century, so it can hardly be considered a text reflecting only the interests and concerns of the common folk. It is possible that the royal patrons, in embracing the text, could have assumed for themselves the role of unofficial and somewhat marginal scholars (over and against the official scholarly elite). In any case, the formulation of both the Primitive Version and the reshaped Bakrī versions likely preceded these royal patrons.

Even though the creators and developers of the discourse remain something of a mystery, a discussion of how different Muslims used this empowering discourse may also help to identify those who perpetuated and popularized the Ibn ᶜAbbās ascension narrative. One can only speculate on the question of what caused this Bakrī version of the Ibn ᶜAbbās ascension discourse to flourish in such a fashion in the seventh/thirteenth century. Nevertheless, the explanation could well revolve around how diverse groups of Muslims used the discourse. Whether it be a tool to be used in intra-Islamic rivalries, a tool for interreligious proselytizing, or a tool for encouraging pious behavior, getting the story's audiences to turn toward the Prophet Muḥammad in the hope of receiving the benefit of his intercession, part of the explanation for the discourse's appeal could be sought in the function that the discourse played when it was put to use by Muslim storytellers, transmitters, and scholars.

Throughout this work, we have seen how the Ibn ᶜAbbās discourse was at the center of intra-Islamic rivalries between competing factions, especially between members of the nascent Sunnī-Shīᶜī factions. The Primitive Version of the narrative circulated in and around the third/ninth century, and ᶜAlī Qummī's text proves that it was known in early Imāmī Shīᶜī circles. The Bakrī reshaped version could have been formulated in these circles as well, but it appears more likely to have been composed as a Sunnī narrative designed precisely to counter the Shīᶜī use of the ascension discourse. Shīᶜīs had seized this discursive terrain early, recognizing its potential for using the voices of the angels, the prophetic progenitors, and God himself to argue on behalf of the special status of ᶜAlī and his descendants. To respond and counter such Shīᶜī use of the ascension narrative, one strategy that some Sunnīs appear to have employed was to co-opt and modify the same Shīᶜī narratives, either completely expunging the explicitly Shīᶜī references or else substituting explicitly Sunnī references in their place. The story of the night journey and ascension thus became a rhetorical battleground over which competing Muslim groups strove to assert their control. While there are significant merits to this explanation for the popularity of the Bakrī narrative, the fact that explicitly partisan Shīᶜī or Sunnī elements first begin to appear in the extant texts of the Ibn ᶜAbbās versions only in the seventh/thirteenth century presents one of this theory's limitations. Isolated fragmentary reports of partisan Shīᶜī ascension accounts are well attested centuries before this pivotal moment, but until the discovery of longer and more complete Shīᶜī versions of the story from the early and early middle period, the idea that these Sunnī Ibn ᶜAbbās ascension discourses of seventh/thirteenth century were composed in response to rival Shīᶜī versions remains somewhat speculative.

The use of the discourse for religious struggle should not be isolated to the Sunnī-Shīᶜī rivalry, however, for there is also evidence to suggest that the Bakrī versions of the Ibn ᶜAbbās ascension discourse were used to engage others, such as Jews, in religious debate. The prophetic figures David and Solomon appear regularly in the later versions of the Ibn ᶜAbbās narratives, and they rarely appear in other similar narratives. They are depicted as joining other biblical figures in affirming Muḥammad's role as the most favored of prophets. For example, Moses not only attests to Muḥammad's superiority, but also proves what a good friend he is to the Muslims by convincing Muḥammad to intercede on their behalf. Moses tells Muḥammad to request a reduction of their ritual obligations, claiming that the Jews had been too weak to fulfill their sacred duties. Further, in Bakrī accounts from the end of the formative period and the two centuries that follow, select narratives incorporate the idea that prior to his return to Mecca, Muḥammad spends time proselytizing among the distant community of faithful children of Israel.[5] These details all point to a Muslim engagement with the Jewish community. When one considers that both Jewish and Christian otherworldly journeys were likely flourishing during the same period in which the Ibn ᶜAbbās discourse developed and spread, one realizes that Muslims may have felt compelled to formulate their own narratives to compete with those of their fellow People of the Book.

This last idea touches upon the general hypothesis that Muslim preachers and storytellers used the discourse in order to attempt to win adherents, from inside or outside the Muslim community. Most versions of the story of Muḥammad's ascension portray a triumphalist image of the Prophet, demonstrating how the rest of God's prophets acknowledge Muḥammad's superiority, showcasing his ability to pass initiatic trials and to secure God's blessings, and illustrating how only the truly pious will accept the veracity of Muḥammad's story and not be swayed be the doubts sown by God's enemies. The Ibn ᶜAbbās narratives in general, and the Bakrī versions in particular, take these features, which are common to the majority of Muslim night journey and ascension accounts, and increase them in scope and intensity.

The examples of this type of triumphalist image of the Prophet abound in the ascension narratives surveyed in this work. Not only does Muḥammad lead the other prophets in prayer, but he also demonstrates his superiority to the rest by recounting the longest list of blessings in the eulogy contest. During the intimate colloquy, God assures the Prophet that he has been granted the equivalent of, and even better favors than, all the rest of the prophets. Not only does Muḥammad overcome the trial by the voices on the road and the test of the appropriate cup from which to drink, but he also overcomes the terror that threatens to destroy him at multiple stages of his journey. Not only does Muḥammad recall mundane details upon his return to prove the truthfulness of his account, but also Gabriel miraculously shows him Jerusalem in order to assist the Prophet in convincing his contemporaries. The Ibn ᶜAbbās narratives portray Muḥammad's station as God's Messenger as being literally inscribed across the faces of otherworldly beings, and etched onto the surfaces of otherworldly monuments. Last but certainly not least, the Bakrī versions graphically illustrate the rewards of paradise and the punishments of hellfire, and they portray otherworldly beings as seeking Muḥammad's intercession with God for the sake of their ultimate salvation. Most Bakrī versions of the Ibn ᶜAbbās ascension narrative include scenes at the end of the intimate colloquy in which Muḥammad proves his ability to petition God on behalf of believers. The concept of intercession suggests to the listener or reader, Muslim or non-Muslim, that one must embrace Muḥammad and his prophetic message if one wishes to avoid burning in hellfire for all eternity. All of these triumphalist features of the Ibn ᶜAbbās ascension narrative could have served as useful tools for a Muslim proselytization effort.

One key to the success of the discourse was its adaptability to diverse proselytizing contexts and needs. For instance, Sunnī Muslims may have used it to attempt to convince a skeptical Jewish audience to accept Islam, to convince a Turkish or Mongol audience to reject other competing religious allegiances in favor of Islam, and also to push a recalcitrant Shīᶜī audience to accept a Sunnī interpretation of Islam. With the rise of illustrated ascension texts at the end of the seventh/thirteenth century, the Ibn ᶜAbbās discourse was able to take on another function related to the conversion process, namely the role of teaching new converts how properly to observe the daily prayer rituals and to recite pious formulae in praise of the deity.[6] In this fashion, the reshaped Ibn ᶜAbbās ascension discourse may have flourished in the seventh/thirteenth century and beyond due to its utility for both sectarian debate and interreligious conversion.

The hypotheses explored in this book each have the merit of explaining aspects of the Ibn ᶜAbbās ascension discourse, especially as it took shape in the versions ascribed to Bakrī. These versions could be modified for use in different contexts. Rather than asserting a single correct interpretation of the origin and use of the Ibn ᶜAbbās ascension discourse, a better approach may be to keep open to the possibility that distinct recensions and redactions of the narrative were likely developed and reshaped with different audiences, and perhaps different purposes, in mind.

The study of premodern Islamic ascension narratives demands a close attention to the unique characteristics of individual texts both on their own terms and in their wider contexts, the latter of which should include the broader history of the formative ascension discourse that I have attempted to sketch in the present study. Much work remains to be done, for the majority of the texts describing Muḥammad's night journey and ascension remain little known and largely unpublished. Nevertheless, this examination of the development of the Ibn ᶜAbbās ascension narrative paves the way for future studies exploring how this fascinating story has been told and retold by diverse groups of Muslims, serving to empower them vis-à-vis both internal and external rivals through a complex discourse extolling the merits of the Prophet and revealing the wonders of his otherworldly journey.

Appendix A
TRANSLATION OF THE PRIMITIVE VERSION

The following represents the first critical translation of the Primitive Version of the Ibn ᶜAbbās ascension narrative. For its base text, this translation makes use of *ḥadīth* report on "The Wonders of the Ascension" (*ᶜAjāʾib al-miᶜrāj*) transmitted by Ibn Ḥibbān (represented in the notes by IḤ) as preserved by Suyūṭī.[1] This base text was compared and amended with the recensions of Qushayrī (QU)[2] and Wāsiṭi (WA).[3] I have added the general title and the headings to the major sections of the text. A discussion of some of the key features of the Primitive Version appears in chapter 2.

"The Wonders of the Ascension,"
the Primitive Version of the Pseudo–Ibn ᶜAbbas Ascension Narrative

[62][4] Ibn Ḥibbān : Muḥammad b. Sudūs Nasawī—Ḥamīd b. Zanjawayh[5]—Muḥammad b. Khudāsh—ᶜAlī b. Qutayba—Maysara b. ᶜAbd Rabbih—ᶜUmar b. Sulaymān Dimashqī—Ḍaḥḥāk [b. Muzāhim]—Ibn ᶜAbbās in a broken chain of transmission (*marfūᶜ*).

[Part One: Journey to the Throne]

[The Messenger of God said:] When I was caused to journey by night to the [first] heaven, in it I saw the wonders of God's servants and creation.

[The Rooster Angel][6]
Among what I saw in the [first] heaven was a rooster that had underfeathers of green and feathers of white. The whiteness of its feathers was the most intense white I had ever seen. Its underfeathers beneath its feathers were the most intense green I had ever seen. Its legs were at the boundaries of the seven lower earths, and its head was beneath the throne of the Merciful, the bend of its neck beneath the throne. It had two wings on its shoulders. When it spread them they reached from the east to the west. When there was little left of the night, it spread its wings, beating them and shrieking out a glorification[7] to God, "Glorified be God, the Great and Exalted! There is no god but he, the Alive and Manifest!" When it did that, all the roosters of earth glorified God and beat their wings and made their rooster calls. When that rooster in the heavens quieted, the roosters of the earth quieted. [. . .][8] While I was observing that rooster, I continued to hope that I might see it again.

[The Half-Fire-Half-Snow Angel]
Next I passed by other strange creatures, among which was an angel half of whose body below its head was of snow, and the other [half] of fire. Between them there was a seam, the fire not melting the snow nor the snow extinguishing the fire. It stood calling in a very loud voice, **[63]** "Glorified be my Lord, who holds back the cold of this snow so that it does not extinguish the heat of this fire! Glorified be my Lord, who holds back the heat of this fire so that it does not melt this snow! O God, the uniter of snow and fire, unite the hearts of your faithful servants!" I asked, "Who is that, Gabriel?" He responded, "An angel that God assigned[9] to the outer limits of the heavens and the extremities of the earths. It is one of the best angelic advisors to the faithful people of earth, petitioning on their behalf with this saying since it was created."

[The Angel of Death]
Then I passed another angel sitting on a throne. All the earth and everything in it was between his knees. In his hands was a written tablet of light. He gazed upon it, not glancing to the right or the left, engaged in it. I asked, "Who is that, Gabriel?" He replied, "That is the Angel of Death, red-faced and sad,[10] the record keeper[11] of the capture of spirits. He is the hardest working of the angels." I queried, "Is this the one, Gabriel, who will capture the spirit of all those possessing spirits who have died or will die in the future?" He replied, "Yes." I asked, "Does he see them wherever they are and witness them by himself?" He answered me,"Yes." I exclaimed, "May [God] protect us from the calamity of death." [. . .][12]

[64] I requested, "O Gabriel, draw me close to the Angel of Death." So he drew me close, and I greeted him. Gabriel called out to him, "This is Muḥammad, the Prophet of mercy whom God sent to the Arabs as a messenger and prophet." He welcomed me and greeted me with peace. He was pleased with my happy demeanor and my joyful tidings. He stated, "Rejoice, Muḥammad, for complete goodness is in your community." I responded, "Praise be to God, the bestower of blessings, that is a mercy from my Lord to me and a blessing upon me."

I asked, "Angel of Death, what is that tablet that is in your hands?" He replied, "Upon [it] is written the times that creatures will die." I asked, "Will you not inform me about those whose spirits you have captured in past ages?" He replied, "Those spirits [are listed] on other tablets of which you have been taught previously." I further questioned, "Angel of Death, how are you able to capture the spirits of all the people of [various] lands and seas on the earth, of its east and west?" He answered, "Do you not see that the entire earth is between my knees and all creatures are in my sight and reach? When the appointed time of a servant passes, I gaze upon him. When I make my angelic representatives aware of my gaze upon one of God's servants, they know that he is captured and they attend to him and bear down upon him, intent upon the extraction of his spirit. When his spirit arrives in the throat, I know of it. No part of this matter is concealed from me. I extend my hand to him and extract his spirit from his body and capture him. That is the matter that takes place between me and those of God's servants who possess spirits." His words [on this subject] made me cry.

[The Guardian of Hellfire]

Then we passed him by and came to an immense angel the likes of which I had never seen among the angels, grave of face, ugly in appearance, intensely strong, and manifestly angry. When I gazed upon him I became frightened, crying out, "Gabriel, who is that, for I am extremely frightened of him." He replied, "It is no wonder that you are frightened of him, Muḥammad, for each of us in your position is frightened of him. He is the angelic Guardian of Hellfire (*Khāzin Jahannam*). He never smiles and, continually from the time that God appointed him to Gehenna, each day he becomes more angry and infuriated with the enemies of God and the people who disobey God in order that God may take vengeance upon them through him. I greeted him, and he returned my greetings. I spoke with him, and he answered me and gave me joyful tidings of paradise. I addressed him, asking, "How long have you been standing at [the gate of] hellfire?" He answered, "Since I was created until now, and thus until the [final] hour." I requested, "Gabriel, go up to him and command him to open a gate of it." He did that, and a blaze shot out from it which spread blackness accompanied by grimy dark smoke that filled the horizons and spread the blaze across the heavens with rumble **[65]** and turmoil. I saw in it abominable terror and a great matter that I am powerless to describe. It almost covered me and made me lose myself. I exclaimed, "Gabriel, go up to him and command him to close it again." So he did.[13]

[Other Angels][14]
We passed him and continued on past many angels, the number of which only God, the One, the King, the Conqueror, knows. Among them was one with many faces between its shoulder blades, and God knows best. After [passing] them, then [I saw] many faces on its chest. In each of those faces were mouths and tongues, and they praised God and glorified him with each of those tongues.

[The Sixth Heaven]
We passed by them from heaven to heaven until through God's power we reached the sixth heaven. In it were numerous creatures beyond description, surging one upon another in multitudes. Each angel among them was filled from his head down to his feet with faces and wings. There was not a single mouth nor head nor face nor eye nor tongue nor ear nor wing nor hand nor leg nor member nor hair that did not glorify God with praise. Each recounted [God with] laud and eulogy, using words that no other member recounted, in voices each of whose timbre did not resemble that of another.[15] They raised their voices, crying for fear of God and in praise of him and his servants. Were the people of earth to hear the voice of one of these angels, they would all die in panic from the intensity of their terror. I asked, "Gabriel, who are they?" He replied, "Glorified be God the Great, these are the 'Ones who Worry' (*Karūbiyyūn*)[16] over their devotions to God, their glorification of him, and their crying for fear of him. They were created just as you see them. No one of them ever speaks to the companion at his side, nor looks at his face. They have not raised their heads up to the seventh heaven since they were created, nor have they looked at the heavens and earths below them out of the humility in their bodies and out of fear of their Lord."

I turned to face them with a greeting of peace, and they made a response to me with a gesture, not speaking to me nor looking at me out of fear. When Gabriel saw that, he told them, "This is Muḥammad, the Prophet of mercy whom God sent to the Arabs as a prophet. He is the seal of the prophets and the master of humanity (*sayyid al-bashar*). Will you not speak with him?" When they heard that [introduction] from Gabriel and his recounting of my status, they turned to face me with good wishes and peace, and they were great in joyful tidings for me. They spoke to me and gave me joyful tidings of goodness for my community. Then they turned to their devotions just as they had been [previously]. I was discharged from abiding with them and gazing upon them in wonder at the greatness of their stature and the favor of their service.

[The Seventh Heaven]
Then we passed them, and Gabriel carried me. He brought me into the seventh heaven, and I saw in it creatures and angels of God's creation about whom I am

not permitted to talk, nor am I permitted to describe them to you. I will inform you that God gave to me at that point the power of all the people of earth, and he increased [such power] in me from him that he knows best. He granted me firmness (*thibāt*) [of vision] and delimited my sight so that I might look upon their light. Were it not for that, I would not have been able to look. So I cried out, "Glorified be God the Great, who created the likes of these!" I asked, "Who are they, Gabriel?" He informed me and told me stories (*qaṣṣa ᶜalayya*) about their wondrous situation. I was not permitted to talk to you about them.

[First Stop in the High Realm: Rows of Angels]
We passed them and Gabriel took my hand, raising me to the High Realm[17] until I was brought to the end at the most noble, most great, leaders of the angels. I gazed upon seventy rows of angels, row after row. Their feet were divided between the boundaries of the seven earths. I passed to where only God knows until I reached "the Despair" (*al-suhūm*), that is, a veil of darkness.[18] Their heads stretched out beyond the high seventh heaven and pierced the upper realm into the atmosphere where God wills. From the middle of their heads to the limits of their feet are faces and the light of wings. Their diverse faces do not resemble one another, their diverse lights do not resemble one another, and their diverse wings do not resemble one another. The vision of those who gaze upon them wavers, so my eyes withdrew from them. When I gazed at the wonders **[66]** of their stature and the intensity of their terror and the gleaming of their light, there stirred in me intense fear of them to the degree that trembling took possession of me. Gabriel looked at me and said, "Do not be afraid, Muḥammad, for God has been generous with you in ways that he has been to no other before you, and has brought you to a place that no other [being] before you has been brought. You will see a great matter and a wondrous creation among the creatures of the Lord of Might, so steady yourself. God says to be strong, for you will see things more wondrous and many times greater than what you have seen."

[Second Stop in the High Realm: Rows of Angels]
Then with God's permission we passed them and [Gabriel] ascended with me to the High Realm until we rose up above them a distance that would take others fifty thousand years. But God gave us such speed that its passage took only an hour of the night. We ended once again at seventy rows of angels, row after row, each row cramped by the row that followed it. I saw in their stature a wondrous wonder in the gleaming of their light and the multitude of their faces and wings and the intensity of their terror. Their voices resounded in glorification of God and eulogy of him. I gazed upon them and praised God for what I saw of his power and the multitude of the wonders of his creation.

[Third Stop in the High Realm: Rows of Angels]
We passed them with God's permission, ascending to the High Realm until we rose[19] above them a distance of fifty thousand years through God's power, by which we were made to journey by night in an hour. We ended at seventy rows of angels, row after row, and like that through seven rows, the distance between each pair of rows being fifty thousand years for a fast rider. Some of them surged into others, and each row was cramped by the row that followed it. They are one layer, some pressed together with others, and some behind others. I was made to imagine (*khuyyila ʿilayya*) that I forgot all of the wonders of God's creation that I had seen besides them.

I was not permitted to tell you about them. Had I been given permission, I would not have been able to describe them to you. But let me inform you that were I to die before my appointed time out of fear of a thing, I would have died from the vision of them and the wonders of their stature and the resounding of their voices and the radiating of their lights. But God, the exalted, strengthened me for that [experience] through his mercy and the completeness of his blessing. He granted me steadiness for what I saw of the radiating of their lights, and I heard the resounding of their voices in glorification. My sight was limited to the vision of them in order not to be dazzled by their lights. They are aligned in rows (*al-ṣāfūn*) around the throne of the Merciful, and those next to them are the glorifiers (*al-musabbiḥūn*) in the heavens. I praised God for what I had seen of the wonder of his creation.

[Fourth Stop in the High Realm: Sea of Light]
We passed them with God's permission, ascending to a high realm until we rose above that and ended at a sea of light that gleamed. One could not see a shore to it, nor an end. When I gazed upon it, my sight was bewildered by it [from seeing] other things, to the point that I thought that everything in my Lord's creation had been filled with light and been made to blaze with fire. My sight almost left me from the intensity of the light of that sea. What I had seen of its gleaming weighed upon me, and it shocked me to the degree that I became very afraid of it. I praised God for what I had seen of the terror of that sea and its wonders.

[Fifth Stop in the High Realm: Sea of Darkness]
We passed it with God's permission, ascending to the High Realm until we ended at a black sea. I gazed and saw that [in it] the darknesses were combined, some above others in a density only God knows. I saw neither a shore nor an end to that sea. When I gazed upon it my sight was darkened, and it covered me to the point that I thought that everything in my Lord's creation had darkened. I became blinded in darkness, not able to see a thing. I thought that Gabriel had left me, which made me fearful and weighed upon me terribly. When Gabriel saw

what I was experiencing, he took me by the hand and began to comfort me and speak to me. He told me, "Do not be afraid, Muḥammad. Rejoice for the favors of God and face them with acceptance. Do you know what you see and where you are being brought? You are going to your Lord, the Lord of Might! Steady yourself when you see the **[67]** wonders of God's creation with which he arouses you." So I praised God for the joyful tidings that Gabriel brought me, and for the wonders of that sea that I had seen.

[Sixth Stop in the High Realm: Sea of Fire]

Then we passed on with God's permission, ascending to the High Realm until we ended at a sea of fire burning brightly, blazing a blaze. It surged in waves, some consuming others. Its fire had rays and radiant flames. It contained din and tumult, and it was terrifying. When I gazed at it I was filled with fear and fright, and I thought that everything that God created had burned up in flames. It covered my sight to the point that I kept bringing my hands up to my eyes when I saw the terror of that fire. I looked at Gabriel and he knew the fear I felt. He addressed me saying, "Muḥammad, do not be afraid, steady yourself and be strong through the strength of God. Know the favor in which you are held, and toward which you are headed. Take the signs and wonders of creation that God shows you with thanks." So I praised God for what I had seen of the wonders of that fire.

[Seventh Stop in the High Realm: Mountains of Ice]

We passed beyond it with God's permission, ascending to the High Realm until we ended at mountains of ice, some behind others. Only God can enumerate them. Lofty, insurmountable peaks pierced the air. Their ice was intensely white, emitting rays like rays of the sun. I gazed, and it trembled as if it were flowing water. My sight was bewildered from the intensity of its whiteness and I was awed by the multitude of mountains and height of the peaks that I saw to the point that I fixed my eyes on them. Gabriel told me, "Do not be afraid, Muḥammad. Steady yourself when God shows you some of the wonders of his creation." So I praised God for what I had seen of the grandeur of those mountains.

[Eighth Stop in the High Realm: Second Sea of Fire]

We passed them with God's permission, ascending to the High Realm until we ended at another sea of fire, its fire increasing many-fold in flaming, flaring, burning, surging, din, turmoil, and terror. The mountains of ice were among the fires, yet they did not extinguish them. When I was made to stand there, and the terror of that fire carried me from fear and fright of that great matter, I was overcome with trembling to the point that I thought that everything in my Lord's creation had burned up in flames. When its matter seemed grave to me and I saw some of the abomination of its terror, Gabriel gazed at me. When he saw the fear and trembling that I experienced, he asked, "Praise be to God, Muḥammad, what has come upon you (*mā laka*)? Are you falling upon this fire? Then what is all this fear? You are in God's favor and are rising up to him so that he may show you some of the wonders of his creation and his greatest signs,[20] so be tranquil through your Lord's mercy and accept that by which he has favored you. You are in a place that no descendant of Adam[21] before you has ever reached. Take what you have been given with thanks, steady yourself when you see some of your Lord's creation, and leave behind your fear. You are a believer in that which you fear. If you think what you see now is wondrous, you will see even more wondrous things after this than what you have seen before." My fright vanished and my soul became calm. I praised God for what I had seen of the wonders of his signs.

[Ninth Stop in the High Realm: Sea of Seas]

We passed that sea [with God's permission], ascending [to the High Realm][22] until we ended at a sea of water. It is the sea of seas. I am not able to describe it to you other than to say that I did not detail any of its regions in the regions I told you about. In it I felt the strongest fright. When I was made to stand on that sea, there was no terror stronger than its terror. The multitude of waves and composition of its breakers—a breaker is a great wave—[are] like immovable mountains, some above others, tightly woven together with crests (*ghawārib*), that is, courses, which are small waves. What I saw of that sea overwhelmed me, to the point that I thought that there did not remain anything in God's creation that was not drowning in that water. Gabriel looked at me and exclaimed, "Muḥammad, do not be afraid of this. If you fear this, what comes after it is even more fearful and more immense. This is something created, but we are going to the creator, my Lord, your Lord and the Lord of all things!" He removed from me the fear that had seized me, and I became tranquil through the mercy of my Lord.

I gazed in that sea **[68]** and saw a strange creature, beyond description. I asked, "Gabriel, where is the limit of this sea, and where is its bottom?" He answered, "Its bottom passes the seven lower earths to where God wills. Impossible, impossible is the subject of this sea. Muḥammad, your Lord's creatures in it are greater and more wondrous than what you have seen." So I cast my glance to its sides.

I found myself standing with angels who had with their stature drowned the stature of all the angels, and with their light surpassed the light of all the angels, through the greatness of their lights and the multitude of their wings. In their various statures, [their wings] spread beyond the limits of the heavens and the earths, outside of space, fluttering in glorification of God, passing beyond space to where God wills. The glow of their light, in its shining, was like the glow of fire. Had God not protected me with his power, granted me firmness, and enveloped me in a garden of his mercy in which he guarded me, their light would have wrested away my sight and their countenances would have burned my body. But through the mercy of God and the completeness of his blessing upon me, the glow of their light was diverted from me and my sight was limited to the vision of them. I gazed upon them in their station, and then the water of the sea, which was the sea of seas in its thickness and multitude of waves and breakers, did not pass their knees.

I asked, "Gabriel, what is this sea which drowns all the seas and exhausts a person with the intensity of its terror a hundred times more wondrous than what I had seen of God's creation, and yet with all its depth it does not pass their knees? Where are the bottoms of their feet?" He replied, "Muḥammad, you have already been informed about the matter of this sea, and about the wonders of this creation in which are the bottoms of their feet at the source of the water which is at the bottom of this sea. The tops of their heads are at the throne of the Lord of might. They thunder in their glorification, and were the people of earth to hear the voice of only one of these angels, they would all be struck down (*saᶜiqūn*) and die. They call out, 'Glorified be God, through his praise! Glorified be God, the Great, the Living, the Manifest! Glorified be God, through his praise! Glorified be God, the Great! Glorified be God, through his praise! Glorified be God, the Holy!'" I praised God for what I had seen of the wonders of that sea and those in it.

[Tenth Stop in the High Realm: Sea of Light]

Then we passed them with God's permission, [ascending] to the High Realm until we ended at a sea of light, its light having risen up and shone throughout the high realm. I saw in the rays of its gleaming a great matter. Were I to strive to describe it to you, I would not be able to do so except to say that its light surpassed all light, drowned out all fire, and went higher than all the rays I had seen previously and told to you. When I looked upon it, its rays took away my sight and indeed everything, covering all else. I could not see a thing, just as if I had been gazing into darkness rather than light. When Gabriel saw what I was experiencing, he called out, "Dear God, make him firm through your mercy, aid him through your power, and complete him in your blessing." When Gabriel petitioned (*daᶜā*) for me in this way, he brought back my sight. God limited it to the vision of the rays of that light, and he granted me the firmness of that [vision].

I gazed upon it, and my sight turned to the shores of that lake. When my eyes filled, I thought that its light colored me from red to yellow to white to green. Then they mixed and put on all [the colors], to the point that I thought it had darkened from the intensity of its glow and the rays of its gleaming and the shining of its light. I looked at Gabriel, and he knew what I was experiencing, so he began to petition for me a second time in a way similar to his first petition. God returned my sight to me through his mercy and limited it to the vision of that. He protected me with his strength until I became firm and arose to [be able to bear the vision], through his beneficence making it seem of little importance to me.

I began to turn my sight toward the breakers of light on that sea, and saw that there were angels standing in it in one row, all pressed together, crowding some against others, surrounding the throne and circling round it. When I gazed **[69]** upon them, I saw wonders of their stature as if I had forgotten all the angels that I had seen before them and that I described to you. When I looked upon the wonders of their stature, I thought that I actually had forgotten all the angels that I had seen previously, out of the wonder of the stature of those angels. I was forbidden to describe them to you. Had I been permitted to do that and striven to describe them to you, I would not have been able to do so. I would not have conveyed one one-hundredth of a portion [of the description]. Praise be to God, the Creator, the Knowing, the Great!

They surrounded the throne and disregarded the sight of anything else. They thunder in their glorification, as if the heavens and the earths and the immovable mountains are joined one with another, or even more than that, and more wondrous than can be described. I listened to their glorification in order that I might understand it. They would cry out, "There is no god but God, Possessor of the Noble Throne! There is no god but God, the High, the Great! There is no god but God, the Alive, the Manifest!" When they opened their mouths in glorification of God, out of their mouths came a shining light like a burning fire. Were it not for the fact that it was through God's power that they surrounded the light of the throne, I would have certainly thought that the light of their mouths would burn the whole rest of God's creation. Were God to order one of them to devour the seven heavens and the seven earths and all the creatures in them in a single bite, it would have done it. It would be easy for it to do through the honor and grandeur of their stature. They are more wondrous, and their matter is greater, than anything that anyone can describe.

I asked, "Gabriel, who are they?" He responded, "Glorified be God the Conqueror above all his servants! Muḥammad, it is not fitting for you to know who they are. Did you not see the inhabitants of the sixth heaven and all that was above them up to these? Did you not see what was between this, and what you did not consider greater or more wondrous? These are [all] Cherubim (*karūbiyyūn*) of diverse kinds.[23] God, exalted in his grandeur and holy in his deeds, made these that you see and favored them in their places and their creation. He made them in their degrees and forms and lights, just as you saw. But what you did not see is even more numerous and [even] more wonderful." I praised God for what I had seen of their affair.

[Beyond the High Realms to the Throne]

We passed them with God's permission, ascending in the atmosphere of the High Realm faster than an arrow and [faster than] wind, with God's permission and power, until I was brought to the throne of [God], the possessor of might, the dear, the one, the conqueror. When I gazed upon the throne, then all of what I had seen of God's creation next to the throne became small of mention, insignificant of account, base in import. In fact, the seven heavens and the seven earths, the layers of hellfire and the degrees of paradise, the covers and the veils, the lights, seas, and mountains which are in the High Realm, and all of the creatures and creation next to the throne of the Merciful were like a small ring of chainmail in the land of a wide open plain, in which you cannot tell one side of [the plain] from the other. Such befits the station of the Lord of Might, to be great in the greatness of his divinity. He is thus and even greater, more grand, more powerful, more noble, more favored. His nature is beyond the description of the describers and beyond the wagging tongues of the talkers.

When I was caused to journey by night to the throne and was opposite it, a green *rafraf* (Q 55:76) descended to me. I cannot describe it to you. Gabriel put me down and sat me upon it. Then he grew small without me, and put his hands up to his eyes in fear for his sight from the flashing of the glittering light of the throne. He began to cry loudly, to glorify God, to praise and to honor him. That *rafraf* raised me up, with God's permission and his mercy toward me, and he completed his blessing upon me with the approach of the master of the throne from above it.

[Part Two: Divine Audience and Tour of Paradise]

[Vision of God]

I saw a great matter, which tongues cannot discuss and imagination cannot reach. My sight was bewildered beside it to the point that I feared blindness, so I closed my eyes and put trust in God. When I closed my eyes, God returned my vision to me in my heart, and I began to gaze with my heart at what I had been gazing at with my eyes. I saw a light[24] gleaming. **[70]** I was forbidden to describe to you what I saw of his grandeur. I asked my Lord to favor me with the steadiness of vision toward him in my heart in order to complete his blessing of me. My Lord did that and favored me with it, and I gazed upon him in my heart until he made it firm, he steadied [my] vision of him. When he was thus, he unveiled his veils from [around] him, sitting on his throne in his dignity, greatness, nobility, and exaltedness. He did not permit to me to describe anything else about him to you. Glorious is he in his majesty, noble in his deeds, his exalted station, and his resplendent light!

He inclined to me from his dignity a slight inclination, and I was brought near to him. That is his saying in his book, as he informs you of his actions with me and his favors to me: "*Possessing strength, he straightened up while he was on the highest horizon, then he drew close and descended and was a distance of two bows or closer*" (Q 53:6–9). That [last phrase] means: where he inclined to me and brought me near to him the distance of what is between two sides of a bow, or rather closer than the middle to the curve of a bow. "*And he revealed to his servant what he revealed*" (Q 53:10). This means: what he decreed of his command that he commissioned to me. "*The heart did not lie in what it saw*" (Q 53:11). This means: my vision of him in my heart. "*He saw some of the greatest signs of his Lord*" (Q 53:18).[25]

[Encounter with God]

When he inclined to me from his dignity, glorified be he, he placed one of his hands between my shoulder blades, and I felt the coldness of his fingers upon my heart for some time. With that I felt his sweetness (*ḥalāwatuhu*), his beautiful fragrance, cool pleasure, and generous vision. All the terror that I had encountered vanished, and all my trembling was driven from me. My heart became calm, and it became filled with delight and consolation. Rejoicing and rapture came upon me, to the point that I began to incline[26] and topple to the right and left, and something like slumber (*al-sibāt*) overtook me. I thought that all those who were in the heavens and earth had died, because I did not hear any of the angels' voices, nor did I see any of his creatures upon the vision of my Lord.[27] My God left me this way as long as God willed, then he returned me to consciousness as if I had been dozing (*mustawsin*). I awoke and came to my senses, feeling calm in the knowledge of my location and my situation of awake nobility and evident affection.

[Heavenly Host Debate]

My Lord, glorified and praised be he, spoke to me saying: "Muḥammad, do you know what the *heavenly host debate?* " (Q 38:69). I replied, "My Lord, you are most knowing in that, and in all things. You are the most knowing of things unseen." He responded, "They debate about the degrees (*al-darajāt*) and the goodnesses (*al-ḥasanāt*). Do you know, Muḥammad, what the degrees and goodnesses are?" I answered, "My Lord, you are most knowing and most wise." He told me, "The degrees (*al-darajāt*) are the washing of ablutions in hated situations (*al-makrūhāt*), walking by foot to congregational prayers (*al-jumuʿāt*),[28] and waiting for prayer after prayer (*al-ṣalāt*). The goodnesses (*al-ḥasanāt*) are feeding food (*al-ṭaʿām*), spreading the peace (*al-salām*), and keeping vigil at night when other people are sleeping (*niyām*)." I never heard anything more consoling nor more sweet than the intonation of his words, and I became comfortable with him out of the sweetness of his intonation.

[Final Verses of the Cow Chapter][29]
Then he asked me, "Muḥammad, does *the Messenger believe . . .* ?"[30] I responded, "*The believers all believe in God and his angels and his books and his messengers. We do not differentiate between any of his messengers* like the Jews and the Christians did." He asked, "And what else do they say?" I answered, "'*They say, We hear* your statement *and we obey* your command." He said, "You speak the truth. Ask and be given." I replied, "*Forgive us, Lord. To you is the arrival*" (Q 2:285). He responded, "I have forgiven you and your community. Ask and be given." I replied, "*Lord, do not blame us when we forget or err, O Lord.*" He responded, "I have raised error and forgetting from you and your community, as well as what you find hateful." I replied, "*Lord, do not make us bear a heavy weight*, that is, a misdeed, *like the one you made those before us bear*, that is, the Jews." He said, "That is for you and your community." I requested, "*Lord, do not make us carry what we are not able.*" He answered, "I have done that with you and your community. Ask and be given." I petitioned, "Lord, *forgive us* for [our] degradation *and pardon us* for [our] defamation *and have mercy on us* for [our] distortion. *You are our master, so give us victory over the unbelievers*" (Q 2:286). He responded, "I have done that for you and your community."

[Favor of the Prophets]
I said, "My Lord, you *took Abraham as an intimate friend* (Q 4:125), and you *spoke to Moses directly* (Q 4:164). You raised Enoch *to a high place* (Q 19:57). You gave Solomon a *kingdom not befitting to anyone after him* (Q 38:35), and you *gave David the psalms* (Q 4:163; 17:55). What is for me, my Lord?"

He replied, "Muḥammad, I took you as an intimate friend just as I took Abraham as an intimate friend. I spoke to you just as I spoke to Moses directly. I gave you the opening of the book and the final verses of the Cow chapter (Q 2:285–86), which were from the treasuries of my throne. I have not given them to a prophet before you. I sent you to all the people of the earth, the white, black, and red, jinn and human. I have never sent a prophet before you to their collectivity. I made the earth, its land and sea, ritually pure and a place of prayer for you and your community."

"I nourished your community with booty (*al-fay*ʾ; Q 59:6–7) such that I did not offer to a community before yours. I gave you victory through dread (Q 59:2), to the point that your enemies flee from you even when there is a month's journey between you and them. I sent down upon you the master of all the books, a protection for them (Q 5:48), and a *Qurʾān which we divided* [into chapters] (Q 17:106). I *raised up for you your mention* (Q 94:4) to the point that I united it with my mention. I am never mentioned in anything of the paths of my religion (*shawāriʿ dīnī*) without you being mentioned with me."[31]

"We verily gave you in place of the Torah the "*couplets*" (Q 15:87),[32] in place of the Gospel the "two hundred,"[33] in place of the Psalms the "seals."[34] I have favored you with favor, so seize with power what *I have given you and be among the thankful* (Q 7:144)."[35]

[Secret Commission and Dismissal]

Then after this he informed me of matters that he did not permit me to tell you about. When he commissioned me with his commission[36] and he left me **[71]** for however long he wished, then he sat upon his throne (*istawā ᶜalā ᶜarshihi*). Glorified be he in his majesty and gravity and might!

I looked, and found that [the situation] had changed between him and me. Beside him was a veil of light burning brightly, no one knows its length except God. Were it to tear in a spot, it would burn up all of God's creatures.[37] The green *rafraf* that I had been sitting upon conveyed me downward, and it began to lower and raise me in the High Realm. At one point it started to raise me as if to fly with me, and at another it lowered me as if to descend with me toward what was below me. I thought that I would be dropped in the atmosphere of the High Realm. The *rafraf* kept doing that with me, descending and ascending, until I was dropped before Gabriel. He picked me up, and the *rafraf* flew upward until it was hidden from my sight.

[Miraculous Vision]

Then my God steadied the vision in my heart such that I could perceive in my heart what was behind me just as I perceive with my eyes what is in front of me. When God favored me with the vision of it, my sight fixed upon it. Gabriel gazed at me, and when he saw what I was experiencing he said to me, "Do not be afraid, Muḥammad. You will become firm through God's power. God will help you with steadiness to allow the vision of the light of the throne, the light of the veils, the light of the seas, the mountains of the High Realm, the light of the Cherubim (*karūbiyyūn*), and what is below that of the wonders of God's creatures to the ends of the earth." I saw all of that, one below the next, after the vision of one of them had broken upon me and diminished my sight from all else.

[Heavenly Voices]

I heard the voices of the Cherubim and those above them, the voice of the throne, the voice of the chair and of the curtains of light,[38] and the voices of the veils. They raised up around me in glorification of God, sanctification of God, and praise of God. I heard diverse voices: chirping, humming, roaring, clanging, and thundering, each different from one another.[39] I was afraid when I heard these wonders. Gabriel told me, "Do not be afraid, Messenger of God. Rejoice! For God has averted all fears and frights from you. I know through certain knowledge that you are his favorite creation and his purest human. He presented you with things that he never presented to any one of his creation, neither near angel nor sent prophet. The Merciful, great and magnificent, brought you close to him near the throne, a place that no one of his creation had ever reached or approached, neither the residents of the heavens nor of the earth. God gladdens you and selects you with his favor. He bestowed upon you the preferred rank and superior favor. Take [all] this in thanks (Q 7:144), for indeed he loves the thankful. His merit to you increases upon thanks from you." So I praised God for the way he selected and favored me.

[Tour of Paradise Begins]
Then Gabriel stated, "Messenger of God, gaze upon paradise until I show you what is yours in it, and what God has prepared for you in it, that you may know your destination after death. Asceticism in the earth increases your asceticism in it, desire in the afterworld increases your desire for it." I replied, "Agreed." So I traveled with Gabriel through praise of my Lord away from the High Realm, dropping exceedingly quickly, faster than an arrow or the wind.

[Questions about the High Realm: The Seas]
The fear that had overtaken me after hearing the Glorifiers around the throne left me, and my heart came back to me. So I spoke to Gabriel and began to ask him about what I had seen in the High Realm. [I posed to him the question,] "Gabriel, what were those seas that I saw, made of light, darkness, fire, water, pearl, ice, and light? He answered, "Glorified be God, those are the pavilions (*sarādiqāt*) of the Lord of Might with which he surrounds his throne. They are his covers, in addition to the seventy veils with which the Merciful veils himself from his creation. Those pavilions are covers for creatures, from the light of the veils to everything below that in God's creation. Messenger of God, how do you think what you saw compared to what was hidden, what you did not see of the wonders of the creation of your Lord in the High Realm?" I cried out, "Glorified be God, the Magnificent! How numerous are the wonders of his creation. I do not wonder at his power given the grandeur of his lordship."[40]

[Questions about the High Realm: The Angels]
Then I asked, "Gabriel, who were the angels that I saw in **[72]** the seas, and between the sea of fire to the sea of those who stand in rows (*al-ṣāfūn*), when they formed rows as if they were a compressed structure, crowding some against others? And who were the ones I saw behind them, like them, standing in formation, row upon row, between them and the others there being a distance, a span, and a remoteness?" He answered, "Messenger of God, did you not hear your Lord when he said in some of [the verses] he sent down to you: '*A day when the spirit and the angels stand in a row*' (Q 78:38)? And he informed you

that the angels said: '*We are those who stand in rows and we are those who glorify*' (Q 37:165). Thus those whom you saw in the seas of the High Realm are *those who stand in rows* around the throne to the end of the sixth heaven. The other ones are *those who glorify* in the heavens. The Spirit (*al-Rūḥ*) is their leader and the largest of all of them. Then Isrāfīl is next [largest]."

I asked, "Gabriel, who is the highest row that is in the highest sea above all the rows that surround the throne and encircle it?" Gabriel replied, "Messenger of God, the Cherubim are the most noble of the angels and largest of them and the leaders of them. Not a single one of the angels dares to gaze at one of the Cherubim. Were one of the angels of the heavens and earth to gaze at a single one of the Cherubim, it would be dazzled and their light would burn its eyes. Not a single one of the Cherubim dares to gaze at a single one of the residents of the highest row, which are the most honored of the Cherubim and the largest of them. They are greater than I am able to describe to you, and it is sufficient that you saw them."

[Questions about the High Realm: The Veils]

Next I asked Gabriel about the veils, and about what I heard of their glorification, exaltation, and adoration of God. He informed me about them, veil by veil and sea by sea, the types of their glorifications in many dialects that contained wonders, every wonder consisting of a eulogy and exultation of God.

[Tour of Paradise Resumes]

Gabriel brought me around in paradise, with God's permission. He left no place that he did not show me and explain to me. I know each step, palace, house, room, tent, tree, river, and spring as well this mosque of mine.

[The Lote Tree of the Boundary]

We continued to circle it until he brought me to the Lote Tree of the Boundary. He said, "Muḥammad, this is the tree that God mentioned in what he sent down, '*At the lote tree of the boundary*' (Q 53:14), [so called] because every near angel and every sent prophet ends at it. No servant, other than you and I these two times, have passed it. Before that, never. At [the Lote Tree] is the boundary of the realm of creatures, with God's permission and his power. In the future, God will decree in it what he wills.

I gazed upon it, and its trunk had a thickness that only God knows. Its branch is in the *garden of the refuge* (Q 53:15), which is the highest of all the gardens. I gazed at the branch of the Lote Tree, off of which other branches grew more numerous than the dust of the earth and its soil. Upon the branches were leaves so numerous only God knows their number. A single one of its leaves could cover the entire earth. It carried different fruits of paradise, in various types and varieties and flavors. Upon each branch was an angel, and upon each leaf was an angel, and upon each fruit was an angel, glorifying God in different voices and various dialects.

Then Gabriel told me, "Rejoice, Messenger of God, for your wives and children and many of your community will have a large kingdom and a momentous way of living in security under this tree. In it no fear will be upon you, nor will you grieve."[41]

[Rivers of Paradise]

I looked and saw a river flowing from the base of the tree, its water was more white than milk and more sweet than honey. It flowed over pebbles of pearl, sapphire, and chrysolite, its banks were as musk in odor and as snow in whiteness. He asked, "Do you see, Messenger of God, the very river that God mentioned in what he sent down to you: '*Indeed we have given you abundance*' (*al-kawthar*, Q 108:1). It is [the river of] *Tasnīm* (Q 83:27), and **[73]** God called it "*Tasnīm*" because it flows abundantly (*yatasannama*) to the people of paradise from under the throne to their houses, palaces, homes, rooms, and tents. In it is mixed their drinks of milk, honey, and wine. That is God's saying: '*A spring from which the servants of God drink, they let it flow in a gush*' (Q 76:6), that is, they direct it [to flow] to their homes. It is among the most honored drinks of paradise."

[Tree of Ṭūbā]

Next he brought me around paradise until we ended at a tree such that I did not see its like in paradise. When I stopped under it and raised my head, I could not see anything else in my Lord's creation because of its enormity. Its branches spread, and I smelled from them a fragrant smell, more fragrant than anything I had smelled in paradise. My glance circled around it, and I saw that its leaves were woven from the rarities of paradise, between white and red and yellow and green. Its fruits were like enormous jugs. God created each fruit in the heaven and earth from various colors and tastes and fragrances. I was pleased with that tree and the good qualities that I saw in it. I asked Gabriel, "What is this tree?" He answered, "This is the one that God mentioned in what he sent down to you: '*Ṭūbā is for them, and a good place of rest*' (Q 13:29). This is *Ṭūbā*, O Messenger of God, you and many of your people and your community will have in its shade the best final destiny and long comfort."

[Residences of Paradise]

Gabriel brought me around paradise until he brought me at last to heavenly palaces of ruby without blemish or crack. Within each of them were seventy thousand palaces, each palace having seventy thousand abodes, each abode having seventy thousand houses. In each house was a tent[42] of white pearl which had four thousand gates. One could see the inside of these tents from the outside and the outside from the inside out of the intensity of its radiance. Within them were beds of gold, that gold casting rays like the rays of the sun. It would reduce the sight of everything else, were it not for the fact that God does not allow such a thing. They were crowned with pearls and gems. Upon them were furnishings, their interiors of brocade and their exteriors of piled light, gleaming above the beds. On the beds were many jewels that I cannot describe to you. They are beyond the description of tongues and the desires of hearts. The jewels of women were on one side, the jewels of men on the other. A canopy was set above them, without covers.

In every palace, abode, house, and tent of paradise there were many trees, their trunks of gold, their branches of gems, their leaves of jewels, and their fruits the size of jugs of various colors, fragrances, and tastes. In the gaps between them were continuously flowing rivers of *Tasnīm*, exquisite wine, pure honey, and delicious milk. Among them was the spring of "*Salsabīl*" (Q 76:18), a spring of camphor, and a spring of wine more tasty that can be described, its fragrance that of musk.

[Heavenly Maidens]

In each house was a tent for the dark-eyed wives. Were one of them to show you [her] heavenly palm, the light of that palm would surpass the radiance of the sun. So how about their faces? They cannot be described by any thing that they would not surpass in beauty and perfection. Each one of [these maidens] has seventy servants and seventy young attendants devoted especially to them, apart from the servants of their husbands. Those servants are clean and good-looking, as God affirms: "*When you see them, you think that they were scattered pearls*" (Q 76:19) and "*around them circle young attendants as if they were hidden pearls*" (Q 52:24).

[Tour of the Palaces]

Then he brought me to stop at a palace. I saw in that palace such goodness, blessedness, freshness, splendor, tranquility, vigor, honor, and favor, such that no eye had seen, no ear had heard, and types of goodness and blessedness that had not been imagined in the human heart. All of that was empty, waiting for its owner from among the friends of God. I was overwhelmed by the wonders that I saw in that palace. I asked, "Gabriel, is there in paradise another palace like this one?" He answered, "Yes, Messenger of God. All **[74]** of the palaces of paradise are like this or better than this. Many palaces are even better than what you have seen. One can see their inside from their outside, their outside from within, and even better." I said, "For one like this, the workers work; in one similar to this, the breathers breathe."

I did not leave behind a place that I did not see, with God's permission. Thus I know every palace, abode, house, room, tent, and tree of paradise as well as I know this mosque of mine.

[Descent and Encounter with the Prophets]

Then he brought me out of paradise. We passed through the heavens, descending gradually from heaven to heaven. I saw our father Adam, and I saw my brother Noah. Then I saw Abraham. Next I saw Moses. Then I saw his brother Aaron, as well as Enoch, in the fourth heaven, his back leaning against the record house of creatures in which their affairs [are recorded]. Next I saw my brother Jesus in the [first] heaven.[43] I greeted each of them, and they met me with joyful tidings and salutations. They each asked me, "What did you do, Prophet of mercy, and where were you brought in the end? What did he do with you?" I informed them, and they celebrated, rejoiced, and praised God for that. They petitioned their Lord, asking him on my behalf for increase and mercy and favor.

We descended gradually from heaven. With me always was my companion and brother Gabriel. He did not leave me, nor I him, until he conveyed me to my place on earth from which he had carried me.

[Conclusion]

Praise be to God for that [journey]! It was all in a single night, with God's permission and power. "*Glorified be the one who caused his servant to journey by night from the sacred place of prayer to the furthest place of prayer . . .* " (Q 17:1), then beyond that, to where God willed.

I am, with God's blessing, the master of the children of Adam, without boasting, in this world and the afterworld. I am a servant, captivated by few things after seeing *some of the greatest signs of* [*my*] *Lord* (Q 53:18) and after meeting my brothers among the prophets. I yearn for my Lord, and for what I saw of his beneficence to his friends (*awliyāʾuhu*). I thrilled in reaching my Lord and meeting my brothers among the prophets whom I saw. What belongs to God is best and most lasting of all.

Appendix B
BAKRĪ'S "TOTAL AND COMPLETE" ASCENSION

The following represents a translation of the majority of the Bakrī "total and complete" (*al-tamām wa'l-kamāl*) ascension narrative, which is contained in the earliest dateable manuscript of this text known at the present. It is based on the manuscript held in Istanbul's Süleymaniye Kütüphanesi, under accession number 95/2 of the Amcazade Hüsayın Paşa collection. Comparisons to other extant Bakrī texts are given in the notes. The title page of this recension gives the following description of the work's contents:

> A book of the ascension of the Prophet, how he was made to ascend through the seven heavens, what he saw of the wonders and creatures, returning to his bed with glory and blessing that same night, and the favors that were conveyed to him. The reports are from him and his family, in the transmission of Abū al-Ḥasan Bakrī.[1]

The chain of transmission on the first page of the text confirms the alleged connection with Bakrī, whom the text presents as a student of the famous early author of the Prophet's biography, Ibn Isḥāq, and someone familiar with the reports of Ibn Isḥāq's contemporary, the famous Qur'ān commentator Muqātil b. Sulaymān (both d. ca. 150/767).[2] I have credited Bakrī with the elaboration of this general group of Ibn ʿAbbās texts that apparently began circulating around the sixth/twelfth or seventh/thirteenth centuries in what I have called the "Reshaped Version." I have added the general title and the headings to the major sections of the text, and have inserted recto (r) and verso (v) references from the source manuscript, Amcazade 95/2. A discussion of some of the key features of this Bakrī reshaped version is presented in chapter 8.

[Part One: The Night Journey to Jerusalem]

[27v] [Muḥammad narrates:] I had entered the house of my cousin Umm Hāniʾ, daughter of Abū Ṭālib, after the evening prayers. I found Umm Hāniʾ already slumbering in her sleeping quarters, so I performed the ritual prayers and then I wanted to seek shelter in [the comfort of] my bed. Suddenly I was in the presence of my beloved, Gabriel. It was a night of intense darkness, the moon having been hidden **[28r]** behind clouds and gloom. Indeed it was a pitch-black night, one of thunder and lightning, one during which neither a rooster crowed nor a donkey brayed nor a dog barked.

[Angels Approach]

The roof of my house was split, and there descended Gabriel in his [resplendent] form. [He wore] the brightest of gowns, lightning of pleat, white of body. His hair was [in braids] like ropes, white like snow. His feet were immersed in yellow [light]. Upon him was a cloak decorated with pearls and pure gold (*ʿiqyān*). Upon his forehead two lines were written, gleaming and shining in light: "There is no god but God" [and] "Muḥammad is the Messenger of God." He had seventy whiskers of musk. His form filled everything between the east and the west. He had five hundred wings. I woke warily, trembling, afraid. He said, "Do not be anxious, Muḥammad, for I am the faithful spirit, the messenger of the Lord of the worlds." Then he embraced me and kissed me between my eyes.

I said to him, "O my beloved Gabriel, did a revelation descend or a command occur or a warning appear?" He replied, "No revelation descended, nor a warning appear, nor a command occur." I said, "Then what is it, brother Gabriel?" He answered, "How praiseworthy it is that God sent me to you, to approach you with greetings of peace. He has commanded me to wake you, so get up and fasten your **[28v]** belt and don your cloak, for indeed tonight you will find yourself at your direction of prayer (*qibla*). A great matter is desired for you [to witness]. Your master, *whom slumber does not overtake, nor sleep* (Q 2:255)[3] will whisper with you. Indeed, God wishes to honor you this night in a way he has never honored anyone else before, nor will he honor anyone else in all of creation in the same way after. Rejoice, Muḥammad, in what he has given you. Make yourself [pure and] good, for you will see tonight some of the wonders of your Lord. You will witness his grandeur, and [the grandeur of] the creatures of his heavens and his angels."

[The Prophet said:] I got up, happy and pleased, and I fastened my belt, performed ablutions, and performed ritual prayer. Then I went out with Gabriel, and found myself with Michael, who was accompanied by 70,000 angels whom I saw in the sky. I greeted them and they returned my greeting, congratulating me on the honor of my Lord and the exaltedness of his contentment. Gabriel took my hand and led me to the Zamzam [well]. He parted my chest, then he put it in order and cleansed it. He circumambulated the House [i.e., the Ka^cba] with me. I prayed at the Station of Abraham (*maqām Ibrahīm*), and then I withdrew.

[The Prophet's Mount, Burāq]

I intended to exit the sacred enclosure when suddenly I found myself with Burāq, **[29r]** whom Gabriel had tied. [Burāq] was a mount smaller than a mule and larger than a donkey. Its face was as the face of a human, and its hindquarters was as the hindquarters of a horse. Its hair was braided just like a string of pearls and emeralds. Its eyes were as brilliant stars, aflame. They sent out rays like the rays of the sun. It was gray, dappled, and snowy white on its legs. Its right [side] was of pearl strung upon pearl and coral. [Its left side] was covered with two stripes, one of gold and the other of silver, arranged with gems. Its soul was as the soul of a human. Its reins were a chain of red gold. Its backside was of emerald. It had two wings like those of an eagle, woven as a brocade of silk. Green of body, it had been formed out of light, a creation of [God,] the all-forgiving king. Its saddle was of gleaming gold, brilliant like a lamp, with two stirrups of pure gold. Its face was that of a person.[4] Its step reached to the limit of its sight. Its bridle was of ruby. Muḥammad said, "Gabriel, what is this mount?" He replied, "Muḥammad, this is Burāq. Ride it, and pass on to see **[29v]** the wondrous command of God." Then Gabriel took its bridle and Michael its stirrups.

[Burāq Shies]

[Muḥammad said:] I put my hand upon the bow of its saddle, intending to ride it, and it neighed, stirred, and jerked around like a fish caught in a net. Gabriel struck its stirrups with his hand, exclaiming, "Calm down, Burāq. Why do you shy? By God, no one more noble than Muḥammad has ever ridden upon you." It answered, "Gabriel, Abraham the intimate friend has ridden upon me in order to sacrifice his son Ishmael. Moses the speaker has ridden upon me, as has Adam the pure and faithful." Gabriel told Burāq, "This is Muḥammad son of ^cAbd Allāh, beloved of the Lord of the worlds, master of all of creation, and possessor of intercession, crowned by the crown of noble favor. To him is the *qibla* of Islam, the favor of [all] beings (*al-an^cām*); the Way and the consensus (*al-sunna wa 'l-jamā^ca*), and the response during the intercession (*al-shafā^ca*). For him are the great phrases, 'There is no god but God, [and] Muḥammad is the Messenger of God.' He was sent to the white and black as a rejoicer and warner, and he is the best of the messengers, leader of the blaze of the noble procession." Burāq asked Gabriel, **[30r]** "This is the possessor of the Yemenī *qibla*, and the community of the faithful (*al-ḥanīfiyya*) who will return creatures into the intercession, paradise on his right and hellfire on his left? Whoever believes him enters paradise, and whoever calls him a liar enters hellfire?" Gabriel answered, "Indeed." Burāq become abashed, to the point that a drop of sweat trickled down [its cheeks].

[Burāq] said, "Gabriel, indeed he has defiled himself with his hand upon gold." Gabriel asked me, "Have you touched gold with your hand, Muḥammad?" I said, "I passed by an idol of the Quraysh which was covered with gold, and I passed my hand over it, saying to it, 'He who worships you is indeed clearly astray.'" Gabriel said, "Burāq, approach the beloved of the Lord of the worlds." Burāq said, "Gabriel, I ask you by God the great, the compassionate and caring, and by the covenant between you and me, will you not ask him to include me in his intercession on the day of resurrection?" The Messenger of God said to it, "Burāq, are you not among the mounts of paradise, free and comfortable from such [fear of hellfire]?" It said, "Messenger of God, I desired to exit from [paradise] while advanced in age, so I will not return to it, just as Iblīs exited and will not return to it. I do not know God's plan." [The Prophet said,] "Be at ease, Burāq, you will be a part of my intercession." When Burāq heard that, **[30v]** it rejoiced and trusted me to ride it.

[The Night Journey]

When I got upon its back, it [proceeded] like the flash of lightning or like the gusting of wind. Gabriel called out to me, "Muḥammad, apply yourself exclusively to Burāq, refusing to respond to anyone on your path." So I applied myself to Burāq, and it placed its hoofs at the limit of its sight. On the journey [on Burāq's back], I encountered neither sensation nor movement; when it descended down into a dried-up riverbed, it lengthened its front legs[5] and shortened its [back] legs, and when it ascended up a mountain, it shorted its front legs and lengthened its [back] legs, until we crossed [the amount of land] that God wills.

Gabriel commanded me, "Muḥammad, descend and pray here two cycles of ritual prayer upon the community of Abraham." [Muḥammad said:] So I descended and prayed two cycles, then I rode [Burāq once again]. I asked Gabriel, "Why did you command me to pray here?" He responded, "Aḥmad, that is Mount *Ṭūr* of Sinai, the spot in which Moses spoke to God."

Then we went on, and the trustworthy Gabriel was hidden from me. Suddenly I heard a voice calling on my right, "Muḥammad, wait so that I may talk to you, for I am a good advisor to you and your community." Burāq continued on without stopping, and I did not respond to it, since Gabriel had made me promise not to, and that was a success granted by God.

[31r] Then we went on, and while proceeding I heard a voice shouting on my left, "Muḥammad, wait, stop so that I may talk to you, for I am the best of creatures in advising you." Burāq continued on without stopping, and I did not respond to it out of my prior promise.

We went on, and suddenly there was a woman immediately in front of me. Her hair was spread out, her frock extended toward me. Upon her were jewels and finery such that I had never seen any creature wear, of resplendent quality and beauty. She stood directly before Burāq, even though it at times flew and at times ran upon the ground, yet it did not turn toward her, and that was a success granted by God.

Then I heard a sound, which almost terrified me to the point that [my reason] flew from me,[6] consisting of a great crashing noise. When I passed it, suddenly I came to the land known as the Province of Syria (*al-Shām*), arriving at the House of Sanctity (*bayt al-maqdis*) [in Jerusalem].

[Jerusalem]

I found myself among Abraham, Moses, Jesus, and all the prophets and messengers, who had appeared from the Furthest [Place of Prayer, *al-Aqṣā*]. They came to me, greeted me, and welcomed me. They said, "Praise be to God who fashioned you as a brother and a crown for us. What a most blessed brother you are, and what a blessed arrival you have had."

[While I was still riding upon Burāq], they brought me to "the Furthest" (*al-Aqṣā*, Q 17:1), and Gabriel said to me, "Muḥammad, did you see anyone **[31v]** or hear anything or glance at anything [on the night journey to Jerusalem]?" I said, "Yes, Gabriel, I heard a caller on my right call to me, 'Muḥammad, wait up! Muḥammad, stop a while, for I am the best of creatures in advising you.' Next I heard something similar on my left. Finally I encountered a woman whose description is such and such." Gabriel asked, "Anything else?" Muḥammad replied, "I heard a crashing." Gabriel queried, "Do you know who the first voice who shouted was?" I answered, "God and his Prophet are most knowing."[7] He said, "That was the caller of the Jews. Had you responded to him, your community after you would have become Jewish until the day of resurrection. As for the shouter on the left, that was the caller of the Christians. Had you responded to him, your community after you would have become Christian until the day of resurrection. As for the adorned woman, she was the world inclining toward you. Were you to have responded to her, your community would have chosen this world over the next, which would have led your community into hellfire."

I responded, "For [only] my Lord's sake is the praise and the thanks.[8] Yet Gabriel, when the woman called out I did respond to her, because I am the one who pities women the most. When she said to me, 'Stop!' I remained upon Burāq. She desired to speak to me, and even began speaking to me, but I was loath to speak to her, and I passed on." Gabriel said, "Muḥammad, your community after you will be tested by the love of the world, until **[32r]** even the wise will extend and incline toward it. Had you not loved it, your community would have been safe from the love of it."[9]

[Gabriel continued,] "As for that [loud] crashing [sound], it is a rock that God sent down into the hellfire known as the 'Blazing fire' (*Hāwiyya*, Q 101:9) seventy thousand years [ago], and it has still not reached the bare desert [at its bottom]. It will fall until the day of resurrection."

Then Gabriel grabbed my hand and told me to descend [from Burāq's back]. He struck his finger into the rock [of the holy sanctuary] and bore a hole into it, into which he sent Burāq.[10]

He said to me, "Enter." So I entered, and found myself with a strikingly handsome youth. He shook my hand so I shook his, he greeted me and I greeted him. He embraced me and then disappeared. Gabriel questioned me, "Who was that, Muḥammad?" I replied, "God knows best." He exclaimed, "God granted you success, for that was Belief, and your religion rests upon belief. Your community will seek the goodness of belief over unbelief." Hearing that, I thanked God many times.

[Prayer with the Prophets]

Then I entered the place of prostration (*al-masjid*), and found myself among the prophets in rows, three-hundred and twelve messengers in all. Gabriel advanced us forward, and called for ritual prayer, [shouting], "Oh elders among the messengers, this is your leader, coming forward." He grabbed my upper arm and advanced me, so I came to the front. He said, "Lead them in prayer, and be quick." So I prayed as the leader of the prophets. I went forward and led them in two cycles of prayer, **[32v]** spreading the peace, and this is no boast upon my brothers. Gabriel had told me, "Muḥammad, My Lord commanded me [to advance you to the front]," and that is no mere boast.

Then they approached me, greeted me, and congratulated me for the favor and honor that God had given me. Gabriel informed me of that, and he informed me of the names of each one of them, until there was not one of the messengers left whom I did not know. They called for increased favors for me, and they congratulated me because my community will enter paradise. Gabriel grabbed my upper arm, and brought me toward the rock.

[Cup Test]

There I found myself faced with three cups, the first of wine, the second of milk, and the third of water. Suddenly a voice called out from above my head, "If Muḥammad drinks the water, his community after him will drown. If he drinks the wine, his community after him will go astray." So I reached out my hand for the milk, and I drank all but a little of it. Then another voice said, "Had Muḥammad drunk all the milk, none of his community would have entered hellfire." I requested, "Gabriel, return the milk to me." He replied, "Impossible, Muḥammad, the matter has been set, and the pen has already written what will be." I asked Gabriel if that had been set down in the Book, and he answered that it had been.

[Part Two: Journey through the Seven Heavens]

Then Gabriel told me to advance to the rock, so I advanced **[33r]** and I found myself at the *mi^crāj* ladder, which had been erected from the rock of the House of Sanctity to the sky of the world [i.e., the first heaven]. I gazed upon beauty such that I had never seen before, making me desirous of gazing upon it another time. It consists of a ladder of gold with supports of silver. Its [initial] rung was yellow, [then] its [next] rung was red, then green, then white, [continuing] through all the colors. [It had] a rung of silver and one of gold, one of sapphire and one of [other] gems. I gazed upon the angels descending and ascending upon it, saying halleluiahs and proclaiming God's greatness, sanctifying and glorifying and praising and extolling the Lord of the worlds.

[Ascending the Mi^crāj-Ladder to the Green Sea]

Gabriel called out to me, "Ascend, Muḥammad, and rejoice at the beneficence of the Lord of the worlds." Then he pressed me to his chest, wrapping me in his wing, and carried me upon the *mi^crāj*. I put my legs down upon the first of its supports, and it pushed upon me as if it blew like a wind, yet I did not separate from it. I did not have the sensation of walking, nor did I find my path tiring, rather it was as if I were a bird or a rising [star]. That was out of the power of my Lord, whom there is no god but he.

Suddenly I found myself with the angels of my Lord. They were seeking to meet me, inquiring about me, and offering me congratulations for what my Lord bestowed upon me of favor and nobility, petitioning for its increase in me.

I proceeded in this fashion until I ended up at a **[33v]** green sea such that I had never seen before. Around it angels were glorifying God. I asked, "My beloved Gabriel, what sea is this?" He replied, "This is the green sea visible to the people of the earth, and it serves as a veil between the earth and sky."[11]

[The Angel of Death]

Then I looked and found myself with a seated angel who had the world between his knees, below whom was a seat (*kursī*) of light. On his right was a tablet, and on his left was a tree, a leaf of which was like the surface of the earth. On his right were angels, and in his hand were a javelin and a cup.[12] He looked long and hard at the tablet, then extended his hand out to the tree. Then he reached his hand to the eastern and western lands of the earth. He appeared to be an enormous angel, whose legs split the lowest earth, and whose head traversed the skies to the base of the throne. Those angels [that I saw under him] were speeding off by his command.

Upon his right were angels as numerous as the population of all the *jinn*, handsome of face, resplendent of light, pleasant of smell. Sight was almost dazzled by the beauty of their faces, and hearts [swooned] from the beauty of their fragrance. Upon his left were angels that were ugly of countenance, black of face, and disgusting of smell. Flames of fire emitted from their nostrils, eyes, and mouths, like the flash of lightning. Souls almost [departed] from the stench of their smell and the ugliness of their demeanor. When I saw them, I trembled with fear, **[34r]** and my heart became afraid.

Gabriel told me, "Muḥammad, greet this angel, for he has a great station with God. Indeed, he is the greatest of angels in obedience, receiving no respite and no rest from what the Lord of the worlds assigned to him." [The Prophet said:] I approached him and greeted him, and he replied to me with [an inclination of] his head, not speaking to me because of his being occupied by what the Lord of the worlds assigned to him. He looked upon the world, the next world, the tablet, and the tree in succession, with no respite and no rest.

Gabriel called out to [the angel], "Will you not reply to the greeting of the master of creation, the Messenger of God, the beloved of the Lord of the worlds, the friend of the faithful?" The angel said, "Who is he, Gabriel?" Gabriel replied, "He is Muḥammad, Messenger of the Lord of the worlds." The angel asked, "Has Muḥammad been sent?" Gabriel responded, "Yes." So the angel said, "Welcome to you, master of the messengers. I see blessedness in you and in your community of the faithful. Thus I see them in this tablet of mine."

[Muḥammad said]:[13] "Gabriel, I have not yet passed a single angel of my Lord who did not smile and joyously greet me except for this one, who never appears laughing or joyous." Gabriel responded, "You **[34v]** are the most favored with God, and were he to laugh with anyone before you, he would have laughed with you. Yet, since the day God created him, he has not laughed, [nor will he ever] until the day the hour comes."

[The Prophet asked,] "Who is he, this angel, and what is his name, for my heart is afraid to look upon him and I tremble with fear out of terror of him." Gabriel replied, "This is ʿAzrāʾīl, the Angel of Death, a powerful angel. One cannot describe the severity and anger in him. He and [another great angel] Mālik, the Guardian of Hellfire, will never laugh with any creature until the final hour comes."

"My beloved Gabriel, inform me about the tablet that is on his right, which he looks at with such long glances, and also about that tree on his left." Gabriel replied, "Muḥammad, as for the tablet on his right, written on its surface are the names of each and every human being from the day that God created them until the day of resurrection. As for that tree, their names are inscribed upon it, too. He glances upon it, and when he sees that a leaf withers and dries up on its branches, he knows that the appointed hour [of death] approaches for that servant. So he strikes it with that javelin of his, and it falls."

[Questions Posed to the Angel of Death]

[The Prophet said,] "Gabriel, I hate to ask him, [but] something occurs to me." **[35r]** Gabriel said, "The matter is with God. He will do what [God] wills." Suddenly a voice cried out, "Muḥammad, advance and ask him what you will, for God has commanded you to ask, and has commanded him to answer."

So [the Prophet] approached him and asked, "Angel of Death, tell me about the man who dies in the east and another dies in the west in the same hour. How do you seize both of their souls?" He said, "Muḥammad, do you not see that the entire world is in my hands, just like a table in one of your hands? I grab what I want from the east to the west of the earth just as one of you grabs a bite from a dish when it is placed in front of him."

I asked further, "Angel of Death, when armies engage in battle, and in a single hour [many] people die, do you seize them all?" He answered, "No creature seizes [souls], with God's permission, apart from me." I asked, "How do you seize them [all]?" He replied, "Muḥammad, I call out to them, with God's permission and power, uttering a single shout over them, rendering them thunderstruck (*yaṣᶜaqūna*). Their souls come faster than the blink of an eye, hearing and obeying, out of fear for the greatness of the Lord of the worlds."

I inquired of him, "ᶜAzrāʾīl, where are those who have passed on, from the first to the last?" He answered, "With me here are their names, **[35v]** written down." I asked, "And [what about the names of those] who remain, among the last ones?" He replied, "I have them on God's *Preserved Tablet*" (Q 85:22). I asked, "How do you know them?" He answered, "The command of the Lord of the worlds descends from year to year, containing the number of those who will die [each year]." I asked, "How do you recognize them?" He said, "Their names descend from the sky, where it is written 'So and so will die, in such and such a country, in such and such a month, on such and such a day, during such and such an hour.'"

I asked, "How do you know the people of paradise from the people of hellfire?" He said, "Oh Muḥammad, it is written on their foreheads: either wretched [i.e., damned] or happy [i.e., saved]." I inquired, "Regarding the happy ones, how do you treat them?" He replied, "I know that they are among the people of paradise, so I send to them those angels who are on my right, who take the form of the angels of paradise. They enter into [their homes], and when the man or woman or child fixes his or her eyes upon them, his or her intellect begins to cry out of the goodness of their easy bearing, the companionability of their faces, and the pleasantness of their form. They come to [the dying soul] early, greet it, and open the door to paradise for it and show it its place in paradise before it dies. This opens its heart, improves its spirit,[14] and gives it confidence to leave [its body], **[36r]** desiring what it saw. When they grasp its spirit through the arteries, limbs, bones, flesh and blood, and when the spirit arrives in the gullet the rest of you at that moment gazing at them the angel waits and I grasp it, I, with my own hands. I lead [the soul] on towards its given fate so that those in the heavens and earth can pray on its behalf. Then I take it into paradise and it is raised up to the high realm. When such a man is prepared and is carried to his fated destiny, an angel stays behind in his house. When [those left behind] cry or wail, that angel calls out to them, 'Oh people of this abode, do not cry or be anxious, for by God, we did not cut off his sustenance, nor did we establish his allotted time. Rather, we acted as we were commanded. Do not cry. Indeed, we shall return to you, and continue returning here until there is not one of you left.'"

[He continued,] "Oh Muḥammad, if the servant [who dies] was wretched, those angels on my left are sent to him, the ones resembling the *Zabāniyya* (Q 96:18) of Jahannam. They are the punishing angels. When [the servant] glances upon them, his eyes become fixated, and his intellect flees from the ugliness of their countenance and the stench of their smell. When they grab his spirit, his intellect goes to his neck until it reaches the gullet. They leave it there, suspended in such a state of great distress. Since I know that, I too grasp it in the hard [portion] of his heart. **[36v]** I force it out of his hard [narrow passage], that is, I push it the hard [way through] the heart, out of hate, with the same ferocity of those angels, until one of them brings it out into the air. Then he repeats [the process].

Next [the wicked soul] is cast into the fire of *Sijjīn* (Q 104:4–5), which is a pit of the deepest hellfire." [The Prophet] asked, "Which hellfire is it, ᶜAzrāʾīl?" He said, "The seventh and lowest. In it is a black, dark, pitch-colored tree, which never sees the light, upon which are many types of tortures."[15] [The Prophet] said: I cried upon hearing that, and Gabriel also cried because of my tears. I said to Gabriel, "My beloved Gabriel, death is sufficient as a warning."

Then I asked, "Angel of Death, how do you distinguish [on your list] those whom you have grasped from those who remain?" He responded, "The one whom I have already grasped from among them, I strike out his name, and the one whom I have not grasped, I do not. I repeatedly cast my glance over the latter, seventy times each day, and never neglect him."

[He cried out,] "Oh Muḥammad, what begins at death is even more terrible and more important." I asked him, "What is it, ᶜAzrāʾīl?" He replied, "The two blue angels who roll up their hair and gnash their fangs at the earth. In their hands are two pillars. Were the greatest mountain on earth to be struck with one, it would crumble. Their eyes gleam like the flash of lightning and their voices boom like the rumble of thunder. **[37r]** Every believer and nonbeliever alike beseeches them, and everyone, obedient or profligate, they terrify in the grave. They make each one sit down in his grave, and then they spread out before him all of his works. They then show him his resting place, whether he be among the people of paradise or the people of hellfire."

The Prophet said, "The two certainly terrify the unbelievers and act in such a fashion with them, but what about with the faithful ones?" He responded, "That is a matter of your Lord. There is no god but He. As for the unbeliever, Muhammad, he will not find any respite from punishment, from the day of his leaving the world to the day of resurrection. As for the faithful, for him you will offer a courage that will shield him from all his disobedient faults in the world.

When he exits from his grave, he will exit from it upon the seat of that courage which he attained."

[The Rooster Angel]

[The Prophet said,] "I bade farewell to ᶜAzrāᵓīl, then I passed on, traversing what God willed. I found myself with an angel in the air in the form of a rooster, its neck under the throne and its legs in the borders of the lowest world. It had feathers of the brightest white. Its backside was yellow. One of its wings was in the east, the other in the west. Its feathers were of every color that God created. I have never seen a creature more eloquent than it, nor more beautiful. **[37v]** Below its wings were [feathers of] white down. When it fluttered and prostrated, it praised God in the midst of its prostrations, crying out, "Glory to the king, the most holy, Lord of the angels and the spirit! Glory to the most high, highest is his glory! Glory to the one whom the birds glorify in different languages! Glory to the one whom the hours of the night and the hours of the day glorify!"

I marveled, standing there gazing at it. I asked, "My brother Gabriel, who is this?" He replied, "This is an angel whom God created in the form of a rooster, as you see. He taught it the stages of the night and the day, and the hours of the ritual prayers. Whenever the hour or the time of ritual prayer arrives, this angel raises its voice and flaps its wings throughout the [east and west]. When it glorifies [God] in the heavens, all of the roosters of the earth also glorify and flap their wings, [continuing] in glorification until the times of prayer are completed during the day. At night, it does the same as during the day, except that it says at the first portion of the night, 'Glorified be the wise one who does not hurry.' In the second [portion of the night], it says, 'Glorified be the generous one over the one who disobeys him.' In the third [portion of the night], it says, 'Wake up, o you negligent ones, this is the time for seeking forgiveness.' When it is time for the call to prayer, the gates of the sky are opened, and the Lord descends to the lowest heaven, calling out to the people of the earth, **[38r]** 'If there is one who repents, then I accept his repentance. If there is one who seeks forgiveness, then I forgive him. I am indeed the most forgiving, the most merciful.' After the call to prayer, that is, the dawn call to prayer, the gates of the sky become closed once again."

[Half-Fire-Half-Snow Angel]

[The Prophet continued,] "Gabriel and I passed on until suddenly we were with another angel, half of whose body was of white snow and the other half of whose body was of blazing fire. Its head was in the snow [portion]. The fire did not melt the snow, nor did the snow extinguish the fire, and one thing did not blend with the other. I asked, "Gabriel, what is the name of this one?" He answered, "Muḥammad, its name is Ḥabīb [Beloved], and it is the best counselor to those of the earth. This angel makes the following supplication: 'My dear God, unite the hearts of the male believers and the female believers [just as I unite fire and snow]. Rectify their essential nature, and improve the actions of the righteous so that they do not cease to perform them. You are powerful over all things.' From the day [this angel] was created until the day of resurrection, it does not cease in uttering this invocation. May God bless this angel for it. The angel looked upon Gabriel and asked, "Gabriel, who is [that man]?" He replied to Ḥabīb, "This is Muḥammad." Then it greeted me, warmly received me, and congratulated me, extolling my name and promising me good things.

[The Guardian of Hellfire]

Gabriel and I walked on, and we found ourselves with an angel seated in the air on a seat (*kursī*) of light, holding in his hands a pillar of fire that would flatten the heavens were he to strike them with it. He was powerful, loud, and intense [**38v**] with sadness and distress. God created his head out of freezing cold, his eyes out of blazing lightning, his sides out of the copper of the *Ḥuṭama* (Q 104:4–5), his chest out of the stone of the *Hāwiya* (Q 101:9), and his wings out of *Sijjīn* (Q 83:7–8).[16] On his right were angels with chains, manacles, and thick shackles. [Also] on his right were [piles of] hooks, irons, swords, chains, manacles, and thick shackles. On his left were [the accursed abodes of] *Jahannam*, *Najjūm*, *Zaqqūm*, *Ḍarīᶜ*, and *ᶜAdhāb*, as well as snakes, scorpions, beasts of prey, dogs, and iron bars. I seek refuge in God from all that.

When I saw him, he terrified me, and I stood transfixed, gazing at him. Then I perceived that Gabriel was saying, "Dear God, do not make him to be upon our path," and I thought to myself, "This angel must indeed be great, since even Gabriel seeks refuge from him." Then I asked, "My beloved Gabriel, who is that?" He replied, "Muḥammad, it is Mālik, the Guardian of Hellfire." My nervousness increased, and I endeavored to stay back from him, but Gabriel said to me, "Approach him and greet him. There is no angel in the heavens who does not seek refuge from him, for he knows your fate." [The Prophet said:] I came close to him and greeted him. He returned [the greeting] with [an inclination of] his head, so Gabriel called out to him, "Mālik, show him honor in greeting." [**39r**] Mālik asked, "And who is he, Gabriel?" "He is Muḥammad, the Beloved of God." So he greeted me, opening the way for me, saying, "Welcome to you, you most noble of human beings. You are the most blessed of prophets, and this is the most blessed of arrivals. I find total goodness in you and in your community, for you are 'most praised' (*Aḥmad*), and they are 'the praising ones' (*al-Ḥāmidūn*). You are 'the faithful' (*al-Amīn*), and they are 'the faithful ones' (*al-Muʾminūn*). You are 'the near' (*al-Qarīb*), and they are 'the near ones' (*al-Muqarrabūn*). Thus God gladdens you with them, and they with you."

I posed questions to him, saying, "Mālik, how long ago were you placed in charge of *Jahannam*?" He responded, "Since the day God created me, he placed me in charge of its affairs." I asked, "So why is it that you are so sad, affected, and full of such care?" He replied, "Muḥammad, it was out of sadness for the one who disobeys [God] until the moment of his arrival. They push such a one to me, and he falls into my hands. When I seize him, I take revenge upon him for what he did." I asked, "O Mālik, why is it that the Guardians of Hellfire do not exit from the hellfire to seek some relief?" He answered, "Muḥammad, God created them in it, and they are comfortable in it. Were they to exit from it, they would die, just as a fish dies when it leaves the water. God made them from fire, Muḥammad, and placed hardness into their hearts, stronger than iron. When a servant receiving punishment petitions them [for mercy], they do not have any mercy for him, nor when he falls to the ground do they talk to him. Night and day they punish he who disobeyed God until they have wreaked their vengeance upon him." I cried, and Gabriel cried too.

[The First Heaven]
Then we proceeded, [**39v**] seeking refuge in God from the hellfire, from its heat, and from Mālik, until we arrived at the [first] heaven. In it were angels of God, and it was a heaven made out of black smoke. Its name is "Elevated" (*al-Rafīʿa*). Its thickness was a journey of five hundred years, and between it and the earth was the same distance. I saw in it stars hanging like lanterns, the smallest of which was the size of a great mountain. I saw that some of them were in motion, and some of them were ornamented. There was no place on them the length of a finger that did not have an angel either kneeling or touching his head down in prostration. We knocked on [the first heaven's] gate, and its guardian called out, "Who is it?" Gabriel answered, "Gabriel." The guardian asked, "And who is with you?" He replied, "Muḥammad." The guardian said, "Welcome to you, Gabriel, and to the one with you," and he opened the gate.

I gazed upon an angel sitting on a seat (*kursī*) of light, with angels in front of him, behind him, and on his right and left, glorifying God and sanctifying him. I said, "My beloved Gabriel, who is that?" He said, "Muḥammad, it is Ismāʿīl, the one in charge of the closest heaven. Approach him and greet him." So I approached him and greeted him, and he replied to my greeting, saying, "Welcome, Muḥammad. You are the best of those beloved [to God], the best of brothers, and your arrival here is the best of arrivals. Rejoice, for complete goodness is in you and your community." [Muḥammad said:] I gazed upon the soldiers of Ismaʿīl [**40r**], under whose command were ninety-thousand angels that were all assigned to the first heaven. They approached me, greeted me, sought forgiveness, and congratulated me.

I gazed upon angels standing in rows, with shoulders equidistant [from one another]. They were the humble ones (*al-ḥāshiʿūn*), ascetic (*al-rāhibūn*), listening, obedient, fearful, and cautious, making a sound like [thunder] through their glorifications when they cry out, "Most glorified and holy is the Lord of the angels and the spirit! Holy, holy is the Lord of Lords! The mighty and munificent! Glorified be the magnificent, the most magnificent! Glorified be the generous, the most generous! Glorified and exalted and elevated and magnified be he!" I asked Gabriel [if he knew] how numerous they were. He replied, "No, Muḥammad, no one knows the number of those [angels] except God who created them: *No one knows the soldiers of your Lord except he*" (Q 74:31). I heard Ismaᶜīl making the following glorification: "Glorified be the most magnificent king! Glorified be the high, the highest! Glorified and exalted be he! Glorified be the one to whom nothing else is resembles! *He is the all hearing, the all seeing*" (Q 17:1).

Then I advanced through the nearest heaven, and I found myself with angels in the form of cows with bodies of light. The sound of their wings was like the sound of thunder. They have [clusters of] two, three, and four wings. [It seemed as if] one angel surged upon another.[17] Their light gleamed, almost blinding my sight. When they saw me, they raised [**40v**] their voices in glorification, to the point that I thought that everyone in the earth would be able to hear them. I was seized by fear and crying at the intensity of their devotions, the absence of any levity [among them], and the number of their strivings. From seeing them, I became filled with awe.

Among these angels, I saw a handsome old man. When he glorified, they glorified. He had an immense light that gleamed from him. Upon both them and him were robes of light. When he saw me, he greeted me. I asked, "My beloved Gabriel, who is this?" He answered, "Muḥammad, this is Noah. Advance to him and greet him. So I did, and he replied, "Welcome to you. You are the righteous child. Rejoice, Muḥammad, for complete goodness is in you and your community." Thus he congratulated me and my community. He continued, "Muḥammad, I have never seen any [works] purer than the works of your community, nor any people more enlightened, not even among those who say there is no god but God, and you are Muḥammad, the Messenger of God."

Then I saw something about which I was not allowed to tell you.[18] Then Gabriel told me, "Advance, Muḥammad, and pray two cycles of prayer for the community of Abraham with the angels of [this] heaven." So I advanced, and led them in ritual prayer.

We continued ascending until we came upon a great sea that was more intensely white than snow. On it the foam accumulated, layer upon layer. I said, "Gabriel, what sea is this?" He replied, "Muḥammad, this is the Sea of Living Creatures (*Baḥr al-ḥayawān*) in which God will bring to life the bones of the dead between [**41r**] the two [trumpet] blows on the day of resurrection."

[The Second Heaven]

Gabriel ascended with me from the First Heaven to the Second Heaven faster than the blink of an eye. Between them was a distance of a five-hundred-year journey, and its width was similar to that distance. I gazed at it and saw that it was of gleaming iron, and its name was "Foremost" (*Qaydūm*). Gabriel knocked on its gate, and an angel responded, "Who is there?" He said, "I am Gabriel." The angel asked, "And who is with you?" Gabriel responded, "Muḥammad, the Messenger of God." The angel cried out, "Praise be to God, Lord of the worlds." He opened the gate for us, and we entered.

We found ourselves with rows of angels upon whom there was dignity, gravity, and the features of ᶜUthmān b. ᶜAffān. I said, "Gabriel, how did these angels arrive to this station?" He replied, "By reciting the Qurᵓān." I saw them in straight rows, in the posture of touching their heads to the ground, with their shoulders touching. Were one to measure the space between their shoulders with a hair, it would not be parted, and it would not fit between them. They were raising their voices in glorification and sanctification of God, the Lord of the worlds, saying, "Glorified be the generous creator! Glorified be the highest of the high! Glorified be the one from whom there is no place to flee or find refuge, nor is there a place to find safety except with him! Glorified be our Lord, and exalted be he!" I said [to Gabriel], "May [my community's] worship be that way." Gabriel replied, "Come, Muḥammad, ask your Lord to grant you and your community what he granted to them." So I petitioned [to God for that].

I advanced and gazed upon thick-bodied angels, of a shape more beautiful than I had ever seen. Their faces **[41v]** were in the shape of eagles (*nusūr*), and their bodies were of light. When the first of them glorified [God], the last of them responded with sanctification, glorification, praise, and magnification of God, Lord of the worlds. They do not abate or become weary of remembering God, the great and exalted. Then I gazed upon [the Second Heaven's] guardian, *ᶜIlliyīn*,[19] who was sitting among them.

Next I gazed upon a sea more enormous than the Sea of Living Creatures. I would not be able to describe it, even were I to struggle with my [best] effort.[20] I asked, "Which sea is this one, brother Gabriel?" He said to me, "Muḥammad, this is the sea from which God sent forth the waters upon the people of Noah and drowned them. O Muḥammad, by the one who sent you with the truth as a prophet, indeed it is larger than the seven earths. Were the Lord to send ten [such floods] upon the world, he would drown it and its inhabitants, rising up to the tips of its mountains [to a height of] seven hundred cubits. Its name is the Sea of Seas (*Baḥr al-buḥūr*)."

Then Gabriel raised me up, and I found myself with two glorious individuals, and I asked about them. He said, "They are John son of Zachariah (John the Baptist) and Jesus son of Mary. Approach them and greet them." So I advanced to them and greeted them. They returned the greeting and congratulated me for what God had granted me of favor and blessing. Then Gabriel advanced me forward and commanded me to pray, so I advanced and led the people of the heaven in two cycles of prayer, without frivolity or pause. I was filled with wonder at the frivolity of the people of the world and the industry of the people of the heavens.

[The Third Heaven]

[42r] We passed on toward to the people of the Third Heaven, ending at it faster than a wink, it being the distance of a five-hundred-year journey, and its width the same in distance. It was of copper, and was called "Powerful" (*Mākūn*). Gabriel knocked on its gate, and an angel among its guardians responded, "Who is there?" Gabriel said, "I am Gabriel." The guardian asked, "And who is with you?" Gabriel replied, "Muḥammad." The gatekeeper queried, "Has Muḥammad been sent?" Gabriel answered, "Yes." The gatekeeper replied, "Praise be to God, Lord of the worlds," opening the gate for us, and we entered through it. In [the Third Heaven] I saw angels who were enormous of stature. I asked about that, and was told to recite, "*Say: He is God, one*" (Q 112:1). Then I advanced, and encountered the guardian of the Third Heaven.[21] He congratulated me for what God had granted to me.

I advanced and found myself with angels in the form of human beings, with bodies of light. I also saw an angel, great of stature, whom the rest encircled. I saw wonders of God's creation, great is his power. I observed that angel, and found him to be the leader of one hundred rows of angels, each row like the *two weighty ones* [in number].[22]

And I gazed upon David and Solomon, about whom Gabriel informed me. I advanced to them and greeted them, and they returned my greeting, shaking my hand and saying, "Praise be to God who made you a crown and brother to us! Congratulations to you for what God granted you of favor and blessing, and congratulations to your community for your intercession [on its behalf] on the day of resurrection." I also heard David glorifying [God], with the angels **[42v]** helping him, calling out, "Glorified be the creator of light! Glorified be he, over what the breasts [of humanity] conceal! Glorified be the one who raises [creatures up] from the graves! Glorified be the one to whom the lights all lead!" Solomon arose, calling out, "Glorified be the king of kings! Glorified be the conqueror of the oppressors! Glorified be the breaker of pharaohs! Glorified be the creator of the creation! Glorified be the spreader of sustenance!" They did not subside with these glorifications, nor did they pause. [Once again] I was filled with wonder at the laxity of the people of the world. Then Gabriel commanded me [to advance], so I advanced and prayed two cycles of ritual prayer.

[The Fourth Heaven]

Then he raised me from the Third Heaven to the Fourth Heaven in the blink of an eye. Between them was the distance of [a] five-hundred-year [journey], and their width something similar [to that in distance]. I looked upon it, and saw that it was made of white silver, gleaming with light that blinded one's sight.

Its name was "Brilliant" (*al-Zāhira*). Gabriel knocked on its gate, and there was a reply by its guardian, whose name was Raḥmānaʾīl.[23] [He asked, "Who is it?" Gabriel replied, "Gabriel."] He asked, "And who is with you?" Gabriel responded, "With me is Muḥammad, the Messenger of God." Raḥmānaʾīl cried out, "Praise be to God." He sprang up to greet me, saying, "Welcome, Muḥammad, what a blessed brother you are! Congratulations to you for all the blessings of God and his contentment [that you have received], and congratulations to your community for your intercession [on its behalf]."

I looked around and found myself with innumerable angels. I had never seen so many in number, nor so many that were so intense in industry [in carrying out their devotions]. Their faces were in the shape of eagles (*ʿiqbān*). When the first of them glorified, the last of them replied, crying out [**43r**] with glorification and sanctification of the Lord of the worlds. They called out in their glorification, "Glorified be the creator of darkness and light! Glorified be the most forgiving king! Glorified be the creator of the sun and the moon! Glorified be the most high, the most sublime! May he be glorified and exalted!" As I looked upon them, I was filled with wonder at how they did not pay attention to each other, nor did they gaze to their right or their left. They were humble, resplendent, and lowly, making humble entreaties to God.

I gazed upon a seat (*kursī*) of light, upon which sat a man ruddy of face, incredibly lean, handsome of cheek, hooked of nose, skilled of tongue, brilliant of eye. He had a jewel of a voice, and very hairy forearms. He was engaged in glorifying [God] amidst the angels. I asked who he was, and Gabriel answered, "That is your brother Moses son of ʿImrān, the one to whom the most merciful spoke. Approach him and greet him." So I did, and he returned the greeting. Then he asked, "Gabriel, who is this? Who is this?" Gabriel replied, "Moses, this is Muḥammad." When he heard that, he asked further, "Has Muḥammad been sent?" Gabriel answered, "Yes."

[**43v**] He sprung up and hugged me, congratulating me and shouted, "O my brother, praise be to God who showed me your ascent and allowed me to witness your journey. Muḥammad, you will arrive at a great place, and you will be given a wish [there], so ask for the reduction [of duties] for your community as much as you can. Know that I imposed upon my community duties that they could not accept. They rejected them and lied, just as prophets before me have been lied to. I found in them only tiredness and fatigue. Muḥammad, your community is the best of communities that has been brought from among humanity, and God has blessed you in ways that he has blessed no prophet before you. He has given you the keys of goodness, and he wishes to impose upon you the requirements of religion and the paths of faith and certainty. He will place conditions upon you and your community, conditions and prayers, and will make them obligatory upon you at all times. So ask your Lord for a reduction, for your community is weak. When you give them such a reduction [of

duties], things will be easier for them, and they will have faith in you and believe in you."

I asked for him to assist me. He cried out, "My beloved Muḥammad, listen to what I say to you. When God imposes upon you one hundred prayers [per day], ask for ten, or less than that. If he imposes upon you fifty, ask him [**44r**] for five or less. God has no need for the [devotions of the people of the] world!" I began to go, but he called out for me to return. He said, "Muḥammad, ask for a reduction as much as you can, for he will impose upon you fasting. If six months [of fasting] per year are commanded of you, ask for one month, or even less than that. Indeed your Lord is forgiving, merciful, generous, and kind with his creation. For you and your community, I am indeed giving the best advice. I came as a prophet to the children of Israel, and found nothing but fatigue in them." I told him, "May God reward you well with the best of rewards, brother Moses, for what you have done for me and my community."

None of the prophets was more friendly, more caring, or more compassionate to my community than Moses was. He did not cease to exhort and to cry for them, out of longing for them to arrive at their [rightful] position with the Lord of the worlds, until what he exhorted settled in my heart and became firmly implanted. His exhortation was a great guide for me, and I did not hear it from any of the other people of the heavens. [. . .][24] [**44v**] I heard my brother Moses calling out in his glorification, "Glorified be the Lord of the great throne! Glorified be the compassionate and caring one! Glorified be the one whom the describers cannot describe! Glorified be the one whose quality, extension, grandeur, and likeness never reach his creation!"

I continued on past him and looked upon the sun, seeing that it was proceeding rapidly through the celestial sphere (*al-falak*), which was a sea as great as could be. It had waves as numerous as the stars of the sky, and upon each of their surfaces was an angel glorifying God and sanctifying him. I saw that the face of the sun to its rim was a fire, and angels were striking it with pieces of ice in order to make its heat bearable to the people of the earth. Glorified be God, the great.

Then Gabriel commanded me to lead the inhabitants of the Fourth Heaven in prayer, so I prayed two cycles of prayer, and I reduced [its heaviness] [**45r**] for them.

[The Fifth Heaven]

Gabriel ascended with me to the Fifth Heaven faster than the blink of an eye. Between it and the Fourth [Heaven] was [a distance of a] five-hundred-year [journey], and its breadth was the same distance. When I approached it, I examined it and saw that it was of red gold, gleaming with such light that it almost blinded one's eyesight. It is called "Ornamented" (*al-Muzayyina*). Gabriel rapped upon its gate, and its guardian, named Shahrabaʾīl, answered.[25]

In [the heaven] were angels of a number known only to God, arranged in rows that were bowing in prayer but not touching their heads to the ground in prostration, and rows touching their heads to the ground but neither bowing nor sitting. Were a bird to fly from one of their shoulders to the other, it would not reach its destination in a hundred years. They did not gaze at one another. [Some said], "Glorified be God, the exalted! Magnificent is his majesty, and great is his praise! There is no dominion except his!" And I heard them glorifying [God also] with the phrases, "Glorified be the mighty, the powerful one! Glorified be the generous, the thankful one! Glorified be the loving, the gentle one, who does what he wills! Glorified be the conqueror, the enormous one! Glorified be the one who gives life to bones when they have decayed! Glorified be the mighty, the wise!"

Among them was a handsome old man who also glorified God and sanctified him. I asked, "Gabriel, who is that?" He replied, "That is Idrīs (Enoch), the one raised up *to a high place* (Q 19:57). Below him were four heavens, and above him were three." [**45v**] Then we went to one side of him, and I suddenly found myself at a seat (*kursī*) of light, upon which was seated the handsomest old man, who similarly raised his voice in his glorification and sanctification. I asked Gabriel who he was, and Gabriel told me, "That is your father Abraham, the *intimate friend*" (Q 4:125). I approached him and greeted him, and he sprung up and embraced me, exclaiming, "Welcome to you, my dear child! Glorified be the one who granted you complete goodness, assisted you with his patience, and made you and your community the best of communities. They will indeed proceed into paradise. He made you the last of the prophets, the medium of his covenant, one devoted to the welfare [of your community], the lamp of their light. You have risen up to a great height, so do not forget your father Abraham. Remember him, and God will not forget you in his mercy when you reach your desired goal." He gently took my hand and embraced me, congratulating and commending me, and Idrīs did also. The two wished me well.

Then I advanced to the middle of the [Fifth] Heaven, and found myself at the largest sea that I had seen thus far. At the shore of that sea, I saw an enormous angel sitting on a seat (*kursī*) of light. Between his eyes was a scale. I swear by the one who sent me in truth as a prophet that his two shoulder blades were as broad as the circumference of the heavens and the earth and their foundations, just as the distance between the east and west. [For this angel] Mikāʾīl, the clouds, [**46r**] the angels, the records of creatures and their sustenance were all subjects that concerned him. He was busy with all his Lord commanded of him, and all that God appointed for him to do. He never took a rest or a break from the remembrance of God. On his right were one hundred rows of angels, and on his left were the same. They were all hastening to execute his orders. I asked who he was. [Gabriel told me that he was the mighty angel, Mikāʾīl]. Gabriel called out to him, "Mikāʾīl, this is Muḥammad." He asked, "Has

Muḥammad been sent?" Gabriel replied, "Yes." He greeted me, congratulating me for the blessings of the Lord that I had received, commending me on behalf of my community. He told me, "Rejoice, for I have not seen in the records of any community in the accounting [of good deeds] anything like what I have seen in the records of yours. Congratulations to you, and to those who obey you and follow you, for indeed I see goodness in you and your community."

I went forward, and found myself with an angel sitting on a seat (*kursī*) of light. Were God to permit it, it could swallow all of the created beings in one gulp out of the enormity of its stature. Then I found myself among other angels around the first one, whose heads were in the seventh heaven. In their hands were hooks and poles with which they struck the reins of the winds. I said, "My brother Gabriel, who is that [seated angel]?" He said, "That is the Spirit (*al-Rūḥ*)."

I advanced past them and encountered a sea of light [**46v**] and blazing fire. It made an incredible noise, its waves crashing together. Angels were standing in it. [Looking upon it, I felt] as if I would almost give up my soul [and die]. Gabriel covered me, and said, "Muḥammad, what is the matter with you? Stay firm to the command of your Lord!"[26] I responded, "Help, Gabriel! What is that sea? Which sea is it?" He answered, "Muḥammad, it is the sea of lightning, and its name is 'Thunderstrike' (*al-Saᶜq*). None except the one who created it can describe it."

[The Sixth Heaven]

He raised me up to the Sixth Heaven, the one called "Pure" (*al-Khāliṣa*). Gabriel knocked at its gate. I regarded it and saw that it was made of gems, gleaming with light. Between it and the Fifth was [a distance of a] five-hundred-year [journey], and its breadth was something similar in distance. Gabriel's knock was answered by its guardian, whose name was Yaʾīl.[27] He called out, "Who is it?" Gabriel responded, "Gabriel." He questioned, "And who is with you?" Gabriel answered, "Muḥammad." He asked, "Has Muḥammad been sent?" Gabrield replied, "Yes." The angel sprang up and opened the gate, greeting me and congratulating me for God's contentment [with me]. I saw in him enormous dignity, and asked how he arrived at it. He replied, "Out of my love for you." I heard him call out in his glorification, "Glorified be the almighty, the generous one! Glorified be the living one who never dies! Glorified be the wise, the generous one! Glorified be [**47r**] the living one who never dies! Glorified be the wise, the generous one! Glorified be the clear light! Glorified be the one who is a god in both the heavens and the earth!" After that he sat in his place.

I went forward and found myself with the angels of the Sixth Heaven, more numerous than what I had seen previously. No one could describe them, nor even approximate one tenth of them. They listened in respect for their Lord, and in their glorification they cried out, "Glorified be the one who is the only one appropriate to glorify! Glorified be the one whom the lion glorifies in its station! Glorified be the one whom all wild beasts glorify, lowering their heads! Glorified be the one whom insects glorify in their tiny homes!" Thus, by God, is [a good example of] obedience, apprehension, and God consciousness.

I advanced and came upon an enormous angel sitting on a seat (*kursī*) of light. On his right were angels, and as he glorified and sanctified God, they responded to him with glorification. Fire almost came out of his mouth during his glorification. When I saw that, I almost fell down, covering myself. Gabriel said to me, "Muḥammad, stay firm to the command of your Lord!" I said, "Gabriel, what is the name of that angel?" He said, "His name is Shajāʾīl, and he is the angel appointed to thunder. Thunder results from the sound of his voice. Approach and greet him." I did so, and he returned my greetings, smiling in my direction and shaking my hands. He boomed, [**47v**] "Welcome, Muḥammad, and congratulations for your Lord's contentment with you! I see that complete goodness is in you and your community!"

I proceeded on and was amazed by the angels of the Sixth Heaven, who were the party of God and his soldiers. Were one of them to be commanded to uproot the heavens and the earth, he would uproot them from their foundations faster than the blink of an eye. Their faces expressed love of the angels, and they had many wings. I said, "Gabriel, I saw the most intense devotions and effort among the angels of the Sixth Heaven." He told me to greet them. After Gabriel had introduced me, I approached and greeted them. They were joyful to see me, and they congratulated me.

I noticed that among them there was a seat (*kursī*) of light, upon which sat a youth, intense in [devotional] effort, humble and submissive. I asked, "Brother Gabriel, who is he?" He replied, "He is Hūd.[28] Greet him, Muḥammad." I approached him and greeted him. He congratulated me and commended me for what God had granted me of favor and blessing.

I continued forward, and then we ascended. I gazed upon angels, some standing on their feet, some kneeling, and some with their heads to the ground. They raised their voices in glorification and sanctification [of God], calling out, "Glorified be the guide, the most knowing! Glorified be the possessor of majesty and nobility! Glorified be the sustainer of birds [**48r**] and of lions! Glorified be the one who knows what is in the wombs, and by whose permission pregnancies take place! [Glorified be he,] possessor of majesty and nobility!"

Then I passed them, ascending higher, and saw a green sea, looking as if it were made of emerald, gleaming with light. Its waves collided, and it almost blinded the observer gazing at it. Upon its waves were angels, as many as I had seen in the previous heavens combined. They were glorifying God in languages that I could not understand, because of the form of the languages and the vast number of them. They encompassed that sea on every side, to the point that the sea's waves were raised up. Upon each wave were more waves, as God willed.

I asked, "What is that sea, Gabriel?" He responded, "The Sea of Wonders (*Baḥr al-ʿajāʾib*). Pray two cycles of ritual prayer, Muḥammad." So I prayed, and I reduced [its heaviness for them].

[The Seventh Heaven]

Gabriel raised me up to the Seventh Heaven faster than the blink of an eye. Between it and the Sixth was a five-hundred-year journey, and its breadth was similar to that in distance. [The Seventh Heaven] is made of white pearl, yet supple like dough, gleaming with light. Its name is "Glistening" (*al-Dāmiʿa*). It almost blinded the gaze of the one who looked upon it. Gabriel knocked on the gate, and its guardian, Rūḥaʾīl, responded, "Who is it?" Gabriel answered, "I am Gabriel." The guardian asked, "Who is with you?" Gabriel said, "Muḥammad." The guardian queried, "Has Muḥammad been sent?" Gabriel replied, "Yes," to which Rūḥāʾīl responded, "Praise be to God, Lord of the worlds." He opened the gate and welcomed me, congratulating and commending me. I saw that he had an enormous reverence, and asked him for what reason God had granted him [**48v**] that [station]. He replied, "As a gift from him. Rejoice, Muḥammad, for the contentment of God, and make your community rejoice because of the mercy and forgiveness of God."

I saw with him seven hundred angels, each one with a hundred thousand angels. They were submissive, devoted, and fearful. They cried out in their glorifications, "Glorified be the one who spread out the earth and the throne! Glorified be the one who raises us above acts of disobedience and conceals them! Glorified be the one who created the planets and made them resplendent! Glorified be the one who created the seas and held them back! Glorified be the one who enchanted the days and concealed them! Glorified be the almighty, the great!" I saw kinds of angels that my Lord forbade me to describe. They have not looked upon the earth since the day God created them, and they know nothing of the disobedience that it contains. Likewise they do not raise their heads to the throne because of the greatness of the Lord of the worlds that rests upon it, magnificent his majesty and powerful his rule. Each one of them has a tongue [the length of which] exceeds five hundred years. They wear green flowing garments (*rafārif*). Blessed be God, the judge on the day of judgment.

When they gazed upon me, they raised their voices in glorification, and I thought that all created beings had died, for nothing hears them and does not perish. I was seized by shaking and crying, and said, "Gabriel, I have never seen in the heavens angels who were more intense in devotion, nor greater in exertion, than the angels of the Seventh Heaven." Gabriel told me to approach [**49r**] and greet them. So I went forward and greeted them, and they returned the greeting to me with a gesture drawn from their devotions. Gabriel said to them, "Angels of the Lord, greet him [properly], for this is the best of creation, Muḥammad son of ʿAbd Allāh son of ʿAbd al-Muṭṭalib." So they greeted me, welcomed me, and congratulated me and my community.[29]

Then I ascended past them and saw angels that caused me to forget all that I had seen out of the enormity of their size, magnitude of their [devotional] exertions, and intensity of their fear. My hair stood on end, my flesh trembled, and my heart stopped. Gabriel said to me, "Muḥammad, be patient in the command of your Lord! Indeed, what lies ahead are such wonders that were I to inform you of them, you would not be able to describe them, not even a tenth of them." I saw among those angels one angel whose head was beneath the throne and whose legs were below the limits of the seventh and lowest earth. Were God to give this angel power over the world, land and sea, it would pulverize them in the blink of an eye. It glorified God, shouting in its glorification, "Glorified be the creator, the great! Glorified be the dear, the wise one! [**49v**] Glorified be the one who veils his light over his creation! Glorified be the one who rains his favor down upon his servants, and showers them with sustenance!"

I saw an angel upon whose body were seventy thousand heads, each head with seventy thousand mouths, each mouth with seventy thousand tongues, each tongue glorifying God with seventy thousand languages, no one language resembling another. I heard them calling out, "Glorified be the highest Lord, who is the highest of the most high! Glorified be the one who arranges all matters! Glorified be the one who is near in approach, and who is the highest in the heights! In resplendence he is the luminous, in command the all powerful, in dominion the most mighty! Glorified be the Lord of each and every thing, its creator, life giver, life taker, and sustainer! Glorified be the one who there is no god but he, who has power over all things!"

I saw another angel [so immense that] were all the seas and rivers of the earth to flow into its stomach, it would not fill it up. It was saying, "Glorified be God the great! Glorified be God the most holy! Glorified be God who is more powerful than all things! Glorified be the one in whose hands lies the forelocks of all creatures, and in whose hand lies the distribution of all sustenance, [**50r**] who has power over all things!"

I saw another angel upon whose body were seventy thousand wings. It entered a sea of light, then it emerged from it. From each feather there dripped a drop, and God created from each drop an angel glorifying God and sanctifying him in every language until the day of resurrection.[30] I heard this angel calling out in its glorification, "Glorified may you be, my master! How high is your station! Glorified may you be, my master! How mighty is your command! Glorified may you be, my master! How merciful you are with your creatures! Glorified may you be, my master! How powerful you are over your servants! Glorified may you be, my master! How numerous are your gracious gifts!"

I saw an angel standing upon a seat (*kursī*) of light, and it had four faces: one face like that of a human being, one face like the face of a lion, one face like the face of a bull, and one face like the face of an eagle.[31] In its glorification it cried out, "Glorified be the generous sustainer of the birds, wild animals, beasts, predators, and humans! The one who looks after their sustenance, and that of [the rest of] his servants without asking for recompense!"

I saw that the angels of the Seventh Heaven were more numerous than the angels of the six [lower] heavens **[50v]** and seventy times more terrifying than the rest of creation. Among them were angels that stand [in their devotions] but never bow, some who bow but never touch their head down [in prostration], some who touch their head down but never raise their heads. They were arrayed in row after row, troop after troop. They raised their voices in glorification, sanctification, magnification, eulogy, and praise to the Lord of the worlds.

I saw an angel standing upon a seat (*kursī*) of light, more enormous than any of the other angels I had seen in the heavens. At its extremity, its two legs were at the limits of the seven lower earths, and the seven heavens were in its grasp, not even reaching its loins. It had two wings, one in the east and the other in the west. I asked Gabriel what this angel was, and he replied, "Muḥammad, this angel has a great position with the Lord of the worlds, so advance and greet it." So I went forward and greeted it, and it returned my greetings with a movement of its head, without speaking. Gabriel spoke to it, saying, "Why did you not respond to the best of creation?" It asked, "Who is that, Gabriel?" He replied, "Muḥammad, the Messenger of God." **[51r]** It asked, "Has Muḥammad been sent?" Gabriel answered, "Yes." It then cried out, "Welcome, Muḥammad! You are the best of the beloved ones, and yours is the best of arrivals. Rejoice, Muḥammad, with the contentment of God and his favor. Have your community rejoice that God has blessed you [all] with a blessing such that he never bestowed upon any before."

Then he stood among the angels and made the call to prayer, and they approached little by little, and I found myself standing alone. Gabriel said to me, "Advance, Muḥammad, and lead these angels in two cycles of prayer." So I did, and I served as the prayer leader for the angels of the heavens, just as I am the prayer leader for the people of earth. After the prayer, angels approached me and congratulated me for what God had granted me, and they rejoiced for my community, and petitioned [God] for increased good works.

[The Inhabited House]

I continued and suddenly I found myself at the Inhabited House (*al-bayt al-ma*ᶜ*mūr*). When I gazed upon it, I found it to be an enormous house with the appearance of the Sacred House [i.e., the Kaᶜba in Mecca], and the Sacred House had the same appearance as it. [The Sacred House] is equivalent to the Inhabited House in the heavens, to the degree that were a drop to fall from the latter, it would fall **[51v]** upon the Sacred Kaᶜba.[32] It has a gate that faces the Throne. The angels circumambulate it just as we humans circumambulate the Sacred House, seventy thousand angels every day circumambulating and never returning to it. Their cohort will not, in fact, come back to visit it until the day of judgment.

I said, "Gabriel, what is this?" He said, "Inhabited House." I asked, "With what is it inhabited?" He replied, "With angels of the lord of the worlds. Would you like me to show you what is inside it?" I answered, "Yes." So Gabriel advanced us forward and called out, "O people of the Inhabited House, this is Muḥammad, the Messenger of God." Before he finished speaking, some angels who took the form of thunderbolts [decorated] with numerous pearls came to us. When they saw me, they all bent down and touched their heads to the ground. Gabriel asked me, "Do you know why they are doing that, Muḥammad?" I replied, "God knows best." Gabriel said, "Out of their joy for seeing you."

Then I looked in the direction of the gate of the house, which was built [facing] the heavens, and there I saw an old man upon whose head was a crown of light, seated on a seat (*kursī*) of light with his back against **[52r]** the Inhabited House. By God, I had never seen anyone more handsome than he. Sometimes he looked to his right and smiled laughingly, and sometimes he looked to his left and began crying. He was calling out, "Glorified be the one who reckons, the one who humbles peoples with his might through their obedience to him, and who humbles peoples through their disobedience to him! Glorified be the one who offers and refuses! Glorified be the one who lays low and raises up! Glorified be the one who grants success to peoples through their obedience to him, those who do what is pleasing to him, and who makes [other] people destitute and calls them to account! Indeed, all will be put to the test!" I asked, "My beloved Gabriel, who is that seated there?" He replied, "That is your father Adam, the father of humankind. Go forward and greet him." So I did so, and he returned the greeting, saying, "Welcome to you, and God's mercy be with you. Which of my children are you? I have never seen anyone who has reached what you have reached." Gabriel replied to him, "Adam, this is Muḥammad, the Messenger of God." When he heard that, he got up to stand. He embraced me, and then seated me upon his lap, kissing me just as a father kisses his child, saying, "Glorified be the one who brought you, and praise be to God **[52v]** who showed you to me! O my son Muḥammad, this night you are favored with an exalted station. You will hear the speech of the generous lord, and will witness the exalted king! When you are with God, my son, do not forget me, but remember me."

Upon hearing this I cried in happiness, and asked, "My father, I see you looking to the right and smiling laughingly, and looking to the left and crying." He explained, "Muḥammad, when I look to the right, I see the *people of the right*[33] of your community and those who are obedient among my children. Their deeds kindle a light, and I laugh out of joy for them. When I look to the left, however, I see the unbelievers and the wicked. Their deeds are sultry and dark, so I become aggrieved out of sadness when I look upon their deeds. Glory be to the one who brought you, Muḥammad. Today you are the greatest among my children, and the most favored of them with God." Then he petitioned [God] on my behalf and lauded me with praise and blessings, saying, "God, you have made him the bridegroom of the people of paradise, so increase in him **[53r]** your goodness, you to whom is the praise and eulogy, and the continuity and eternity." Then he cried out, "Glorified be God! Praise be to God! There is no god but God! God is great! There is no might nor power except in God, the high and exalted!" He told me, "Muḥammad, memorize these phrases, for they are righteous and abiding, and to those who say them come blessings whose number is known only to God."

Then I glanced to my right, and I saw the gate to the paradise called *Firdaws* (Q 18:107; 23:11), whose base was of gold and whose crenellations were of pearl. Its dirt was of musk, its grass was of saffron, its soil was of ambergris, and its land was of pearl and sapphire. The base of its trees was of pure gold, and their branches were of emeralds mixed with pearl and sapphire. Their fruits were sweeter than honeycomb, smoother than butter, more wholesome than honey, and more fragrant than the finest musk.

Then I proceeded and saw a tree whose trunk was like the breasts of a human, and it was surrounded by young children. I asked Gabriel about the tree and the children **[53v]** around it, and he told me, "They are the children of your community who died while still [in the age of] suckling. Abraham is their father and Sarah is their mother. God created this tree for them and their development."

[Part Three: Beyond the Seventh Heaven to the Throne]

Gabriel grabbed my hand and brought me tearing past veils and pavilions, while I looked upon rows of angels on my right and left. I had never seen so many angels, and I asked Gabriel what they were called. He replied, "Muḥammad, they are the *Rūḥāniyyūn*, of whom only God who created them knows their number." Then he continued to tear forward and traverse with me through the rows, veils, and pavilions, while I heard glorifications and sanctifications [praising God]. I thought that I had become the wind or a bird.[34] I saw veils of darkness, fog, fire, light, snow, and cold, and of every variety of precious gem that God created. There were veils of emerald and veils of green light. No one knows their number except God. Between each veil and the next were innumerable angels, **[54r]** wave upon wave, each of them drenched in light. Their feet rested on the lowest earths and their heads were beneath the throne.[35] I swooned, because I was almost overcome with the experience. Gabriel said to me, "Steady yourself, Muḥammad, and have patience with God's command."

[Lote Tree of the Boundary]

I stayed that way until we came upon the Lote Tree of the Boundary (*sidrat al-muntahā*). I gazed upon it, an enormous lote tree that defies any description. Its fruits were like jugs of stone, and its leaves were larger than the ears of elephants, leaves of every color in God's creation. The length of its shadow was the distance of [a journey of] five hundred years. On every branch I saw something incredible: one thousand rows of angels bowing down their heads to God, sanctifying, magnifying, and extolling him with their voices raised in diverse languages. Below the roots of [the lote tree] a river flows, making such a sound that I thought that all of creation must be able to hear it.

I asked Gabriel what that lote was, and he replied, "It is the Lote Tree of the Boundary." I wondered why it was called that, and he responded, "Because **[54v]** actions of the servants, and indeed all matters of created beings end at it. Neither a sent prophet nor any of the angels that you have seen has passed beyond it. That river is called the River Abundance (*Kawthar*), which is for you, master of the messengers, one who is without [equal] among all of the prophets. This is what God granted to the people of God in his saying, "*Indeed we have given you Kawthar*" (Q 108:1). I said, "For [only] my Lord's sake is the praise and the thanks."

[Gabriel Stays Behind]

Then I advanced forward a little, and then turned back and did not see Gabriel. That worried me, and I cried out, "My beloved Gabriel!" He replied to me from his station, the majesty of the Lord of might having turned his wing, fixed his spear, and lowered his head, "Here I am, beloved of God." I exclaimed, "I see that you have tarried behind me in that place. The intimate friend needs his intimate! Do not leave me and tarry behind!" Gabriel answered, "Here the lover approaches his beloved."

Moreover, Gabriel, upon him be peace, continued, "Muḥammad, it weighs heavily upon me to tarry behind you, I swear by the one who sent you with the truth as a prophet. But '*there is none among us who does not have a known station*' (Q 37:164). Were I to have advanced from here the distance of a fingertip, I would have burned up from the intensity of the lights."

[55r] I said, "Gabriel, do you have a parting farewell for me? What is it?"

He said, "Do you remember when Abraham was thrown into Nimrod's furnace and I was opposite him, my beloved, when he was descending into the raging fire. I asked him, 'Abraham, do you need anything?' He replied, 'How about you?' For on that day I was not composed of light. His chief that is, Abraham's father provided [the fire] in secret. [Gabriel replied,] 'I will extinguish it for you myself in order to requite you with it in this *praised station*'" (Q 17:79).

[Muḥammad reiterated,] "Gabriel, do you have any need from God?"

On that matter, someone recorded the following lines of poetry:

> I traveled by night and Gabriel was my close friend,
> whom I approached both ascending and after,
> Ages passed, o sea of generosity,
> but debts remained, o obliterator. . . .

And regarding the meaning of that [are other lines of poetry]:

Gabriel journeyed by night and stopped
and did not cross the Lote Tree of the Boundary,
This is what your Lord granted [Muḥammad]:
authority, exaltedness, and greatness—be he congratulated!

[55v] [Gabriel said,] "Muḥammad, one does not overstep this lote tree, nor does one guide except at the direction of the Lord." The Messenger of God said, "Gabriel, I am journeying from this lote tree, without being guided by anything except the direction of my Lord. I do not see an angel journeying with me, nor does any spiritual angel (*rūḥānī*) set my aim." Gabriel replied, "You are correct, Muḥammad, no one that you have yet seen is able to cross this lote tree. From here parts the matter of all created beings, and you must follow the command of your Lord."

[When the Prophet heard this, he became fearful, as he said in his own words:] I got to my knees, and wanted to fall flat on my face in a faint. Gabriel set me aright and embraced me, telling me, "Muḥammad, you should have no fear, for you are the most noble and favored of beings." Whatever [fear] I had been experiencing went away. While I was in that state, a voice suddenly cried out from before the divine throne saying, "Gabriel, push Muḥammad, my beloved, [forward]." So Gabriel took my hand, then he pushed me forward, and I broke through [as many] veils as God willed.

[On the Green Rafraf Past Seas]

While I was **[56r]** in the midst of that, I thought that all those who were in the heavens and earth had died, for I did not hear any trace of them. Suddenly I saw a green *rafraf* (55:76) in the shape of a seat, and a voice called out to me, "Ride it." When I sat upon that *rafraf*, it flew with me like an arrow shot from the string of a bow, or even faster than that.

It stopped with me at a white sea. Upon that sea, I found myself with an angel of a shape whose like I had never seen. Were a fast bird to fly between the shoulders of this angel, it would not reach from one shoulder to the other in five hundred years. Behind it were one hundred thousand rows of angels. It was glorifying and sanctifying God, while the angels behind followed it.

Next, I saw a second sea that was green like an emerald. On its edge stood an angel that, were God to allow it to gulp down the heavens and the earth, it would be easy for it to do so. The *rafraf* flew on, and everything that I traversed, there I found an angel pointing to me and greeting me. Veils were rolled up between my hands, and I continued in that way until I had crossed seventy thousand seas. Upon each one of those seas, I had seen some of the wonders (*ᶜajāʾib*) of the angels that I am not able to describe.

[56v] Then I gazed upon rows of the Cherubim (*al-Karūbiyyūn*), and I heard their glorifications and the variety of their languages. They humbled themselves out of fear of God, Lord of the worlds, glorified and exalted beyond what the wrongdoers say, high and grand.

[The Archangel Isrāfīl]

The *rafraf* flew with me between their rows until it came to Isrāfīl. With one of his wings, he blocked the east and the west. His legs reached the extremes of the seventh and lowest earth, while his head rested below the divine throne. He had a thousand wings, and each wing had a thousand heads, each head with a thousand faces, each face with a thousand tongues, and each tongue glorified God in a thousand languages, no one language resembling another.

Then I looked and saw that I was upon a throne on the base of his neck. The trumpet was to his right, and it was a horn made of light that revolved around him like the revolution of the heavens. It had holes in it that numbered as many as the souls of creation. He had one leg forward and the other back behind, and he was waiting upon [God's] command. The Preserved Tablet (*al-lawḥ al-maḥfūẓ*, Q 85:22) hung between his eyes. The width of the tablet was the distance from the east to the west. When I looked at him, my muscles quivered, **[57r]** my heart was afraid, and I desired to cover myself. I heard a voice call out saying, "Muḥammad, have no fear, this is Isrāfīl. Approach him and greet him." My fear went away, and I approached Isrāfīl, calling out to him, "Peace be upon you, Isrāfīl, and God's mercy and blessings." He called back to me in a voice like thunder, "And upon you be peace, Muḥammad, and God's mercy and blessings. Welcome, by God, welcome! Make yourself at ease. What a blessed brother you are, and what a blessed arrival this is. Rejoice in God's pleasure, for you have arrived at a place where no human or *jinn* has set foot, nor any of the nearest of angels." I asked, "Isrāfīl, why are you in this place?" He replied, "O Aḥmad, this is my station since God created me, and I will not leave it until the day of judgment. God has raised me and favored me over all others, for I hear the speech of my Lord." I asked, "How does it sound to you?" He answered, "Nothing is like him, nor does he resemble anything." I said, "Isrāfīl, in what place am I now?" He replied, "Raise your head!" So I raised my head, and I found myself among the bearers of the divine throne. They. . . .[36] **[57v]**

[Vision of the Divine Throne]

[Next to the throne,] everything that I had seen in the seven heavens I considered as no more than a ring of chainmail in an open plain on the earth.[37] Such befits the throne of the compassionate Lord of the worlds. No one can describe it. I saw a snake wrapped around it, its head made to meet its tail. When the throne glorified [God], it covered all of creation, and when that snake glorified

[God], it raised its voice even louder [than the throne].[38] I looked and saw wonders.

Then Isrāfīl called out, "Proceed, Muḥammad, by your Lord's command!" I replied, "O Isrāfīl! O Isrāfīl! Help! My heart has left me from what I have just seen of God's power!" He answered, "Muḥammad, strengthen yourself by your Lord's command. No one else has been permitted here, and no other has ascended to this place. That is among the ways that God has favored you."

[Upper Seas]

Then the *rafraf* was pushed forward, and it flew rising up with me until it brought me to a sea blazing with fire. I gazed at its waves, one upon another, and saw that it contained countless angels whose number was known only to God. I looked at Isrāfīl, who had not moved away from me, and I was amazed at that sea and the wonders of God that were in it.

[58r] Then we crossed it, ascending beyond it to a black and murky sea. In it were forms whose speech I could not hear. I thought that [all of] creation had died. Then I heard someone call out, "Have no fear, Muḥammad. These angels that you see are the *Rūḥāniyyūn*. Among all the folk of the heavens, they restrain their voices the most, lowering their heads out of humility toward God." I saw other strange things from God's creation that I was not permitted to inform you about, and even were I to try my hardest to describe them, I still would not be able to do so. Blessed be God as a king, most majestic as a commander, most noble and yet most frightening as a ruler. There is no rule except his rule, nor any kingdom except his.

We continued on and crossed seven seas, the length and breadth of each spanning the distance between east and west, and their depths being as the distance between heaven and earth. In each of the seas were as many angels as were in the heavens, and even many times more.

[Traversing Veils]

I was made to traverse sea after sea until I was brought to the veil of power, the veil of might, and the veil of glory. I was made to cast them aside. Then I saw veils of **[58v]** sapphire, green coral, silver, gold, [ruby], pure gold, as well as veils of coldness, of light, and of every material in all of creation. From the intensity of its rays and brilliance, each veil gleamed with a light that almost blinded the vision of anyone who looked upon it. Angels kept guard at each veil. Were God to command any one of these angels to take all the heavens and the earth in its hand, it would do so.

Then I was brought to stop at a veil unlike the others I had seen, and Isrāfīl rustled it. Its guardian asked [from the other side], "Who is it?" He responded, "Isrāfīl." The guardian asked, "And who is with you?" Isrāfīl replied, "Muḥammad." The guardian queried, "Has Muḥammad been sent for?" Isrāfīl answered, "Yes." Then the guardian of the veil exclaimed, "Praise be to God, Lord of the worlds!" He reached out his hand, took my arm, and drew me through, leaving Isrāfīl behind. After my parting from him, I continued to see things and hear voices that caused me to say, "Help! Help!" The guardian of the veil replied, **[59r]** "Muḥammad, have no fear. Isrāfīl is no longer with you, for he does not have permission, nor any station, to be in this place. Indeed, above me, no one in all of creation except you has permission to go. How much God has generously favored you, and how much he has bestowed upon you with what he has granted you. Proceed forward, and do not be afraid."

So I did, and it was as if I were flying, and the guardian of that veil continued to lead me through faster than the blink of an eye to a veil of fire, whose guardian asked, "Who is it?" He replied, "The guardian of the first veil." The guardian of the veil of fire asked, "Who is with you?" He replied, "Muḥammad." The guardian of the veil of fire asked, "Has he been sent for?" He responded, "Yes." The guardian of the veil of fire exclaimed, "Praise be to God, Lord of the worlds." Then he reached out his hand, took my arm, and pulled me through to him. He congratulated me and welcomed me. I crossed through [that] veil to another veil that I am unable to describe, for my Lord forbade me to describe it to you. I kept crossing through veil after veil, each of which dazzled my sight, and rendered me completely terrified with what I had seen. Each **[59v]** guardian comforted me and quelled my terror, and I proceeded [past them].

I raised my head, and found myself at a seat (*kursī*) set with white pearls, decorated with green emeralds. The angel took me by the hand and said to me, "Sit here, Muḥammad." I sat, and became afraid for I thought that all the people of the heavens and earth had died. While I was in that state, with the angels of the veils congratulating and welcoming me, a voice from above my head called out, "Peace be upon you, Muḥammad." I raised my head, and found myself with an angel more intensely white than snow, clad in green spotted with red, and crowned in yellow. He was the prayer leader of the [highest] angels, and all of them were in his form. He gestured to me and stated, "Welcome to you, beloved of the most powerful [Lord]. Incline your heart and ears this way as I approach your Lord." Then he said, "Congratulations for that [place] to which God will bring you." The folk of that *rafraf* congratulated me, and I was shown a multitude of wonders.

That angel brought me through a thousand veils of excellent smelling musk **[60r]**, of pungent saffron, of milky-white pearls, gems, other pearls, and pure gold. Then I was brought to the veil of enormity, then of magnificence, then of completeness, then of oneness (*waḥdāniyya*). This last one was a veil of white pearls, gleaming with light that almost blinded the sight of one who looked upon it.

When I was there, a voice called out to the guardian of the veil of oneness, saying, "Raise the veil from between me and my beloved." The veil was raised, and I saw angels bent down, never raising their heads out of humility before God, and angels touching their heads down, never sitting up, glorifying, sanctifying, magnifying, and praising God in strange languages. They never raise their heads out of fear of the majesty of God, nor do they gaze upon the earth because of what it contains of wrongdoing and disobedience. While I stood at the veil of oneness, my sight being nearly blinded by the light of the veil, a voice cried out, "Come forward, Muḥammad." I went forward, step after step, overcome by an intense fear, when I heard some movement coming from the veil of oneness. **[60v]** It gleamed with incredible whiteness, and I saw written upon it the lines, "There is no god but God, and Muḥammad is the Messenger of God." When I heard [and saw] that, my heart flew from me, and my body trembled. Then I heard a voice call out, "Have no fear."

[Part Four: The Divine Audience]

The *rafraf* swept out from under me, and my feet came to rest on something solid. I went forward and found myself on the carpet of power. My tongue was paralyzed. Then a drop fell onto my lips, and I found it delicious and sweet. My tongue began to move again, and I sang with all the praises and knowledge that my Lord had taught to me.

I tried to look, but the light dazzled and blinded my eyes. Nevertheless, vision was returned to me in my heart, and I saw my Lord in my heart, not with my eyes. I was not permitted to tell you what I saw of God. No one can describe nor even approximate [God], for he is not like any created thing, nor can his eternal essence or his unique qualities be admitted into rational faculties. "Above," "below," and "in front" cannot delimit or define him. God is exalted above any [formulation of] extension, **[61r]** companionship, or progeny.

I stopped when I was permitted to, and I spoke saying, "Salutations to God, good tidings and blessed prayers." A voice called out, "Peace be upon you, Muḥammad." I was inspired to respond, "Peace be upon us, and upon God's righteous servants. You are my God and master, you are peace, from you proceeds peace, and to you returns peace."

Then I was inspired to take off my sandals. A voice called out, saying, "My beloved, do not take off your sandals." I replied, "My Lord, you trained me in polite behavior, indeed you are the best of my instructors. I feared the punishment of contradicting you, were it to be said to me what was said to my brother, Moses, '*Take off your sandals, for you are in the sacred valley of Ṭuwā*'" (Q 20:12). The voice responded, "My beloved, how do you compare to Moses? I said to Moses '*Take off your sandals*' in order to honor the ground that I made holy through him not stepping on it with his sandals. But you, when you step on a ground, you make its soil pure for your community out of the glory of your power. So by my might and glory, I promised Mount *Ṭūr* of Sinai that I would honor it by the step of Moses' [bare] feet, and I promised the carpet **[61v]** of my power that it would become honored through the tread of your sandals. Approach me, for tonight there is no intermediary between us. I am God and you are Muḥammad."

So I approached by a step, and I heard a voice call out, "Approach me!" I continued approaching until I was as near to my Lord as *the distance of* [*two*] *bow*[*s*] *or closer* (Q 53:9). My terror left me, and I was filled with joy, pleasure, and gladness. Something took me by the arm and sat me upon a seat (*kursī*). I never saw its shape. I sought forgiveness for myself through the words of my Lord, when a voice like the first called out, "Peace be upon you, Prophet, and the mercy and blessings of God." I had never heard anything more delicious or sweet than those words. I said, "My master, you are peace, from you proceeds peace, and to you returns peace." A voice called out, "O Aḥmad," and I replied, "Here I am, at your service, Lord." The voice asked, "How did you know that I was your Lord and master?" I said, "The sweetness of belief, and your kindness toward your servant indicated you to me."

[Final Verses (Seals) of The Cow Chapter]

[God asked:] "*Does the Messenger believe in what has been sent down to him from his Lord?*" I was inspired **[62r]** to reply, "[*The believers all believe in God, his angels, his books, and his messengers. We do not differentiate between any of his messengers. They say,*] '*We hear and obey.' Forgive us, Lord. To you is the arrival.*" God said, "*God does not burden a soul beyond what it can bear. It has what it has earned, and upon it is what it earned.*" [I said,] "*Lord, do not blame us* [*when we forget or err*]" (Q 2:285). [God responded,] "Muḥammad, ask and be given! Muḥammad, I have raised error and forgetfulness from you. Is there anything more?" I was inspired to say, "*Lord, do not make us bear a heavy weight like the one you made those before us to bear.*" The voice called out, "I have done that. Anything else?" My Lord inspired me to say, "*Lord, do not make us carry what we are not able. Forgive us and pardon us and have mercy upon us. You are our master, so give us victory over the unbelievers*" (Q 2:286). He said, "I have done that, Aḥmad. Take these [verses and dispensations], which are from the treasuries of paradise." I took them from my Lord, and between him and me there was a revelation through them. I said, "My Lord and master, for you is the praise, and for your sake is the thanks."

He queried, "Do you see me?" I answered, "My master, my sight has become blinded by the light of your majesty." He asked, "Do you find me?" I replied, "No one finds you, nor accounts for you. *Sight does not encompass* (Q 6:103) you. You are the king, **[62v]** the mighty." He affirmed, "Aḥmad, majestic is my praise, elevated is my station. No eye will see me, for I am God, there is no god but me, the mightiest of the mighty, the king of kings, the Lord of this world and the next, the most merciful of this world and the next." I said, "Exalted are you, and powerful over all things."

[Heavenly Host Debate]
Then I heard the speech of the Lord of the worlds, saying, "Muḥammad, do you know what the *heavenly host debate?"* (Q 38:69). He inspired me to say, "My God and master, they debate about the penitential acts (*kaffarāt*) [and the degrees (*darajāt*)]. [The former involve] going by foot to the [Friday] assemblies (*al-jamā*ᶜ*āt*), [waiting for] prayer after prayer, and performing ablutions even in hateful situations (*al-makārih*)." He said, "You have spoken the truth. Convey that from me to your community. What are the degrees (*darajāt*), Muḥammad?" I said, "Feeding food, spreading the peace, and praying at night while others are sleeping." He said, "You have spoken the truth, Muḥammad. Convey that from me. You will have from me the ability to intercede on the day of judgment until you reach contentment and even beyond." I said, "For [only] my Lord's sake is the praise and the thanks."

[Favor of the Prophets]
Then a voice called out, "Muḥammad, make a request!" I said, "My Lord, what should I request, since you *spoke to Moses directly* (Q 4:164), and you *took Abraham as an intimate friend* (Q 4:125), and you gave Solomon a great *kingdom* [*not befitting to anyone after him*]" (Q 38:35). A voice called out, "Aḥmad, **[63r]** if I took Abraham as an intimate friend, I took you as a beloved. If I gave Solomon the *obedience of the wind* on a day like *a month* (Q 34:12), I caused you to journey by night from your house to my carpet of power in a single evening. If I spoke to Moses directly, I spoke to him on Mount *Ṭūr*, and I speak to you here on the carpet of light and power. My beloved, do not mention Moses, or Jesus, or any of the messengers [as superior to you]. I swear by my might and majesty, when I created you, I took a handful of my light and I gazed upon it. From the terror of my gaze, one hundred and fourteen thousand drops formed [from it], out of each of which I created a prophet. When I created you and all of them, I weighed you and them, and you outweighed all the rest, so I favored you over and above the rest. The rest requested my contentment, but I request your contentment, Muḥammad. You have come for your contentment, so your Lord will give you contentment."

"People dispute about you until it exhausts you, and yet through it all you ask for my contentment.[39] Those who revile you [also] revile me, and those who reject you reject me. Your people say about you, 'Indeed, he is a poet,' and I responded for you, '*We have not taught him poetry, nor would that be appropriate for him*' (Q 36:69). Your people say, **[63v]** 'You are crazy,' and I responded for you, '*Your companion is not crazy*' (Q 81:22). Your people say about you, Muḥammad, 'He is astray or misled,' and I responded for you, '*By the star when it sets, indeed your companion is not astray nor misled*' (Q 53:1–2). Your people say, 'His Lord withdrew from him and dislikes him,' since the majesty of your power is from me. But, my beloved, I did not withdraw from you nor did I dislike you nor did I exile you, so I responded for you in the clear portion of the book, '*By the daybreak and the night when it becomes quiet, your Lord did not bid you farewell, nor does he dislike you*' (Q 93:1–3). Abū Lahab reviled you when he said, 'May your hands perish, Muḥammad,' and I responded for you, '*Perish the hands of Abū Lahab, and may he perish. His possessions and what he gained do not make him wealthy. . . . His wife will carry the firewood, a noose around her neck*'" (Q 111:1–2, 4–5).

[Gifts and Praise for the Prophet and the Muslim Community]
"My beloved, Muḥammad, request and it will be sent down to you. By my might and grandeur I swear that I never created a creature more favored by me than you. I addressed every prophet by name. I said, '*Adam, settle down . . .* ' (Q 2:35 and 7:19). '*John, take the book with power*' (Q 19:12). '*David, we have made you a viceregent over the earth . . .* ' (Q 38:26). And I addressed you [as well]: '*O Prophet, I sent you as a witness, a conveyer of good news and warner*' (Q 33:45). '*O Prophet, struggle against the unbelievers and the hypocrites*' (Q 9:73). '*O Prophet, why do you forbid* [*that which God makes lawful for you*]*?*' (Q 66:1). And in magnifying [your status], '*Indeed God and his angels pray over the Prophet. O you who believe, pray over him and wish him peace*' (Q 33:56). I mentioned you [repeatedly] in **[64r]** the Qur'ān, verse after verse. I said, '*Do not turn your eyes . . .* ' (Q 15:88 and 20:131). '*We have made* [the Qur'ān] *easy through your language . . .* ' (Q 19:97 and 44:58). '*But spread your wings . . .* ' (Q 15:88 and 26:215). '*Did I not open your chest for you* [*and removed the weight*] *that had burdened your back, and raised up your mention*' (Q 94:1–4). '*Do not walk too cheerfully upon the earth*' (Q 17:37). '*The heart did not lie in what it saw*' (Q 53:11). The faithful spirit descended upon your heart, my beloved. By my might and majesty, were it not for you, I would not have created Adam, not even one particle of him, but rather I would have filled the earth with angels just as I did the heavens."[40] I said, "For [only] my Lord's sake is the praise [and the thanks]."

Then I heard a voice call out, "Muḥammad, I have made your community great and magnificent. I have also borne witness to your community, saying, '*You were the best of communities brought forth among humanity*' (Q 3:110). I helped them to thrive, saying, '*You were commanded to do what is right and avoid what is hateful*' (Q 3:110). Once again I bore witness to them when I said, '*You are witnesses* [*to the truth*] *for humanity*, and *the Messenger is a witness for you*' (Q 22:78). I consider them the most honorable of communities. In their favor, I sent down to them the Opening of the Book, which is divided between me and my servants. For me is the portion: *'Praise be to God, Lord of the worlds. The compassionate and caring, master of the day of judgment'* (Q 1:2–4). For my servants among your community the portion is: *'You do we worship, and from you we seek help. Guide us along the straight path.* **[64v]** *The path of those whom you have favored, not those who have incurred your anger, nor of those who have gone astray'* " (Q 1:5–7).

"I have made them the last community in the order of civilizations so as not to prolong their standing during the reckoning, and so they may not greet me with numerous misdeeds. I also made them the very last community so as not to prolong their time buried under the ground. Furthermore, I multiplied their good deeds. If one of my servants among them intends to do a good deed and does not do it, I write down one good deed for him; if he does it, I write down ten. If he considers a bad deed, I only record one for him if he does it; if he does not do it, a good deed is written down for him. That is a favor that I give to you and your community."

I requested, "My Lord, raise their swords up from them." And at that point I saw the sword hanging in the pavilions (*sarādiq*) of the throne. A voice called out, "Muḥammad, I sent you with it, and with it you will become victorious." I said, "For you [alone] is the praise for your decree."

[Imposition of Duties]

The voice called out, "Muḥammad, I have imposed upon you and your community fifty prayers. Offer them to me complete, through performing their ablutions, kneelings, prostrations, and standings, and they will receive from me the exaltation of the degrees (*al-darajāt*) and the multiplication of the goodnesses (*al-ḥasanāt*)."

I remembered the sound advice that I had received from Moses, so I said, "Lord, my community is weak, and you are merciful and kind to them, so please reduce [the burden] for them. Your servants are **[65r]** weak, and they do not have any other God besides you." He said, "Muḥammad, I impose upon you and your community forty prayers." I said, "My Lord, reduce it for them, for you are merciful." He said, "Muḥammad, I have imposed thirty prayers." I thought about Moses' advice some more, and I said, "My Lord, reduce it for them, for they are your servants, and you are kind and merciful." He said, "I have imposed upon them twenty prayers." I said, "That is a lot for them, since my community is weak. I wish for you to reduce it further."

God said, "Muḥammad, I have imposed upon you and upon them five prayers. Offer them completely, through kneeling, prostrating, and standing, and inform them that I will write for them the reward of performing the fifty prayers that I originally imposed upon them. My decision has been decreed upon them, and my favor upon them did not decrease. Through five prayers, I will reward them the equivalent of the performance of fifty prayers. '*Whoever comes with a good deed, he will have ten like them*; *whoever comes with a bad deed will receive no more than its equivalent*' (Q 6:160). Muḥammad, whoever raises up [his behavior striving] for the good deeds, they will be granted to him, and he will be happy (i.e., will enjoy salvation). Whoever's good overcomes his evil, he too will be happy."

"Muḥammad, there has been imposed upon you and your community the fasting of six months each year." I remembered **[65v]** the sound advice of my brother Moses, so I petitioned, "My Lord, my community is weak, so reduce [this burden] for them. They are your servants, and you are merciful to those who believe in you." [. . .][41] God said, "Muḥammad, imposed upon you and your community are five ritual prayers each day and night, and the fasting of one month every year, the month of Ramaḍān. Are you content, Muḥammad?" I said, "Yes, my Lord and master, I am content, and beyond content." [. . .][42]

[I asked,] "My Lord and master, what will be given to my community when they fast and pray the amount you have imposed upon them?" God responded, "Muḥammad, I will give them **[66r]** for every prayer that they complete the reward of ten prayers, and I will protect them from every error that they would make between every two prayers. If they fast one month each year, I will give them the reward of the [six] months that had been imposed upon them. Also, for every night in the month of Ramaḍān [that your community fasts], I will free six hundred thousand [souls] from hellfire of those who were to have received torture. If it is one of the nights at the end of the month, for every person [who fasts] I will free from your community six hundred more of those bound for the fire. Are you content with that, Muḥammad?" "My Lord and master, I am content, and beyond content."

I had the intention of asking my Lord for [further] reduction for my community so that there would be imposed only two ritual prayers, no more than the ritual prayer at the beginning of the night and the one at the beginning of the day. Thus I wished to befriend them and reduce [the burden] for them, and to receive [such duties] as a dispensation and mercy not given to any prophet before me. However, when I had decided to ask my Lord, [I recalled how] he had argued with me over giving [reductions], and I became too shy to ask him about it.

[Advice and Commission]

My Lord said, "Muḥammad, forgiveness will be for the one who knows me through [my] oneness, and takes nothing as a partner next to me. One who does not know me through oneness, I will forbid **[66v]** him from my paradise, and prevent him from receiving my mercy. His destiny will be toward hellfire, abiding there continuously for eternity."

"Muḥammad, forgive and you will be forgiven. Be toward orphans like a merciful father, and toward widows like a devoted husband. I will incline toward my paradise anyone who does these things. Among my decisions, Muḥammad, is that paradise will be forbidden to all communities until you and your community enter into it. Muḥammad, I have sent to you my mercy and to your community their ease. Muḥammad, I have granted you a station that no one else has reached, neither the first people nor the last. Muḥammad, call your community to my worship and remind them of my punishment. Be patient with what befalls you for my sake, for the patient ones will be given their reward, without reckoning. Muḥammad, call upon me when I send you down with my command, for indeed I am near and responsive to the one who calls. When one calls upon me for your sake, [especially] the call of someone oppressed, indeed I will reply to it, even were the request from a disbeliever for disbelieving in me. Muḥammad, my peace and mercy are upon you until the day of resurrection. Look at such a station I caused you to ascend, and at such a station I spoke with you. I only did so because you are my beloved, and I wished to make manifest your favor and make clear your influence **[67r]** with me. So ask of me what you wish, for there is no intermediary between us here, neither revelation nor [angelic] messenger [separates us].

[Favor of the Prophets Reprise and Intercession]
I said, "My Lord, you *created Adam with* your *hand* (Q 38:75), you *breathed into him some of your spirit* (Q 15:29; 32:9; 38:72), you caused your *angels to touch their heads to the ground* (Q 2:34; 38:72, et al.) before him, *caused him to dwell* (Q 2:35; 7:19) in the abode of your favor, and paired him with the life of your nation [Eve]. What, then, have you granted this night to your servant Muḥammad?"

God said, "Muḥammad, I created Adam with my hand, I breathed into him some of my spirit, I paired him with the life of my nation, [Eve] and I caused him to dwell in the abode of my favor. Yet I also sent him out of my paradise because of his wrongdoing, for I will not allow one who disobeys me to live near me. As for you, I have conjoined your name with my name, for I am not mentioned without you being mentioned with me. I have even made your name to proceed mine in the phrase, 'Muḥammad, the Messenger of God.' I am the one praised [*Maḥmūd*], you are one greatly praised [*Muḥammad*], and the people of your community are the ones who praise [*al-ḥāmidūn*]."

"If I took Abraham as an *intimate friend* (Q 4:125), I have also taken you as a beloved. I ransomed Ishmael with a great sacrificial ram, and I am ransoming your community from the fires of hell with the idolaters. If I carried Noah upon the [Ark] *of planks and calk* (Q 54:13), I carried you on the Burāq and thus folded up the heavens for you. If **[67v]** I raised up Idrīs (Enoch) '*to a high place*' (Q 19:57), I have also raised you, Muḥammad, to a place where no sent prophet nor near angel has trod, and here you are, '*a distance of two bows or closer*' (Q 53:9) from me. If I *gave David the psalms* (Q 4:163; 17:55), I gave you *seven rhymed* [verses] (Q 15:87) and the great Qurʾān. And if I forgave a single one of his misdeeds, I have '[*opened*] *your chest for you and removed the weight* [that had burdened your back], *and raised up your mention*' (Q 94:1–4) above each noble creature. Furthermore, I have forgiven you of all your misdeeds, both previous and subsequent."

"If I gave Solomon command over created things, I have made the earth pure and a place where you and your community may touch your heads to the ground in ritual prayer. I have sworn that you and your community would inherit it from all other created things. If I created Jesus by *breathing into* him *some of my spirit* (Q 21:91), [and if] he spoke to me, I split your name from mine, and I granted you a river named *Kawthar* (Q 108:1). Its banks are made out of pearls and sapphires, and on **[68r]** its sides runs water that is more intensely white than snow, more sweet than honey, and more fragrant than fine musk. I also gave you the spring *Salsabīl* (Q 76:18), intercession on the day of resurrection, and an exalted and mediating rank, and the *praised station* (Q 17:79). I rewarded you with Ramaḍān, something I had not given to any before you. Moreover, I made you the seal of the messengers (*khātim al-rusul*)."

I said, "For [only] my Lord's sake is the praise. My Lord, forgive my community." He replied, "Done. I have forgiven seventy people of your community of those who deserved hellfire. I said, "For [only] my Lord's sake is the praise and the thanks."[43]

[Prelude to the Tours of Paradise and Hellfire]

My Lord said, "Muḥammad, would you like to cast your eyes upon what I have prepared for you and your community in paradise?" I said, "My Lord and master, I would indeed like that." Then a voice called out, "Iṣṭīfyaʾīl!" An angel replied, "Here I am, at your service." The voice said, "This is Muḥammad. Convey him to Gabriel. Command [Gabriel] to show him what I have prepared for him and his community, and bring him into paradise with my permission."

So Iṣṭīfyaʾīl took me by the arm. [Despite having seen] what I had seen of my Lord's angels, **[68v]** I had never seen any creature more enormous in stature, more handsome of face, nor more pleasant of fragrance than he. He transported me from the presence of my Lord, great be his greatness, high be his command, and mighty be his matter. He had given me all goodness, and increased for me all goodness, making me content and even beyond content. Iṣṭīfyaʾīl rent the veils faster than the blink of an eye, by God's permission, until I arrived back with Gabriel who was at the Lote Tree of the Boundary, watching for me. Iṣṭīfyaʾīl said to him, "Gabriel, God commands you to bring Muḥammad into paradise and to show him the rich blessings and magnificent angels that God has prepared for him and his community."

When Gabriel saw me, he drew near and embraced me, then drew me to him a second time in an intense embrace, and kissed me between the eyes. He congratulated me for the favor and blessing that God had bestowed upon me, saying, "Congratulations, Muḥammad, for what took place tonight, and for what you have witnessed of your Lord's power. Indeed you stepped foot in a place where **[69r]** no person before you or after you has arrived, you heard the speech of your Lord, he sat you upon the seat (*kursī*) of his favor, and he granted you intercession."

Muqātil b. Sulaymān said: Thus did I hear [this story] from Wahb b. Munabbih, who reported it from ᶜAbd Allāh Ibn ᶜAbbās, and thus also [narrated] Ḍaḥḥāk and Muzāḥim, who reported it from Ibn ᶜAbbās.

[. . .][44]

Glossary: Key Themes and Tropes in the Ibn ᶜAbbās Ascension Narratives

Angels, Major: The Ibn ᶜAbbās narratives tend to include four major angels that appear at the very beginning of the Primitive Version, namely the Rooster angel, the angel made half out of fire and half out of snow (the "Half-Fire-Half-Snow angel"), the Angel of Death (Azrāʾīl), and the Guardian of Hellfire (Mālik). In addition to these four, two of the highest of all the angels, Isrāfīl and Mikāʾīl, often appear in the vicinity of God's throne.

Bargaining Scene: The vast majority of ascension reports, including those in the major Sunnī *ḥadīth* collections, discuss how during the climax of the ascension, God commands Muḥammad and his community to observe fifty ritual prayers each day and night. Upon the advice of Moses, Muḥammad asks for a reduction in the number, and eventually God reduces the duty from fifty prayers to five (each one worth the merit of ten) per day. This trope appears in most Ibn ᶜAbbās recensions as well, but it loses some of its emphasis with the fuller development of rest of the "intimate colloquy" (q.v.). In addition, the reshaped versions often append to this bargaining over the number of ritual prayers an exchange in which God and Muḥammad bargain over the number of months per year that the Muslim community should fast during daylight hours.

Belief Personified: In certain reshaped versions of the Ibn ᶜAbbās narrative, especially those ascribed to Bakrī (see chapter 8), Muḥammad encounters a handsome youth upon his arrival to Jerusalem. He embraces the youth, who subsequently vanishes. Gabriel informs him that by embracing the youth, he and his community will embrace right belief (*īmān*). This trope should be viewed as an extension of the more common "tempting figures" trope (q.v.), contrasting with the personifications to be avoided therein.

Cold Hand: In the Primitive Version and some later recensions of the Ibn ʿAbbās discourse, upon Muḥammad's arrival into God's presence, God reaches out and touches Muḥammad, who feels the coolness of his touch upon his back. The touch either removes the fear that Muḥammad had been feeling or it conveys to him some special form of knowledge. Compare this trope with the "sweet drop" (q.v.). The trope appears outside the ascension context in a "heavenly host debate" *ḥadīth* report transmitted in the sound Sunnī collection by Tirmidhī, discussed in chapter 5.

Cup Test: At some point in his journey, often in Jerusalem but in some versions at the Inhabited House in the seventh heaven, Gabriel and/or another angel bring Muḥammad a series of cups, and he is asked to choose one to drink. Usually there are three cups, often filled with either water, wine, honey, or milk (milk is always present, and always the correct choice). Muḥammad chooses the milk and hears that he was "rightly guided" to do so. Had he chosen another beverage, there would have been dire consequences for him and his community. In the reshaped Ibn ʿAbbās texts, sometimes Muḥammad is said to have left behind a portion of the milk, and finds out that if he had finished it off, his entire community would have been spared from the hellfire.

Eulogy Contest: In some of the extended narratives transmitted by Ṭabarī, when Muḥammad joins the rest of the prophets in Jerusalem, they each take turns recounting the manner in which God had favored them, citing qurʾānic passages as evidence. Muḥammad eulogizes himself last, and Abraham and others agree that God favored him the most. This scene bears direct comparison with the "favor of the prophets" trope.

Favor of the Prophets: During his conversation with God (see "intimate colloquy"), and usually near its end, Muḥammad lists the various ways that God has shown favor or distinction to prophets that had preceded him, and he asks God how he, Muḥammad, will be honored in a similar fashion. God replies by enumerating the ways that Muḥammad has been granted favors equal to or better than those granted to other prophets. Often this conversation topic transitions into a "gifts" or "intercession" section, with God bestowing more favors upon Muḥammad and/or allowing him to petition for dispensations on behalf of his community.

Final Verses (Seals) of the Cow Chapter: Drawn from Q 2:285–86, these two verses that end the longest chapter of the Qur᾽ān are here adapted to form a part of the actual dialogue exchanged between Muḥammad and God in their "intimate colloquy." The verses are cited in full in chapter 1.

Heavenly Host Debate: Drawing on Q 38:65–70, in this portion of the "intimate colloquy" conversation, God asks Muḥammad if he knows what the heavenly host debate. Usually Muḥammad replies in the negative, and God teaches him the content of the debate through the use of rhyming catch-words such as "the degrees" (*darajāt*) and "the goodnesses" (*ḥasanāt*), sometimes after touching him with the cold hand (*q.v.*).

Intercession: Usually introduced by the phrase "Ask and be given," in this part of the "intimate colloquy" (q.v.) Muḥammad petitions God on behalf of a certain portion of the Muslim community. In later recensions, this scene becomes more and more elaborate, with God promising entrance into paradise to a larger and larger group of the devout.

Intimate Colloquy: This dialogue between Muḥammad and God on the night of the ascension becomes a central and distinctive feature of the Ibn ᶜAbbās discourse. It almost always contains three major topics, each of which are described above, in some form or another: the "heavenly host debate," the "final verses (seals) of the Cow chapter," and the "favor of the prophets." Afterward God showers Muḥammad with gifts, allows him to intercede on behalf of the Muslim community, and imposes ritual obligations.

Opening of Muḥammad's Chest: In some versions of the night journey narrative, soon after the angels arrive in Mecca to fetch Muḥammad, they are said to open up his chest and to wash his heart, returning it to its place cleansed and purified before the journey begins. This scene, which appears in a number of the ascension narratives from the Sunnī sound *ḥadīth* collections, is incorporated in only a select few of the Ibn ᶜAbbās ascension texts.

Prayer Stops: On the way to Jerusalem during the night journey, in some narratives Muḥammad is told to "descend and pray two cycles of ritual prayer" in one or more locations. He is afterward informed what makes the site(s) particularly sacred, namely its connection to one of the major prophets preceding Muḥammad, usually Moses or Jesus. This idea, which first appears in a *ḥadīth* reported by Nasāʾī (see chapter 5), finds its way into many of the reshaped versions of the Ibn ʿAbbās discourse. Compare the "tempting figures."

Sandals: In some late recensions of the Ibn ʿAbbās ascension narrative, probably beginning with Bakrī (see chapter 8), God sometimes commands Muḥammad not to remove his sandals as he approaches the divine presence in order to bless this exalted site with the dust from his shoes. This idea makes an explicit contrast between the way God treats Moses on Sinai and the way God treats Muḥammad at the divine throne.

Sweet Drop: As Muḥammad nears the divine throne in later versions of the Ibn ʿAbbās narrative, a drop of sweet liquid often falls from the throne onto his tongue. It either removes his fear and makes it easier for him to address the divinity, or else it conveys to him some type of secret knowledge. In that sense, the function of the sweet drop is analogous to that of the "cold hand" (q.v.).

Sword: During the "intimate colloquy" (q.v.) in some late Ibn ʿAbbās narratives, Muḥammad notices a sword hanging from the side of the divine throne, sometimes given a particular name (e.g., "The Sword of Vengeance"), sometimes described as "dripping blood." Muḥammad requests that God remove this sword from his community, and God refuses, informing him that his community was sent with the sword and will achieve victory with the sword.

Tempting Figures: While on the road to Jerusalem during the night journey, Muḥammad is addressed by voices on the right and left, calling upon him to stop or turn toward them. He also encounters a beautiful woman decked out in finery and jewels, who appears before him in the road. He refuses to allow himself to be distracted by any of these figures, and Gabriel later informs him that his community would have inclined toward other allegiances (the Jews, the Christians, or "the world") had he done so. Distinctive to some later reshaped versions of the Ibn ʿAbbās narrative is the idea that Muḥammad did actually turn briefly toward the beautiful woman, or at least he desired to do so. Some recensions also append to this scene the "belief personified" trope (q.v.).

Veils: Beginning with the Primitive Version, the Ibn ʿAbbās ascension narratives often describe a series of seas, mountains, and other types of "veils" that separate the Lote Tree of the Boundary from the divine throne. In some versions the veils take the form of actual partitions, sometimes composed of a material substance such as fire or precious gems, other times composed of some abstract quality such as "majesty" or "oneness." In the reshaped version, the latter veils set boundaries that even the highest of angels cannot cross, the guardians of each veil having to reach under and pull Muḥammad past it.

Notes

Introduction

1. Qur'ān, *sūra* (chapter) 17, "The Night Journey," *āya* (verse) 1. All such qur'ānic citations in the body of the text will hereafter employ the shorthand "(Q 17:1)." Quotations or allusions from the Qur'ān appear in *italics*. Unless otherwise stated, translations in this book are my own.

2. The dating convention used throughout this book is to first give the Muslim date according to the lunar years after the pilgrimage to Medina (AH), followed by the common era dating (CE or AD) after a slash to separate the two. Thus 150 AH, which corresponds roughly with 767 CE, will be rendered (150/767), a date that falls in the middle of the second/eighth century.

3. Pierre Bourdieu, *Outline of a Theory of Practice*, trans. Richard Nice (Cambridge: Cambridge University Press, 1977), 164–71.

4. Muḥammad Sa'īd Ramaḍān Būṭī, *Fiqh al-sīra*, 7th ed. (Beirut: Dār al-Fikr, 1978), 154–55; quoted by Khālid Sayyid 'Alī, *al-Isrā' wa'l-mi'rāj: mu'jiza wa ḥaqā'iq, asrār wa fawā'id* (Damascus and Beirut: al-Yamāma, 1998), 30.

5. Jamel Eddine Bencheikh, "L'Aventure de la Parole," 238, from an essay appearing at the end of id., *Le Voyage nocturne de Mahomet* (Paris: Imprimerie Nationale, 1988), 231–90.

6. Ibid., 284.

7. Michael Sells, "3 Enoch (*Sefer Hekhalot*) and the Mi'rāj of Abū Yazīd al-Bisṭāmī," a paper read at the Annual Meeting of the American Academy of Religion, 1989, unpublished copy, 10.

8. For instance John Collins, in his introduction to the groundbreaking study of the apocalyptic genre (*Apocalypse: The Morphology of a Genre*, *Semia* 14 [1979]), excludes any consideration of Muslim sources. The collection *Death, Ecstasy, and Other Worldly Journeys* that Collins coedited with Michael Fishbane similarly pays scant attention to Islamic ascension narratives.

9. E.g, see the recent work of Brooke Vuckovic and Christiane Gruber, both mentioned below.

10. For a useful overview of the history of scholarly approaches to the Qur'ān, see Andrew Rippin, "Western Scholarship and the Qur'ān," in *The Cambridge Companion to the Qur'ān*, ed. Jane D. McAuliffe (Cambridge: Cambridge University Press, 2006), 235–51.

11. Brooke Olson Vuckovic, *Heavenly Journeys, Earthly Concerns: The Legacy of the Miʿrāj in the Formation of Islam* (New York and London: Routledge, 2005).

12. In particular, see the outstanding work by Christiane Gruber, as well as the articles that she and I have coedited in the forthcoming volume *The Prophet Muḥammad's Ascension: New Cross-Cultural Encounters* (Bloomington: Indiana University Press, expected 2009).

13. See Christiane Gruber, "The Prophet Muḥammad's Ascension (*Miʿrāj*) in Islamic Art and Literature, 1300–1600," (PhD diss., University of Pennsylvania, 2005); id., *The Ilkhanid Book of Ascension: A Persian-Sunni Prayer Manual* (London: I. B. Tauris and BIPS, forthcoming).

CHAPTER 1. MUḤAMMAD'S NIGHT JOURNEY IN THE QUR'ĀN

1. See Sells, *Approaching the Qur'ān* (Ashland, OR: White Cloud, 1999), 20; Neal Robinson, *Discovering the Qur'ān*, 2d ed. (Washington DC: Georgetown University Press, 2003), 224–40; Farid Esack, *The Qur'ān: A User's Guide* (Oxford: Oneworld, 2005), 73–74.

2. For examples of this position, see Richard Bell, "Muḥammad's Visions," *The Moslem World* 24 (1934):145–54; John Wansbrough, *Qur'ānic Studies*, 67–69; Mordechai Nissan, "Notes on a Possible Jewish Source for Muhammad's Night Journey," *Arabica* 47, no. 2 (2000):274–77.

3. See especially the reference to Moses leading the Exodus from Egypt: Q 20:77, 26:52, 44:23. The verb also appears twice in reference to the nocturnal flight of Lot, Q 11:81 and 15:65.

4. Angelika Neuwirth, "From Sacred Mosque to the Remote Temple," 388f. Neuwirth explains apparent connections with Moses as attempts to link Muḥammad with previous prophets.

5. My work in this way parallels the recent work of Brooke Olson Vuckovic and its concern with "reception theory." See the introduction to her *Heavenly Journeys, Earthly Concerns*, 10–12.

6. See Neuwirth, "From Sacred Mosque to the Remote Temple," 401, n.30.

7. A. Guillaume attempts to decode this qur'ānic phrase by a study of early historical sources; see his "Where was al-Masyid al-Aqsa," *Andalus* 18 (1953):323–36. Once again let me emphasize that this study does not attempt to uncover original historical fact but rather trace the history of Muslim interpretations. Since no major Muslim storyteller or Qur'ān commentator entertained the thesis that Guillaume defends

—namely that the "*furthest place-of-prayer*" was none other than the town of Jiᶜrāna, not far from Mecca—this intriguing idea will not concern us here.

8. Such an identification appears in both the Qurʾān commentary of Muqātil b. Sulaymān and in Ibn Hishām's recension of Ibn Isḥāq's biography of Muḥammad, both discussed in what follows. This position gains support from the qurʾānic phrase "*whose precincts we have blessed*," an idea that the Qurʾān often connects with the land of Israel / Palestine (Neuwirth, "From the Sacred Mosque to the Remote Temple," 382–83).

9. See the *ḥadīth* reports of the night journey discussed in chapter 5. Some of the first European scholars to study the night journey and ascension narratives, for example Schrieke in "Die Himmelsreise Muhammeds" (*Der Islam* 6 [1916]: 1–30) and Horowitz in "Muhammeds Himmelfahrt" (*Der Islam* 9 [1919]: 159–83), privilege as foundational those versions of the story that ignore Jerusalem in favor of an ascension to heaven directly from Mecca.

10. See chapter 3. Note that both Muqātil b. Sulaymān and Ibn Saᶜd treat the two events as separate, and Ibn Saᶜd even proposes separate dates for the two journeys.

11. The term *miᶜrāj* properly refers to a "ladder," but Arabic sources use it as shorthand for the heavenly ascension itself. See the discussion of the term and references provided in Vukovic, *Heavenly Journeys and Earthly Concerns*, 2–3.

12. See my translation of Sulamī, *The Subtleties of the Ascension* (Louisville, KY: Fons Vitae, 2006), sayings 16 and 24.

13. This translation of Q 81:15–24 is by Michael Sells, from his *Approaching the Qurʾān* (Ashland, OR: White Cloud, 1999), 48.

14. Geo Widengren traces the trope of the heavenly commission through a series of Near Eastern narratives. See *The Ascension of the Apostle and the Heavenly Book* (Uppsala: A. B. Lundequistska, 1950); id., *Muhammad, the Apostle of God, and His Ascension* (Uppsala: A. B. Lundequistska, 1955), especially 9–10 and 96f.

15. Josef van Ess, "Vision and Ascension: *Sūrat al-Najm* and Its Relationship with Muhammad's *miᶜrāj*," *Journal of Qurʾānic Studies* 1 (1999):49–50.

16. See al-Ṭabarī, *Tafsīr al-Ṭabarī* (*Jāmiᶜ al-bayān fī taʾwīl ay al-qurʾān*). vol. 11 (Beirut: Dār al-Kutub alᶜIlmiyya, 1992), 503–19 (*tafsīr* 53:1–18).

17. Van Ess, "Vision and Ascension," 49.

18. Ibid., 47–62, where van Ess argues that what was originally interpreted as a vision of God, later was explained as a vision of Gabriel, the change due to rising concerns over the theological problem of the representation of God in a physical form (*tashbīh* and *tajsīm*).

19. See al-Ṭabarī, *Tafsīr al-Ṭabarī*, vol. 11, 512–13 (*tafsīr* 53:11).

20. Ibid., 514. This is the very same Ibn ᶜAbbās in whose name the most detailed Islamic ascension accounts will be transmitted, discussed below in chapters 2 and 8.

21. Van Ess, "Vision and Ascension," 50.

22. In addition to the scholars van Ess lists, see also Guillaume, "Where Was al-Masyid al-Aqsā?"

23. The issue of the original meaning of the qurʾānic phrase will not concern us here, but one cannot deny the near Muslim unanimity in placing the Lote Tree's location in the upper heavens. Sells and others note the parallels between some descriptions of the Lote Tree and descriptions of the tree of paradise from the book of Genesis (e.g., see Sells, *Early Islamic Mysticism*, 326 n.20).

24. There is an intriguing parallel between, on the one hand, the above idea of God's descent on the Lote Tree and addressing Muḥammad from there and, on the other, the scene from the Hebrew Bible, Exodus 3, in which God addresses Moses from out of a burning bush.

25. This other tree is called "Goodness" (*ṭūba*), and is discussed in the following section.

26. Neuwirth, "From Sacred Mosque to Remote Temple," 398.

27. I render the phrase "*al-bayt al-maᶜmūr*" as "The Inhabited House," both due to my dissatisfaction with the more common but confusing "Frequented House," and to my desire to choose a passive participle that stays faithful to the original Arabic root. The ascension narratives place this "house" in the seventh heaven, where the prophet Abraham is frequently depicted as leaning his back against it and where angels enter and perhaps worship. In this way, the Inhabited House appears as a type of heavenly Kaᶜba, analogous to Jewish descriptions of the temple in the heavens that mirrors the Solomonic temple in Jerusalem.

28. See the discussion of this term by Walid Saleh, *The Formation of the Classical Tafsīr Tradition: The Qurʾān Commentary of al-Thaᶜlabī* (Leiden: E. J. Brill, 2004), 119–24. Compare the name of another paradisiacal river, "Fullness" (*Tasnīm*, Q 83:27), that appears in the Qurʾān more explicitly with reference to paradise (although not necessarily a river).

29. Some later ascension narratives interpret this term *rafraf* as a proper name for a winged mount, playing a role analogous to the one that Burāq plays during Muḥammad's journey to Jerusalem.

30. For instance Miguel Asín Palacios, one of the first to discuss the Primitive Version of the Ibn ᶜAbbās narrative, sees in these qurʾānic allusions at the end of the narrative a transparent attempt to lend what was originally a non-Islamic narrative some Islamic credentials. See Asín Palacios, *La escatalogía musulmana en la Divina Comedia*, 2d ed. (Madrid, Granada: Consejo Superior de Investigaciones Científicas, 1943), 40–41. I offer a full English translation of this passage in my "Constructing an Islamic Ascension Narrative: The Interplay of Official and Popular Culture in Pseudo-Ibn ᶜAbbās" (PhD diss., Duke University, 2002), 23.

31. Compare a different but similar verse: "*Say: I do not say to you that I possess the treasures of God, nor do I have knowledge of the hidden, nor do I say to you that I am an angel*" (Q 6:50).

32. Two Arabic terms are used for this concept, based on the same Arabic root: *mundhir* (Q 38:65) and *nadhīr* (Q 38:70).

33. See the *ḥadīth* report from Tirmidhī's sound *ḥadīth* collection, discussed in chapter 5, and the adaptation of this scene to the divine colloquy at the climax of Muḥammad's ascension.

34. Since portions of qurʾānic chapters were sometimes revealed at different times according to traditional Muslim theories of gradual revelation, it also remains possible for a Muslim to imagine that the final two verses of the Cow chapter are, in fact, Meccan verses.

35. See the evidence assembled by Neuwirth, "From the Sacred Mosque to the Remote Temple," 396–97, who cites the following qurʾānic passages: Q 15:14–15, Q 17:93, Q 6:35, and Q 6:125. One could also add other passages, such as references to Pharaoh's attempt to build a tower to ascend to heaven: Q 40:36–37, Q 28:38–40; cf. Q 38:10–11.

36. In addition to the passages cited by Neuwirth as mentioned in the previous note, see also Q 43:33–35, as well as Q 52:44 and Q 17:90–92.

37. The Arabic phrase is *al-samāʾ al-dunyā*, literally the "nearby heaven" or the "the sky of this [lower] world." I have followed the exegetical tradition of the ascension literature, however, in which this phrase becomes a technical term to refer to the first of seven heavenly realms.

38. See the article by David Halperin, "Ascension or Invasion: Implications of the Heavenly Journey in Ancient Judaism," *Religion* (1988):47–67, on Moses and the Evening Star; see also id., *Faces of the Chariot*, 486; the Hekhalot texts themselves contain plenty of warnings for those who would dare to ascend to the heavens without the proper knowledge, purity, or aptitude. See, for example, *Hekhalot Rabbati*, summarized in Ithamar Gruenwald, *Apocalyptic and Merkavah Mysticism* (Leiden: E. J. Brill, 1980), 150–73.

39. The word *miʿrāj* never itself appears in the Qurʾān, just as the word *isrāʾ* never appears there, but the verbs formed from the roots of these two words do indeed appear in the text.

40. Note that the Arabic word *maʿārij* represents the plural form of the word *miʿrāj*. While the plural form is translated as "steps" or "stairs," it could also be rendered "ladders" or "ascensions."

41. On this chapter of the Qurʾān, and the qurʾānic use of the concept of "spirit" as infused in key boundary moments, see the commentary by Michael Sells, *Approaching the Qurʾān*, 183–204.

42. A related but distinct type of hyperbole appears in the ascension narratives associated with Ibn ʿAbbās, in which physical distances get reported in terms of years of travel. See Halperin, *Faces of the Chariot*, Index 6, s.v. "Five-hundred-year-Journey."

43. Neuwirth, "From the Sacred Mosque to the Remote Temple," 397.

44. A large number of later Ibn ʿAbbās ascension narratives conclude their accounts with a reference to this verse, and one may theorize that they do so not only to justify the controversy that took place in Mecca upon Muḥammad's recounting his tale the next morning, but also in order to justify the pro-Sunnī position they seek to reinforce.

45. Neuwirth, "From the Sacred Mosque to the Remote Temple," 378.

CHAPTER 2. ORALITY AND THE PRIMITIVE VERSION OF THE IBN ᶜABBĀS ASCENSION NARRATIVE

1. Jan Vansina, *Oral Tradition as History* (London: James Currey, 1985), 13.
2. Ibid., 69.
3. Ibid., 30, 53, 167f.
4. Ibid., 92–100, 196.
5. Richard Bulliet, in his *Islam: The View from the Edge* (New York: Columbia University Press, 1994), 27–34, asserts that *ḥadīth* reports can be understood as answers to questions that Muslims, and particularly new converts, were asking.
6. Arabic biographical sources on the life of Ibn ᶜAbbās from the formative period include: Ibn Saᶜd, *al-Ṭabaqāt al-kubrā*, vol. 2, 365–72; Ibn ᶜAbd al-Barr, *al-Istiᶜāb fī maᶜrifat al-aṣḥāb*, ed. Bajawī, vol. 3, 933–39; Ibn Athīr, *Usd al-ghāba fī maᶜrifat al-ṣaḥāba*, vol. 3, 290–94; Ibn Khallikān, *Wafayāt al-aᶜyān wa anbāʾ al-zamān*, ed. Iḥsān ᶜAbbās, vol. 3, 62–64.
7. Ibn ᶜAbd al-Barr, *al-Istiᶜāb*, vol. 3, 934 and 937–38; Ibn Athīr, *Usd al-ghāba*, vol. 3, 292–93.
8. Claude Guillot, "Portrait 'mythique' d'Ibn ᶜAbbās," *Arabica* 32, no. 2 (1985): 127–84.
9. E.g., Ibn Athīr, *Usd al-ghāba*, vol. 3, 292.
10. Guillot, "Portrait 'mythique' d'Ibn ᶜAbbās," 179–80.
11. See Andrew Rippin, "Ibn ᶜAbbās' *al-Lughat fīʾl-qurʾān*," *Bulletin of the School of Oriental and African Studies* 44 (1981):15–25; id., "Ibn ᶜAbbās' *Gharīb al-qurʾān*," *Bulletin of the School of Oriental and African Studies* 46 (1983):332–33; id., "Tafsīr Ibn ᶜAbbās and Criteria for Dating Early Tafsīr Texts," *Jerusalem Studies in Arabic and Islam* 18 (1994): 38–76.
12. See Ṭabarī, *Jāmiᶜ al-bayān fī taʾwīl ay al-qurʾān* (hereafter: *Tafsīr*), vol. 11, 507–9 (commentary on Q 53:8–9) and 512–14 (commentary on Q 53:13).
13. Gordon Newby, *The Making of the Last Prophet* (Columbia: University of South Carolina Press, 1989), 10.
14. The three sources are the following: a *ḥadīth* deemed "weak" by Ibn Ḥībbān Bustī (d. 354/965), apparently only preserved in full by Suyūṭī (d. 911/1505) in his *Lālī al-maṣnūᶜa fī aḥādīth al-mawḍūᶜa*, ed. Abū ᶜAbd al-Raḥmān Ṣalāḥ b. Muḥammad b. ᶜUwayḍa (Beirut: Dār al-Kutub al-ᶜIlmiyya, 1996), 62–75; a *ḥadīth* from Abū al-Qāsim Qushayrī (d. 465/1072), "*Kitāb al-miᶜrāj*," Bankipore, Kahuda Bakhsh Oriental Public Library MS 1891, fols. 25v–30r (cf. the printed ed. in id., *Kitāb al-miᶜrāj*, ed. ᶜAbd al-Qādir, 56–62); a *ḥadīth* from ᶜAbd al-Raḥmān b. ᶜAbd al-Muḥsin Wāsiṭī (d. 744/1343), "*Sharḥ asmāʾ Rasūl Allāh*," Damascus, Maktabat al-Asad al-Waṭaniyya MS 6840, fols. 34v–51r.
15. An abbreviated reference appears in Ibn Ḥibbān's *al-Majrūḥīn min al-muḥaddithīn*, vol. 2 (Riyāḍ: Dār al-Sumayᶜī, 2000), 344–45, s.v. "Maysara b. ᶜAbd Rabbih."

16. Suyūṭī, *al-Lālī al-maṣnūʿa*, 62. On the symbolism of the Rooster, see Roberto Tottoli, "At Cock-Crow: Some Muslim Traditions about the Rooster," *Der Islam* 76 (1999):139–47.

17. Suyūṭī, *al-Lālī al-maṣnūʿa*, 62–63. This angel will variously be given the name "Spirit" (*rūḥ*) or "Beloved" (*ḥabīb*) in other sources. See Muqātil, *Tafsīr Muqātil*, vol. 4, 565–66 (*tafsīr* of Q 78:38) and ibid., vol. 4, 772 (*tafsīr* to the end of Q 97); see also Qummī, *Tafsīr Qummī*, 371.

18. This interview with the Angel of Death becomes especially developed and refined in the later reshaped versions of the Ibn ʿAbbās ascension narrative.

19. The scene depicts Muḥammad as looking into the hellfire, but no specific scenes of torture are described at this point, and no actual tour of hellfire follows. This account of the angel Mālik, Guardian of Hellfire, appears to have been widely known in the early period, perhaps circulating as an independent report. Ibn Hishām's description of the scene closely resembles that of the Primitive Version, and he claims to have received it from "a certain [unnamed] person of knowledge" (see chapter 3). Ibn Hishām's reticence to name his source raises the question of whether he may have drawn the report from an early version of the Ibn ʿAbbās *ḥadīth*.

20. Suyūṭī, *al-Lālī al-maṣnūʿa*, 65.

21. Qushayrī, "*Kitāb al-miʿrāj*," fols. 27v–28r. On the textual foundation of these three topics in the colloquy between Muḥammad and God, see both chapter 1 and chapter 5. Most reshaped versions of the Ibn ʿAbbās ascension narrative contain all three of these main intimate colloquy elements.

22. See van Ess, "The Youthful God: Anthropomorphism in Early Islam," Ninth Annual University Lecture in Religion, Arizona State University, 1988 (photocopy); id., "Vision and Ascension," 47–62; id., "Le *Miʿrāǧ* et la Vision de Dieu," passim; id., "Le théologie et le Coran: *miʿrāǧ* et le débat sur l'anthropomorphisme," chap. 2 in *Les Prémices de la Théologie musulmane* (Paris: Albin Michel, 2002); Gimaret, *Dieu à l'image de l'homme: Les anthropomorphismes de la* sunna *et leur interprétation par les théologiens* (Paris: CERF, 1997).

23. E.g., Qurʾān 76:19 and 52:24, passages cited in the Primitive Version (see Appendix A).

24. Ibid., 74. In this passage, Muḥammad sees Adam in the highest heaven and Jesus in the lowest heaven as he descends back to earth. Compare the reshaped version translated in Appendix B, where Adam similarly appears in the highest heaven.

25. This phrase was coined by Michael Sells, "3 Enoch (Sefer Hekhalot) and the *Miʿrāj* of Abū Yazīd Bisṭāmī," unpublished paper read before the American Academy of Religion, 1989.

26. See, for instance, the famous "*Hekhalot Rabbati*," summarized in Ithamar Gruenwald, *Apocalyptic and Merkavah Mysticism* (Leiden: E. J. Brill, 1980), 150–73.

27. See ibid.; Colby, "Constructing an Islamic Ascension Narrative," 244–49; on the allegorical dimension, see Peter Heath, *Allegory and Philosophy in Avicenna (Ibn Sīnā)*, and Ibn Sīnā's *Miʿrājnāma* discussed in chapter 9.

28. For instance, the angels that appear in the extended narratives of Anas b. Mālik in the two major Sunnī sound *ḥadīth* collections are often left unnamed and indistinct, in sharp contrast to the approach in the Primitive Version.

29. The term *ᶜiliyyūn* appears in Q 83:18, where it seems to indicate the location where the ledgers of good works performed by the righteous are kept.

30. One potential early exception appears in the *ḥadīth* report attributed to Ibn ᶜAbbās and Abū Ḥabba Anṣārī that Muḥammad reached the level in which he was able to hear "the scratching of the pens" (Muslim, *Īmān*, no. 263; also quoted twice in Bukhārī; for both, see chapter 5). The later traditionist Najm al-Dīn Ghayṭī (d. 984/1576) insists that this latter station remains within the bounds of the Lote Tree, however, and that Muḥammad never passed beyond it.

31. Later versions of the Ibn ᶜAbbās ascension narrative often replace many of these terrifying seas and mountains with a whole series of less threatening veils. Nevertheless, the element of fear and danger remains (see chapters 8 and 9). Again the Jewish ascension texts offer some potential parallels to the dangers and trials faced by the one ascending (see the summaries in Gruenwald, *Apocalyptic and Merkavah Mysticism*), and this topic merits further study.

32. Suyūṭī, *al-Lālī al-maṣnūᶜa*, 70.

33. On the concept of *fanāᵓ* in early Sufism, see Michael Sells, *Early Islamic Mysticism* (New York: Paulist Press, 1996), 119–21, 222–24, 259–65.

34. For one example, see the mystical commentary in Sulamī's gloss on Q 7:143 attributed to Jaᶜfar Ṣādiq, translated in Sells, *Early Islamic Mysticism*, 80.

35. See Sells, *Early Islamic Mysticism*, 249. The whole of the narrative and the accompanying commentary appear in ibid., 242–50.

36. See Sulamī, *The Subtleties of the Ascension*, trans. and annotated by Frederick Colby (Louisville, KY: Fons Vitae, 2006), 12–13.

37. For instance, Furāt Kūfī in his *Tafsīr* interprets Q 2:285–86 with reference to the intimate dialogue during Muḥammad's ascension. See my article, "The Role of Imāmī Shīᶜī Narratives in the Construction of and Contestation over the Story of Muḥammad's Ascension," in *The Prophet Muḥammad's Ascension: New Cross-Cultural Encounters*, edited by Frederick S. Colby and Christiane Gruber (forthcoming from Indiana University Press); id., "Constructing an Islamic Ascension Narrative," 147–49; see also below, chapter 4.

38. As mentioned above, chapter 1 n. 30, Asín looks suspiciously on the amount of qurᵓānic allusion in the Primitive Version, seeing in it a transparent attempt to add Islamic legitimacy to an otherwise non-Islamic narrative. Though I agree that aspects of the narrative may have been drawn from the common stock of images from the ascension "language world" that are not only Iranian but also from further afield hermetic traditions, it would nevertheless be a mistake to see the Primitive Version as a wholesale importation from any one non-Islamic source.

39. Sells, *Early Islamic Mysticism*, 249, where Bisṭāmī is said to encounter the "spirits of the prophets" at the end of his dream ascension.

40. Later Ibn ᶜAbbās narratives collate the fantastic wonders of the Primitive Version together with the more typical scenes from other ascension accounts in which Muḥammad meets one or more prophets in each heaven as he ascends. Even in the later reshaped Ibn ᶜAbbās ascension narratives, however, the question of the order in which Muḥammad encounters each of the prophets in the heavens remains remarkably fluid; see chapters 8 and 9.

41. Suyūṭī, *al-Lālī al-maṣnūᶜa*, 74.

42. Ibid.

43. Ibid., 74–75.

44. Asín Palacios, *Escatalogía musulmana*, 40–41. The translation in this passage is my own.

45. Van Ess, "Le *Miᶜrāǧ* et la Vision de Dieu," 44–45.

46. Ibid., 51.

47. Ibid., 45, n.94.

48. Ṭabarī's use of the phrase "you did this and that" (*wa faᶜalta wa faᶜalta*) here and in what follows functions like the phrase "et cetera," and proves that Ṭabarī knew more details of this narrative than he chooses to include.

49. Ṭabarī, *Tafsīr*, vol. 11, 510 (commentary on Q 53:11).

50. Cf. the second *isnād* attributed to the Qurʾān commentator Ibn Marduwayh (d. 410/1019) in Suyūṭī, *al-Lālī al-maṣnūᶜa*, vol. 1, 74. Suyūṭī states that Ibn Marduwayh preserved the text "in its [full] length (*bi-ṭūlihi*)." Unfortunately, Ibn Marduwayh's *Tafsīr* is no longer extant, so it is not possible to verify this statement or compare the latter's recension to those of the three in my possession. Even so, a close comparison of the second *isnād* that Suyūṭī ascribes to Ibn Marduwayh's recension of the Primitive Version to the *isnād* that Ṭabarī cites above suggests that one of these chains may well be a corrupted form of the other. For instance, several of the names in the chains differ from one another only slightly in terms of orthography: Aḥmad instead of Muḥammad, Saᶜīd b. Rāzīn instead of Saᶜīd b. Zarbī, etc.

51. Suyūṭī, *al-Lālī al-maṣnūᶜa*, 70.

52. Ibid., 74.

53. For Tirmidhī's *ḥadīth* reports, see chapter 5. For some discussion of the image of God's cold hand in Sulamī's work *The Subtleties of the Ascension*, see my article "The Subtleties of the Ascension: al-Sulamī on the Miᶜrāj of the Prophet Muḥammad," *Studia Islamica* 94 (2002):167–83. The image of the cold hand appears in later texts based upon the Bakrī version.

54. Richard Bulliet, *Islam: The View from the Edge*, 27–34.

55. As chapter 6 will show, the fact that later scholars either appended the Primitive Version to the end of other accounts or collated it with other accounts gives credibility to the idea that these scholars found in the Primitive Version valuable supplemental material. Qushayrī transmits the Primitive Version after citing the reports of Mālik b. Ṣaᶜṣaᶜa, Anas b. Mālik, and others; see Qushayrī, "*Kitāb al-miᶜrāj*," fols. 5r–11v (ᶜAbd al-Qādir ed., 29–38); Wāsiṭī and Qummī combine the Primitive Version with the

Abū Sa^cīd Khudhrī *ḥadīth*, while Tha^clabī combines it with the Abū Hurayra *ḥadīth* (on the Khudrī and Abū Hurayra reports, see chapter 6).

56. On Muqātil's background and works, and particularly on his relationship with the *quṣṣāṣ*, see *EI*², s.v. "Mukātil b. Sulaymān," by M. Plessner and Andrew Rippin.

57. With few exceptions, Muqātil's account of the night journey and ascension does not cite its sources or oral chains of transmission. For this reason, along with other charges (i.e., that Muqātil was a sectarian, or anthropomorphist, or that he overly relied upon Jewish and Christian tales, etc.), Muqātil's *Tafsīr* was not widely used by later scholars, and some viewed it as unreliable. For rejoinders to such criticism, see Ibn Khallikān, *Wafayāt al-a^cyān*, edited by Iḥsān ᶜAbbās (Beirut: Dār Ṣādir, 1977), vol. 5, 255–57; *EI*², s.v. "Mukātil b. Sulaymān."

58. Muqātil, *Tafsīr Muqātil*, vol. 2, 513 (*tafsīr* of Q 17:1).

59. Ibid., 516.

60. Ibid., 517.

61. Muqātil's description of Burāq offers perhaps the earliest example of a text in which Burāq is said to be more than a riding beast and even to have human features such as a human face. Later Ibn ᶜAbbās narratives, such as the reshaped version ascribed to Bakrī (see chapters 8 and 9, and Appendix B) similarly treat Burāq as a rational being with human features.

62. Ibid., 516. Compare ibid., vol. 4, 603 (*tafsīr* of Q 81:21), which bears a close resemblance to the account in Ibn Hishām's recension of Ibn Isḥāq's night journey account.

63. Ibid., vol. 4, 161. The Arabic term *rafraf* appears once in plural form in the Qur'ān (Q 55:76), where the verse describes a scene in paradise with the phrase, "*they lean on green rafrafs*." Muqātil's identification of the one of the "*greatest signs*" on the ascension with a "green *rafraf*" was made by others, including ᶜAbd Allāh Ibn Mas^cūd in a *ḥadīth* from Bukhārī, book *Tafsīr*, chapter *Sūrat al-Najm*, no. 4 (no. 4858); see also Ṭabarī, *Tafsīr*, vol. 11, 519 (commentary on Q 53:18), where all such reports trace back to reports from Ibn Mas^cūd.

64. Ṭabarī, *Tafsīr*, vol. 11, 510–14, commentary on Q 53:11, 13.

65. The word *ṭūbā* ("goodness") appears in the Qur'ān in 13:29, and it comes to be connected with a tree of paradise that is distinct from the famous Lote Tree of the Boundary. As we shall see in chapter 4, Shī^cī exegetes often understand special significance in the *Ṭūbā* tree because of its connection with anecdotes about the birth of Muḥammad's daughter Fāṭima, wife of ᶜAlī.

66. Muqātil, *Tafsīr Muqātil*, vol. 4, 565–66 (*tafsīr* of Q 78:38); an abbreviated reference to this same angel appears in ibid., vol. 4, 772 (*tafsīr* to the end of Q 97).

67. See Charles Pellat, *EI*², s.v. "Ḳāṣṣ."

68. Van Ess, "Le *Mi^crāǧ* et la Vision de Dieu," 45.

69. El-Azmeh, *al-Mi^crāj wa-'l-ramz al-ṣūfī*, 16.

70. Pellat, *EI*², s.v. "Ḳāṣṣ," 734.

CHAPTER 3. EARLY HISTORICAL DESCRIPTIONS OF MUḤAMMAD'S JOURNEY

1. On Ibn Bukayr's recension, see Guillaume, *New Light on the Life of Muḥammad*, 58; van Ess, "Le Miᶜrāj et la vision de Dieu dans les première spéculations théologique en Islam," in Amir-Moezzi, ed. *Le Voyage initiatique en terre d'Islam* (Louvain, Paris: Peeters, 1996), 47 n.109 and ibid., 50. I am aware of two printed editions of Ibn Bukayr's recension of Ibn Isḥāq: *Kitāb al-sīra wa'l-maghāzī,* ed. Suhayl Zakkār (Beirut: Dār al-Fikr, 1978); *Sīrat Ibn Isḥāq,* ed. Muhammad Ḥamīd Allāh (Rabat: Maᶜhad al-Dirasāt wa'l-Abḥāth lil-Taᶜrib, 1976).

2. Ibn Isḥāq (in the recension of Ibn Bukayr), *Kitāb al-Sīra wa'l-maghāzī*, edited by Suhayl Zakkār, 295; Ibn Isḥāq (in the recension of Ibn Hishām), *Sīrat Rasūl Allāh*, ed. Wüstenfeld, vol. 1 / I, 262. Ibn Hishām's recension appends to the citation of this verse a more expanded account, describing the sending down of additional and related qur'ānic verses. See the English translation in Guillaume, *The Life of Muḥammad* (Oxford: Oxford University Press, 1955), 181.

3. Ibn Isḥāq (recension of Ibn Bukayr), *Kitāb al-Sīra wa'l-maghāzī*, 295; Ibn Isḥāq (recension of Ibn Hishām), *Sīrat Rasūl Allāh*, ed. Wüstenfeld, vol. 1 / I, 263. Whenever I refer to Ibn Isḥāq's *Sīra* without specifying a particular recension, it is to Ibn Hishām's more widespread version.

4. Ibid. for both sources. While I generally agree with Guillaume that "the author means to leave open the question of whether it was an actual physical journey or a nocturnal vision" (Alfred Guillaume, *The Life of Muḥammad*, 182, note 1), the journey of the spirit mentioned in the anecdote that follows makes it seem as if Ibn Isḥāq himself favors the latter explanation.

5. Ibn Isḥāq (recension of Ibn Bukayr), *Kitāb al-Sīra*, 295, where that *ḥadīth* report appears immediately after the introduction to the night journey and in lieu of any more specific accounts; compare Ibn Isḥāq [recension of Ibn Hishām], *Sīrat Rasūl Allāh*, vol. 1 / I, 263–65, where at least four *ḥadīth* reports precede this anecdote, including a long account attributed to Ḥasan al-Baṣrī.

6. Ibn Isḥāq (recension of Ibn Bukayr), *Kitāb al-Sīra*, 295.

7. Josef van Ess, "Le *Miᶜrāǧ* et la Vision de Dieu," in *Le Voyage Initiatique en Terre d'Islam*, ed. Mohammad Ali Amir-Moezzi (Louvain-Paris: Peeters, 1996), 47 n.109 as well as ibid., 50.

8. Ibn Isḥāq (recension of Ibn Bukayr), *Kitāb al-Sīra*, 297.

9. Ibn Isḥāq (recension of Ibn Hishām), *Sīrat Rasūl Allāh*, ed. Wüstenfeld, vol. 1 / I, 263.

10. Ibid., 263–64.

11. Ibid., 265. At this point in the narrative, the author quotes Q 17:60, linking the night journey to the idea of a vision that God grants which causes strife (*fiṭna*) among people.

12. Ibid., 267–68.

13. Unlike the typical role that Abū Bakr comes to play in these scenes, the model of the true believer for later Muslims, here when some Meccans tell Abū Bakr what Muḥammad has been telling them, he immediately accuses them of lying (ibid.).

14. Ibid. Compare the translation of this passage in Guillaume, *The Life of Muḥammad*, 183, and the other later authors who rely on Guillaume, e.g., Sells, *Early Islamic Mysticism*, 327 n.34; Vuckovic, *Heavenly Journeys, Earthly Concerns*, 91. Guillaume and his followers read the passage as if the narrator, al-Ḥasan Baṣrī, was raised up in the air in order to better see Muḥammad. Instead, I contend that the narrative describes how the city of Jerusalem was raised up (by Gabriel or God) for Muḥammad.

15. The ascension *ḥadīth* in these collections will be described in chapter 5.

16. Ibn Isḥāq (recension of Ibn Hishām), *Sīrat Rasūl Allāh*, 263 and 266.

17. See the summary of Hūd b. Muḥakkam Hawwārī's version of Muḥammad's ascension in my dissertation "Constructing an Islamic Ascension Narrative," 191–96; Claude Gilliot has made a study of Hawwārī's Qur᾽ān commentary: "Le Commentire Coranique de Hūd b. Muḥakkam / Muḥkim," *Arabica* 44, no. 22 (1997):179–233. Regarding Ṭabarī, see chapter 6.

18. For an English translation, see Guillaume, *The Life of Muḥammad*, 184–87.

19. Ibn Isḥāq (recension of Ibn Hishām), *Sīrat Rasūl Allāh*, 268; Guillaume, *The Life of Muḥammad*, 185. On the reference to Ismāᶜīl, see the discussion of Ṭabarī's report of Abū Saᶜīd Khudrī's ascension *ḥadīth*, chapter 6.

20. On Zayd b. Ḥāritha, Muḥammad's adopted son, see Vuckovic, *Heavenly Journeys, Earthly Concerns*, 104–5; on the story of the marriage, see Ṭabarī, *The History of al-Ṭabarī*, vol. 9, *The Last Years of the Prophet*, trans. Ismail Poonawala (Albany: State University of New York Press, 1990), 134; Fatima Mernissi, *The Veil and the Male Elite*, trans. Mary Jo Lakeland (Reading, MA: Addison-Wesley, 1991), 104 and 175.

21. Ibn Isḥāq (recension of Ibn Hishām), *Sīrat Rasūl Allāh*, 268–69; cf. the translation by Guillaume, *The Life of Muḥammad*, 185. This anecdote is discussed briefly by Vuckovic, *Heavenly Journeys, Earthly Concerns*, 38–39.

22. On Ibn Saᶜd and the importance of his biographical dictionary, see Muḥammad Siddiqi, *Ḥadīth Literature*, 96–100.

23. Ibn Saᶜd, *al-Ṭabaqāt al-kubrā*, vol. 1, 213–14.

24. For instance, Ibn Kathīr and others ask why Muḥammad did not recognize the prophets in the heavens if he had just met them and prayed with them in Jerusalem. See Ibn Kathīr, *Tafsīr al-qur᾽ān al-ᶜaẓīm*, ed. Salāma (Riyadh: Dār al-Ṭayba, 1997), vol. 5, 31 (tafsīr Q 17:1).

25. These represent two holy sites within the enclosure of the Kaᶜba in Mecca.

26. The association of the phrase "scratching of the pens" with the heavenly ascension appears in Sunnī official *ḥadīth* collections, often linked to Ibn ᶜAbbās. For example, see Muslim, *Ṣaḥīḥ*, book of *Īmān*, chapter of *al-Isrā᾽*, no. 5 (no. 263 overall); Bukhārī, *Ṣaḥīḥ*, book of *Ṣalāt*, no. 1 (no. 349); ibid., book of *al-Anbiyā᾽*, no. 5 (no. 3442 overall). This detail could preserve a distant echo of the idea in the Ibn ᶜAbbās ascen-

sion narratives (see chapters 2 and 8) that Muḥammad could not hear any created thing just prior to entering the divine audience.

27. Ibn Saᶜd, *al-Ṭabaqāt al-kubrā*, vol. 1, 213.

28. On this theme, see Harris Birkeland, *The Legend of the Opening of Muḥammad's Breast* (Oslo: I Kommisjon Hos Jacob Dybwad, 1955).

29. Ibid. The *isnād* for the Ibn ᶜAbbās chain is: ᶜAbd Allāh b. Jaᶜfar Zakariyya b. ᶜAmr Ibn Abī Mulayka Ibn ᶜAbbās.

30. Ibn Saᶜd, *al-Ṭabaqāt al-kubrā*, vol. 1, 214.

31. I would like to thank Marion Katz for calling my attention to the correct interpretation of the phrase "*shiᶜib Abī Ṭālib*," a reference to a geographical location near Mecca.

32. Ibn Saᶜd, *al-Ṭabaqāt al-kubrā*, vol. 1, 214–15. Recall that the same detail appears in one report transmitted in Ibn Hishām's recension of Ibn Isḥāq's text, Ibn Isḥāq (recension of Ibn Hishām), *Sīrat Rasūl Allāh*, ed. Wüstenfeld, vol. 1 / I, 267.

33. Vuckovic, *Heavenly Journeys, Earthly Concerns*, 77–79.

34. Ibid., 79.

35. Ibn Kathīr, *Tafsīr*, cited in Vuckovic, *Heavenly Journeys, Earthly Concerns*, 79.

36. Ibn Saᶜd, *al-Ṭabaqāt al-kubrā*, vol. 1, 215.

37. Another anecdote, ibid., describes how Muḥammad worries to Gabriel before arriving home in Mecca, "My community will not believe me!" and Gabriel assures him that Abū Bakr will.

38. Ibid. See the discussion of the Ibn Hishām and Ibn Saᶜd versions in Vuckovic, *Heavenly Journeys, Earthly Concerns*, 91–92.

39. See Muslim, *Ṣaḥīḥ*, book of Īmān, chapter on the night journey, no. 278; compare Ibn Saᶜd, *al-Ṭabaqāt al-kubrā*, vol. 1, 215.

40. See Ibn Saᶜd, *al-Ṭabaqāt al-kubrā*, vol. 1, 214–15; compare Ibn Isḥāq (recension of Ibn Hishām), *Sīrat Rasūl Allāh*, ed. Wüstenfeld, vol. 1 / I, 266; Ibn Isḥāq (recension of Ibn Bukayr), *Kitāb al-Sīra*, 295–96; Guillaume, *The Life of Muḥammad*, 183–84.

41. This detail appears in an independent fragment reported in Ibn Isḥāq (recension of Ibn Bukayr), *Kitāb al-Sīra*, 296.

42. Ibn Saᶜd, *al-Ṭabaqāt al-kubrā*, vol. 1, 215–16; see also the parallel *ḥadīth* in Muslim cited above, *Ṣaḥīḥ*, book of Īmān, chapter on the night journey, no. 278.

CHAPTER 4. PROTO-SHĪᶜĪ NARRATIVES OF HEAVENLY ASCENT

1. Nawbukhtī, *Firaq al-shīᶜa*, ed. Helmut Ritter (Istanbul: Maṭbaᶜat al-Dawla, 1931), 34; cf. Ashᶜarī, *Maqālat al-islāmiyyīn*, 9. For other sources, see "Constructing an Islamic Ascension Narrative," 140, n.171.

2. For a discussion of ᶜIjlī and his ascension in Western literature, see Amir-Moezzi, "L'Imam dans le Ciel," 112; van Ess, "Le *Miᶜrāj* et la Vision de Dieu," 51–52;

id., *Theologie und Gesellschaft*, vol. 1, 377; Widengren, *Muḥammad, the Apostle of God, and His Ascension*, 33; Tucker, "Abū Manṣūr al-ᶜIjlī and the Manṣūriyya: A Study in Medieval Terrorism," *Der Islam* 54 (1977):66–76; Samarrai, *Theme of the Ascension*, 196; Merkur, *Gnosis*, 202.

3. Note that Asín Palacios, van Ess, and others study the chain of transmission attached to the primitive version of the Ibn ᶜAbbās ascension narrative and conclude that the story was likely fabricated around the turn of the first century AH, that is, by someone who flourished contemporaneously with ᶜIjlī. See Miguel Asín Palacios, *La escatalogía musulmana*, 40–41, translated in my "Constructing an Islamic Ascension Narrative," 21; van Ess, "Le *Miᶜrāǧ*," 44–45.

4. Muṭṭahir b. Ṭāhir Maqdīsī, *Kitāb al-badᵓ wa'l-tarīkh*, ed. Clément Huart, vol. 5, 130–31, trans. Widengren, *Muḥammad, the Apostle of God, and His Ascension*, 86; see ibid., 31–32.

5. In some variants this sweet drop calms Muḥammad's nerves, while in others it transmits to him a wealth of knowledge, not unlike what Bazīgh reportedly claimed to have received.

6. Ṣaffār Qummī, *Baṣāᵓir al-darajāt*, ed. Mīrzā Muḥsin Kuchebāghī Tabrīzī (Qum: Maktabat Āyat Allāh al-ᶜUẓmā Marᶜashī Najafī, 1982). On this work and its contents, see Mohammad Ali Amir-Moezzi, "al-Ṣaffār al-Qummī (m. 290/902–3) et son *Kitāb Baṣāᵓir al-Darajāt*," *Journal Asiatique* 280, nos. 3–4 (1992):221–50; id., "L'Imam dans le Ciel," 110–11 and passim; Meir M. Bar-Asher, *Scripture and Exegesis in Early Imāmī Shīᶜism* (Leiden: E. J. Brill, 1999), 8.

7. Ṣaffār Qummī, *Baṣāᵓir al-darajāt*, 79 (sec. 2, chap. 10, no. 10); cf. the French translation in Amir-Moezzi, "L'Imam dans le Ciel," 114. Amir-Moezzi points out that variations of this same anecdote appear in the work of other later Imāmī Shīᶜī scholars including the tenth-century theologian Ibn Bābūya Ṣaddūq (d.381/991) and the sixteenth-century compiler Muḥammad b. Bāqir Majlisī (d. 1111/1699).

8. The idea that Muḥammad ascended to heaven on multiple occasions appears in other works, not only those of Shīᶜī authors but also those by Sunnīs. One noteworthy example appears much later in the Sunnī Qurᵓān commentary by Ibn Kathīr, who uses the "multiple ascension" hypothesis to explain variations in Sunnī canonical sound *ḥadīth* reports.

9. On this debate in the early period, see Bar-Asher, *Scripture and Exegesis*, chap. 4.

10. Ṣaffār Qummī, *Baṣāᵓir al-darajāt*, 107 (sec. 2, chap. 20, no. 3). Chapter 20 begins with the heading, "A chapter on how the Imams were shown the Angelic-realm of the heavens and the earth, just as the Prophet was shown [them], to the point that they looked upon what was above the throne." Cf. the commentary by ᶜAlī b. Ibrāhīm Qummī to Q 53:13–15 in *Tafsīr Qummī*, vol. 2, ed. Ṭayyib Mūsa Jazāᵓirī (Najaf: Maṭbaᶜat Najaf, 1976), 335–36, where this narrative is divided into smaller narrative fragments, and where ᶜAlī joins Muḥammad on the ascension not in body but in form (*mithāl*).

11. It is thus that I understand the reference to the "second residence." Given that the Jewish ascension narratives sometimes describe the various stages of the journey as palaces (*hekhalot*), this idea may well have been shared across religious boundaries.

12. Ṣaffār Qummī, *Baṣā'ir al-darajāt*, 107 (sec. 2, chap. 20, no. 1).

13. Ibid., sec. 2, chap. 20, no. 2.

14. On the question of the relative rank of the knowledge accorded to angels, prophets, messengers, and Imams, see Bar-Asher, *Scripture and Exegesis*, 144f. Regarding Abraham's ascension as it plays a role in Isma‘īlī Shī‘ī discussions of the ascent, see Lisa Alexandrin, "Prophetic Ascent and the Individual Initiatory Experience in Qadi al-Nu'man's *Asas al-ta'wīl*," in *The Prophet Muḥammad's Ascension: New Cross-Cultural Encounters*, ed. Frederick Colby and Christiane Gruber (Bloomington: Indiana University Press, forthcoming).

15. Ṣaffār Qummī, *Baṣā'ir al-darajāt*, 416–18 (sec. 8, chap. 18, no. 11).

16. Ibid. Section 8 contains numerous other anecdotes that depict ‘Alī as the one who will have the authority to separate those bound for paradise and those bound for hellfire, earning him the title "divider of paradise and hellfire" (*qāsim al-janna wa'l-nār*).

17. This allusion to Q 42:51, "*It is not for a human being that God should speak to him except in revelation* (waḥy) *or from behind a veil*," is here inserted into the key verse from Q 53:10, "*He revealed* (awḥā) *to his servant what he revealed*." The verses are linked by "revelation" (*waḥy*).

18. An allusion to Q 57:3, "*He is the first and the last, the manifest and the hidden, and he is of all things the most knowing*," most commonly understood as references to the divinity.

19. Ṣaffār Qummī, *Baṣā'ir al-darajāt*, 514–15 (sec. 10, chap. 18, no. 36); cf. the French translation in Amir-Moezzi, "L'Imam dans le Ciel," 104.

20. Such confusion on the part of Muḥammad over ‘Alī's status may help to explain the "unusual tradition" that Bar-Asher cites from ‘Alī b. Ibrāhīm Qummī's work, *Tafsīr Qummī*. Bar-Asher labels this report, "Doubts (or Grief) of Muḥammad When Hearing God Praise ‘Alī." See Bar-Asher, *Scripture and Exegesis*, 225–32.

21. I am thinking of Abū Yazīd Bisṭāmī and his ascension (see Sells, *Early Islamic Mysticism*, chap. 7), as well as some of the sayings recorded by Sulamī that depict Muḥammad as taking on divine qualities (see *The Subtleties of the Ascension*, sayings 6, 9, 10, 11, 13, 23, 35, etc.).

22. Bar-Asher, *Scripture and Exegesis*, 30.

23. Furāt Kūfī, *Tafsīr Furāt al-Kūfī*, no. 234 (commentary on Q 10:94).

24. For an example from a century later, see the prayer niche (*mihrāb*) in Cairo's Ibn Ṭulūn mosque, dated ca. 1094, pictured in Renard, *Seven Doors to Islam* (Berkeley: University of California Press, 1996), 29.

25. For instance, see Furāt Kūfī, *Tafsīr Furāt al-Kūfī*, vol. 2, 372–74, no. 503 (commentary on 39:74); see also ‘Alī b. Ibrāhīm Qummī's interpretation of Q 53:1–8,

Tafsīr Qummī, vol. 2, 336–37. As we will see, such inscriptions serve as sites for theological and sectarian competition.

26. Furāt Kūfī, *Tafsīr Furāt al-Kūfī*, no. 272 (commentary on Q 13:7).

27. The tree of *Ṭūba* (Q 13:29) is here conflated with the Lote Tree of the Boundary (Q 53:14).

28. The phrase reminds one of the seal of prophecy often said to appear on Muḥammad's back, but it is also quite similar to the language used in the heavenly host debate trope in which God is sometimes depicted as touching Muḥammad between his shoulder blades with his cold hand.

29. Furāt Kūfī, *Tafsīr Furāt al-Kūfī*, vol. 1, 211 (commentary on 13:29). Many more narratives on the heavenly origin of Fāṭima's seed can be found in ibid., 207–17.

30. The question of the date of Muḥammad's ascension arises here, for clearly such anecdotes could not sustain what becomes the mainstream Sunnī date for the ascension: just a year before the emigration to Medina, and not long after the death of Khadīja.

31. Furāt Kūfī, *Tafsīr Furāt al-Kūfī*, vol. 1, 74–75, no. 48 (commentary on Q 2: 285–86). There are references to this and other related passages in Amir-Moezzi, "L'Imām dans l'Ciel," 103 n.18.

32. In fact, Furāt Kūfī himself offers two different versions of this report, one longer than the other. Compare ibid., nos. 47 and 48.

33. See Uri Rubin, "Pre-existence and Light: Aspects of the Concept of Nur Muhammad," *Israel Oriental Studies* 5 (1975):62–119. Rubin discusses these luminous figures in ibid., 99–100, where he translates the phrase *ashbāh al-nūr* as "luminous reflections." See also Bar-Asher, *Scripture and Exegesis*, 136–39; Amir-Moezzi, "L'Imam dans L'Ciel," 107–8 (especially n.35, where he lists other parallel sources); Halperin, "Hekhalot and *Miʿrāj*," 271 and 279.

34. The appearance of the Mahdi next to the throne here, exalted as the defender of God's friends and foe to God's enemies, may explain the appearance of the sword hanging from God's throne in later versions of the Ibn ʿAbbās ascension narrative (a brief example appears in Appendix B).

35. Furāt Kūfī, *Tafsīr Furāt al-Kūfī*, vol. 2, 372–74, no. 503 (commentary on Q 39:74). The scene draws its humor from the idea that the angels and others would have asked Muḥammad for his intercession, which proves that such an idea must have been in circulation by the end of the third/ninth century.

36. Ibid., 374. Compare the Jewish idea that God created an image of Jacob engraved upon the throne; see Halperin, "Hekhalot and *Miʿrāj*," 275.

37. While there are certainly Christian resonances to this image, there may be some Jewish overtones as well. For instance, Halperin theorizes that the transformation of Enoch into the "lesser YHWH" Metatron in the Jewish Hekhalot literature helps one to understand these Shīʿī ascension anecdotes. See Halperin, "Hekhalot and *Miʿrāj*," 273. Notice that in the reshaped version of the Ibn ʿAbbās ascension, the divine voice commands Muḥammad to sit on a bejeweled *kursī* in the vicinity of the divine throne (see Appendix B).

38. In most other Islamic references to this trope, the angel is not given any specific name, rather it is mentioned that this angel greeted a prophet while still seated (a symbol of arrogance and dominion) and thus was forced to stand. See Furāt Kūfī, *Tafsīr Furāt al-Kūfī*, vol. 1, 75, no. 49 (commentary on 2:285); cf. Hawwarī, *Tafsīr Kitāb Allāh al-ᶜAzīz*, vol. 2 (Beirut: Dār al-Gharab al-Islāmī, 1990), 406 (commentary on 17:1); Qummī, *Tafsīr Qummī*, 372 (commentary on 17:1); Halperin, "Hekhalot and *Miᶜrāj,"* 274.

39. Furāt Kūfī, *Tafsīr Furāt al-Kūfī*, vol. 2, 372–74, no. 503 (commentary on 39:74).

40. The image of a sword of vengeance (*sayf al-nuqma*) being wielded near the divine throne will later be transformed in Sunnī narratives that describe that sword hanging from the divine throne.

41. Najāshī, *Rijāl*, 305; see Amir-Moezzi, "L'Imam dans le Ciel," 100; van Ess, "Le *Miᶜrāǧ* et la Vision de Dieu," 53; id., *Theologie und Gesellschaft*, vol. 1, 345, and ibid., vol. 5, 69.

CHAPTER 5. CANONICAL SUNNI *ḤADĪTH* REPORTS ON MUḤAMMAD'S JOURNEY

1. For a general overview of this formative history, see Marshall Hodgson, *The Venture of Islam*, vol. 1. Josef van Ess offers a more detailed study of early figures and theological trends in his monumental series *Theologie und Gesellschaft*. The literature on the early development of *ḥadīth* literature is vast. For two contrasting views, see Joseph Schacht, *The Origins of Muḥammadan Jurisprudence* (Oxford: Oxford University Press, 1959; Muhammad Zubayr Siddiqi, *Ḥadīth Literature: Its Origin, Development, and Special Features*, edited and revised by Abdal Hakim Murad (Cambridge, UK: Islamic Texts Society, 1993). See also the useful introduction and appended bibliography assembled in *Ḥadīth: Origins and Developments*, ed. Harold Motzki (Burlington, VT: Ashgate, 2004), liv–lxiii.

2. I have in mind here the theological notion that all Muslims of the first generations reliably told the truth (*taṣdīq al-ṣaḥāba*), a practical doctrine that rests upon a principle of faith.

3. For instance, the measure of the reliability of particular transmitters was partially determined by their reputation among other Muslims, a variable that could easily become dependent upon subjective factors such as whether the transmitters' religious or theological loyalties were similar to those passing judgment on their reputation.

4. In bracketing the question of the beginnings, origins, or truth of these narratives, I am following the basic approach discussed in my "Constructing an Islamic Ascension Narrative" (Duke University PhD diss., 2002), and that of Brooke Olson Vuckovic, *Heavenly Journeys, Earthly Concerns*. Some Muslim scholars likewise call for the study of the night journey and ascension narratives as literature and intellectual

legacy, independent of the question of provenance or validity. See Nazeer El-Azmeh, *Mi^crāj wa'l-ramz al-ṣūfī* (Beirut: Dār al-Bāḥith, 1973); Jamel Eddine Bencheikh, *Le Voyage nocturne de Mahomet* (Paris: Imprimerie Nationale, 1988).

5. Since I concentrate this chapter on those ascension-related reports that come to have an impact on the telling of the story of Muḥammad's journey, it does not make reference to many of the other intriguing narratives that appear in the numerous *ḥadīth* collections that I consulted, including those of Ibn Ḥanbal, Abū Daʾwūd, ʿAbd al-Razzāq, Ibn Abī Shayba, Ṭayālisī, etc.

6. By "extended narrative," I mean those reports that present a full narrative of the events of the evening, with a beginning, middle, and end. By fragment or anecdote, I mean those reports that discuss only a single scene or portion of the narrative. By this definition, in Muslim's *Ṣaḥīḥ* (collection of sound *ḥadīth*), book *Īmān*, in its chapter entitled "The Night Journey" (*al-isrāʾ*), there are four extended accounts (nos. 259, 262, 263, and 264; on which, see below) and ten fragmentary shorter anecdotes: three on the opening of Muḥammad's chest (nos. 260, 261, 265) and seven on the physical description of Moses and/or Jesus (nos. 266, 267, 268, 269, 270, 271, 272).

7. On the biography of Anas, see the revised edition of the *Encyclopaedia of Islam* (*EI*²), s.v. Anas b. Malik; see also Siddiqi, *Ḥadīth Literature*, ed. Abdal Hakil Murad (Cambridge: Islamic Texts Society, 1993), 20–21. In light of the fact that all of the extended ascension *ḥadīth* reports in Bukhārī and Muslim were transmitted by this single individual, one wonders why the extended reports of other transmitters were excluded from these collections. In terms of chains of transmission, there appears to be no clear reason why Bukhārī and Muslim would privilege Anas' extended ascension accounts above those of other reliable companions, and I would contend that these traditionists made use of selective criteria other than sound chains of transmission.

8. Muslim, *Ṣaḥīḥ*, book *Īmān*, chapter *al-Isrāʾ*, no. 259 (hereafter Muslim no. 259 or simply "no. 259"); there is no parallel *ḥadīth* in Bukhārī. The full chain of transmission is the following: Shaybān b. Furūkh—Ḥammād b. Salama—Thābit al-Bunānī—Anas b. Mālik—Messenger of God.

9. Muslim, *Ṣaḥīḥ*, book *Īmān*, chapter *al-Isrāʾ*, no. 262; Bukhārī, *Ṣaḥīḥ*, book *Manāqib*, no. 24; the full version appears in Bukhārī, *Ṣaḥīḥ*, book *Tawḥīd*, no. 37. The chain of transmission for the version in Muslim no. 262 is as follows: Hārūn b. Saʿīd al-Aylī—Ibn Wahab—Sulaymān b. Bilāl—Sharīk b. ʿAbd Allāh b. Abī Namir—Anas b. Mālik. The chain of transmission for the full version in Bukhārī is as follows: ʿAbd al-ʿAzīz b. ʿAbd Allāh—Sulaymān—Sharīk b. ʿAbd Allāh—[Anas] Ibn Mālik.

10. Muslim, *Ṣaḥīḥ*, book *Īmān*, chapter *al-Isrāʾ*, no. 263; Bukhārī, *Ṣaḥīḥ*, book *Ṣalāt*, no. 1; ibid., book *al-Anbiyāʾ*, no. 5. The chain of transmission for the version in Muslim no. 263 is as follows: Ḥarmala b. Yaḥyā al-Tujībī—Ibn Wahb—Yūnus—Ibn Shihāb—Anas b. Mālik—Abū Dharr—Messenger of God. The chain of transmission in Bukhārī, *Ṣalāt*, no. 1, is as follows: Yahyā b. Bukayr—al-Layth—Yūnus—Ibn Shihāb—Anas b. Mālik—Abū Dharr—the Messenger of God. The chain of transmission in Bukhārī, *al-Anbiyāʾ*, no. 5, is twofold: ʿAbdān—ʿAbd Allāh—Yūnus—al-Zuhrī and

Aḥmad b. Ṣāliḥ—ʿAnbasa—Yūnus Ibn Shihāb—Anas [b. Mālik]—Abū Dharr—Messenger of God.

11. Muslim, *Ṣaḥīḥ*, book *Īmān*, chapter *al-Isrāʾ*, no. 264; Bukhārī, *Ṣaḥīḥ*, book *Badʾ al-Khalq*, chapter *Dhikr al-Malāʾik* (no. 6), no. 1; ibid., book *Manāqib al-Anbiyāʾ*, chapter *al-Miʿrāj* (no. 42), no. 1. The chain of transmission for the version in Muslim no. 264 is as follows: Muḥammad b. al-Muthannā—Ibn ʿAdiyy b. Saʿīd—Qatāda—Anas b. Mālik (who perhaps said)—Mālik b. Ṣaʿṣaʿa (a man of his tribe)—Prophet of God. The chain of transmission in Bukhārī, book *Badʾ al-Khalq*, chapter *Dhikr al-Malāʾik*, no. 1, is twofold: Hudba b. Khālid—Hammām—Qatāda—Anas b. Mālik—Mālik b. Ṣaʿṣaʿa—The Prophet; and Yazīd b. Zurayʿ—Saʿīd and Hishām—Qatāda—Anas b. Mālik—Mālik b. Ṣaʿṣaʿa—The Prophet. The chain of transmission in Bukhārī, *Manāqib al-Anbiyāʾ*, chapter *al-Miʿrāj* (no. 42), no. 1, is the first of the two chains just mentioned, as follows: Hudba b. Khālid—Hammām b. Yaḥyā—Qatāda—Anas b. Mālik—Mālik b. Ṣaʿṣaʿa—The Prophet.

12. Compare Moses receiving the duty of establishing ritual prayer directly from God at the burning bush, Q 20:14, quoted by Olson Vuckovic, *Heavenly Journeys, Earthly Concerns*, 65.

13. On the reactions of the Muslim community upon Muḥammad's return and its significance, see Vuckovic, *Heavenly Journeys, Earthly Concerns*, chap. 3. Apart from the extended narratives described above, Bukhārī does include a single anecdote on the community reaction in his section discussing Q 17:1 (*Ṣaḥīḥ*, book *Tafsīr Sūrat Banī Isrāʾīl*, chapter *Asrā bi-ʿAbdihi*, no. 2). In this anecdote, the Quraysh accuse Muḥammad of lying about his journey, and God reveals Jerusalem to him so that he is able to describe it to them while looking at it. Compare another version of this trope at the end of Ibn Hishām's account of the night journey.

14. As mentioned above, this detail is missing in Muslim, *Ṣaḥīḥ*, book *Īmān*, chapter *al-Isrāʾ*, no. 259, but the latter *ḥadīth* appears to be missing its beginning, for it mentions nothing about the Prophet's location or state when Burāq was brought to him.

15. This "opening of the chest" scene may well have begun as an anecdote that was unconnected to the night journey and ascension. For an overview of the various positions, see Vuckovic, *Heavenly Journeys, Earthly Concerns*, 18–25.

16. See, for instance, the fragmentary anecdotes mentioned above, especially those at the end of Muslim's section on the night journey, *Ṣaḥīḥ*, book *Īmān*, chapter *al-Isrāʾ*, nos. 266, 267, 268, 269, 270, 271, 272.

17. Muslim, *Ṣaḥīḥ*, book *Īmān*, chapter *al-Isrāʾ*, no. 266. Compare the descriptive section between the night journey and ascension accounts in Ibn Hishām's recension of Ibn Isḥāq, discussed above. On Mālik and al-Dajjāl, see Vuckovic, 36–39. Mālik plays a key role in the Ibn ʿAbbās ascension narratives, often answering Muḥammad's questions and/or ushering him on a tour of hellfire; see chapters 2 and 8.

18. See, for instance, the *ḥadīth* reports that immediately follow the previous accounts of the night journey in Muslim, *Ṣaḥīḥ*, book *Īmān*, chapter *al-Isrāʾ*, nos. 267–72 (end of the chapter).

19. Muslim, *Ṣaḥīḥ*, book *Īmān*, chapter *al-Isrāʾ*, nos. 268–69.

20. Muslim, *Ṣaḥīḥ*, book *Kitāb al-faḍāʾil*, chapter "*Min faḍāʾil Mūsā*," no. 164; cf. Ibn Ḥanbal, *Musnad*, edited by Aḥmad Muḥammad Shākir (Cairo: Dār al-Maʿārif, 1950); Nasāʾī, *Sunan*, vol. 3, 215. The passage is described by Vuckovic, *Heavenly Journeys, Earthly Concerns*, 62.

21. Heribert Busse cites these *ḥadīth* reports as part of his argument that the night journey and ascension narratives originally described the same apocalyptic journey to the holy sanctuary in heaven, only later being treated as separate narratives. See especially 12–13 of his study "Jerusalem in the Story of Muḥammad's Night Journey and Ascension," *Jerusalem Studies in Arabic and Islam* 14 (1991):1–40.

22. Muslim, *Ṣaḥīḥ*, book *Īmān*, chapter "*Fī dhikr sidrat al-muntahā*," 1; Nasāʾī, *Sunan*, vol. 1, book *Ṣalāt*, chapter "Farḍ al-Ṣalāt," no. 4 (no. 455 in the collection), 72–73, making use of the second *isnād* chain that Muslim cites; compare Tirmidhī, *Sunan*, book *Tafsīr al-Qurʾān*, chapter *Tafsīr Sūrat al-Najm* (Q 53), no. 1, discussed below.

23. On the concept of intercession, see *EI*², s.v. "*shafāʿa*." Many of the Sunnī *ḥadīth* collections have short chapters devoted to Muḥammad's intercession. An account attested twice in Ibn Māja's work proves how highly Muslims had come to esteem Muḥammad's ability to intercede, for it depicts Muḥammad as refusing God's offer to admit half of all Muslims automatically into paradise in favor of instead receiving the ability to intercede (see Ibn Māja, book of *Zuhd*, chapter on *Shafāʿa*, 634 and 636).

24. Muslim, *Ṣaḥīḥ*, book *Īmān*, chapter "*Ithbāt al-Shafāʿa*" to the end of the book *Īmān*.

25. Muslim, *Ṣaḥīḥ*, book *Īmān*, chapter "*Dalīl ʿalā dukhūl ṭawāʾif min al-Muslimīn al-Janna bi-ghayr ḥisāb wa lā ʿadhāb*." Cf. Tirmidhī, *Sunan*, book *Ṣifat al-Qiyāma*, chapter *Lamma Usriya biʾl-nabī*, no. 1; the *Sunan* collection of Dārimī, vol. 2 (n.p.: Dār Iḥyā al-Sunna al-Nabawiyya, n.d., 2 vols. in 1), book *Raqāʾiq*, chapter "*Yadkhulu al-Janna Sabaʿūn Alf*," 328.

26. Nasāʾī's *Sunan* can be found in the lists of the "Six Books," and according to Azamī, some scholars even considered Nasāʾī more knowledgeable in *ḥadīth* than Muslim (Azamī, *Studies in Ḥadīth Methodology and Literature*, 97).

27. Notice that the first *ḥadīth* in Nasāʾī's section on Muḥammad's night journey and ascension is essentially the same as Muslim, *Ṣaḥīḥ*, no. 264. Compare Nasāʾī, *Sunan*, vol. 1 (Liechtenstein: Thesaurus Islamicus Foundation, 2000), book *Ṣalāt*, chapter "Farḍ al-Ṣalāt," no. 1 (no. 452 in the collection), 70; Muslim, *Ṣaḥīḥ*, book *Īmān*, chapter *al-Isrāʾ*, no. 264; Bukhārī, *Ṣaḥīḥ*, book *Badʾ al-Khalq*, chapter *Dhikr al-Malāʾik* (no. 6), no. 1; ibid., book *Manāqib al-Anbiyāʾ*, chapter *al-Miʿrāj* (no. 42), no. 1.

28. Nasāʾī, *Sunan*, vol. 1, book *Ṣalāt*, chapter "Farḍ al-Ṣalāt," no. 3 (no. 454 in the collection), 72.

29. As the "three mosques" *ḥadīth* makes clear, the idea of pilgrimage to these other holy places was a matter of contention among Muslims in the early period. See M. J. Kister, "You shall Only Set Out for Three Mosques," *Le Museón* 82 (1969):173–96.

30. Vuckovic, *Heavenly Journeys, Earthly Concerns*, 34.

31. Notice that the above anecdote forms just one part of a longer report that appears in Nasāʾī's collection under the rubric of "the duty of ritual prayer."

32. Vuckovic, *Heavenly Journeys, Earthly Concerns*, 34.

33. The only way to explain Vuckovic's remark that this prayer stop trope "only appears in the . . . *Sunan* of Nasāʾī" (*Heavenly Journeys, Earthly Concerns*, 33) is to take into account the select number and type of sources she consults in her study (ibid., 5–6).

34. Qummī, *Tafsīr*, vol. 2, 3–4 (cf. idem., 1895 lithograph, 368); compare Thaʿlabī's *Tafsīr*, vol. 6, 58; id., "*Ḥadīth al-masrā*," fol. 32r.

35. For the full account, see Tirmidhī, *Sunan*, book *Tafsīr al-Qurʾān*, chapter *Tafsīr Sūrat Banī Isrāʾīl* (Q 17), no. 19 (no. 3440 in the collection). Its chain of transmission is the following: Ibn Abī ʿUmar—Sufyān—Misʿar—ʿĀṣim b. Abī al-Nujūd—Zirr b. Ḥubaysh—Ḥudhayfa b. al-Yamān. Cf. Ibn ʿArabī Mālikī, *ʿĀriḍat al-aḥwazī bi-sharḥ ṣaḥīḥ al-Tirmidhī*, ed. Hishām Bukhārī (Beirut: Dār Iḥyāʾ al-Turāth al-ʿArabī, 1995), book on *Tafsīr al-Qurʾān*, chapter on *Tafsīr Sūrat Banī Isrāʾīl* (Q 17), no. 17 (no. 3159 in the collection). Compare Ṭabarī, *Tafsīr al-Ṭabarī*, vol. 8, 15 (*tafsīr* Q 17:1).

36. See Tirmidhī, *Sunan*, book *Tafsīr al-Qurʾān*, chapter *Tafsīr Sūrat al-Najm* (Q 53), no. 1. The chain of transmission for this anecdote is Ibn Abī ʿUmar—Sufyān—Mālik b. Mighwal—Ṭalḥa b. Muṣarrif—Murra—ʿAbd Allāh [Ibn Masʿūd]; compare Nasāʾī, *Sunan*, vol. 1, book *Ṣalāt*, chapter "Farḍ al-Ṣalāt," no. 4 (no. 455 in the collection), 72–73, quoted above.

37. See Tirmidhī, *Sunan*, book *Ṣifat al-Qiyāma*, chapter *Lamma Usriya biʾl-nabī*, no. 1; compare the parallel reports in Muslim, *Ṣaḥīḥ*, book *Īmān*, chapter "*Dalīl ʿalā dukhūl ṭawāʾif min al-Muslimīn al-Janna bi-ghayr ḥisāb wa lā ʿadhāb*"; the *Sunan* collection of Dārimī, vol. 2, book *Raqāʾiq*, chapter "*Yadkulu al-Janna Sabaʿūn Alf*," 328. Prior to this *hadith*, each of these traditionists records other types of reports about intercession. Tirmidhī's narrative described above has been partially translated and discussed by Vuckovic, *Heavenly Journeys, Earthly Concerns*, 63, 101–2.

38. Regarding ʿAbd Allāh b. ʿAbd al-Raḥmān Dārimī (d. 255/868), see Ṣiddīqī, *Ḥadīth Literature*, 68–69. The author points out that Dārimī's work "is generally accepted as an important source, and has been regarded by some traditionists as the sixth of the canonical collections" (ibid., 69).

39. In some texts Muḥammad intercedes for seventy individuals who would otherwise be damned, in others, for seventy million, but the concept is still the same. See chapters 8 and 9.

40. Cf. the eschatological reports in Ibn Māja, *Sunan*, book of *Zuhd*, *Sunan Ibn Maja* (Liechtenstein: Thesaurus Islamicus Foundation, 2000), 625–41; Dārimī, *Sunan*, vol. 2, book of *Raqāʾiq*, 329–40; ʿAbd al-Razzāq, *Musannaf*, vol. 11 (Beirut: al-Majlis al-ʿIlmī, 1972), book of *Jāmiʿ*, 289–end.

41. Tirmidhī, *Sunan*, book *Tafsīr al-Qurʾān*, chapter *Tafsīr Sūrat Banī Isrāʾīl* (Q 17), no. 20. Its chain of transmission: Ibn Abī ʿUmar—Sufyān—ʿAli b. Zayd Ibn Jaʿdān—Abū Naḍra—Abū Saʿīd al-Khudrī. The "no boast" phrase similarly appears in

reference to Muḥammad's ability to intercede in Ibn Māja, book of *Zuhd*, chapter on *Shafāʿa*, 634 and 635–36.

42. Tirmidhī, *Sunan*, book *Tafsīr al-Qurʾān*, chapter *Tafsīr Sūrat Banī Isrāʾīl* (Q 17), no. 20; compare the related *ḥadīth* recorded by Ibn Māja, book of *Zuhd*, chapter on *Shafāʿa*, 634–35.

43. Recall that the early source of this *ḥadīth*, Anas, is the same companion who transmitted the majority of extended ascension *ḥadīth* in Bukhārī and Muslim's collections. Ibn Māja's version of this same account, cited in the previous note, contains parallel details and is similarly ascribed to Anas; it could therefore be seen as a potential source for the addition in Tirmidhī's account.

44. Ibid. In Tirmidhī's version, which is presented as a dream (unlike the version in Ibn Māja, mentioned below), the additional chain is given as ʿAlī b. Zayd Ibn Jaʿdān—Anas [Ibn Mālik].

45. Ibn Māja, book of *Zuhd*, chapter on *Shafāʿa*, 635.

46. Tirmidhī, *Sunan*, book *Tafsīr al-Qurʾān*, chapter *Tafsīr Sūrat Ṣad* (Q 38), nos. 3, 4, and 5. The last of these versions is deemed substantially sound (*ḥasan ṣaḥīḥ*), and related through multiple chains of transmission, the primary one being Muḥammad b. Bashshār—Zayd b. Sallām—Abū Sallām—ʿAbd al-Raḥmān b. ʿAʾish Ḥaḍramī—Mālik b. Yukhāmir Saksakī—Muʿādh b. Jabal—Muḥammad. Dārimī also records this "Heavenly Host Debate" *ḥadīth* in his *Sunan*, vol. 2, 126, with the following chain of transmission: Muḥammad b. Mubārak—Abū Walīd—His father—Jābir—Khālid b. Jallāj—Makḥūl—ʿAbd al-Raḥmān b. ʿĀʾish—Muḥammad.

47. The rhyme, based on words ending with the feminine sound plural (*-āt*), appears throughout the exposition of the meaning of the catch-words, and suggests the oral origins of this anecdote. Other versions of this scene sometimes include different catch-words such as *al-ḥasanāt* ("the goodnesses"); see, for example, the Primitive Version (chapter 2 and Appendix A). Later accounts expand the list of rhyming catch-words to three or even four terms, harmonizing the variations, but the main content remains substantially the same. Interestingly, none of these accounts ever explains exactly why the angels would debate the meritorious acts of human devotion, such as the observance of ritual prayer under difficult conditions, feeding the poor, etc.

48. Van Ess, "The Youthful God," passim; id., "Le *Miʿrāǧ* et la Vision de Dieu," in *Le Voyage Initiatique*, ed. Amir-Moezzi, 27–56; id., "Vision and Ascension: Sūrat al-Najm and Its Relationship with Muḥammad's *miʿrāj*," *Journal of Qurʾānic Studies* 1 (1999):47–62.

49. Qummī, *Tafsīr Qummī*, 572–73, commentary on Q 38 (*Ṣad*):67–70.

50. Daniel Gimaret, seeking to discover the Arabic antecedents of the Latin *Liber Scale* traces this "interpolated *ḥadīth*" back as far as Qushayrī (d. 465/1072). See his "Au coeur de *Miʿrāǧ*, un *ḥadīth* interpolé," in *Le Voyage Initiatique*, ed. Amir-Moezzi, 67–82. While I am indebted to Gimaret's work for introducing me to this trope and pointing me to its sources in Tirmidhī's collection, Qummī's use of the *ḥadīth* proves that the link between this trope and ascension narratives must have taken place much earlier than Gimaret supposed.

CHAPTER 6. THE USE AND APPROPRIATION OF THE IBN ᶜABBĀS DISOURSE IN COMMENTARIES

1. See, for instance, Mahmoud Ayoub, *The Qurʾān and Its Interpreters*, vol. 1 (Albany: State University of New York Press, 1984), 3–4. Ṭabarī's pivotal status has been called into question by Walid Saleh, *The Formation of the Classical Tafsir Tradition: The Qurʾān Commentary of al-Thaᶜlabī* (Leiden: E. J. Brill, 2004), 10.

2. The Ṭabarī passage in question here was quoted at the end of chapter 2.

3. Ṭabarī, *Tafsīr*, vol. 8, 4, commentary on Q 17:1. After recounting other divergent reports, Ṭabarī declares the above anecdote to be "on the mark" (*bi-'l-sawāb*, ibid., 6).

4. Ibid., 4–6; compare to Muslim no. 262 (summarized in chapter 5). In this variation on the Anas *ḥadīth*, three angels awake Muḥammad as he sleeps between two companions in the mosque of the Kaᶜba.

5. Ṭabarī, *Tafsīr*, vol. 8, 6.

6. See Ṭabarī, "Muḥammad's Night Journey and Ascension," trans. Rueven Firestone, in *Windows on the House of Islam*, 336–45; Étienne Renaud, "Le Récit du miᶜrāj: une version arabe de l'ascension du Prophète, dans le Tafsīr de Tabarī," in *Apocalypses et Voyages dans l'Au-Delà*, ed. Claude Kappler (Paris: CERF, 1987), 267–90; Asín Palacios, *La escatología musulmana en la Divina Comedia*, q.v. "the unique redaction of cycle 3," 440–43.

7. Ṭabarī, *Tafsīr*, vol. 8, 7: "Abū Hurayra or another, Abū Jaᶜfar [Ṭabarī] expressed his doubt."

8. In the edition of Ṭabarī's *Tafsīr* I am using, the text extends from pages 7–12 of volume 8.

9. In his other major work, *Tārīkh al-umam wa 'l-mulūk*, Ṭabarī similarly places the night journey and ascension near the beginning of Muḥammad's prophetic career. See *The History of al-Ṭabarī*, vol. 6, *Muḥammad at Mecca*, trans. Montgomery Watt and M. V. McDonald (Albany: State University of New York Press, 1988), 78–80.

10. This scene from Abū Hurayra's narrative in Ṭabarī's *Tafsīr*, which does not appear in many other narratives and thus can be used to identify those who cite Abū Hurayra's account, draws its inspiration from Q 50:30, in which God addresses *jahannam* and it asks after more victims. Vuckovic, who discusses this verse in *Heavenly Journeys, Earthly Concerns*, 113, appears unaware of the Abū Hurayra version of the scene, which predates the Ibn Kathīr version by centuries.

11. I would suggest that the "spirits of the prophets" device was employed here to explain how the prophets could have appeared both here and in the various heavens, and explain why Muḥammad did not recognize the prophets when he subsequently encounters them in the heavens.

12. In comparing the Islamic narratives to Dante's *Divina Comedia*, Asín Palacios focuses particular attention on this series of scenes from the Abū Hurayra narrative. Regarding the "moral concerns of the medieval elite," see Vuckovic, *Heavenly Journeys, Earthly Concerns*, chap. 4.

13. Martha Himmelfarb examines such "measure-for-measure" punishments in the tours of hell of late antiquity in her *Tours of Hell: An Apocalyptic Form in Jewish and Christian Literature* (Philadelphia: University of Pennsylvania Press, 1983).

14. See Vuckovic, *Heavenly Journeys, Earthly Concerns*, 119–20. On the Ibn Hishām recension, see chapter 3; on the Abū Sa^c^īd Khudrī ascension narrative, see below.

15. For example, when in a later narrative one finds a scene in which Muḥammad comes upon a piece of wood blocking his path, an object explained allegorically as representing the obstructionists and slanderers within Muḥammad's community, it offers a strong hint that the compiler or editor used the Abū Hurayra *ḥadīth* as one of his or her sources.

16. Ṭabarī, *Tafsīr*, vol. 8, 10 (commentary on Q 17:1). Cf. Ṭabarī, "Muḥammad's Night Journey," in *Windows on the House of Islam*, 342; Renaud, "Le Récit du mi^c^rāj," in Claude Kappler, ed., *Apocalypses et Voyages dans l'Au-delà* (Paris: Éditions du CERF, 1987), 283.

17. Ibid.

18. Maria Subtleny has recently argued that the later famous illustrated Timurid *Book of the Ascension* should be understood as a work intended for Muslims proselytizing among Jews. See her "Islamic Ascent Narrative as Missionary Text: The Timurid *Mi'rajnama*," in *The Prophet Muḥammad's Ascension*, ed. Colby and Gruber.

19. Renaud, "Les Récit du Mi^c^rāj," 270.

20. These seven "couplets" or "rhymed verses" mentioned in Q 15:87 are frequently interpreted as a reference to the seven verses in the opening sūra of the Qur^ɔ^ān, Q 1.

21. On the multivalency of this term, see Walid Saleh, *The Formation of the Classical Tafsir Tradition*, 119–24.

22. Ṭabarī, *Tafsīr*, vol. 8, 11 (commentary on Q 17:1). Cf. Ṭabarī, "Muḥammad's Night Journey," in *Windows on the House of Islam*, 343–45; Renaud, "Le Récit du mi^c^rāj," 285–86.

23. Ṭabarī, *Tafsīr*, vol. 8, 10 (commentary on Q 17:1). Cf. Ṭabarī, "Muḥammad's Night Journey," in *Windows on the House of Islam*, 343; Renaud, "Le Récit du mi^c^rāj," 284.

24. The reference to the drink being pure (*ṭuhūr*), an adjective drawn from the same root as the word for the state of ritual purity (*ṭahāra*), together with the association of this drink with the rewards of paradise, commends this qur^ɔ^ānic reference for use in this anecdote.

25. This trope does not appear independently in the collections of sound Sunnī *ḥadīth*, and my research into hundreds of manuscripts and printed versions of Arabic ascension narratives leads me to the hypothesis that this concept derives from the Abū Hurayra report.

26. See Ṭabarī, *Tafsīr*, vol. 8, 12 (commentary on Q 17:1); cf. Hawwārī, *Tafsīr Kitāb Allāh al-^c^Azīz*, ed. Ḥāj b. Sa^c^īd Sharīfī, vol. 2 (Beirut: Dār al-Gharb al-Islāmī, 1990), 401; Bayhaqī, *Dalā^ɔ^il al-nubuwwa*, vol. 2, 390–91.

27. Ṭabarī, *Tafsīr*, vol. 8, 12 (commentary on Q 17:1).

28. Asín Palacios focuses on these allegorical "tempting figure" encounters for a different purpose, namely to compare them to scenes from Dante's *Divina Comedia* (see Asín Palacios, 440f.).

29. This anecdote does in fact appear in the early version of the Khudrī *ḥadīth* transmitted by Hūd b. Muḥakkam Hawwārī, *Tafsīr*, 404, as well as in the later version transmitted by Bayhaqī, *Dalāʾil*, vol. 2, 394.

30. Since the scene does not appear in Ibn Hishām or Ṭabarī's version of Abū Saʿīd Khudrī's *ḥadīth*, one might hypothesize that the idea was borrowed from the Abū Hurayra *ḥadīth* and collated into select recensions of the Khudrī narrative.

31. Ṭabarī, *Tafsīr*, vol. 8, 14; Hawwārī, *Tafsīr*, 405; Bayhaqī, *Dalāʾil*, vol. 2, 394. Note the parallel between Muḥammad's ritual cleansing in this passage and that associated with the opening of Muḥammad's chest at the beginning of the night journey.

32. Ibid.

33. The same anecdote appears in Ibn Hishām's version of Ibn Isḥāq, *Sīrat rasūl allāh*, vol. 1 / I, 270, which similarly draws upon Khudrī's account.

34. See the discussion of Ibn Isḥāq's narrative in chapter 3 for references on Zayd b. Ḥāritha.

35. See Qummī, *Kitāb tafsīr ʿAlī b. Ibrāhīm* (Tabriz lithograph: n.p., 1895), hereafter "1895 lithograph," 368–76; id., *Tafsīr Qummī*, ed. Ṭayyib Mūsā Jazāʾirī (Najaf: Manshūrāt Maktabat al-Hudā, 1387 / 1967–68), hereafter "*Tafsīr*," vol. 2, 3–14.

36. Qummī's narrative does, however, contain details that derive not from Khudrī's account but rather from that of Abū Hurayra. For instance, Muḥammad hears a rock falling into *Jahannam* (Qummī, *Tafsīr*, vol. 2, 3–4; id., 1895 lithograph, 368–69; cf. Ṭabarī, *Tafsīr*, vol. 8, 8–9).

37. Amir-Moezzi, "L'Imām dans le Ciel," 100, n.6. In the same note, Amir-Moezzi also points out that Majlisī reproduces this same *ḥadīth* nearly verbatim in his text *Biḥār al-anwār* (Tehrān-Qumm: Ḥaydarī, 1956–72), vol. 18, 319–31. The latter narrative has been translated by James Merrick in *The Life and Religion of Muḥammad* (Ḥayāt al-qulūb) (Boston: Phillips, Sampson, 1850), vol. 2, 192–99.

38. Qummī, *Tafsīr*, vol. 2, 4–7 (cf. id., 1895 lithograph, 369–71); compare Ṭabarī, *Tafsīr*, vol. 8, 13; Ibn Hishām, *Sīra*, vol. 1 / I, 268–69; id., *The Life of Muḥammad*, 185–86. The whole section of the Jaʿfar Ṣādiq *ḥadīth* from Qummī's *Tafsīr* dealing with the encounters of the first heaven has been translated in Colby, "Constructing an Islamic Ascension Narrative," 206–10.

39. Qummī, *Tafsīr*, vol. 2, 6–7 (cf. id., 1895 lithograph, 370–71); compare Ibn Ḥibbān, transmitted in Suyūṭī, al-*Lālī*, 62–64; recall that the Half-Fire-Half-Snow angel was mentioned by Muqātil b. Sulaymān (see chapter 2), but the latter did not explicitly connect this angel with Muḥammad's ascension.

40. Qummī, *Tafsīr*, vol. 2, 7–8 (cf. id., 1895 lithograph, 371–72); compare the same angels in the Primitive Version recorded by Ibn Ḥibbān, transmitted in Suyūṭī, al-*Lālī*, 65 (see Appendix A).

41. An extra detail added to Qummī's Jaʿfar narrative, however, is the mention of "angels of humility" (*al-malāʾika al-khushūʿ*) at the end of the description of each heaven.

42. Qummī, *Tafsīr*, vol. 2, 9–10 (cf. id., 1895 lithograph, 373); compare Ibn Ḥibbān, transmitted in Suyūṭī, al-*Lālī*, 66–67.

43. Qummī, *Tafsīr*, vol. 2, 10 (cf. id., 1895 lithograph, 374); compare Ibn Ḥibbān, transmitted in Suyūṭī, al-*Lālī*, 62.

44. Qummī's *Tafsīr* elsewhere preserves an independent account of the Heavenly Host Debate trope, presenting it along with its qurʾānic proof text, Q 38: 67–70 (see Qummī, 1895 lithograph, 572–73). Unlike its version of the Jaᶜfar ascension narrative, Qummī's version preserves a Shīᶜī partisan slant. See my "Constructing an Islamic Ascension Narrative," 213–15.

45. Qummī, *Tafsīr*, vol. 2, 3 (cf. id., 1895 lithograph, 368).

46. Seyyed Hossein Nasr, *Sufi Essays* (London: George Allen & Unwin, 1972), 109–10.

47. The Night Journey Verse, Q 17:1; recall that the other key ascension passage from the Star chapter also makes reference to the "signs" that Muḥammad sees (Q 53:18).

48. For example, the Ibn Hishām recension of the Ibn Isḥāq narrative states that Muḥammad "was shown the signs of what was between the heavens and the earth" (Ibn Hishām, *Sīra*, vol. 1 / I, 263). As in the latter account, the angelic guardian of the first heaven is named Ismāᶜīl, a detail to which Halperin, "Hekhalot and Miᶜrāj," 274–75, unconvincingly attributes Jewish influence.

49. The Primitive Version begins, "When I was caused to journey by night to the heaven, in it I saw the wonders of God's servants and creation" (Ibn Ḥibbān, transmitted in Suyūṭī, al-*Lālī*, 62).

50. Qummī, *Tafsīr*, vol. 2, 3–4 (cf. id., 1895 lithograph, 368); compare Thaᶜlabī's *Tafsīr*, vol. 6, 58; id., "*Ḥadīth al-masrā*," fol. 32r. For the Nasāʾī *ḥadīth*, see chapter 5.

51. Qummī's commentary on the night journey verse concludes with the elaboration of a second ascension-related *ḥadīth* ascribed to Jaᶜfar Ṣādiq, one that is not a complete narrative but that adds supplementary details to the extended narrative that precedes it. This second *ḥadīth* is not crucial for the argument at hand, and it will not be analyzed here, nor will references to the night journey in other sections of Qummī's *Tafsīr*, such as the "unusual" *ḥadīth* about Muḥammad's envy of ᶜAlī during the ascension that is discussed by Meir Bar-Asher in his *Scripture and Exegesis in Early Imāmī Shiism*, 225–32 (based on the exegesis of Q 10:94–95).

52. See Thaᶜlabī's *Tafsīr*, vol. 6, 54–69; cf. id., "*Ḥadīth al-masrā wa'l-miᶜrāj bi-Rasūl Allāh*," MS 2137 Feyzullah, Beyezit Kütüpanesı, Istanbul, fols. 24r–54r.

53. Thaᶜlabī's *Tafsīr*, vol. 6, 55; id., "*Ḥadīth al-masrā*," fol. 24v. I am grateful to Walid Saleh for providing me with copies of the pages from the printed version of the text, as well as pages from manuscripts of the work in his possession different from that of MS 2137 Feyzullah.

54. The multiple chains of transmission that Thaᶜlabī gives at this point appear in a highly abbreviated fashion in the recent printed edition of the *Tafsīr* (pp. 55–56),

which presents only two partial *isnāds* instead of the original seventeen. There is no note to indicate the omission.

55. One of the two chains originating with Abū Hurayra closely resembles the *isnād* attached to the Abū Hurayra ascension *ḥadīth* as reported by Bayhaqī (see below). Of the four Ibn ᶜAbbās chains, two resemble the *isnāds* attached to the Primitive Version.

56. Thaᶜlabī's *Tafsīr*, vol. 6, 57; id., "*Ḥadīth al-masrā*," fol. 29v; compare Ṭabarī, *Tafsīr*, vol. 8, 8. Unlike in the Abū Hurayra *ḥadīth*, Thaᶜlabī's account of the night journey contains the prayer stop trope (*Tafsīr*, vol. 6, 58; id., "*Ḥadīth al-masrā*," fol. 32r) that was discussed in chapter 5 with reference to the *ḥadīth* collection of Nasāʾī. The Jaᶜfar Ṣādiq *ḥadīth* in Qummī's *Tafsīr* similarly incorporates that anecdote, and it will appear again in the reshaped Ibn ᶜAbbās narratives (see chapters 8 and 9).

57. Thaᶜlabī's *Tafsīr*, vol. 6, 57–58; id., "*Ḥadīth al-masrā*," fol. 31r–32r; compare Ṭabarī, *Tafsīr*, vol. 8, 8–9.

58. Thaᶜlabī's *Tafsīr*, vol. 6, 58–59; id., "*Ḥadīth al-masrā*," fol. 32v–34v; compare Ṭabarī, *Tafsīr*, vol. 8, 9.

59. In Thaᶜlabī's famous work on the stories of the prophets (*Qiṣṣāṣ al-anbiyāʾ*) entitled *ᶜArāʾis al-majālis* (Beirut: Maktabat al-Thaqāfa, n.d.), 11, the same name is given for this angel in the midst of Thaᶜlabī's description of the seven heavens. See Colby, "Constructing an Islamic Ascension Narrative," 223–25; Jean-Patrick Guillaume, trans., "Extraits des Récits sur les prophètes de Thaᶜlabī" in *Le Livre de L'Échelle de Mahomet*, ed. Gisele Besson and Michele Brossard-Dandré (Paris: Librarie Générale Française, 1991), 355–72.

60. Thaᶜlabī's *Tafsīr*, vol. 6, 60–61; id., "*Ḥadīth al-masrā*," fol. 36r–39v; compare Ibn Ḥibbān, transmitted in Suyūṭī, al-*Lālī*, 62–65.

61. Thaᶜlabī's *Tafsīr*, vol. 6, 62–63; id., "*Ḥadīth al-masrā*," fol. 41v–42v; compare Ṭabarī, *Tafsīr*, vol. 8, 10.

62. Thaᶜlabī's *Tafsīr*, vol. 6, 63; id., "*Ḥadīth al-masrā*," fol. 43r–44r; compare Ibn Ḥibbān, transmitted in Suyūṭī, al-*Lālī*, 69–70; given the discussion of veils rather than seas and multitudes of angels in this section of the text, Thaᶜlabī shows a less slavish reliance on the Primitive Version at this point but reminds one instead of various later versions of the same discourse ascribed to both Ibn ᶜAbbās and Ibn Isḥāq, such as that by Abū Ḥasan Bakrī (see chapter 8).

63. Thaᶜlabī's *Tafsīr*, vol. 6, 63–64; id., "*Ḥadīth al-masrā*," fol. 44r–44v; compare this trope in Bakrī's text, and see the translation in my "Constructing an Islamic Ascension Narrative," 232.

64. Qushayrī's recension was introduced in chapter 2 and will be discussed in more detail in the following chapter. Significantly the chain of transmission that Qushayrī gives at the start of his recension of the Primitive Version relies on a figure named Abū Ḥudhayfa Isḥāq b. Bishr Qurashī, a scholar also mentioned in one of the chains of transmission given by Thaᶜlabī.

65. Ibn Ḥibbān was a Shāfiᶜī traditionist of Nishapur from a generation or two prior to Thaᶜlabī. Recall that both Thaᶜlabī and Qushayrī were similarly Shāfiᶜīs from

Nishapur, and they presumably were heirs to the same intellectual tradition of which Ibn Ḥībbān was a part. The contention that Thaᶜlabī's version of the ascension narrative draws directly from the same narrative strand as that one recorded in Ibn Ḥibbān's collection can be proven by noticing that Thaᶜlabī's text includes a passage that makes sense only with reference to the latter. After his divine colloquy, Gabriel takes Muḥammad to paradise, and there he explains to Muḥammad the significance of the seas that he had crossed and the angels he had met in the last stages of his journey to the divine throne. What makes this passage problematic in Thaᶜlabī's narrative as it stands is that Thaᶜlabī's ascension *ḥadīth* had never mentioned these upperworldly seas prior to this point. Both the elaborate presentation of these seas prior to the divine colloquy and this later exegetical passage explaining their significance appear in Ibn Ḥibbān's recension of the Primitive Version. Thaᶜlabī likely excerpted this passage from the common source, and he (or a later editor) simply failed to remove those details that were not similarly collated into his composite account. In other words, I propose that Gabriel's explanations to Muḥammad were copied from the Primitive Version into Thaᶜlabī's narrative along with the rest of the intimate colloquy scene, despite the fact that the preceding scenes on which Gabriel's explanations were predicated were not also collated into it. Gabriel's explanations in Thaᶜlabī's ascension narrative make little sense without the missing scenes that Ibn Ḥibbān's recension of the Primitive Version supplies.

66. Abū al-Futūḥ Rāzī, *Tafsīr rūḥ al-jinān waʾl-rawḥ al-janān* [*al-Rawḍ al-jinān*], ed. Abū al-Ḥasan Shaᶜrānī and ᶜAlī Akbar Ghaffārī, vol. 7 (Tehran: Kitabfurūshī Islāmiyya, 1965), 167–87. Portions of Rāzī's section on the night journey and ascension were translated into Italian by A. M. Piemontese, *Oriente Moderno* 60 (1980):225–43; the latter was translated into French by Claude Kappler in id., ed., *Apocalypses et Voyages dans l'Au-Delà* (Paris: Editions of CERF, 1987), 293–320. These earlier translators did not apparently realize the degree to which Rāzī's narrative draws directly on the Arabic account in Thaᶜlabī's *Tafsīr*.

67. See the discussion in "Constructing an Islamic Ascension Narrative," 250–52. Thaᶜlabī's mistake in including Gabriel's interpretation of the meaning of the heavenly seas that were not themselves described (see above, n. 65) is reproduced wholesale in Rāzī's Persian translation of Thaᶜlabī's account.

68. The two chains are the following: Sulaymān Aᶜmash and ᶜAṭāʾ Sāʾib—the Commander of the Faithful [ᶜAlī b. Abī Ṭālib]; someone—ᶜAbd Allāh Ibn Masᶜūd. These fragmentary chains of transmission should be compared to the chains of transmission that precede a different ascension narrative in the *Kitāb al-miᶜrāj* of Qushayrī, ed. ᶜAbd al-Qādir, 43 (Bankipore MS, 15r); cf. Bayhaqī, *Dalāʾil al-nubuwwa*, vol. 2, 404–5.

CHAPTER 7. CONTESTING THE PRIMITIVE VERSION IN NISHAPUR

1. On the historical context in which these scholarly elite of Nishapur lived and worked, see Richard Bulliet, *The Patricians of Nishapur* (Cambridge: Harvard University Press, 1972).

2. Bulliet, *Patricians of Nishapur*, 14.

3. Hodgson, *The Venture of Islam*, vol. 2, 36–39.

4. Bulliet, *Patricians of Nishapur*, 38.

5. Samarrai, *The Theme of Ascension*, 20–27.

6. On the life of Ibn Ḥibbān, see Dhahabī, *Siyar aʿlām al-nubalāʾ*, vol. 10, 166–69; *EI*², s.v. "Ibn Ḥibbān," by J. W. Fück.

7. Ibn Ḥibbān's collection of works are too numerous to be listed here, but lists of his extant works can be found in Kahhāla, *Muʿjam al-muʾallifīn*, vol. 3, 207–8; Brockelmann, *GAL*, vol. 1, 164, and supplement vol. 1, 273; *Ṣaḥīḥ Ibn Ḥibbān*, ed. Shuʿayb Arnaut and Ḥusayn Asad, vol. 1 (Beirut: Muʾassasat al-Risāla, 1984–), 15–18.

8. See Ibn Ḥibbān, *Ṣaḥīḥ Ibn Ḥibbān*, ed. Arnaut and Asad. The work *Mawārid al-zaman ʿalā zawāʾid Ibn Ḥibbān* (Cairo: Maktabat al-Salafiyya, [1961]), ed. Muḥammad ʿAbd al-Razzāq Ḥamza, compiles those reports included in Ibn Ḥībbān's *ṣaḥīḥ* collection that do not appear in the collections of sound reports by Bukhārī and Muslim.

9. The work *Kitāb al-majrūhīn* has been published numerous times in the past few decades; the edition I consulted was edited by Ḥamdī ʿAbd al-Majīd Salafī (Riyādh: Dār al-Sumayʿī, 2000), 2 vols. It appears that the work *Gharāʾib al-akhbār* is no longer extant.

10. Ibn Ḥibbān, *al-Majrūhīn*, vol. 2, 344–45.

11. I have recently translated, annotated, and edited these sayings in Sulamī, *The Subtleties of the Ascension*, Louisville, KY: Fons Vitae, 2006.

12. See my discussion of this trope in Sulamī, *Subtleties of the Ascension*, 16–17.

13. Sulamī, *Subtleties of the Ascension*, 61 (saying no. 15).

14. Sulamī's collection contains a saying that presupposes a knowledge of the cold hand trope that originally was linked to the heavenly host debate trope (see, for example, the discussion of the Tirmidhī versions in chapter 5): "Muḥammad was strengthened by the vision of the heavens and the earths, and the placing of the palm [of his hand]. After these, he was capable of [bearing] each thing received by his secret-heart from the command of his Lord" (Sulamī, *Subtleties of the Ascension*, 73, saying no. 20).

15. Sulamī, *Subtleties of the Ascension*, 132 (saying 49).

16. Qushayrī, *Kitāb al-miʿrāj*, ed. ʿAlī Ḥusayn ʿAbd al-Qādir (Cairo: Dār al-Kutub al-Ḥadītha, 1964); id., "[*Kitāb al-miʿrāj*]," MS 990, Bankipore, dated 880/1475. The printed edition contains numerous mistakes and small but significant omissions and should thus be used in consultation with the original manuscript. Samarrai devotes chap. 7 of his work *The Theme of Ascension in Mystical Writings* to Qushayrī's *Kitāb al-miʿrāj*.

17. Roughly half of the sayings that Sulamī records appear in a subsection of Qushayrī's work entitled "What the Sufi Shaykhs Say about [the Subtleties of the Ascension]"; see Qushayrī, *Kitāb al-miʿrāj*, ed. ʿAbd al-Qādir, 100–16; id., "[*Kitāb al-miʿrāj*]," MS 990, Bankipore, fol. 50v–61r. At the very end of the section, Qushayrī appends a single *ḥadīth* transmitted on the authority of Sulamī.

18. Qushayrī, *Kitāb al-miʿrāj*, ed. ʿAbd al-Qādir, 75–76; id., "[*Kitāb al-miʿrāj*]," MS 990, Bankipore, fol. 37v–38r. The only specific case the work mentions is the dream

vision ascribed to Abū Yazīd Bisṭāmī (for an example of which, see Sells, *Early Islamic Mysticism*, 242–50).

19. Qushayrī, *Kitāb al-miᶜrāj*, ed. ᶜAbd al-Qādir, 85–92; id., "[*Kitāb al-miᶜrāj*]," MS 990, Bankipore, fol. 42v–46b. The other prophets are Idrīs/Enoch, Abraham, Elijah, Moses, and Jesus.

20. Qushayrī, *Kitāb al-miᶜrāj*, ed. ᶜAbd al-Qādir, 27–64; id., "[*Kitāb al-miᶜrāj*]," MS 990, Bankipore, fol. 4r–31r. As mentioned in chapter 5, Anas b. Mālik receives the honor of having the majority of extended sound Sunnī ascension *ḥadīth* reports ascribed to him.

21. Samarrai states, "Al-Qushayrī collected Traditions of the *Miᶜrāj* from the different books of Tradition, in particular the *Musnad* of Abū ᶜAwāna. These Traditions were transmitted to him by Abū ᶜAwāna's great-nephew, Abū Nuᶜaym ᶜAbd al-Malik b. al-Ḥasan al-Isfarāʾinī (d. 400/1010)" (Samarrai, *The Theme of Ascension*, 246).

22. Saleh, *Formation of the Classical Tafsīr Tradition*, 27.

23. The Muᶜtazilī position might well be associated with the majority of the Hanafīs of Nishapur, who in this period were locked in a bitter political rivalry with the majority of the Shāfiᶜīs of Nishapur, most of whom associated with Ashᶜarī theology over and against Muᶜtazilī theology. On this rivalry and its political implications, see Bulliet, *Patricians of Nishapur*, 36f. Against Samarrai's interpretation of Qushayrī composing the work to counter his Karrāmī opponents (Samarrai, *The Theme of Ascension*, 260–61), the text offers no explicit evidence to suggest that Qushayrī addressed his critiques to the Karrāmīs rather than the Shīᶜīs, Hanafīs, or Muᶜtazilīs.

24. Qushayrī, *Kitāb al-miᶜrāj*, ed. ᶜAbd al-Qādir, 26; id., "[*Kitāb al-miᶜrāj*]," MS 990, Bankipore, fol. 3v.

25. For example, contrast Qushayrī, *Kitāb al-miᶜrāj*, ed. ᶜAbd al-Qādir, 83; id., "[*Kitāb al-miᶜrāj*]," MS 990, Bankipore, fol. 42r, in which Abū Bakr's name is added to the testimony of witness, a modification of parallel Shīᶜī reports ascribed to ᶜAlī, discussed in chapter 4. Qushayrī discusses Abū Bakr's unique qualities in ibid., 72–73; id., "[*Kitāb al-miᶜrāj*]," MS 990, Bankipore, fol. 36r.

26. Shiblī recounted that [Muḥammad] said, "I was passing several paths, when a voice called out, 'O Abū Bakr!' so I turned toward it, and I did not see anyone. A speaker spoke, saying, 'One who turns this way or that, he is not one of us'" (Qushayrī, *Kitāb al-miᶜrāj*, ed. ᶜAbd al-Qādir, 103; id., "[*Kitāb al-miᶜrāj*]," MS 990, Bankipore, fol. 52r). This scene obviously plays upon the tempting figures trope (q.v.), here adding an antisectarian spin to it.

27. The chain of transmission for these anecdotes is the same as the Zaydī line of the first Imāms, as follows: Zayd b. ᶜAlī [Zayn al-ᶜAbdidīn] b. al-Ḥusayn—his father [ᶜAlī Zayn al-ᶜAbdidīn]—his grandfather [al-Ḥusayn]—ᶜAlī b. Abī Ṭālib. See Qushayrī, *Kitāb al-miᶜrāj*, ed. ᶜAbd al-Qādir, 39–42; id., "[*Kitāb al-miᶜrāj*]," MS 990, Bankipore, fol. 11v–15r.

28. At the conclusion of the Sunnī section, Qushayrī quotes his teacher, Abū ᶜAlī Daqqāq, as saying, "These are the reports (*akhbār*) mentioned in the sound collections (*ṣiḥāḥ*)" (Qushayrī, *Kitāb al-miᶜrāj*, ed. ᶜAbd al-Qādir, 38; id., "[*Kitāb al-miᶜrāj*]," MS

990, Bankipore, fol. 11v). The latter phrase implies that Qushayrī organizes the *ḥadīth* he transmits on a spectrum from most reliable to most questionable, thereby casting some doubt on the Shīʿī and unofficial Sunnī narratives that follow this statement. See Qushayrī, *Kitāb al-miʿrāj*, ed. ʿAbd al-Qādir, 38; id., "[*Kitāb al-miʿrāj*]," MS 990, Bankipore, fol. 11v. Qassim Samarrai, in his work *The Theme of the Ascension in Mystical Writings* (Baghdad: National Printing Company, 1968), 260–63, suspects that some of the reports in this "Shīʿī section" of Qushayrī's *Kitāb al-miʿrāj*, and specifically what I am calling the Extended Cosmological *ḥadīth*, reflect later interpolations into Qushayrī's text. This point of view has some merit, and I will discuss it further below.

29. Qushayrī, *Kitāb al-miʿrāj*, ed. ʿAbd al-Qādir, 38–39; id., "[*Kitāb al-miʿrāj*]," MS 990, Bankipore, fol. 11v–12r. This detail appears in the early Shīʿī ascension reports such as the one collated into the Jaʿfar Ṣādiq *ḥadīth* that ʿAlī Qummī records in his commentary on Q 17:1 (*Tafsīr*, vol. 2, 11–12 ; cf. id., 1895 lithograph, 375). Although Qushayrī cites this anecdote as if he considers it relatively trustworthy, he does offer the caveat that even if the narrative is authentic, it still must be interpreted, for he insists that Muḥammad going behind a veil does not necessitate that God is confined to that single place. He furthermore insists that an angelic intermediary rather than God responds to the lines in the call to prayer. See Qushayrī, *Kitāb al-miʿrāj*, ed. ʿAbd al-Qādir, 39; id., "[*Kitāb al-miʿrāj*]," MS 990, Bankipore, fols. 12r–12v.

30. Qushayrī, *Kitāb al-miʿrāj*, ed. ʿAbd al-Qādir, 39–42; id., "[*Kitāb al-miʿrāj*]," MS 990, Bankipore, fol. 12v–15r.

31. The "People of the House" in Shīʿī parlance is a reference to the family of the Prophet and his descendants, those favored and supported by the Shīʿīs as the rightful leaders of the community. The reference to the touch of the angels seems to be a relatively transparent reinterpretation of the cold hand trope, avoiding ascribing anthropomorphic qualities to the divinity by assigning to angels instead of to God the role of calming Muḥammad through touch. In an anecdote reported by Furāt Kūfī, *Tafsīr Furā al-Kūfī*, vol. 1, 211 (*tafsīr* of Q 13:29), Gabriel is the one who places his hands upon Muḥammad to calm him in this way. Later in his book, Qushayrī analyzes the cold hand by maintaining that it must be understood metaphorically (Qushayrī, *Kitāb al-miʿrāj*, ed. ʿAbd al-Qādir, 95–96; id., "[*Kitāb al-miʿrāj*]," MS 990, Bankipore, fol. 48v).

32. One might be tempted to speculate that they were inserted into the work by a later transmitter. Although that is the position taken by Samarrai regarding the Primitive Version and Extended Cosmological *ḥadīth* (see the following section) in his work *The Theme of Ascension*, 258–61, Samarrai appears to accept that Qushayrī himself included these anecdotes, while registering his doubt at their authenticity (ibid., 246–47). Without another copy of Qushayrī's text to verify the theory of interpolation, such a position would be difficult to prove definitively.

33. See above, recalling that Bayhaqī reports an instance of the transmission of this narrative but refrains from transmitting the narrative himself. In Qushayrī's text, the Extended Cosmological *ḥadīth* spans pages 43–56 in the printed version, folios 15r–25v in the manuscript.

34. Qushayrī, *Kitāb al-mi^crāj*, ed. ^cAbd al-Qādir, 43; id., "[*Kitāb al-mi^crāj*]," MS 990, Bankipore, fol. 15r. Compare the more complete chains of transmission cited in Bayhaqī, *Dalā^ʾil*, vol. 2, 404–5. Because of the multiple correspondences between this Extended Cosmological *ḥadīth* and the Ibn Hishām recension of the Ibn Isḥāq ascension narrative, and because of the presence of Ibn Isḥāq in the list of transmitters in the Cosmological *ḥadīth*, it becomes tempting to postulate that the latter narrative represents little more than an expanded version of Ibn Isḥāq's account. In my previous work, in fact, I referred to the Extended Cosmological *ḥadīth* as the "Revised Ibn Isḥāq" narrative. The fact that some later ascension works in Bakrī's reshaped tradition (see chapter 9) similarly trace their narratives back to Ibn Isḥāq sometimes in lieu of Ibn ^cAbbās raises the question of whether these reworked "Ibn Isḥāq" ascension narratives form a related but distinct genre. At this point I am convinced that these later "Ibn Isḥāq" texts deserved to be considered together with the other reshaped Ibn ^cAbbās ascension texts as part of a single genre.

35. Unlike the standard trope of the five-hundred-year journey, this narrative substitutes the number four hundred for five hundred. Since it also places four hundred thousand angels on either side of the ladder (Qushayrī, *Kitāb al-mi^crāj*, ed. ^cAbd al-Qādir, 45; id., "[*Kitāb al-mi^crāj*]," MS 990, Bankipore, fol. 16v–17r), the number four hundred seems to have some symbolic significance to the author of this account.

36. Qushayrī, *Kitāb al-mi^crāj*, ed. ^cAbd al-Qādir, 45–46; id., "[*Kitāb al-mi^crāj*]," MS 990, Bankipore, fol. 17r.

37. The name of the first gatekeeper is the same here as in the Abū Sa^cīd Khudrī version of the ascension narrative as transmitted in the Ibn Isḥāq and ^cAlī Qummī accounts. Ismā^cīl also appears in the Bakrī recensions of the ascension narrative, discussed in chapter 8.

38. See the chart listing these and other details from Ibn ^cAbbās texts in chapter 9.

39. Qushayrī, *Kitāb al-mi^crāj*, ed. ^cAbd al-Qādir, 46–48; id., "[*Kitāb al-mi^crāj*]," MS 990, Bankipore, fol. 17r–18v.

40. Qushayrī, *Kitāb al-mi^crāj*, ed. ^cAbd al-Qādir, 48–49; id., "[*Kitāb al-mi^crāj*]," MS 990, Bankipore, fol. 19r–19v. Mention of Fāṭima here offers further evidence to suggest the ^cAlīd loyalty of this *ḥadīth*'s transmitter.

41. Qushayrī, *Kitāb al-mi^crāj*, ed. ^cAbd al-Qādir, 49–51; id., "[*Kitāb al-mi^crāj*]," MS 990, Bankipore, fol. 20r–21v. In the Bakrī recensions, the angel Isrāfīl assumes the role granted here to the angel *Rūḥ*. The name *Rūḥ* is assigned to different angels in other ascension narratives. For instance, it is the name of one of the leaders of the archangels in the Primitive Version of the Ibn ^cAbbās narrative (see Ibn Ḥibbān in Suyūṭī, al-*Lālī*, 72); on the other hand, Muqātil considers it the name of the Half-Fire-Half-Snow angel in *Tafsīr Muqātil*, vol. 4, 565–66 (*tafsīr* of Q 78:38).

42. Qushayrī, *Kitāb al-mi^crāj*, ed. ^cAbd al-Qādir, 53–54; id., "[*Kitāb al-mi^crāj*]," MS 990, Bankipore, fol. 23r–23v.

43. Qushayrī, *Kitāb al-mi^crāj*, ed. ^cAbd al-Qādir, 54; id., "[*Kitāb al-mi^crāj*]," MS 990, Bankipore, fol. 23v. Samarrai, The *Theme of Ascension*, 248, cites ^cAbd al-Ghanī

as quoted in Suyūṭī, al-*Lālī*, vol. 1, 83–85, insisting that this report is a forgery. Halperin, "Hekhalot and *Mi*ʿ*rāj,*" traces the anecdote to rabbinic legends.

44. Qushayrī, *Kitāb al-mi*ʿ*rāj*, ed. ʿAbd al-Qādir, 54; id., "[*Kitāb al-mi*ʿ*rāj*]," MS 990, Bankipore, fol. 23v.

45. Qushayrī, *Kitāb al-mi*ʿ*rāj*, ed. ʿAbd al-Qādir, 54–55; id., "[*Kitāb al-mi*ʿ*rāj*]," MS 990, Bankipore, fol. 24r–24v. Compare the version transmitted by Ibn Hishām; see chapter 3.

46. Qushayrī, *Kitāb al-mi*ʿ*rāj*, ed. ʿAbd al-Qādir, 46; id., "[*Kitāb al-mi*ʿ*rāj*]," MS 990, Bankipore, fol. 17r.

47. Qushayrī, *Kitāb al-mi*ʿ*rāj*, ed. ʿAbd al-Qādir, 56; id., "[*Kitāb al-mi*ʿ*rāj*]," MS 990, Bankipore, fol. 25v.

48. See Bayhaqī, Abū Bakr Aḥmad b. Ḥusayn. *Dalāʾil al-nubuwwa wa ma*ʿ*rifat aḥwāl ṣāḥib al-sharī*ʿ*a*, ed. ʿAbd al-Muʿṭī Qalʿajī, vol. 2 (Beirut: Dār al-Kutub al-ʿIlmiyya, 1985), 354–65 (night journey) and 366–405 (ascension). In his two chapters devoted to Muḥammad's night journey and ascension, Bayhaqī privileges the official Sunnī ascension reports, as one would expect.

49. Bayhaqī, *Dalāʾil al-nubuwwa*, vol. 2, 404–5.

50. Samarrai, The *Theme of Ascension*, 247, 252. Between pages 247–60, Samarrai advances arguments to support his contention that this Extended Cosmological *ḥadīth* has no basis in authentic *ḥadīth* reports and that Qushayrī could thus not have included it in his original work.

51. Samarrai, The *Theme of Ascension*, 251.

52. Ibid., 247–49 and 260–61.

53. Ibid., 260, 262.

54. Bayhaqī, *Dalāʾil al-nubuwwa*, vol. 2, 404–5.

55. Qushayrī, *Kitāb al-mi*ʿ*rāj*, ed. ʿAbd al-Qādir, 56–57; id., "[*Kitāb al-mi*ʿ*rāj*]," MS 990, Bankipore, fol. 25v.

56. See my "Constructing an Islamic Ascension Narrative," 173–74.

57. Bayhaqī, *Dalāʾil al-nubuwwa*, vol. 2, 390–96 (Abū Saʿīd Khudrī *ḥadīth* as transmitted by Abū Hārūn ʿAbdī) and 396–403 (Abū Hurayra). Bayhaqī appears to associate the title *Ithbāt al-masrā wa'l-mi*ʿ*rāj* with the former narrative, ibid., vol. 2, 405.

58. Bayhaqī, *Dalāʾil al-nubuwwa*, vol. 2, 405. Ibn Kathīr, *Tafsīr al-Qurʾān al-*ʿ*Aẓīm*, vol. 5, 26, also reports this dream vision, quoting it from Bayhaqī.

59. Unlike Bayhaqī, Ibn Ḥibbān does quote the work at length. His position toward the narrative remains unambiguous, however, since the work in which he cites the Primitive Version is dedicated to reporting forged (*maṣnū*ʿ) reports.

CHAPTER 8. BAKRI'S TOTAL AND COMPLETE IBN ʿABBĀS DISCLOSURE

1. Resolving the debate on the historicity of Abū al-Ḥasan Bakrī awaits the detailed study of scholars able to scrutinize the disparate unpublished works attributed to

him in various manuscript collections around the world (Rosenthal, "al-Bakrī," EI^2). Boaz Shoshan has recently renewed the assertion, first proposed a century earlier, that a person we might call the "historical Bakrī," who seems to have authored an early version of a biography of Muḥammad known as *al-Anwār*, flourished in the middle of the third/ninth century. This hypothesis is based on the notion that the historical Bakrī likely composed his works prior to the death of one Abū Rifāʿa ʿUmāra b. Wathīma Fārisī in 289/902 (Shoshan, *Popular Culture in Medieval Cairo*, 35–36), whose work contains selections apparently indebted to the former. Others such as Brockelmann (*GAL Suppl.*, vol. 1, 616) and Rosenthal (EI^2) have placed Bakrī's life in the seventh/thirteenth century, based on a work attributed to this Bakrī in the Vatican archives (Vatican MS Borg 125) dated 694/1295. Since it is beyond the scope of this chapter to resolve this debate, it will accept Shoshan's reasoning that "if indeed a man named Abū 'l-Ḥasan al-Bakrī ever ('ever' meaning early Islamic time) existed and was the author or transmitter of a [*Life of the Prophet Muḥammad*], his name was deliberatly cited . . . as the source of much later, popular stories" (Shoshan, *Popular Culture in Medieval Cairo*, 36). Taking that position as a starting point, and based on the evidence Shoshan discusses, this study will proceed with the hypothesis that an early and historical "Bakrī" did exist and that in later centuries more expansive works were attributed to him.

2. The choice of Ibn Isḥāq here is not coincidental, for a series of Ibn ʿAbbās ascension narratives, especially those somehow related to Bakrī, invoke Ibn Isḥāq's name as well. It is as if Bakrī's contribution was to take Ibn Isḥāq's text as the general basis for a fantastic novella.

3. While I contend that it is crucial to avoid simplistic models of "influence," as if Islamic ascension works contain little but the recycled materials of some other apocalyptic tradition (the attitude of Culianu, *Out of This World*, for instance, or even of Halperin, "Hekhalot and Miʿrāj"), more detailed studies of the connections between specific tropes across religious and cultural traditions such as initiated by Halperin will certainly enrich our understanding of these tropes.

4. Until recently, Western scholars have only been aware of a single recension of this text, namely Paris Bibliothèque Nationale MS Arabe 1931 (hereafter Ara.1931), fols. 70r–91r (see Brockelmann, *GAL* S1, 2d ed., 616), undated. My research has uncovered four other copies of texts explicitly invoking Bakrī's name, one of which is directly related to Ara.1931 and will be considered a part of the same recension: Cairo Dār al-Kutub MS Tārīkh Taymūr 738/8 (hereafter T.T.738/8), fols. 292v–313r, undated. The other three recensions are the following: Istanbul Süleymaniye Kütüphanesi MS Amcazade Hüsayın Paša 95/2 (hereafter Amc.95/2), fols. 26v–82v, undated, but likely from the end of the seventh/thirteenth century; Istanbul Süleymaniye Kütüphanesi MS Ayasofya 867 (hereafter Aya.867), fols. 170r–78v, dated 886/1481; Damascus Maktabat al-Asad al-Waṭaniyya MS 6093 (hereafter Asad6093), fols. 1v–31v, dated ca. 1156/1743.

5. The single recension that includes two manuscripts, Ara.1931 and T.T.738/8, both carry vague titles: The former bears the label "*Qiṣṣat al-miʿrāj*," while the latter appears to refer to itself by the title "*Miʿrāj al-nabī*."

6. Ibn Isḥāq is given as a source in Asad 6093, fol. 1v, and presented as a direct source for Bakrī in Amc.95/2, fols. 27r–27v.

7. Shoshan, *Popular Culture in Medieval Cairo*, 32, argues that the "detailed and unique descriptions" along with the "obvious mythological treatment" of Muḥammad's biography serve as indicators of the "popular" nature of Bakrī's biography of the Prophet, entitled *al-Anwār*.

8. The date of Amc.95/2 remains uncertain, but given that the text appears to be written in the same hand as the text that precedes it in the manuscript, and given that the latter dates from 679/1280 (see the discussion below), this recension of Bakrī's "Total and Complete" report of the ascension also likely was copied in the last quarter of the seventh/thirteenth century. It therefore may be considered the earliest version extant.

9. Amc.95/2, 27v–28r. See the translation of a major portion of Amc.95/2 in Appendix B, and compare it to another recension of Bakrī's work (Aya.867) translated in Appendix 2 of my "Constructing an Islamic Ascension Narrative," 442–62. In the discussion that follows here, I will treat Amc.95/2 as the "base text" for Bakrī's ascension work, unless otherwise noted.

10. Amc.95/2, fol. 28r.

11. Amc.95/2, fol. 60v.

12. Amc.95/2, 28r–28v.

13. Aya.867, 170r, translated in "Constructing an Islamic Ascension Narrative," 442–43; T.T.738/8, fol. 293v; Ara.1931, 71v; cf. Asad6091, 2r, which mentions an unspecified *burda*.

14. Amc.95/2, fol. 28v, where the scene spans less than two lines, and nothing is mentioned about what Gabriel extracts from or inserts into Muḥammad's chest.

15. Ṭabarsī, *Majmaʿa al-bayān*, 395; I discuss this passage and Ṭabarsī's analysis of the night journey and ascension more generally in "Constructing an Islamic Ascension Narrative," 254f.

16. See Appendix B for one example of a rich description of Burāq. Other recensions agree with the version in Amc.95/2 in general tenor, if not always in exact detail.

17. Amc.95/2, fol. 29v; Asad6093, fol. 3v; T.T.738/8, fol. 294v; Ara.1931, fol. 72v.

18. Amc.95/2, fol. 29v; Asad6093, fol. 3v; the latter trope appears in the ascension narrative presented in Thaʿlabī's *Tafsīr*, vol. 6, 56; id., "*Ḥadīth al-masrā*," 28r–28v; see chapter 6.

19. The only exception appears in Asad6093, fol. 3r, where the description of Burāq is cut short in favor of presenting two different narratives explaining why Burāq shied. The depiction of Burāq with a human face and human soul also appears in Qushayrī's "Extended Cosmological" *ḥadīth* in his *Kitāb al-miʿrāj*, ed. ʿAbd al-Qādir, 44 (Bankipore MS., fol. 15v); see chapter 7.

20. Amc.95/2, fol. 29v–30r; Asad6093, fols. 3r–3v; T.T.738/8, fols. 293v–295r; Ara.1931, fols. 71v–72v; Aya.867, fols. 170r–170v.

21. As we shall see, the Persian *Mi^c^rājnama* found in Istanbul Süleymaniye Kütüphanesi MS Ayasofya 3441 (hereafter Aya.3441), the text of which Christiane Gruber has recently translated, takes this same impulse to its logical extreme, with each of the angels, from the lowest to the most exalted, begging Muḥammad to include them within his intercession. See Gruber's forthcoming book *The Ilkhanid Book of Ascension.*

22. Amc.95/2, fol. 30r. The matter on which the belief or unbelief rests might well be the question of the veracity of Muḥammad's account of his night journey and ascension. The Bakrī narratives, as other Islamic ascension narratives, graphically depict this test of faith through the contrast between the support of Abū Bakr on the one hand and the opposition of Abū Jahl on the other. Some versions, such as Aya.3441, reduce the matter to a simple statement similar to the passage quoted above: "Every person who denies the Prophet's ascension is an unbeliever" (Aya.3441, 1v–2r, translated by Gruber, quoted in her study "The Prophet Muḥammad's Ascension (Mi^c^rāj) in Islamic Art and Literature, ca. 1300–1600," 124).

23. Amc.95/2, fol. 29v.

24. See the discussion of the first heavens as depicted in Amc.95/2, and compare the similarly partisan statements in the conclusion to Aya.3441, "Praise be to God who made us part of *ahl al-sunnat wa jamā^c^at* by means of the *mi^c^rāj*" (Aya.3441, 60v, translated by Gruber in "The Prophet Muḥammad's Ascension *(Mi^c^rāj)* in Islamic Art and Literature, ca. 1300–1600," 129.

25. On the latter, see Gruber, "The Prophet Muḥammad's Ascension," 127–28.

26. For Khudrī's version of the scene, for example, see Ṭabarī, *Tafsīr*, vol. 8, 12.

27. Amc.95/2, fols. 31v–32r; T.T.738/8, fol. 295v; Ara.1931, fol. 73v; cf. Aya.3441, 12r.

28. See the discussion of the choice of cups trope, below, and more generally the fact that Muḥammad fears for his life repeatedly during the ascension, requiring the angels or the "voice from above" to reassure and comfort him, reminding him that he has nothing to fear.

29. See above, chapter 5; the same *ḥadīth* is cited in Ibn Diḥya, *al-Ibtihāj*, 112–13.

30. Qummī, *Tafsīr*, vol. 2, 3–4 (cf. id., 1895 lithograph, 368); Tha^c^labī, *Tafsīr*, vol. 6, 58 (*tafsīr* to Q 17:1; cf. id., "*Ḥadīth al-masrā*," fol. 32r); for both, and for a discussion of the Abū Hurayra account in Ṭabarī's commentary that also includes this anecdote, see chapter 6.

31. Amc.95/2, fol. 30v; Asad6093, fol. 4r; Aya.3441, fol. 14r; in T.T.738/8 and Ara.1931; Muḥammad is called to descend and pray at both Sinai and Bethlehem, although the third site mentioned in Nisā^ɔ^ī's *ḥadīth*, Medina, does not appear.

32. Amc.95/2, fol. 31r. In this version, the immense "crashing" (*hadda*) Muḥammad hears comes from the sound of the rock that God threw into *al-Hāwiyya* seventy thousand years ago. It will not hit the bottom until judgment day, offering a hyperbolic description of the immense depth of this pit of Hell (see ibid., fol. 32r). Cf. Asad6093, fols. 4v–5r, in which the rock has been falling for only seventy years; T.T.738/8, fol. 296r, and Ara.1931, fols. 73v–74r, in both of which it reports that God threw the rock down

"upon the people of the hellfire" three hundred seventy thousand years ago, and it had not yet reached bottom until now; Aya.3441, fol. 14r, in which the rock was dropped on the day that hellfire was created and it finally reached the bottom on the night of Muḥammad's journey.

33. Amc.95/2, fol. 32r, where the youth is said to represent belief (*īmān*) personified, which both Muḥammad and his community will embrace; Asad6093, fol. 5v, where the good-smelling youth calls out to Muḥammad in a manner directly parallel to the tempting figures, and where Gabriel interprets him as representing "God's religion, Islam," which Muḥammad and his community will follow until judgment day, when they will be resurrected in such a beautiful form and will be granted entrance to paradise; Aya.867, fol. 170v, where the youth represents "God's religion."

34. It is tempting to see in this handsome "belief personified" youth a type of Muslim version of the ancient Zoroastrian notion of the *daena*, the embodiment of one's deeds whom a person meets after death, handsome or ugly depending on the goodness of one's actions in life. The version of the trope in Asad6093, fol. 5v, particularly lends itself to such an interpretation.

35. Amc.95/2, fols. 32r–32v.

36. Amc.95/2, fol. 32v; cf. Aya.867, fols. 170v–171r; T.T.738/8, fol. 296v; Ara.1931, fol. 74r.

37. See Ibn Hishām, *Sīra*, vol. 1/I, 263; compare Qummī, *Tafsīr*, vol. 2, 4.

38. Shoshan, *Popular Culture in Medieval Cairo*, 33.

39. Amc.95/2, fol. 33r; cf. Asad.6093, fol. 5v; Aya.867, fol. 171r.

40. Amc.95/2, fols. 33v–39v; cf. Ibn Ḥibbān, 62–65. The famous Andalusian translation known as *Liber Scale* similarly depicts these angels between the earth and the first heaven (chapters 6–11; see Hyatte, 110–15), and merits close comparison with Amc.95/2.

41. Asad6093, fols. 7v–10r, in which the encounter with Mālik, the Guardian of Hellfire, is deferred until the elaborate "tour of hellfire" section at the end of the text (fols. 22r–25v)

42. For example, in Aya.867, fols. 171v–172r, the Angel of Death appears in the fourth heaven, the Guardian of Hellfire in the fifth heaven, the Half-Fire-Half-Snow angel in the sixth heaven, and the Rooster angel in the highest realms just before the divine throne; cf. T.T.738/8, fols. 298r–301v; Ara.1931, fols. 75v–79r; Aya.3441, fols. 25r–27v.

43. Amc.95/2, fols. 42r–42v; Asad6093, fols. 10r–10v; Aya.867, fols. 171r–171v; T.T.738/8, fol. 297v; Ara.1931, fol. 75v.

44. In most, these archangels both appear at the climax of Muḥammad's ascent as he nears the divine throne. One exception appears in Amc.95/2, fols. 45r–46v, where Mikāʾīl appears in the fifth heaven instead of in the high realms, other details from the highest realms being collated into the description of Muḥammad's vision in the fifth heaven.

45. Amc.95/2, fols. 56v–58r (missing the account of Mikāʾīl, described in previous note); Asad6093, fols. 14v–15r (missing the account of Mikāʾīl); Aya.867,

fols. 174v–175r; T.T.738/8, fols. 303r and 305r–6r (Mikāʾīl-Isrāfīl unit appearing twice in two separate versions); Ara.1931, fols. 81r–81v and 83r–84r (Mikāʾīl-Isrāfīl unit appearing twice in two separate versions); Aya.3441, fols. 47r–48r; Gaya.241, fols. 4r–6v.

46. Amc.95/2, fol. 60v; T.T.738/8, fols. 306v–307r; Ara.1931, fol. 85r; Aya.3441, fol. 51v, with explanations of its function on fol. 53v.

47. Muḥammad finds himself inspired to say, "Salutations (*taḥiyyāt*) to God. . . ." God greets Muḥammad, "Peace be upon you (*salām ʿalayka*)," to which Muḥammad responds, "Peace be upon us, and upon God's righteous worshippers." See Amc.95/2, fol. 61r; Asad6093, fol. 16r; Aya.867, fol. 175v; T.T.738/8, fol. 307r; Ara.1931, fol. 85r; Aya.3441, fol. 51v.

48. Amc.95/2, fol. 61r–61v.

49. Amc.95/2, fols. 61v, 62r–62v; Asad6093, fols. 16r–16v; cf. Gaya.241, fol. 8r.

50. This idea is indebted to Gruber's argument that Aya.3441 and other middle-period ascension works were used as devotional "prayer manuals" to instruct recent converts on the conventions of Muslim worship (see Gruber, "The Prophet Muḥammad's Ascension," chapter 3).

51. Amc.95/2, fol. 64v; Asad6093, fol. 18v; Aya.867, fol. 176r; T.T.738/8, fol. 308r; Ara.1931, fol. 86r. Only the version in Aya.867 offers an alternate rationale for the need of the use of the sword, proclaiming its eschatological function: "The world will only pass away with the sword" (cf. the sword of the Mahdi mentioned in the Shīʿī version; an echo of the sword wielded by the Messiah in the Christian New Testament book of Revelation/Apocalypse of John?).

52. Asad6093, fol. 19r; Aya.867, fol. 176r.

53. Amc.95/2, fols. 64r–64v (Q 1 only), 67v (both Q 1, in the form of 7 *mathānī*ʾ, and entire Q); Asad6093, fol. 19v (both); Aya.867, fol. 167v (both); Aya.867, fol. 176v (both); T.T.738/8, fol. 308v (both); Ara.1931, fol. 86v (both). This passage can be read, but need not be, as indicating that Muḥammad had already received the entire Qurʾān by the time of his heavenly ascension.

54. Amc.95/2, fol. 63r; Asad 6093, fol. 19v. These references invoke the concept of the so-called Muḥammadan Light, on which see Uri Rubin, "Pre-existence and Light."

55. Amc.95/2, fol. 68r.

56. Aya.867, fol. 176v, translated in "Constructing an Islamic Ascension Narrative," 459.

57. T.T.738/8, fol. 309r; Ara.1931, fol. 87r.

58. E.g., the work of ʿAbd al-Raḥmān Bisṭāmī (d. 858/1454) entitled "*al-Kawkab al-wahhāj*," Cairo Dār al-Kutub MS B 20919 (hereafter B.20919), 15r, translated in "Constructing an Islamic Ascension Narrative," 324–25. See also, for example, the recension copied by one Zayn al-Dīn b. Ḥasan b. Zayn al-Dīn in the year 1003/1594, Cairo Dār al-Kutub MS Majāmiʿ 829 (hereafter Maja.829), fol. 176v, discussed in "Constructing an Islamic Ascension Narrative," 337f.; God positively replies to Muḥammad's expression "increase it for me" a dozen times in the text ["*Miʿrāj al-nabī*"] ascribed to

Abu Dharr and copied in 1000/1592, Damascus Asad Library MS 1426 (hereafter Asad 1426) and id., Damascus Asad MS 9608 (hereafter Asad.9608).

59. Amc.95/2, fol. 65v; Asad6093, fols. 17v–18r. Interestingly Aya.867, fol. 176v, mentions a two-month fast as one of the unique *gifts* that God grants to the Muslim community rather than a duty imposed. Consequently Aya.867 has no discussion of the reduction of this two-month fast. Similarly, Asad6093, fol. 20r, recounts the benefits of fasting during a whole series of times, including important holidays as well as the two months of Rajab and Shaᶜbān. On the six-month duty and its reduction, see also the work of Mūsā Iznīqī (d. ca. 833/1429), who adopts it into his *Kitāb al-miᶜrāj*, Istanbul Marmara Üniversitesı Ilahiyat Oğüt MS 1277 (hereafter Ilah.1277), dated 1095/1684, discussed in "Constructing an Islamic Ascension Narrative," 309f.

60. E.g., Bisṭāmī (B.20919), fol. 15v; compare the text copied by Mulla Ibn al-Ḥājj Maḥmūd Ibn al-Ḥajj in 908/1503, "*Miᶜrāj al-nabī ᶜalā al-tamām wa'l-kamāl*," Istanbul Süleymaniye Kütüphanesi MS Ibrahim Efendi 852/3 (hereafter Ibr.852/3), fol. 23v.

61. Amc.95/2, fols. 71v–82r.

62. Asad6093, fols. 20v–25v; cf. T.T.738/8, fols. 299v–301v (tour of hellfire) and fols. 310r–11r (tour of paradise); Ara.1931, fols. 77r–79r (tour of hellfire) and fols. 88r–89r (tour of paradise).

63. Aya.867, fols. 172r–73r (tour of hellfire) and fol. 177r (tour of paradise).

64. Aya.3441, fols. 28r–34v (tour of hellfire) and fols. 42v–45v and 53v–57r (tour of paradise).

65. I consider a detailed study of these scenes, perhaps along the lines of Martha Himmelfarb's study of such tours in Jewish and Christian apocalyptic literature (see her *Tours of Hell* [Philadelphia: University of Pennsylvania Press, 1983]), a desideratum.

66. On the history of illustrated *Miᶜrāj* works between 1300 and 1600 CE, see Gruber, "The Prophet Muḥammad's Ascension," passim, especially chapter 3.

67. The date 679/1280 appears in the colophon to Ibn Rasūl's *Kitāb ᶜarbaᶜīn ḥadīth al-muẓaffariyya* (Istanbul Süleymaniye Kütüphanesi MS Amcazade Hüsayın Paša 95/1, hereafter Amc.95/1), fol. 26r, immediately prior to the frontispiece to the Bakrī *miᶜrāj* text on fol. 26v. I offer my profound thanks to Christiane Gruber for examining the manuscript and helping me to reach this hypothesis about the manuscript's origins.

68. On Sultan Muẓaffar, the second member of the Yemenī Rasūlid dynasty that flourished in the seventh/thirteenth and eighth/fourteenth centuries, see Ziriklī, *al-Aᶜlām*, 2d ed., vol. 9 (Cairo: n.p., 1954–59), 321; *al-ᶜUqūd al-luʾluʾa fī akhbār al-dawla al-rasūliyya*, vol. 1, 43–88; the latter text was translated by J. W. Redhouse, *The Pearl-Strings* (London: H. A. R. Gibb Memorial, 1906–13).

69. Amc.95/1, fol. 1r.

70. Amc.95/1, fol. 26r, where Sultan Yūsuf b. ᶜUmar, apparently in his own handwriting, gives the scholar named Najm al-Dīn ᶜUmar b. Muḥammad Damāmīsī (or Damāmītī?) permission to transmit the work. This permission (*ijāza*) is dated to Rabīᶜ I in the year 679/1280.

71. Both Amc.95/1 and Amc.95/2 are written in dark ink in *naskh* script, with seventeen lines per page. Comparison of the handwriting style in the formation of key letters, such as the kaf, ha, and dhāl, among others, suggest that a single hand copied the entire manuscript.

72. For a comparison, see David James, *Qur᾿āns of the Mamluks* (New York: Thames and Hudson, 1988); see also Martin Lings, *The Qur᾿ānic Art of Calligraphy and Illumination* (London: World of Islam Festival Trust, 1976); Adam Gacek, "Arabic Bookbinding and Terminology as Portrayed by Bakr al-Ishbīlī in His *Kitāb al-Taysir fī Ṣināʿat al-Tafsīr*," *Manuscripts of the Middle East* 5 (1990–91): 106–13.

73. Cited first in Dhahabī's (d. 748/1348) *Mīzān al-iʿtidāl*, ed. Muḥammad Badr al-Dīn Ghassānī Ḥalabī, vol. 1 (Cairo: Maṭbaʿat al-Saʿāda, 1902), 53; Rosenthal, EI^2, s.v. "Bakrī, Abū al-Ḥasan"; Shoshan, *Popular Culture in Medieval Cairo*, 23, who there refers to anti-Bakrī polemics by other fourteenth-century scholars such as Ṣafadī (d. 764 /1363) and Ibn Kathīr (d. 774/1373).

74. I refer to Aya.867, dated in its colophon, fol. 177v, to Jumāda II of the year 886/1481, the base text I took as the "Reshaped Version" and translated in Appendix 2 of "Constructing an Islamic Ascension Narrative," 442–62.

75. EI^2, s.v. "Bakrī, Abū al-Ḥasan."

CHAPTER 9. THE CIRCULATION AND DIFFUSION OF BAKRĪ'S VERSIONS

1. Ibn Sīnā, "*Miʿrājnāma*," ed. N. Māyel Heravī (Mashhad: Islamic Research Foundation, 1996), the edition I use in the discussion that follows. See also Peter Heath, *Allegory and Philosophy in Avicenna (Ibn Sīnā)* (Philadelphia: University of Pennsylvania Press, 1992); Tobias Nünlist, *Himmelfahrt und Heiligkeit im Islam* (Bern: Peter Lang, 2002). The earliest extant copy of this treatise appears in Tehrān MS. Sanā 219, dated 584/1188. For the present purposes I will accept the conclusions of Heath and others that the work is genuine. On the question of the work's attribution, see Heath, *Allegory and Philosophy in Avicenna*, Appendix B.

2. See Heath, *Allegory and Philosophy in Avicenna*, 22 and 206. He sums up his argument on the issue of the attribution of the text as follows: "If one cannot prove the attribution of the *Miʿrāj Nāmā* to Avicenna conclusively, the bulk of the evidence suggests that the work is indeed his and that he wrote the treatise soon after his arrival at Iṣfahān" (ibid., 206). On the Kākūyid court, see C. E. Bosworth, "Dailamīs in Central Iran," in id., *The Medieval History of Iran, Afghanistan, and Central Asia* (London: Variorum Reprints, 1977), 73–95.

3. Ibn Khafīf Shīrāzī (d. 371/982), Ibn Bābūya Ṣadūq (d. 381/991), and Abū ʿAbd al-Raḥmān Sulamī (d. 412/1021) all composed entire treatises devoted to Muḥammad's night journey and ascension not long before this time.

4. Ibn Sīnā, *Miʿrājnāmā*, 79, translated in Heath, *Allegory and Philosophy in Avicenna*, 111.

5. In Appendix D of *Allegory and Philosophy in Avicenna*, 211–13, Heath offers an English translation of this "base narrative," derived by extracting the base text from its surrounding commentary in Ibn Sīnā's *Miᶜrājnāmā*.

6. Ibn Sīnā, *Miᶜrājnāmā*, 101–2; Heath, *Allegory and Philosophy in Avicenna*, 211.

7. Ibid.

8. Ibn Sīnā, *Miᶜrājnāmā*, 104; Heath, *Allegory and Philosophy in Avicenna*, 211.

9. Ibn Sīnā, *Miᶜrājnāmā*, 105–6; Heath, *Allegory and Philosophy in Avicenna*, 211–12.

10. Ibn Sīnā, *Miᶜrājnāmā*, 106; Heath, *Allegory and Philosophy in Avicenna*, 128–29.

11. See a discussion of this trope in chapter 8, and the examples presented in Amc.95/2, fols. 31v–32r; T.T.738/8, fol. 295v; Ara.1931, fol. 73v; cf. Aya.3441, 12r.

12. Ibn Sīnā, *Miᶜrājnāmā*, 109–15; Heath, *Allegory and Philosophy in Avicenna*, 212–13. Muḥammad's reactions upon entering into God's presence, from not hearing a sound or sensing a movement to becoming as if intoxicated, likewise find parallels in the Primitive Version.

13. Ibn Sīnā, *Miᶜrājnāmā*, 109; Heath, *Allegory and Philosophy in Avicenna*, 212. Compare not only the Bakrī versions but also the Ibn Hishām recension of Ibn Isḥāq (which draws upon Khudrī's *ḥadīth*) on this angelic guardian of the first heaven named Ismaᶜīl.

14. Ibn Sīnā, *Miᶜrājnāmā*, 110; Heath, *Allegory and Philosophy in Avicenna*, 212. The Bakrī versions frequently place Mālik and the tour of hellfire in the fifth heaven. For instance, see figure 8.1; Aya.867, fols. 172r–73r; T.T.738/8, fols. 299v–301r; Ara.1931, fols. 77v–78v; Aya.3441, fols. 28v–34v. Heath translates Mālik's proper name as "the proprietor" (Heath, 212).

15. In the Bakrī narratives, Mikāᵓīl explains to Muḥammad the meaning of his name and those of other archangels. Here Mikāᵓīl merely tells Muḥammad his name, and offers a related but more general willingness to answer questions: "Whatever is difficult for you [to understand], ask of me. Whatever you desire, seek of me so that I can show to you the intended aims of everything" (Ibn Sīnā, *Miᶜrājnāmā*, 115, translated in Heath, *Allegory and Philosophy in Avicenna*, 213). The depiction of Mikāᵓīl as possessing a scale, measuring the waters in select Bakrī narratives such as Aya.867, fol. 174r, may be related to the depiction of a separate angel in the same sea in Ibn Sīnā's base text "who was pouring water from the sea into a stream" (Ibn Sīnā, *Miᶜrājnāmā*, 113–14; Heath, *Allegory and Philosophy in Avicenna*, 213).

16. Ibn Sīnā, *Miᶜrājnāmā*, 116–18; Heath, *Allegory and Philosophy in Avicenna*, 213.

17. See Amc.95/2, fol. 60v; Aya.867, fol. 175v; T.T.738/8, fol. 306r; Ara.1931, fol. 84v. The latter two texts specifically state that Muḥammad experienced "neither sensation (*ḥiss*) nor movement (*ḥaraka*)," the same phrase employed in Ibn Sīnā's base text (*Miᶜrājnāmā*, 116; Heath, *Allegory and Philosophy in Avicenna*, 213).

18. See the discussion of this *ḥadīth* report in my translation and annotated edition of Sulamī's *The Subtleties of the Ascension* (Louisville, KY: Fons Vitae, 2006), especially with regard to sayings 39, 40, and 46. See also the treatise "*Shajarat al-Kawn*," ascribed to Ibn ʿArabī, 17. The reference to the "praise" passage appears on page 157 of the translation of the latter treatise by Arthur Jeffery, "Ibn ʿArabī's *Shajarat al-Kawn* [Part Two]" *Studia Islamica* 11 (1959):113–60.

19. Ibn Sīnā, "*Miʿrājnāmā*," 118; Heath, *Allegory and Philosophy in Avicenna*, 213.

20. It may be noted, however, that this remark and the role of Mikāʾīl in answering Muḥammad's questions resembles the role played by the angel of revelation in the Jewish *hekhalot* "*Sar Torah*" (Prince of the Torah) scenes. See David Halperin, *The Faces of the Chariot*, 430–37.

21. Muḥammad encounters some of the prophets on his final descent through the heavens in the Primitive Version (see Suyūṭī, *al-Lālī*, Ibn Ḥibbān narrative, 74), although this inclusion at the very end does have the air of a later insertion (cf. Qushayrī, "*Kitāb al-miʿrāj*," fol. 30v).

22. See *al-Isrāʾ ilā al-maqām al-asrāʾ*, ed. Suʿād Ḥakīm (Beirut: Dandara li-'l-Ṭabāʿa wa'l-Nashr, 1988; ʿAbd al-Ḥamīd Ibn Zayd, *Miʿrāj Ibn ʿArabī: min al-ruʾyā ilā al-taʿbīr* (Ṣafāqis: Kuliyyat al-Ādāb wa'l-ʿUlūm al-Insāniyya, 2004).

23. See James Morris, "The Spiritual Ascension: Ibn ʿArabī and the Miʿrāj, Part I," *Journal of the American Oriental Society* 107, no. 4 (1987):629–52; id., "The Spiritual Ascension: Ibn ʿArabī and the Miʿrāj, Part II," *Journal of the American Oriental Society* 108, no. 1 (1988):63–77.

24. See *Shajarat al-kawn* (Cairo: Bulāq, 1875), 14–18; Arthur Jeffery, "Ibn ʿArabī's *Shajarat al-Kawn*," *Studia Islamica* 11 (1959):145–60.

25. *Shajarat al-kawn*, 17; Jeffery, "Ibn ʿArabī's *Shajarat al-Kawn*," 157.

26. See the summary in the Spanish-language appendix to Asín Palacios, *La escatología musulmana en la Divina Comedia*, 2d ed. (Madrid and Granada: Consejo Superior de Investigaciones Científicas, 1943), 438–39. Sincere thanks are due to Maria Bollo-Panadero for her assistance in securing a copy of this fragmentary manuscript, Madrid Real Academía MS Gayangos 241 (hereafter in the notes: Gaya.241), fols. 1r–7v.

27. I am indebted to Christiane Gruber for her observations regarding the stylistic properties of the handwriting in Gaya.241. According to Asín Palacios, *Escatalogía musulmana*, 438, this manuscript proves "the popularity and spread of this fantastic *ḥadīth* [i.e., the Primitive Version] in the Middle Ages (at least in the twelfth century) in Spain."

28. Asín Palacios made some mistakes in his review of the text, stating, for example, that the account begins in the fifth heaven, even though the text makes it clear at the end of the first heaven described that the preceding action had taken place in the fourth (Gaya.241, fol. 1v). Moreover, there is ample evidence that the text's account of the fifth heaven must have been recorded on one or more folios, now missing, that followed fol. 1v and preceded fol. 2r (note the repetition of the line "and its width is simi-

lar to that" at both the bottom of 1v and the top of 2r, and the end of the heaven at 2r line 5 describing Muḥammad praying with the angels of the *sixth* heaven). Asín Palacios falsely claims that Mālik, the Guardian of hellfire, appears in the "fifth" heaven in the extant text, along with the Angel of Death. While this angel is briefly mentioned by name along with the Azrāʾīl as an angel who never laughs, Muḥammad's encounter with this angel does not in fact appear in the extant fragments of Gaya.241. I conjecture that Mālik may well be expected in the fifth heaven of the text by comparison with some of the other Bakrī versions (refer to figure 8.1), but unfortunately the description of this heaven is completely missing in Gaya.241, lost along with the folio(s) that preceded the extant fol. 2r.

29. Gaya.241, fol. 1r; cf. Ibn Ḥibbān, 63–64; Amc.95/2, fols. 33v–37r; Asad 6093, fols. 7v–9r; cf. *Liber Scale*, chaps. 6–8.

30. Aya.867, fol. 171v; T.T.738/8, fols. 298r–99r; Ara.1931, fols. 75v–77r; cf. Aya.3441, 25r–27r.

31. As mentioned above, the account of the fifth heaven, introduced on Gaya.241, fol. 1v line 12 and thus expected on fol. 2r is unfortunately missing. Gaya.241 fol. 2r line 1 begins the account of the sixth heaven. The fact that the account of the fifth heaven in Gaya.241 must have taken up the front and back of one or more folios suggests that it may have been one of the longer accounts in Gaya.241, and thus may well have contained the encounter with Mālik, the Guardian of Hellfire, and the tour of hellfire anticipated from the pattern established by other related texts.

32. Gaya.241, fol. 2r. The name assigned to this angel does not correspond to any of the names given to the angels in other ascension texts I have consulted, including the "Extended Cosmological" *ḥadīth* and Aya.3441, both of which are particularly rich in such names.

33. This polycephalous angel appears in the seventh heaven in Amc.95/2, fol. 49v; T.T.783/8, fol. 302r; Ara.1931, fol. 80r; Aya.867, fol. 173v. Many similar polycephalous angels inhabit the seventh heaven in the "Extended Cosmological" *ḥadīth*, recorded by Qushayrī, "*Kitāb al-miʿrāj*," fol. 20v. As with its sixth-heaven location in Gaya.241, the polycephalous angel appears in the sixth heaven in Aya.3441, fol. 35v. A composite version of the same angel can be found in the first heaven in *Liber Scale*, chap. 12.

34. Gaya.241, fol. 2v.

35. Gaya.241, fol. 7v.

36. Gaya.241, fols. 5r–6v. This snake anecdote also appears in Amc.95/2, fol. 57v, as well as later works based on the Bakrī version, such as the ninth/fifteenth-century ascension work by Mūsā Iznīkī.

37. The literature on this *Liber Scale Machometi* (herein simply "*Liber Scale*") is vast and continues to grow. See Enrico Cerulli, *Il "Liber della Scala" e la conoscenza dell'Islam in occidente* (Vatican, Biblioteca apostolica vaticana, 1949); José Muños Sendino, *La Escala de Mahoma* (Madrid: Ministerio de Asuntos Exteriores, 1949); Peter Wunderli, *Le Livre de l'Eschiele Mahomet* (Bern: Francke, 1968); Ṣalāḥ Faḍl, *Taʾthīr*

al-thaqāfa al-islāmiyya fī'l-kūmidiyya al-ilāhiyya li-Danti (Cairo: Dār al-Shurūq, 1980); Tijani El-Miskin, "The *Mi^crāj* Controversy: Dante, Palacios and Islamic Eschatology," *International Journal of Islamic and Arabic Studies* 4 n.1 (1987):45–53; Jamel Eddine Bencheikh, *Le Voyage nocturne de Mahomet* (Paris: Imprimerie Nationale, 1987), especially 271f.; Dieter Kremers, "Islamische Einflüsse auf Dantes '*Göttliche Komödie,*'" in *Orientalisches Mittelalter*, ed. Wolfhart Heinricks, 202–15 (Wiesbaden: AULA-Verlag, 1990); Gisele Besson and Michele Brossard-Dandré, *Le Livre de L'Échelle de Mahomet* (Paris: Librarie Générale Français, 1991); Daniel Gimaret, "Au coeur du *Mi^crāǧ*, un *Ḥadith* Interpolé," in *Le Voyage Initiatique en Terre d'Islam*, ed. Mohammad Amir-Moezzi, 67–82 (Louvain-Paris: Peeters, 1996); Jean-Patrick Guillaume, "Moi, Mahomet, Prophète et Messager de Dieu," in *Le Voyage Initiatique*, 83–98; Reginald Hyatte, *The Prophet of Islam in Old French* (Leiden: E. J. Brill, 1997). Hyatte's text offers a English translation, while that of Besson and Brossard-Dandré presents the Latin text and a French translation.

38. The Old French edition of the text, preserved in the Bodleien Library, Oxford MS Laudensis Misc. 537, carries the date 1264 in its colophon. On the question of dating the translations of *Liber Scale*, see Besson and Brossard-Dandré, *Le Livre de L'Échelle de Mahomet*, 20–22.

39. Bodleien Library, Oxford MS Laudensis Misc. 537, translated into English by Reginald Hyatte, *The Prophet of Islam in Old French*, 97–198. I will here use Hyatte's translation as the basis for my study of the text.

40. Although the Arabic texts use the first person, they do not do so in the explicit and overbearing way that one finds in the *Liber Scale*. Guillaume, "Moi, Mahomet, Prophète et Messager de Dieu," 92–98, explores the implications of the formulation "I, Muḥammad, Prophet and Messenger of God" that was repeatedly inserted in *Liber Scale* in the process of translation.

41. Hyatte, *Prophet of Islam*, 105; *Liber Scale*, chap. 1; Amc.95 / 2, fol. 27v; Asad6093, fol. 2r; T.T.738 / 8, fol. 293r; Ara.1931, fol. 71r. Note that *Liber Scale* erroneously identifies Umm Hāni' as Muḥammad's wife instead of merely his cousin.

42. Hyatte, *Prophet of Islam*, 105; *Liber Scale*, chap. 1; Amc.95 / 2, fols. 28r–28v; Asad6093, fols. 2v–3r; Aya.867, fol. 170r; T.T.738 / 8, fols. 293r–293v; Ara.1931, fols. 71r–71v. Bencheikh, *Le Voyage Nocturne*, 271, notes that the only one of the "popular" texts he utilizes—the late work of Barzanjī (d. 1317 / 1899)—contains the opening of the chest scene, and he comments that "one might say that this legend does not constitute an essential element of the story." Indeed, the absence of this scene from the majority of Ibn ^cAbbās and Bakrī texts is striking, and the purpose for the omission of what otherwise must have been a well-known trope has yet to be explained.

43. Hyatte, *Prophet of Islam*, 106; *Liber Scale*, chap. 2; Amc.95 / 2, fol. 29r; Aya.867, fols. 170r–170v; T.T.738 / 8, fol. 293v; Ara.1931, fol. 71v. As mentioned above, Burāq is also given such a description in select esoteric sources such as Muqātil's *Tafsīr* and the Extended Cosmological *ḥadīth*, in Qushayrī's "*Kitāb al-mi^crāj*," fol. 15v.

Liber Scale erroneously describes Burāq as a "male mallard," probably due to a translation error, as proposed by Enrico Cerulli (see Hyatte, *Prophet of Islam*, 106 n.6).

44. Hyatte, *Prophet of Islam*, 107; *Liber Scale*, chap. 3; Amc.95/2, fols. 31v–32r; T.T.738/8, fol. 295v; Ara.1931, fol. 73v; cf. Aya.3441, 12r. The language in Amc.95/2, fol. 31v, is particularly close to the general meaning conveyed in the *Liber Scale* text: "When she said to me, 'Stop!' I remained upon Burāq. She desired to speak to me, and began speaking to me, but I hated to speak to her, and I passed on." Significantly, unlike in all the Islamic ascension texts of which I am aware, *Liber Scale* puts a positive spin on the fact that Muḥammad waited for the woman to approach: "Since you waited and stopped for her, know truly that your people will have greater joy and delight than all other peoples who ever were or will be" (Hyatte, *Prophet of Islam*, 108).

45. Hyatte, *Prophet of Islam*, 108; *Liber Scale*, chap. 4. Compare Amc.95/2, fol. 32v: "Then they approached me, greeted me, and congratulated me for the favor and honor that God had given me. Gabriel informed me of that, and he informed me of the names of each one of them, until there was not one of the messengers left whom I did not know. They called for increased favors for me, and they congratulated me for paradise [being granted] to my community."

46. Compare how Muḥammad interacts with these angels (particularly how he questions ᶜAzrāʾīl and Mālik) in Hyatte, *Prophet of Islam*, 110–15 (*Liber Scale*, chaps. 4–11) together with Amc.95/2, fols. 33v–39r. The handsome and ugly angels accompany ᶜAzrāʾīl in both texts.

47. Hyatte, *Prophet of Islam*, 116; *Liber Scale*, chap. 12; Amc.95/2, fols. 40r–40v.

48. See Hyatte, *Prophet of Islam*, 126 and 158–60; *Liber Scale*, chaps. 20 and 50–51; cf. Amc.95/2, fol. 64v; Asad 6093, 17v–18r; Aya.867, fol. 176v;

49. One commonly cited example is that the *Liber Scale* depicts Muḥammad's encounter with the Rooster angel and the Half-Fire-Half-Snow angel two times each: just before the first heaven (Hyatte, 113; chap. 9) and again in the seventh heaven (Hyatte, 134–35; chap. 29). The Rooster is mentioned again as being immediately under God's throne in chap. 69; that is not a new encounter but rather a description of how the Rooster fits into the structure of the universe according to the *Liber Scale*'s complex and somewhat convoluted cosmological system. Bencheikh, *Le Voyage Nocturne*, 273, argues that the composite nature of the text reflects a deliberate desire on the part of the compiler to compose a new and definitive summation of Muslim otherworldly beliefs.

50. Although Bencheikh constructed his French "reimagination" of a full *Liber Scale* by supplementing it with the modern Ibn ᶜAbbās and the Paris MS of Bakrī (Ara.1931), among others, and noting the close connections between the Bakrī and modern Ibn ᶜAbbās versions, he did not conclude from his meditations in "L'Adventure de la Parole" anything specific about the relationship between the *Liber Scale* on the one hand and the Bakrī text(s) on the other. In his study of the *ḥadīth* of the trope I have been calling the heavenly host debate, Gimaret traces its interpolation in ascension narratives beginning with Qushayrī's *Kitāb al-miᶜrāj* and ending with *Liber Scale*, noticing its

appearance in the Ara.1931, fols. 85r–85v. He too, however, refrains from drawing any conclusions about the Bakrī text(s), stating only that one might be able to date the formulation of the original version of the *Liber Scale* to the fifth / eleventh century, between the death of Ṭabarī (since he fails to note the presence of the heavenly host debate trope in the latter's *tafsīr)* and the death of Qushayrī (Gimaret, "Au coeur du Miʿrāğ," 81–82).

51. Aya.3441, a text that has been analyzed by Gruber, "The Prophet Muḥammad's Ascension," chap. 3.

52. Istanbul Süleymaniye Kütüphanesi MS Ayasofya 3441 (herein Aya.3441). Although I discussed some basic features of the text in my "Constructing an Islamic Ascension Narrative," 306–9, Gruber examines and analyzes the work much more thoroughly and indicates its importance in the history of Islamic ascension narratives; see chap. 3 of "The Prophet Muḥammad's Ascension," and especially 119–30. Gruber's translation of the work, *The Ilkhanid Book of Ascension: a Persian-Sunni Prayer Manual* is forthcoming from I. B. Taurus Press, and I thank her for sharing a draft of this project with me.

53. Gruber, "The Prophet Muḥammad's Ascension," 130.

54. Aya.3441, fols. 3r–6r. The text here alludes to the idea that all people can and do experience a type of ascension in sleep, and it makes a reference to the idea that Sufis such as Abū Yazīd Bisṭāmī (Bayezid) were granted ecstatic visionary ascensions.

55. Aya.3441, fols. 7r–7v. Gruber maintains that many details within Aya.3441 could be said to reflect an engagement with Eastern, especially Chinese Buddhist, ideas.

56. Gruber rightly points out that drawing such a sharp contrast between two camps serves the text's purpose of promoting what it casts as the faithful Sunnī position over and against all other positions, Muslim and non-Muslim. While Abū Bakr is certainly cast in virtually every Islamic ascension narrative in the role of the person who, upon Muḥammad's return to Mecca, vigorously testifies in favor of the Prophet's veracity, the juxtaposition between the supporters of Abū Bakr and the supporters of the enemies of Islam here is no accident, since one major rift between the camps that later came to be known as the Sunnīs and the Shīʿīs formed precisely over the issue of Abū Bakr's right to lead the Muslim community upon Muḥammad's death. Abū Bakr, then, becomes a symbol not only for the true believer who asserts the truth of Muḥammad's ascension but also the true Muslim leader who deserves the support of the Muslim community as a whole.

57. Given the absence of the opening of the chest scene from the majority of Bakrī versions of Muḥammad's ascension, however, it appears that some Muslims objected to the scene on other grounds beyond the question of its reasonableness, such as the idea that Muḥammad's inherently sinless nature (*ʿiṣma*) obviated the need for such a process of purification.

58. See Aya.3441, fols. 8v–9r, translation by Gruber, modified and adapted by me. The text then introduces a list of four lessons (fols. 9r–10r) occasioned by the mere mention in the base narrative of Gabriel's appearing to Muḥammad in his true created form, a scene that is first explained through an exegesis of Q 53:7–9 (fols. 8r–8v).

59. In this sense, the *Liber Scale* and Aya.3441 deserve to be studied together. Some of the similarities between the two works and that of the modern printed Ibn ᶜAbbās narrative have been noted by Gruber, "The Prophet Muḥammad's Ascension," 122–23. Correspondences between the tour of hellfire scenes in the *Liber Scale* and Aya.3441 were alluded to in my "Constructing an Islamic Ascension Narrative," 307, n.11.

60. Gruber, "The Prophet Muḥammad's Ascension," chap. 3.

CONCLUSION

1. The potential connection between the Crusades and the spread of Islamic ascension narratives both in the central lands and westward is an intriguing idea that merits further research.

2. On the apocalypse genre, see John Collins, ed., *Apocalypse*. Ioan Culianu treated the Muslim narratives as derived from Jewish apocalyptic; see his *Psychanodia I* (Leiden: E. J. Brill, 1983), 56–61; id., *Expérience de l'Exase* (Paris: Payot, 1984), 171–72. See also Heribert Busse, "Jerusalem in the Story of Muḥammad's Night Journey and Ascension," *Jerusalem Studies in Arabic and Islam* 14 (1991):1–40.

3. See David Halperin, *The Faces of the Chairot*, 437–46.

4. Steven Wasserstrom, *Between Muslim and Jew*, 211–12.

5. See Christiane Gruber, *The Book of Muhammad's Ascension (Miᶜrajnama): A Study in Text and Image* (Valencia, Spain: Patrimonio Ediciones, expected 2008), chap. 3; see also Maria Subtleny, "The Islamic Ascent Narrative as Missionary Text," in *The Prophet Muḥammad's Ascension: New Cross-Cultural Encounters*, ed. Frederick Colby and Christiane Gruber (Bloomington: Indiana University Press, forthcoming).

6. Gruber, "The Prophet Muḥammad's Ascension," chap. 3; id., *The Ilkhanid Book of Ascension: A Persian-Sunni Prayer Manual.*

APPENDIX A. TRANSLATION OF THE PRIMITIVE VERSION

1. Suyūṭī, *al-Lālī al-masnūᶜā fī aḥādīth al-mawḍūᶜa*, ed. Abū ᶜAbd al-Raḥmān Ṣalāḥ b. Muḥammad b. ᶜUwayḍa, vol. 1 (Beirut: Dār al-Kutub al-ᶜIlmiyya, 1996), 62–74 (hereafter: IḤ). Suyūṭi's additional commentary criticizing the authenticity of the *ḥadīth* continues from 74–75.

2. Qushayrī, "[*Kitāb al-miᶜrāj*]," MS 1891, Kahuda Bakhsh Oriental Public Library, Bankipore, fols. 25v–30r (hereafter: QU). This recension condenses the narrative, replacing large sections of text with short summaries. Consult with caution the printed version of this manuscript, Qushayrī, *Kitāb al-miᶜrāj*, ed. ᶜAlī Ḥusayn ᶜAbd al-Qādir (Cairo: Dār al-Kutub al-Ḥadītha, 1964), 56–62.

3. Wāsiṭī, "*Sharḥ asmāʾ Rasūl Allāh*," MS 6840, Maktabat al-Asad al-Waṭaniyya, Damascus, fols. 34v–51r (hereafter: WA). This text is marred by two missing folios: be-

tween 46v and 47r (in the midst of the intimate colloquy) and between 50v and 51r (immediately preceding the end of the work). This "*Wonders of the Ascension*" section is preceded by the ascension *ḥadīth* of Abū Saᶜīd Khudrī.

4. Page references that I give in the text refer to Ibn Ḥibbān's recension of the Primitive Version (IḤ) as appearing in Ṣalāḥ b. Muḥammad's edition of Suyūṭī's *al-Lālī al-masnūᶜā*.

5. This is the name as it appears in IḤ; perhaps it should be read as Zanjawī, a person of Zanj.

6. The headings in this translation are inserted for ease of reference and are not part of the original text.

7. The term *tasbīḥ*, derived from the same root as the term *subḥāna* or "glorified be," stands for pious phrases that one says in praise or glory to God. The recording of these "glorifications" (Ar. sing. *tasbīḥ*, pl. *tasbīḥāt*) of the angels and prophets is key to many later Ibn ᶜAbbās texts.

8. Ibn Ḥībbān interjects at this point, noting that the preceding account was part of the long ascension *ḥadīth* that stretched "approximately twenty folios." From this detail one might conjecture that a very long narrative that combined the *Wonders of the Ascension* together with the other ascension narratives was in circulation during the time that Ibn Ḥibbān was writing. After this remark, Ibn Ḥibbān inserts an alternate Rooster description that adds little to the narrative, and is not included in WA and QU, which I will therefore skip over in this translation.

9. Preferring here WA, "assigned him" (*wakkalahu*) to IḤ, "made him arrive or join" (*waṣṣalahu*).

10. This phrase is found in both WA and QU, not in IḤ.

11. IḤ and QU have *dāʾib*; WA has *dāʾim*.

12. At this point IḤ records a lengthy report describing what the spirit experiences after death, beginning with its encounter with the angels Munkir and Nakīr and the questions they pose to it (IḤ, 63–64). QU glosses the entire section with the phrase "and he mentions the '*ḥadīth* of the question,'" suggesting that it as an independent *ḥadīth* interpolated into the Primitive Version.

13. This passage draws upon the *ḥadīth* about Mālik, Guardian of the Hellfire. The parallel passage in Ibn Hishām's recension of Ibn Isḥāq, reported anonymously from Ibn Isḥāq via "a certain person of knowledge" (*baḍ ahl al-ᶜilm*), is particularly close to the above version. Ibn Hishām's description of how the flames "rose until I thought (*ḥatta ẓannantu*) that they would consume what I saw" (Ibn Hishām, *Sīra*, vol. 1 / I, 269) bears comparison with the terminology later in the Primitive Version regarding the Prophet's experiences at the terrifying seas of fire.

14. This section is missing in both WA and QU.

15. The final phrase of this sentence is found only in WA.

16. The Arabic term *karūbiyyūn* is very likely a loan word from the Hebrew term *cherubim*, and similar angels appear in Hekhalot texts. Significant here, however, is the

attempt to derive the meaning of their name from the Arabic root *k-r-b*, signifying "to worry, distress, grieve."

17. The word for "High Realm" is *ᶜiliyyūn*, a term found in Q 83:18, where it signifies the location where the books (i.e., ledgers of deeds) of the righteous will be kept. Whether or not the term was borrowed from another language, the Arabic term derives from the root for "high, exalted," *ᶜ-l-y*, and here stands for a high heavenly realm beyond the seventh sphere. There are ten divisions or stops in this "High Realm" in IḤ, only seven of which (1, 2, 3, 4, 7, 8, 10) appear in WA. QU skips them entirely, jumping directly to the lote tree of the boundary.

18. The name *al-suhūm* and the phrase "veil of darkness" are replaced in WA by the term "the heavens" (*al-samawāt*).

19. Thus in WA, parallel to the previous section. IḤ gives *ashrafnā*, "we were honored."

20. This phrase alludes to phrases from the two key passages in the Qurʾān that are understood to refer to God's purpose behind the night journey and ascension, both Q 17:1, ". . . *in order to show him some of our signs*," and Q 53:18, "*he saw some of the greatest signs of his Lord*."

21. The word here is *adamī*, "Adamite." It could be translated as "human," but I prefer to retain the original connotation. For a parallel passage in the ascension vision of Abū Yazīd Bisṭāmī and the Enoch literature, see Sells, "3 Enoch," 3, 5.

22. These formulaic phrases are missing in IḤ, and the entire passage is missing in WA.

23. Compare the use of the term *karūbiyyūn* in the sixth heaven.

24. IḤ simply states he saw "a light" (*nūr*); in contrast, WA once again is much more specific: "I saw the Merciful (*al-Raḥmān*)."

25. Notice that the exegesis jumps at this point to the end of the passage from *Sūrat al-Najm*, probably because the narrative has not yet described the lote tree of the boundary (from 53:14), which is instead mentioned in the following section of the Primitive Version.

26. QU adds at this point "like a candle inclines" (fol. 27a).

27. The phrase "any of his creatures" comes from WA; IḤ has "unjust crimes" (*ajrām al-ẓulma*), which makes little sense in the context.

28. QU gives *ilā jamāᶜāt*, "to the assemblies," the same term appearing in Tirmidhī's versions of the dream vision containing the heavenly host debate (see chapter 5).

29. This section, presenting the final verses (seals) of the Cow chapter, is recorded only in QU, fols. 27v–28r. It therefore may not represent the earliest strand of the Primitive Version. Certainly by the time of Qushayrī (d. 465/1072) and thereafter, however, it had become a standard part of the intimate dialogue section in Ibn ᶜAbbās narratives. As one might expect, it appears in the *Tafsīr* of Thaᶜlabī (d. 427/1036; commentary on Q 17:1) with exactly the same wording as in QU.

30. This phrase and the rest of the paragraph is a dialogue created out of the two final verses of the second chapter of the Qur^cān, 2:285–86. At some points in the passage, words that are not part of the verses are inserted into the text as exegetical glosses. Italics will be reserved for words from the Qur'ān. While the contrast between italics and lack thereof should be sufficiently clear, readers unfamiliar with the passage are advised to refer back to chapter 1.

31. Thus in IḤ, which ends God's list of "gifts" to the Prophet at this point. QU has simply: "*We raised up for you your mention* to the point that you are mentioned whenever I am mentioned."

32. These "couplets" (*al-mathānī*), said in the verse to be seven in number, are often understood as a reference to the first *sūra* of the Qur'ān, *Sūrat al-Fātiḥa.*

33. Probably a reference to the Qur'ān, *Sūra* 3 (*Āl ᶜImrān*), which contains two hundred verses. A number of commentators associate the circumstances in which this chapter of the Qur'ān was revealed with the visit of a Christian delegation from Najrān to the Muslim community. See Ayoub, *The Qur'ān and Its Interpreters*, vol. 2, 1–6.

34. The *khawātīm* or "seals" could once again allude to the "seals of the Cow chapter," although it could also refer to *Sūra*s 113 and 114, which are sometimes given this same title for their role as "seals" for the entire text of the Qur'ān.

35. This entire paragraph is not found in IḤ or WA.

36. The word is *ᶜahd*, which can also mean "contract" or "covenant." QU precedes this sentence with the explicit commission itself: "Then he said to me, 'Return to your people and inform them about me.'" Thaᶜlabī transmits this commission as well, but precedes it with the standard episode that is surprisingly absent from all three recensions of the Primitive Version: "Then there was imposed upon me and my community fifty prayers every day and night."

37. See Muslim, *al-Īmān* no. 291; cf. Ibn Māja, I, 44, translated in James Morris, "The Spiritual Ascension, Ibn ᶜArabī and the Miᶜrāj, Part II," 69 n.172: "God has seventy veils of light and darkness; if He were to remove them, the radiant splendors of His Face would burn up whoever was reached by His Gaze."

38. The latter phrase is absent in IḤ, but found in both WA and QU.

39. The previous sentence is found only in IḤ, missing in WA and QU.

40. This paragraph and the three that follow it are missing in WA and summarized by a single sentence in QU. They represent an obvious interruption of the standard tour of paradise and are helpful in identifying cases in which later narratives draw directly from the Primitive Version.

41. The end of the sentence contains an allusion to the qur'ānic phrase that appears more than a dozen times in the Qur'ān, almost half the instances of which come in *Sūra* 2 (e.g., 2:38, 2:62).

42. Thus in WA, a superior reading to IḤ, "bed," especially given the following phrases.

43. The account of prophets trails off at this point in IḤ, never specifying exactly who resides in which of the lowest heavens. WA does not help us in our reconstruction of the passage because it is missing this folio. Likewise QU is too abbreviated an account to be of help in this regard: "We descended slowly from heaven to heaven, and I saw all of the prophets, who greeted me with salutations" (QU, fol. 30v).

APPENDIX B. BAKRĪ'S "TOTAL AND COMPLETE" ASCENSION

1. Amc.95/2, fol. 26v.

2. The *isnād* appears as follows: "Bakrī said that Muḥammad b. Isḥāq heard ᶜAbd al-Malik saying, regarding the *ḥadīth* report on the night journey from Muqātil b. Sulaymān and Muḥammad b. al-Sāᵓib and al-Kalbī and ᶜUthmān b. Ṭulayq, transmitted from ᶜĀᵓisha, mother of the believers, and ᶜAbd Allāh Ibn ᶜAbbās, and some of it transmitted by ᶜIkrama, Saᶜīd b. Jubayr, and others." (Amc.95/2, 27r). Note the reference to Muqātil, Ibn ᶜAbbās and others below, at the end of the excerpt.

3. The same reference to the "verse of the throne" (*ayat al-kursī*), and a similar commission, appear in Aya.867, fol. 170r. Aya.867 is a later recension of the Bakrī narrative translated in its entirety in Appendix 2 of my "Constructing an Islamic Ascension Narrative," dated 886/1481.

4. The fact that this description of Burāq's human face appears twice in this passage (see the first instance in the passage's beginning) suggests the likelihood that several different reports of Burāq's description were collated together here.

5. Translating "hands" as "front legs" here, since Burāq is depicted as a quadrupedal mount.

6. Supplied by comparison with T.T.738/8, fol. 296r, and with A1931, fol. 73v, given a likely copyist error in Amc.95/2, fol. 31r ("It flew to him to me").

7. This statement is ironic, for it makes little sense that the Prophet himself would claim ignorance by invoking the Prophet, along with God, as most knowing. It points to the fact that this phrase must have been so formulaic at that time that the copyist did not notice the ironic disparity.

8. This refrain of thanks is a common feature in the Bakrī texts, at this point and later in the narrative (e.g., when Muḥammad encounters the river *Kawthar*, Amc.95/2, fol. 54v; or when God replies to the heavenly host debate, ibid., fol. 62v; or when God replies to the favor of the prophets trope, ibid., fol. 67v). Compare, for example, Aya.867, fols. 170v and 176v; T.T.738/8, fols. 296r, 309r, and 310r; Ara.1931, fols. 74r, 87r, and 88r. It finds its way in other later versions of the Ibn ᶜAbbās ascension narrative, as well as disparate ascension texts such as that known as "The Secrets of Revelation" (*Asrār al-waḥy*).

9. This general idea, in which Muḥammad responds to the temptation of the alluring woman who represents the world, appears in the description section (but not

Gabriel's explanation section) of the woman in T.T.738/8, fol. 295v (where Muḥammad grasps Burāq), and Ara.1931, fol. 73v (where Muḥammad tells Burāq, "Stop!"). In all of these cases, Burāq continues on past the woman, despite Muḥammad's wishes to the contrary.

10. This detail is curious, given that more commonly Gabriel uses the hole to secure Burāq's chain, not to store Burāq itself.

11. Cf. Asad 6093, fol. 6r; Aya.3441, 19v. The latter gives this green sea the name *al-Qāḍiyya*, a title drawn from Q 69:26–27. For a discussion of this sea as it appears in Aya.3441, see Gruber, "The Prophet Muḥammad's Ascension," 146.

12. Cf. Asad 6093, fols. 6r–6v.

13. This section makes reference to Muḥammad in the third person more times than elsewhere in the narrative, suggesting an independent report was interpolated here in the text.

14. The original word here is *nafs*, living spirit or breath, the active force of physical life.

15. Here one finds a reference to the seven layers of hellfire, realms that are each given their own name and described in the tour of hellfire scenes of the later Ibn ᶜAbbās texts. Regarding the names for the layers, see Thomas O'Shaughnessy, "The Seven Names for Hell in the Qur᾽ān," *Bulletin of the School of Oriental and African Studies* 24 no. 3 (1961):444–69. In Amc.95/2, a very brief description of hellfire appears here, followed by a more extensive tour in fols. 80r–82r.

16. The body of Mālik, the Guardian of Hellfire, here is said to be composed of different layers of the hellfire over which he presides.

17. Compare the angels of the sixth heaven in the Primitive Version, translated in Appendix A.

18. Compare the Primitive Version, where after encountering the fearful angels (*al-Karūbiyyūn*) in the sixth heaven, he passes to the seventh and encounters "creatures and angels of God's creation about whom I am not permitted to talk, nor am I permitted to describe them to you."

19. The name of this guardian angel of the second heaven, meaning "height" or "high realm," is a term that appears in Q 83:18–20 as a register of the deeds of the righteous. The Primitive Version uses this term repeatedly for each "high realm" beyond the seventh heaven.

20. This indescribable "Sea of Seas" appears in a slightly different fashion in the "ninth stop in the high realm" in the Primitive Version.

21. Unlike in the previous heavens, the name of this guardian does not appear in the text.

22. The "two weighty ones" (*al-thaqalāni*) are mentioned in Q 55:31. Though they have been given different interpretations, here they stand for the totality of human beings and the *jinn*.

23. The name for this guardian angel of the fourth heaven derives fairly transparently from the divine name "the compassionate" (*al-raḥmān*). Although an inves-

tigation of the angelology of this and other ascension narratives goes beyond the scope of this work, it certainly would be fruitful to examine such names in light of the parallel Jewish Hekhalot narratives in which one frequently finds elements of the divine name (such as the tetragrammaton Y-H-W-H) reflected in the composite angelic names. It would be worth considering the significance of such an angel who partakes of the divine name appearing in the fourth heaven, where one might expect to find Metatron in some of the Hekhalot texts (see, for example, Halperin, "Hekhalot and Mi^crāj").

24. At this point in the narrative, the editor inserts a short but digressive report about the reason why Moses called Muḥammad to return to him (fol. 44r l.14 to fol. 44v l.4). Instead of translating this extra report, we will continue with the main textual strand.

25. Presumably the typical formulaic exchange took place before Gabriel and Muḥammad were admitted to the fifth heaven, but that dialogue was omitted in this case.

26. Compare the Primitive Version, Gabriel's reaction to Muḥammad's fear at the Sea of Fire in the "eighth stop in the high realm," Appendix A.

27. This is the generic suffix for angelic names in this text, and in Aya.3441. One could surmise that one of the names of God was supposed to precede this suffix.

28. Hūd is an Arabian prophet mentioned in the Qur^ʾān, sent to the tribe of ^cĀd. See Q 11:50f.

29. Compare the angels of the sixth heaven in the Primitive Version.

30. This trope of the angel who bathes and sheds drops from which God creates more angels appears in early Shī^cī texts (e.g., see ^cAlī Qummī's *Tafsīr*, discussed in chapter 4); according to David Halperin, "Hekhalot and Mi^crāj," it stems from passages circulated in rabbinic circles.

31. The description of this four-faced angel is parallel to the living creatures of Ezekiel 1:5–14.

32. This idea appears in popular tales about how the Ka^cba lies directly below the heavenly temple. A parallel narrative is told in rabbinic stories about how the Temple of Solomon is the exact replica of the heavenly temple, the former situated directly underneath the latter.

33. In several places, the Qur^ʾān juxtaposes the righteous "*people of the right*" with the wicked "*people of the left*." See, for example, Q 90:18–19.

34. Recall that in his dream ascension, Abū Yazīd Bisṭāmī experiences himself being transformed into a bird as he ascends to the highest spheres. See Sells, *Early Islamic Mysticism*, chap. 7.

35. Compare the angels in the "first stop in the high realm" in the Primitive Version.

36. It looks like a line or two was accidentally omitted at this point due to scribal error at the transition between the front and back of a single folio.

37. The same simile appears in the Primitive Version, Appendix A, as well as in a number of other ascension texts (e.g., the Abū Hurayra narrative in Ṭabarī's *Tafsīr*, discussed in chapter 6).

38. This curious snake appears in only a handful of Islamic ascension texts (see, for instance, "[*Kitāb al-miʿrāj*]," Real Academía MS Gayangos 241, fols. 5r–6v). Whenever this snake does appear in Islamic ascension texts, its purpose seems to be to instill humility in the divine throne, which might otherwise become proud thinking itself the most magnificent entity in creation.

39. This section, in which God explains how he comes to Muḥammad's defense through the verses of the Qurʾān, is rarely found in any other Islamic ascension text. In fact, although the Bakrī texts commonly contain a "gift" section following closely upon the "favor of the prophets" discussion, the degree of citation from the Qurʾān here and in what follows far exceeds the norm.

40. An allusion to a famous *ḥadīth qudsī*, that is, a *ḥadīth* report attributed to the divine voice, stating that God created the entire universe for Muḥammad's sake.

41. At this point in the text, the copyist accidentally copied the same lines as previously appeared.

42. Here the text records the more typical account of the bargaining scene, in which Muḥammad descends to Moses and then returns to the Lote Tree before the bargaining over the duties ensues.

43. In contrast with the unusually long gift and favor of the prophets sections above, this intercession passage is unusually short in comparison with other Bakrī recensions.

44. A different anecdote, on the issue of Muḥammad's vision of God, intervenes at this point in the narrative. Afterward, Amc.95/2 continues for another 13 folios with Muḥammad's intricately described visits to paradise and hellfire, then wraps up on fols. 82r–82v with an extremely concise conclusion describing Muḥammad's return to Mecca. The colophon on fol. 82v contains no specific information about the recension's copyist or date. I would like to express my sincere thanks to Christiane Gruber for reading and commenting on an early draft of this translation.

Works Cited

The following includes an alphabetical listing of sources cited in the text, whether they be in European or non-European languages, and whether they be printed or manuscript sources. The only exception is that articles from the *Encyclopaedia of Islam, New Edition* (Leiden: E. J. Brill, 1960–), are not listed individually below; rather, references to entries appear in the notes, following the abbreviation *EI*². Arabic and Persian sources are listed under the *kunya*, family name, title, or name under which the author is conventionally known. In names from these languages, the definite article "al-" or "el-" will be ignored for the purposes of alphabetization.

ᶜAbd al-Razzāq b. Hammām. *al-Musannaf.* Edited by Ḥabīb al-Raḥmān Aᶜẓāmī. 11 vols. Beirut: al-Majlis al-ᶜIlmī, 1972.

Alexandrin, Lisa. "Prophetic Ascent and the Individual Initiatory Experience in Qadi al-Nuᵓman's *Asas al-taᵓwīl*," in *The Prophet Muḥammad's Ascension: New Cross-Cultural Encounters*, edited by Frederick S. Colby and Christiane Gruber. Bloomington: Indiana University Press, expected 2009.

ᶜAlī, Khālid Sayyid. *al-Isrāᵓ wa'l-miᶜrāj: muᶜjiza wa-ḥaqāᵓiq, asrār wa-fawāᵓid.* Damascus and Beirut: al-Yamāma, 1998.

Amir-Moezzi, Mohammad Ali. "L'Imam dans le Ciel." In *Le Voyage initiatique en terre d'Islam*, edited by id., 99–116. Louvain-Paris: Peeters, 1996.

———. "al-Ṣaffār al-Qummī (m. 290/902–3) et son *Kitāb Baṣāᵓir al-Darajāt.*" *Journal Asiatique* 280, nos. 3–4 (1992):221–50.

Anonymous. "[*Kitāb al-miᶜrāj*]." Real Academía de Madrid. MS Gayangos 241. Madrid, Spain.

Anonymous. "[*Miᶜrāj nameh*]." Süleymaniye Kütüphanesi. MS Ayasofya 3441. Istanbul, Turkey. In Persian.

Asín Palacios, Miguel. *La escatalogía musulmana en la Divina Comedia.* 2d ed. Madrid, Granada-Consejo Superior de Investigaciones Científicas, 1943.

Ashᶜarī, Abu al-Ḥasan ᶜAlī b. Ismāᶜīl. *Maqālat al-islāmiyyīn wa ikhtilāf al-muṣakkīn.* Edited by Helmut Ritter. Vol. 1. Weisbaden: Dār al-Nashr Franz Shtaynir, 1963.

Ayoub, Mahmoud. *The Qurʾān and Its Interpreters*. Vol. 1. Albany: State University of New York Press, 1984.

Azamī, M. M. *Studies in Ḥadīth Methodology and Literature*. Indianapolis, IN: American Trust Publications, 1977: reprint 1992.

El-Azmeh, Nazeer. *Miʿrāj wa'l-ramz al-ṣūfī*. Beirut: Dār al-Bāḥith, 1973.

Bakrī, Abū al-Ḥasan Aḥmad b. ʿAbd Allāh. *al-Anwār wa-miṣbāḥ* (or *miftāḥ*) *al-surūr* (or *al-asrār*) *wa'l-afkār fī dhikr* (*sayyidinā*) *Muḥammad al-muṣṭafā al-mukhtār*. Biblioteca Vaticana. MS Borg125. Vatican City. 694/1295.

———. "*Qiṣṣat al-miʿrāj*" or "*Ḥadīth al-miʿraj ʿalā 'l-tamām wa 'l -kamāl.*" Bibliothèque Nationale. MS Arabe 1931. Paris, France.

———. ["*Kitāb fīhi miʿrāj al-nabī*"] or ["*Ḥadīth al-miʿraj ʿalā 'l-tamām wa 'l -kamāl.*"] Dār al-Kutub al-Miṣriyya. MS Tārīkh Taymūr 738/8. Cairo, Egypt.

———. "*Kitāb fīhi miʿrāj al-nabī*" or "*Ḥadīth al-miʿraj ʿalā 'l-tamām wa 'l -kamāl.*" Süleymaniye Kütüphanesi. MS Amcazade Hüsayın Paša 95/2. Istanbul, Turkey.

———. "*Ḥadīth al-miʿraj*" or "*Ḥadīth al-miʿraj ʿalā 'l-tamām wa 'l -kamāl.*" Süleymaniye Kütüphanesi. MS Ayasofya 867. 886/1481. Istanbul, Turkey.

———. "*Ḥadīth al-isrāʾ w'al-miʿraj ʿalā 'l-tamām wa 'l -kamāl.*" Maktabat al-Asad al-Waṭaniyya. MS 6093. Damascus, Syria. 1156/1743.

Bar-Asher, Meir M. *Scripture and Exegesis in Early Imāmī Shīʿism*. Leiden: E. J. Brill, 1999.

Bayhaqī, Abū Bakr Aḥmad b. Ḥusayn. *Dalāʾil al-nubuwwa wa maʿrifat aḥwāl ṣāḥib al-sharīʿa*. Vol. 2. Edited by ʿAbd al-Muʿṭi Qalʿajī. Beirut: Dār al-Kutub al-ʿIlmiyya, 1985.

Bell, Richard. "Muḥammad's Visions." *The Moslem World* 24 (1934):145–54.

Bencheikh, Jamel Eddine. *Le Voyage nocturne de Mahomet*. Paris: Imprimerie Nationale, 1987.

Besson, Gisele, and Michele Brossard-Dandré. *Le Livre de l'échelle de Mahomet*. Paris: Librarie Générale Français, 1991.

Bevan, A. A. "Mohammad's Ascension to Heaven." *Studien zur semitischen Philologie und Religionsgeschichte*. Edited by Karl Marti. Giessen: Alfred Topelman, 1914: 49–61.

Birkeland, Harris. *The Legend of the Opening of Muḥammad's Breast*. Oslo: I Kommisjon Hos Jacob Dybwad, 1955.

Bisṭāmī, Abd al-Raḥmān (d. 858/1454). "*al-Kawkab al-wahhāj fi aḥādīth al-miʿrāj.*" Cairo Dār al-Kutub al-Miṣriyya. MS B 20919. Cairo, Egypt.

Bosworth, C. E. "Dailamīs in Central Iran," in id., *The Medieval History of Iran, Afghanistan, and Central Asia*. London: Variorum Reprints, 1977.

Bourdieu, Pierre. *Outline of a Theory of Practice*. Translated by Richard Nice. Cambridge: Cambridge University Press, 1977.

Brockelmann, Carl. *Geschichte der arabischen litteratur*. Vol. 1. Leiden: Brill. 1943–.

———. *Geschichte der arabischen litteratur: Supplementband*. Vol. 1. Leiden: Brill, 1937–42.

Bukhāri, Abū ᶜAbd Allāh Muḥammad b. ᶜIsmāᶜil. *Ṣaḥīḥ Bukhārī.* Edited by Muhammad Nizār Tamīm and Haytham Nizār Tamīm. Beirut: Sharikat Dār al-Arqam b. Abī Arqam, n.d.

Bulliet, Richard. *Islam: The View from the Edge.* New York: Columbia University Press, 1994.

———. *The Patricians of Nishapur.* Cambridge: Harvard University Press, 1972.

Busse, Heribert. "Jerusalem in the Story of Muḥammad's Night Journey and Ascension." *Jerusalem Studies in Arabic and Islam* 14 (1991):1–40.

Būṭī, Muḥammad Saᶜīd Ramaḍān. *Fiqh al-sīra.* 7th ed. Beirut: Dār al-Fikr, 1978.

Cerulli, Enrico. *Il "Liber della Scala" e la conoscenza dell'Islam in occidente.* Vatican, Biblioteca apostolica vaticana, 1949.

Colby, Frederick S. "Constructing an Islamic Ascension Narrative: The Interplay of Official and Popular Culture in Pseudo-Ibn ᶜAbbās." PhD diss., Duke University, 2002.

———. "The Role of Imāmī Shīᶜī Narratives in the Construction of and Contestation over the Story of Muḥammad's Ascension," in *The Prophet Muḥammad's Ascension: New Cross-Cultural Encounters*, edited by Frederick Colby and Christiane Gruber. Bloomington: Indiana University Press, forthcoming.

———. "The Subtleties of the Ascension: al-Sulamī on the Miᶜrāj of the Prophet Muḥammad." *Studia Islamica* 94 (2002):167–83.

Colby, Frederick S., and Christiane Gruber, editors. *The Prophet Muḥammad's Ascension: New Cross-Cultural Encounters.* Bloomington: Indiana University Press, forthcoming.

Collins, John, ed. *Apocalypse: The Morphology of a Genre. Semeia* 14 [S.I.]: Society of Biblical Literature, 1979.

Collins, John, and Michael Fishbane, editors. *Death, Ecstasy, and Other Worldly Journeys.* Albany: State University of New York Press, 1995.

Culianu [Couliano], Ioan P. *Expérience de l'Exase: Extase, Ascension et Récit Visionnaire de l'Hellénism au Moyen* Age. Paris: Payot, 1984.

———. *Out of This World: Otherworldly Journeys from Gilgamesh to Albert Einstein.* Boston: Shambhala, 1991.

———. *Psychanodia I: A Survey of the Evidence Concerning the Ascension of the Soul and Its Relevance.* Leiden: E. J. Brill, 1983.

Dārimī, ᶜAbd Allāh b. ᶜAbd al-Raḥmān. *Sunan al-Dārimī.* 2 vols. N.p.: Dār Iḥyāᵓ al-Sunna al-Nabawiyya, 1970?.

Dhahabī, Muḥammad b. Aḥmas. *Siyar aᶜlām al-nubalāᵓ.* Vol. 10. Edited by Shuᶜayb Arnaᶜūt and Ḥusayn Asad. Beirut: Muᶜassasat al-Risāla, 1982–1983.

———. *Mīzān al-iᶜtidāl.* Vol. 1. Edited by Muḥammad Badr al-Dīn Ghassānī Ḥalabī. Cairo: Maṭbaᶜat al-Saᶜāda, 1902.

Dimnātī, ᶜAlī b. Sulymān. *Nūr miṣbāḥ al-zujāja ᶜala Sunan Ibn Māja.* [Cairo]: al-Maṭba ᶜa al-Wahbiyya, 1881.

Esack, Farid. *The Qurᵓān: A User's Guide.* Oxford: Oneworld, 2005.

Ess, Josef van. "Le *Mi^{c}rāǧ* et la Vision de Dieu." In *Le Voyage Intitiatique*, edited by Mohammad Ali Amir-Moezzi, 27–56. Louvain-Paris: Peeters, 1996.

———. "Le Théologie et le Coran: *mi^{c}rāǧ* et le débat sur l'anthropomorphisme." In *Les Prémices de la Théologie musulmane.* Paris: Albin Michel, 2002.

———. *Theologie und Gesellschaft im 2. und 3. Jahrhundert Hidschra: eine Geschichte des religiosen Denkens im frühen Islam.* Berlin, New York: de Gruyter, 1991–1997.

———. "Vision and Ascension: *Sūrat al-Najm* and Its Relationship with Muhammad's *mi^{c}rāj*." *Journal of Qur$^{\circ}$ānic Studies* 1 (1999):47–62.

———. "The Youthful God: Anthropomorphism in Early Islam." Paper presented at the Ninth Annual University Lecture in Religion, Arizona State University, 1988 (photocopy).

Faḍl, Ṣalāḥ. *Ta$^{\circ}$thīr al-thaqāfa al-islāmiyya fī'l-kūmidiyya al-ilāhiyya li-Danti.* Cairo: Dār al-Shurūq, 1980.

Gacek, Adam. "Arabic Bookbinding and Terminology as Portrayed by Bakr al-Ishbīlī in His *Kitāb al-Taysir fī Ṣinā^{c}at al-Tafsīr*." *Manuscripts of the Middle East* 5 (1990–91):106–13.

Gilliot, Claude. "Le Commentire Coranique de Hūd b. Muḥakkam / Muḥkim." *Arabica* 44, no. 22 (1997):179–233.

———. "Portrait 'mythique' d'Ibn ^{c}Abbās." *Arabica* 32, no. 2 (1985):127–84.

Gimaret, Daniel. "Au coeur de *Mi^{c}rāǧ*, un *Hadīth* Interpolé." In *Le Voyage Initiatique*, edited by Amir-Moezzi, 67–82. Louvain-Paris: Peeters, 1996.

———. *Dieu à l'image de l'homme: Les anthropomorphismes de la sunna et leur interprétation par les théologiens.* Paris: CERF, 1997.

Gruber, Christiane J. *The Book of Muhammad's Ascension (Mi^{c}rajnama): A Study in Text and Image.* Valencia, Spain: Patrimonio Ediciones, expected 2008.

———. *The Ilkhanid Book of Ascension: A Persian-Sunni Prayer Manual.* London: I. B. Tauris and BIPS, expected 2008.

———. "The Prophet Muhammad's Ascension (*Mi^{c}rāj*) in Islamic Art and Literature, ca. 1300–1600." PhD diss., University of Pennsylvania, 2005.

Gruenwald, Ithamar. *Apocalyptic and Merkavah Mysticism.* Leiden: E. J. Brill, 1980.

Guillaume, Alfred. *New Light on the Life of Muḥammad.* Cambridge, Mancester: Mancester University Press, 1960.

———. "Where Was al-Masyid al-Aqsa," *Andalus* 18 (1953):323–36.

Guillaume, Jean-Patrick. Translated by *id.* "Extraits des Récits sur les prophètes de Tha^{c}labī." In *Le Livre de L'Échelle de Mahomet*, edited by Gisele Besson and Michele Brossard-Dandré, 355–72. Paris: Librarie Générale Française, 1991.

———. "Moi, Mahomet, Prophète et Messager de Dieu." In *Le Voyage Initiatique*, edited by Amir-Moezzi, 83–98. Louvain-Paris: Peeters, 1996.

Halperin, David. "Ascension or Invasion: Implications of the Heavenly Journey in Ancient Judaism." *Religion* (1988):47–67.

———. *Faces of the Chariot: Early Jewish Responses to Ezekiel's Vision.* Tübingen: J. C. B. Mohr, 1988.

———. "Hekhalot and *Miʿrāj*: Observations on the Heavenly Journey in Judaism and Islam." In *Death, Ecstasy, and Other Worldly Journeys*, edited by John Collins and Michael Fishbane, 269–88. Albany: State University of New York Press, 1995.

Hawwarī, Hūd b. Muḥakkam. *Tafsīr Kitāb Allāh al-ʿAzīz*. Edited by Ḥāj b. Sa ʿīd Sharīfī. Vol. 2. Beirut: Dār al-Gharb al-Islāmī, 1990.

Haythamī, ʿAlī b. Abī Bakr. *Mawārid al-zamān ilā zawaʾid Ibn Ḥibbān*. Edited by Muḥammad ʿAbd al-Razzāq Ḥamza. Cairo: Maṭbaʿa al-Salafiyya, 1961.

Heath, Peter. *Allegory and Philosophy in Avicenna (Ibn Sīnā)*. Philidelphia: University of Pennsylvania Press, 1992.

Himmelfarb, Martha. *Tours of Hell: An Apocalyptic Form in Jewish and Christian Literature*. Philadelphia: University of Pennsylvania Press, 1983.

Hodgson, Marshall. *The Venture of Islam*. Vols. 1–3. Chicago, IL: University of Chicago Press, 1958.

Horowitz. J. "Muhammeds Himmelfahrt." *Der Islam* 9 (1919):159–83.

Hyatte, Reginald. *The Prophet of Islam in Old French*. Leiden: E. J. Brill, 1997.

Ibn ʿAbbās, ʿAbd Allāh. *al-Isrāʾ waʾl-miʿrāj*. Susa, Tunis: Dār al-Maʿārif, 2000.

Ibn ʿAbd al-Barr. *al-Istiʿāb fī maʿrifat al-aṣḥāb*. Edited by Bajawī. Vol. 3. Cairo: Maktabat Nahḍat Miṣr, n.d.

Ibn ʿArabī Mālikī. *ʿĀriḍat al-aḥwazī bi-sharḥ ṣaḥīḥ al-Tirmidhī*. Edited by Hishām Bukhārī. Beirut: Dār Iḥyāʾ al-Turāth al-ʿArabī, 1995.

Ibn ʿArabī, Muḥyī al-Dīn. *al-Isrāʾ ilā al-maqām al-asrāʾ*. Edited by Suʿād Ḥakīm. Beirut: Dandara li-'l-Ṭabāʿa wa'l-Nashr, 1988.

———. *Shajarat al-kawn*. Cairo: Bulāq, 1875.

Ibn Athīr, ʿIzz al-Dīn. *Usd al-ghāba fī maʿrifat al-ṣaḥāba*. Vol. 3. Cairo?: Kitāb al-Shalb, 1970.

Ibn Diḥya, Abū al-khaṭṭāb ʿUmar Kalbī. *al-Ibtihāj fī aḥādīth al-mi ʿrāj*. Edited by Rif ʿat Fawzī ʿAbd al-Muṭṭalib. Cairo: Maktabat al-Khānjā, 1996.

Ibn al-Ḥājj, Maḥmūd Ibn al-Ḥajj. "*Miʿrāj al-nabī ʿalā al-tamām wa'l-kamāl*." Süleymaniye Kütüphanesi. MS Ibrāhīm Efendi 852/3. Istanbul, Turkey.

Ibn Ḥanbal. *Musnad*. Edited by Aḥmad Muḥammad Shākir. Cairo: Dār al-Maʿārif, 1950.

Ibn Ḥibbān, Muḥammad Bustī. *al-Majrūḥīn min al-muḥaddithīn*. Vol. 2. Edited by Ḥamdī ʿAbd al-Majīd Salafī. Riyāḍ: Dār al-Sumayʿī, 2000.

———. *Ṣaḥīḥ Ibn Ḥibbān*. Edited by Shuʿayb Arnaʿūt and Ḥusayn Asad. Vol. 1. Beirut: Muʾassasat al-Risāla, 1984– .

Ibn Hishām, ʿAbd al-Malik. *Kitāb Sīrat Rasūl Allāh: Das Leben Muhammed's nach Muhammed Ibn Isḥāk bearbeitet von Abd el-Malik Ibn Hischām*. Edited by Ferdinand Wüstenfeld. Vol. 1/I. 1856.

———. *The Life of Muḥammad*. Translated by Alfred Guillaume. Oxford: Oxford University Press, 1955.

Ibn Isḥāq, Muḥammad. *Kitāb al-sīra wa'l-maghāzī* [recension of Ibn Bukayr]. Edited by Suhayl Zakkār. Beirut: Dār al-Fikr, 1978.

———. *Sīrat Ibn Isḥāq* [recension of Ibn Bukayr]. Edited by Muhammad Ḥamīd Allāh. Rabat: Maᶜhad al-Dirasāt wa'l-Abḥāth lil-Taᶜrib, 1976.

Ibn Kathīr. *Tafsīr al-qurʾān al-ᶜaẓīm*. Edited by Salāma. Riyadh: Dār al-Ṭayba, 1997.

Ibn Khallikān. *Wafayāt al-aᶜyān wa anbāʾ al-zamān*. Edited by Iḥsān ᶜAbbās. Vol. 3. Beirut: Dār Sadir, 1977.

Ibn Māja, Muḥammad b. Yazīd. *Sunan Ibn Māja*. Liechtenstein: Thesaurus Islamicus Foundation, 2000.

Ibn Rasūl, Abū Manṣūr Yūsuf al-Muẓaffar b. ᶜUmar b. ᶜAlī (d. 694/1295). "*Kitāb ᶜarbaᶜīn ḥadīth al-muẓaffariyya*." Süleymaniye Kütüphanesi. MS Amcazade Hüsayın Paša 95/1. Istanbul, Turkey. 679/1280.

Ibn Saᶜd. *al-Ṭabaqāt al-kubrā*. Vol. 2. Beirut: Dār al-Ṣādir, 1957–68.

Ibn Sīnā, Ḥusayn b. ᶜAbd Allāh (d. 428/1037). "*Miᶜrājnāma*." Sanā. MS 219. Tehran, Iran. 584/1188.

———. *Miᶜrāj Nāma*. Edited by Najīb Heravī. Mashhad: Islamic Research Foundation Astan Quds Razavi, 1996.

Ibn Zakkār, Suhayl, ed. *Kitāb al-Sīra wa'l-maghāzī*. Beirut: Dār al-Fikr, 1978.

Ibn Zayd, ᶜAbd al-Ḥamīd. *Miᶜrāj Ibn ᶜArabī: min al-ruʾyā ilā al-taᶜbīr*. Ṣafāqis: Kuliyyat al-Ādāb wa'l-ᶜUlūm al-Insāniyya, 2004.

Iznīqī, Mūsā (d. ca. 833/1429). "[*Kitāb al-miᶜrāj*]." Marmara Üniversitesı Ilahiyat Oğüt. MS 1277. Istanbul, Turkey. 1095/1684.

James, David. *Qurʾāns of the Mamluks*. New York: Thames and Hudson, 1988.

Jeffery, Arthur. "Ibn ᶜArabī's *Shajarat al-Kawn*." *Studia Islamica* 10 (1959):44–77.

———. "Ibn ᶜArabī's *Shajarat al-Kawn*." *Studia Islamica* 11 (1959):113–60.

Kahhāla, ᶜUmar Riḍā. *Muᶜjam al-muʾallifīn*. Vol. 3. Beirut: Muʾassasat al-Risāla, 1993.

Kappler, Claude, ed. *Apocalypses et voyages dans l'Au-delà*. Paris: Editions of CERF, 1987.

Kister, M. J. "You Shall Only Set Out for Three Mosques." *Le Museón* 82 (1969):173–96.

Kremers, Dieter. "Islamische Einflüsse auf Dantes '*Göttliche Komödie*.'" In *Orientalisches Mittelalter*. Edited by Wolfhart Heinricks. Wiesbaden: AULA-Verlag, 1990.

Kūfī, Furāt b. Ibrāhīm Ibn Furāt. *Tafsīr Furāt al-Kūfi*. Edited by Muhammad Kāẓim. Beirut: Muʾassasat al-Nuᶜmān, 1992.

"*Liber Scale Machometi*." Bodleien Library. MS Laudensis Misc. 537. Oxford, England. 1264.

Lings, Martin. *The Qurʾānic Art of Calligraphy and Illumination*. London: World of Islam Festival Trust, 1976.

Majlisī Muḥammad Bāqir. *Biḥār al-anwār*. Vol. 18. Edited by Jawād ᶜAlawī and Muḥammad [al-Akhwandī]. Tehrān-Qumm: Haydarī, 1956–72.

Merkur, Dan. *Gnosis: An Esoteric Tradition of Mystical Visions and Unions*. Albany: State University of New York Press, 1993.

Mernissi, Fatima. *The Veil and the Male Elite*. Translated by Mary Jo Lakeland. Reading, MA: Addison-Wesley, 1991.

Merrick, James. *The Life and Religion of Muḥammad* (Ḥayāt al-qulūb). Vol. 2. Boston: Phillips, Sampson, 1850.
El-Miskin, Tijani. "The *Mi*ᶜ*rāj* Controversy: Dante, Palacios and Islamic Eschatology." *International Journal of Islamic and Arabic Studies* 4, n.1 (1987):45–53.
Morris, James. "The Spiritual Ascension: Ibn ᶜArabī and the Miᶜrāj, Part I." *Journal of the American Oriental Society* 107, no. 4 (1987):629–52.
———. "The Spiritual Ascension: Ibn ᶜArabī and the Miᶜrāj, Part II." *Journal of the American Oriental Society* 108, no. 1 (1988):63–77.
Motzki, Harold, ed. *Ḥadīth: Origins and Developments*. Burlington, VT: Ashgate, 2004.
Muqātil b. Sulaymān. *Tafsīr Muqātil b. Sulaymān*. 4 vols. Edited by ᶜAbd Allāh Maḥmūd Shaḥātā. Cairo: al-Hayᶜa al-Miṣriyya al-ᶜĀmma liᵓl-Kitāb, 1979–88.
Muslim b. Ḥajjāj Qurashī Naysabūrū (d. 261/875). *Ṣaḥīḥ Muslim bi-sharḥ al-Nawawī*. Beirut: Dār al-Kitāb al-ᶜArabī, 1987.
———. *Ṣaḥīḥ Muslim*. 2 vols. Liechtenstein: Thesaurus Islamicus Foundation, 2000.
Najāshī, Aḥmad b. ᶜAlī. *Kitāb al-Rijāl*. Tehran: Markaz-i Nashr-i Kitāb, 1960?.
Nasāᵓī, Abū ᶜAbd al-Raḥmān. *Sunan al-Nasāᵓī*. 8 vols. Cairo: Muṣtafā al-Bābī al-Ḥalabī, 1964.
———. *Sunan al-Nasāᵓī*. 2 vols. Liechtenstein: Thesaurus Islamicus Foundation, 2000.
Nasr, Seyyed Hossein. *Sufi Essays*. London: George Allen & Unwin, 1972.
Nawbukhtī, Ḥasab b. Mūsa. *Firaq al-shīᶜa*. Edited by Helmut Ritter. Istanbul: Maṭbaᶜat al-Dawla, 1931.
Neuwirth, Angelika. "From Sacred Mosque to the Remote Temple." In *With Reverence for the Word: Medieval Scriptural Exegesis in Judaism, Christianity, and Islam*. Edited by Jane McAuliffe, Barry Walfish, and Joseph Goering, 376–407. Oxford: Oxford University Press, 2003.
Newby, Gordon. *The Making of the Last Prophet*. Columbia: University of South Carolina Press, 1989.
Nissan, Mordechai. "Notes on a Possible Jewish Source for Muhammad's Night Journey." *Arabica* 47, no. 2 (2000):274–77.
Nünlist, Tobias. *Himmelfahrt und Heiligkeit im Islam*. Bern: Peter Lang, 2002.
Nwyia, Paul. *Exégèse coranique et langage mystique*. Beirut: Dar el-Machreq, 1970.
O'Shaughnessy, Thomas. "The Seven Names for Hell in the Qurᵓān." *Bulletin of the School of Oriental and African Studies, University of London* 24, no. 3 (1961): 444–69.
Piemontese, A. M. "Una versione persiana della storia del 'miᶜrag'." *Oriente Moderno* 60 (1980): 225–43.
[Pseudo-Bukhārī]. "[*Mi*ᶜ*rāj al-nabi]*." Maktabat al-Asad al-Waṭaniyya. MS 1426. Damascus, Syria.
———. Maktabat al-Asad al-Waṭaniyya. MS 9608. Damascus, Syria.
Qummī, ᶜAli b. Ibrāhīm. *Tafsīr Qummī*. Tabrīz: n.p., 1895 lithograph.
———. *Tafsīr Qummī*. Vol. 2. Edited by Ṭayyib Mūsa Jazāᵓirī. Najaf: Manshūrāt Maktabat al-Huda, 1967–8.

Qushayrī, Abū al-Qāsim. "*Kitāb al-miʿrāj*." Kahuda Bakhsh Oriental Public Library. MS 1891. Bankipore, India.

———. *Kitāb al-miʿrāj*. Edited by Ali Ḥasan ʿAbd al-Qādir. Cairo: Dār al-Kutub al-Ḥadītha, 1964.

Rāzī, Abū al-Futūḥ. *Tafsīr rūḥ al-jinān waʾl-rawḥ al-janān* [*al-Rawḍ al-jinān*]. Vol. 7. Edited by Abū al-Ḥasan Shaʿrānī and ʿAlī Akbar Ghaffārī. Tehran: Kitabfurūshī Islāmiyya, 1965.

Redhouse, J. W. *The Pearl-Strings*. London: H. A. R. Gibb Memorial, 1906–13.

Renard, John. *Seven Doors to Islam: Spirituality and the Religious Life of Islam*. Berkeley: University of California Press, 1996.

Renaud, Étienne. "Le Récit du miʿrāj: une version arabe de l'ascension du Prophète, dans le Tafsīr de Tabarī." In *Apocalypses et voyages dans l'Au-Delà*, edited by Claude Kappler, 267–90. Paris: CERF, 1987.

Rippin, Andrew. "Ibn ʿAbbās' *al-Lughat fīʾl-qurʾān*." *Bulletin of the School of Oriental and African Studies* 44 (1981):15–25.

———. "Ibn ʿAbbās' *Gharīb al-qurʾān*." *Bulletin of the School of Oriental and African Studies* 46 (1983):332–33.

———. "Tafsīr Ibn ʿAbbās and Criteria for Dating Early Tafsīr Texts." *Jerusalem Studies in Arabic and Islam* 18 (1994):38–76.

———. "Western Scholarship and the Qurʾān." In *The Cambridge Companion to the Qurʾān*, edited by Jane D. McAuliffe, 235–51. Cambridge: Cambridge University Press, 2006.

Robinson, Neal. *Discovering the Qurʾān*. 2d ed. Washington DC: Georgetown University Press, 2003.

Rubin, Uri. "Pre-existence and Light: Aspects of the Concept of Nur Muhammad." *Israel Oriental Studies* 5 (1975):62–119.

———. *The Eye of the Beholder*. Princeton, NJ: Darwin, 1995.

Ṣaffār Qummī, Muḥammad b. Ḥasan. *Baṣāʾir al-darajāt*. Edited by Mīrzā Muḥsin Kuchebāghī Tabrīzī. Qum: Maktabat Āyat Allāh al-ʿUẓmā Marʿashī Najafī, 1982.

Saleh, Walid. *The Formation of the Classical Tafsīr Tradition: The Qurʾān Commentary of al-Thaʿlabī*. Leiden: E. J. Brill, 2004.

Samarrai, Qassim. *The Theme of Ascension in Mystical Writings*. Baghdad: National Printing and Publishing, 1968.

Schacht, Joseph. *The Origins of Muḥammadan Jurisprudence*. Oxford: Oxford University Press, 1959.

Scherberger, Max. *Das Miʿrājnāme*. Würzburg: Ergon, 2003.

Schrieke. B. J. O. "Die Himmelsreise Muhammeds." *Der Islam* 6 (1916):1–30.

Sells, Michael. "3 Enoch (*Sefer Hekhalot*) and the Miʿrāj of Abū Yazīd al-Bisṭāmī." Paper presented at the annual meeting of the American Academy of Religion, Anaheim, CA., 1989.

———. *Approaching the Qurʾān*. Ashland, OR: White Cloud, 1999.

———, trans., ed. *Early Islamic Mysticism: Sufi, Qur'an, Miraj, Poetic and Theological Writings.* New York: Paulist, 1996.

Sendino, José Muños. *La Escala de Mahoma.* Madrid: Ministerio de Asuntos Exteriores, 1949.

Shoshan, Boaz. *Popular Culture in Medieval Cairo.* Cambridge: Cambridge University Press, 1993.

Siddiqi, Muḥammad Zubayr. *Ḥadīth Literature: Its Origin, Development, and Special Features.* Edited by Abdal Hakil Murad. Cambridge, UK: Islamic Texts Society, 1993.

Subtleny, Maria. "The Islamic Ascent Narrative as Missionary Text." In *The Prophet Muḥammad's Ascension: New Cross-Cultural Encounters*, edited by Frederick Colby and Christiane Gruber. Bloomington: Indiana University Press, expected 2009.

Sulamī, Abū ᶜAbd al-Raḥmān. *The Subtleties of the Ascension.* Edited and translated by Frederick S. Colby. Louisville, KY: Fons Vitae, 2006.

Suyūṭī, Jalāl al-Dīn. *al-Lālī al-maṣnūᶜa fī aḥādīth al-mawḍūᶜa.* Edited by Abū ᶜAbd al-Raḥmān Ṣalāḥ b. Muḥammad b. ᶜUwayḍa. Beirut: Dār al-Kutub al-ᶜIlmiyya, 1996.

Ṭabarī, Muḥammad Ibn Jarīr. *The History of al-Ṭabarī.* Vol. 6, *Muḥammad at Mecca.* Translated by Montgomery Watt and M. V. McDonald. Albany: State University of New York Press, 1988.

———. *The History of al-Ṭabarī.* Vol. 9, *The Last Years of the Prophet.* Translated by Ismail Poonawala. Albany: State University of New York Press, 1990.

———. "Muḥammad's Night Journey and Ascension." Translated by Rueven Firestone. In *Windows on the House of Islam*, edited by John Renard, 336–45. Berkeley: University of California Press, 1998.

———. *Tafsīr al-Ṭabarī (Jāmiᶜ al-bayān fī taʾwīl ay al-qurʾān).* Beirut: Dār al-Kutub al-ᶜIlmiyya, 1992.

Ṭabarsī, Faḍl b. Ḥasan (d. 548 / 1153). *Majmaᶜa al-bayān fī tafsīr al-Qur'ān.* Qum: Manshūrāt Maktabat Ayat Allāh al-ᶜUẓmā al-Marᶜashī al-Najafī, 1936.

Thaᶜlabī, Abū Isḥāq Aḥmad b. Muḥammad. "*Ḥadīth al-masrā wa'l-miᶜrāj bi-Rasūl Allāh.*" Beyezit Kütüpanesi. MS Feyzullah 2137. Istanbul, Turkey.

———. *al-Kashf wa-al-bayān ᶜan Tafsīr al-Qur'an.* Vol. 6. Edited by Imām Abī Muḥammad b. ᶜAshūr. Beirut: Dār Iḥyāᶜ al-Turāth al-ᶜArabī, 2002.

———. *Qiṣṣāṣ al-anbiyāʾ al-musammā ᶜArāʾis al-majālis.* Beirut: Maktabat al-Thaqāfa, n.d.

Tirmidhī, Abū ᶜĪsā (d. 279 / 892). *Jāmiᶜ ṣaḥīḥ.* In *ᶜĀriḍat al-aḥwzī bi-sharḥ ṣaḥīḥ al-Tirmidhī* by Ibn ᶜArabī al-Mālikī, edited by Hishām Samīr Bukhārī. Beirut: Dār Iḥyāʾ al-Turāth alᶜArabī, 1995.

———. *Sunan al-Tirmidhī.* 2 vols. Liechtenstein: Thesaurus Islamicus Foundation, 2000.

Tucker, W. "Abū Manṣūr al-ᶜIjlī and the Manṣūriyya: A Study in Medieval Terrorism." *Der Islam* 54 (1977):66–76.

Vansina, Jan. *Oral Tradition as History.* London: James Currey, 1985.

Vuckovic, Brooke Olson. *Heavenly Journeys, Earthly Concerns: The Legacy of the Miᶜrāj in the Formation of Islam*. New York and London: Routledge, 2005.

Wansbrough, John. *Qurʾānic Studies: Sources and Methods of Scriptural Interpretation*. Oxford: Oxford University Press, 1977; reprint Amherst, NY: Prometheus, 2004.

Wāsiṭī, ᶜAbd al-Raḥmān b. ᶜAbd al-Muḥsin. "*Sharḥ asmāʾ Rasūl Allāh*." Maktabat al-Asad al-Waṭaniyya. MS 6840. Damascus, Syria.

Wasserstrom, Steven. *Between Muslim and Jew*. Princeton, NJ: Princeton University Press, 1995.

Widengren, Geo. *The Ascension of the Apostle and the Heavenly Book*. Uppsala: A. B. Lundequistska, 1950.

———. *Muhammad, the Apostle of God, and His Ascension*. Uppsala: A. B. Lundequistska, 1955.

Wunderli, Peter. *Le Livre de l'Eschiele Mahomet*. Bern: Francke, 1968.

Zayn al-Dīn b. Ḥasan b. Zayn al-Dīn (fl.1003/1594). "*al-Najm al-wahhāj fīʾl-masrā waʾl-miᶜrāj . . . ᶜalā al-tamām waʾl-kamāl*." Dār al-Kutub al-Miṣriyya. MS Majāmīᶜ 829. Cairo, Egypt.

Ziriklī, Khayr al-Dīn. *al-Aᶜlām: qamūs tarājim al-ashhar al-rijāl wa-'l-nisā min al-ᶜArab wa-'l-mustaᶜrabīn wa-'l-mustashriqīn*. 2d ed. 10 vols. Cairo: n.p., 1954–59.

Index

The letter *f* following a page number denotes a figure, the letter *n* denotes a note, and the letter *t* denotes a table.

Index of Qurʾānic Verses

This index only lists the pages of those verses mentioned in the body of the text and the accompanying notes, not those mentioned in either of the two appendices.